DREAMS
DIE
HARD

DREAMS
DIE
HARD
DAVID HARRIS

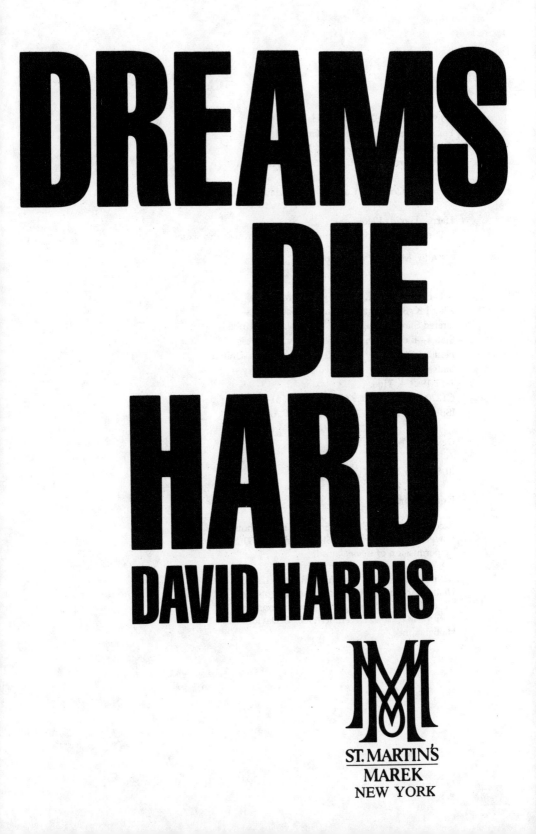

ST. MARTIN'S
MAREK
NEW YORK

Library of Congress Cataloging in Publication Data

Harris, David, 1946-
    Dreams die hard: three men's journey through the sixties.

    "A St. Martin's/Marek book."

    1. Harris, David, 1946-   2. Lowenstein,
Allard K. 3. Sweeney, Dennis. 4. Journalists—
United States—Biography. 5. Legislators—United
States—Biography. 6. United States. Congress.
House—Biography. 7. Civil rights workers—United
States—Biography. 8. United States—History—
1961-1969. I. Title.
CT220.H35   973.9'092'2 [B]   81-23279
ISBN 0-312-21956-3   AACR2

Design by Manuela Paul

10 9 8 7 6 5 4 3 2 1

First Edition

Excerpts from "A Chance Encounter" by Thomas
Powers, *Commonweal* 107:261–2 (April 11, 1980), used
by permission of *Commonweal*.

Acknowledgment is gratefully made to David
Halberstam for permission to use excerpts from
"The Man Who Ran Against Lyndon Johnson,"
Harper's Magazine, December 1968, © David
Halberstam.

To Wallace Turner

whose advice kept me
from falling into any holes
deeper than I could climb out of

DREAMS DIE HARD

1

I would have left this story alone if it weren't for the ending Dennis wrote to it all so much later in our lives. What he finally did to Allard finished off a decade long gone but still much too important to ignore.

Those days are remembered vaguely now as "the Sixties," but quick captions tend to be glib and miss all the actual vastness that coming of age in such times implied. Dennis Sweeney, Allard Lowenstein, and I were all in the thick of things while they lasted. Lots of people lost one another along the way, and that certainly was true for the three of us. Ten years after the Sixties ended, our mutual pasts had long since receded into the landscape behind me. When I suddenly wanted to remember them, I had to look back across a long plain and against a fierce glare. Naturally enough, the story was dominated at first glance by the conclusion in its foreground.

On Friday, March 14, 1980, at 4 P.M., Dennis Sweeney, 37, entered the Rockefeller Center law office where he had an appointment with Allard Lowenstein. The two men had seen each other only three or four times in the fifteen years since they went their separate ways in the heyday of the civil rights movement. For the last three years, Sweeney had been earning a living in Connecticut as a free-lance carpenter. Most of his friends from the Sixties had heard nothing from him since 1973, and it was widely rumored among them that he had committed suicide years earlier. On that Friday in March, he was carrying a brand new seven-shot Llama .380 automatic in his windbreaker pocket. It was loaded.

Lowenstein, 51, was, as always, busy. After talking with Dennis he planned to meet a candidate for the Democratic nomination in one of Manhattan's upcoming congressional primaries and inform the man that he would be in the race as well. It would be Allard's eighth such race in 12 years. The *New York Times* had recently referred to him as a "perennial candidate," but he was still widely esteemed for the felling of Lyndon Johnson in 1968 and his one term in Congress shortly thereafter. The Manhattan law office was less a vocation than the latest perch from which Lowenstein was pursuing left Democratic politics.

He had spent most of the previous month campaigning for Ted Kennedy's presidential bid. He kept his appointment with Sweeney on March 14 because they had once been close, and Allard wanted to help Sweeney if he could.

Allard shook Dennis's hand, ushered him into a private office, and closed the door.

Fifteen minutes later, shooting erupted behind the closed door. When Dennis Sweeney emerged, he laid the now empty automatic in the receptionist's "out" tray, sat down, lit a cigarette, and waited silently for the police to arrive. Allard Lowenstein lay on the office floor, calling for help and bleeding profusely from his chest.

Until the news reached me three hours later, Allard Lowenstein and Dennis Sweeney were wisps out of some time long ago. By March 14, 1980, I had been a journalist working out of San Francisco for seven years, first with *Rolling Stone* and then, for the last two years, with the *New York Times Magazine*. Allard and Dennis entered my life again when a reporter friend called my home and read me the news off the wire copy: Former Congressman Allard K. Lowenstein had been rushed to St. Clare's Hospital with severe bullet wounds. His assailant was under arrest and had been identified as one Dennis Sweeney. My automatic surge of adrenaline stunned me for a moment. Then I answered her questions. I would do the same thing with a succession of reporters until midnight, California time. I provided what information I could:

I had once been close to Allard, during 1965. I had been part of his ever changing army of student protégés. So had Dennis Sweeney. I had been close to Dennis during 1966 and 1967. Allard had introduced us both to politics. Dennis had become Stanford University's foremost civil rights hero, I its first and only student body president to be imprisoned for willful refusal to submit to conscription.

I suppose the three of us, each in his own approximate way, typified three strands of behavior that, when wrapped about one another, made the decade what it was. Allard was the older liberal, wedded to the Democratic party, convinced that the citadels of power could be stormed from the inside out, his world view framed by a belief that articulate reason, recourse to the constitution, benign leadership, and enlightened self-interest were the ultimate hole cards. Dennis was the young man, idealistic, moved by the sufferings of others, and disillusioned with the compromise inherent in the liberal approach. He divorced himself from the status quo and eventually became consumed with the need to create a communal identity in which he could submerge himself in the radical task of immense change on all fronts. I was the even younger man, romantic too, disturbed by the hypocrisy of what was and unwilling to accept the degradation of making my separate peace with it. I was drawn to the exemplary existential act as a means of transforming both myself and the world around me. We three had made brief but intense common cause, but those connections had eventually dissolved one after another in the wake of disputes over politics and identity. It was a time when ideologies emerged and then failed, attempts at heroism were made and then abandoned, but the belief in beliefs and heroes remained paramount.

I had seen Allard once in the last ten years, at a meeting of the California Democratic party in 1977. The last I'd heard of Dennis was when his mother and stepfather tried to commit him to an Oregon mental institution in 1973. At the time, I was told that he had torn out the denture bridge spanning the middle of his upper jaw with his bare hands. He apparently thought it was picking up radio signals from the CIA. Allard had probably directly influenced more young people during the Sixties than anyone else I knew, and Dennis was one of the first. Allard had introduced Dennis to the civil rights movement in Mississippi, but their relationship had ended in bitterness before I met either of them.

The questions that day and night, March 14, 1980, were interspersed with eruptions out of the forgotten past. A lawyer I'd last seen with Allard at the 1966 National Student Association congress called to ask whether I thought Dennis was "working for someone." A mathematician I'd last seen in a crowd chasing the Vice President of the United States across a vacant lot at Stanford in 1967 called to ask the same question. A high government official who had helped with The Dump Johnson and McCarthy for President campaigns in 1968 called to say Allard was "irreplaceable," both personally and politically. A former 1964 Mississippi Summer Project worker who had later burned his draft card outside the Pentagon told me he wasn't surprised at what had happened, only that Dennis had done it. A Connecticut reporter told me he'd been trying for three hours to contact Sweeney's mother in Portland, Oregon. He finally got the phone number of a neighbor through the church where Dennis's stepfather's funeral had been held two weeks earlier. When the neighbor answered the phone, she asked whom Sweeney had shot. When she heard the name Lowenstein, the neighbor snorted and reportedly said, "He had it coming." She refused to explain or comment further.

At 11 P.M. E.S.T., the *New York Times* city desk called with news that Allard Lowenstein had died after five and a half hours of emergency surgery.

A snapshot of Allard lodged in my mind for the next hour. The face would have been ugly if it weren't for the presence he generated. The hair was dark, thin, and scattered. His glasses were plastic-rimmed, the lenses thick as Coke-bottle bottoms. Behind them, set deep in black pouches of sleeplessness, were large dark eyes that tended to bulge. In contrast to his wrestler's body, they seemed remarkably fragile. His attractiveness was not readily apparent until he opened his mouth, but then it was overwhelming. Allard Lowenstein was as good a talker as any I had ever heard.

The last phone call of the evening was from someone who'd known both Allard and Dennis at Stanford in the days before the civil rights movement. He remembered Dennis as gentle, shy, and at one time "devoted to Al." It was almost midnight.

"So how did it all end up like this?" the caller asked.

I have been trying to answer that question ever since.

It is not easy. I cannot remember Dennis and Allard without remembering myself, and consequently my recollections are refracted at one end by who I was becoming at the time and at the other by who I have become since. They are sensitive memories as well. Predictably, those years of my youth have become an increasingly intimate possession as they have drawn further and further away. To recount them, whether easy or not, is to reveal myself in ways I never could have then. I now marvel at how young I was and how much happened to me. I started the decade a boy from farm country, and before the decade was over I had cut a path for myself that I could never have imagined for anyone before it began. Like many other people, I brought my own need to be honest, true, and manly to a public arena where the stakes were high and very visible and where my own future was in jeopardy. Like Allard, I made a name for myself, but, like Dennis, I was never completely comfortable with that. It now seems like a lot to go through just to grow up. By the age of 21, I was comfortable making definitive statements about important subjects to large groups of people who were prepared to believe me, but I have no such statements to make about Allard and Dennis. At the age of 36, my precociousness is gone and their ending is too sad, the rest too complicated, and I am now old enough to know better. I only want to backtrack and string it all together piece by piece.

The story did not start out at all the way it ended. Allard and Dennis met as dean and student at Stanford University in 1961. Allard Lowenstein, the new 32-year-old assistant dean of men, director of Stern Hall, and lecturer in the Political Science Department, sought out and attracted bright young men who cared about making the world better, and Dennis Sweeney, just a freshman and 18 years old, was one of them. It seemed inconceivable they would unravel into victim and assassin two decades later. The tracks leading up to such senselessness were mingled with thousands of others. Back then, we all still pictured dreams of a better world as simple and inevitably redemptive. We chased after them ferociously and with an intensity that dominated every aspect of our lives. Few of us had yet seen visions warp under the pressure they attract. That experience was still over the horizon, waiting after years of political upheavals that would leave Allard Lowenstein a legend, Dennis Sweeney a casualty, and everyone else different from what they would otherwise have been.

At one time or another, I thought I knew each of us well.

2

In 1958, on the verge of turning 30, Allard K. Lowenstein was already being referred to as "the world's oldest student leader." Dennis Sweeney was 15 at the time and I, 12.

The second of three children born to a doctor-turned-restaurateur, Allard had been raised in Westchester County, New York. At the age of 10, he charted daily changes in the battle lines of the Spanish Civil War on his bedroom wall. Young Allard reportedly wept when the Loyalist democrats and Socialists finally surrendered after betrayal by their Communist allies.

Allard's only recorded comment about his parents came in the next-to-last paragraph of the author's note to *Brutal Mandate*, the one book he would manage to write in his life. The manuscript was also his last project before he reported to his new job at Stanford University in 1961. In this author's note Allard's mother is referred to with distant respect: "There is my mother," he wrote, "gracious and loving through long years of raising unpredictable children, patient despite the strains of running a household constantly invaded by all kinds of unexpected guests." This reserved and functional description stands in sharp contrast to his adulation for his father. "And my father," Allard continued, "more vigorous in his seventies than any of his offspring: how proud I am to be his son, and how fortunate that he, more than any other man, lives that his family may enjoy life. There is nothing a son can say to a man whose heart is such that taking nothing, he feels privileged to give; nothing except that his children wish the roles could be reversed so he could know how reciprocal is this love and all its by-products."

Dennis Sweeney was born in Oregon in 1943, but Sweeney was not his original surname. In the two years I knew him, he never told me his real one, even though he didn't lose it until he was a teenager. He had no brothers or sisters, and his natural father had provided only a brief glimpse of himself in Dennis's childhood.

According to an account published in the *Village Voice* after Dennis shot Allard:

> His parents separated shortly after he was born . . . and his father, a career military man, left for England alone. He did not return or visit until his son was two, and then stayed one month. . . . He promised to send Dennis a letter . . . but no letter ever arrived. Dennis never saw his father again. In the early 50's, the family received word that he had been killed in Korea.

> Raising a child by herself was difficult for his mother, and, despite moving in with his grandmother, the "difficulty" remained. Eventually, Dennis was sent off to some kind of "boys' ranch" for more than a year. Although the reason for that childhood exile can only be speculated at, he would later tell friends that, at the time, he considered it "punishment."

Lowenstein's parents seem to have been concerned but tolerant about their son's decision to forgo the Ivy League after graduation from Horace Mann School and pursue his undergraduate education at the University of North Carolina at Chapel Hill. The decision reflected the typically eclectic mixture of elements that Allard would always be. He chose Chapel Hill because of both its liberal president and its intercollegiate wrestling team. Throughout his life, wrestling was one of Lowenstein's passions. When I first met him, 15 years after his varsity career was over, he challenged me to wrestle within hours. Allard would return regularly to Chapel Hill to grapple with the UNC squad until well into his forties. Among his much lesser claims to uniqueness is the distinction of being probably the only varsity wrestler ever to read the *New York Times*, front to back, virtually every day of his life.

The *Times* was another Lowenstein obsession. Throughout his life, it would be virtually impossible to find him without at least one copy nearby. He himself was first mentioned in the paper while still a student and wrestler at UNC. More than 30 years later, when I requested my editors at the *New York Times Magazine* to photocopy the paper's clip file on Lowenstein, I was told that doing so would require three days of solid xeroxing. Aside from the sheer volume, the most remarkable aspect to the accumulated notices of three decades of public life would be the uniformity of their political configuration. The direction of Lowenstein's politics seems to have been well set by the early 1940s. The *Times*'s first mention of Allard made that much clear.

The reference appeared on August 2, 1947, in the fourth paragraph of an inside column about the Encampment for Citizenship, a conference of some 150 young people of "different races, colors, and creeds," held at Fieldston School in Riverdale and sponsored by the Ethical Culture Society and various labor unions and political groups. It was designed to promote learning a "way to practice democratic ideals" and widen "the social viewpoint of American citizens," and its guest speakers included Eleanor Roosevelt, Henry Wallace, and a number of other prominent figures to the left of Franklin Roosevelt in the Democratic party. Allard would inhabit that political turf for the rest of his life. In 1947 he was identified as the undergraduate who had been selected to preside over that year's Encampment. Young Lowenstein was credited with having "successfully led a movement to open the North Carolina Student Legislature to students of Negro colleges" the year before. He was not quoted. Before adjourning, the assembled young people passed a resolution to "return home" and pursue "a program of national unity built on social justice." No doubt Allard himself helped construct the wording. Except for the assumption of a stable homesite, the line is one way of describing the rest of his life.

A more precise means of locating Lowenstein politically is through his pantheon of idols. Until Bobby Kennedy was shot in 1968, Allard only had three. Politically, they would always be the stars by which he steered himself. Personally, they were among the few people Allard identified as his betters.

One was Frank Porter Graham, the man whose presidency had drawn Lowenstein to UNC and later an appointee to a fraction of one term representing North Carolina in the United States Senate. Allard served as Graham's special Senate assistant during 1949. In Lowenstein's eyes, Graham epitomized the intelligent man risking person and power to uphold right under adverse circumstances. "If iron could be gentle," Lowenstein claimed in the author's note to *Brutal Mandate*, "it would be Frank Graham, a man who could lose his seat in the United States Senate . . . rather than filibuster in violation of his conscience or cheat a Negro boy of his due."

Norman Thomas was a second. Six-time Socialist party candidate for President, Thomas also ran twice for governor of the state of New York and once for mayor of New York City. His political curve had much of both the influence and shortfall that would be reflected in Allard's own. Allard revered him as a monument to the value and dignity of persistent service.

Eleanor Roosevelt was the third of Allard Lowenstein's idols and by far the most important. Her mention in the *Brutal Mandate* author's note immediately preceded his parents':

> There is Mrs. Franklin D. Roosevelt, the greatest of human
> beings, if greatness can be measured by numbers of people
> helped and quantities of energy guided to useful purpose.
> This feeling I share with so large a part of the human race
> that it would be presumptuous to mention it here, were it not
> that my debt to her is particularly great. . . . Eleanor
> Roosevelt expects no gratitude for great things done. In fact, I
> have no idea how one would go about trying to express
> gratitude to her, unless it's to try to help along as best one
> can the sort of things to which she gives her life.

Allard spent his early adulthood apprenticing for precisely that task.

Lowenstein was elected president of the National Student Association in 1950. Yale Law School followed, interrupted by a term as president of Students for Stevenson; after law school he spent two years as an enlisted man in the United States Army. Work for the College Council for the United Nations and a year of graduate study in history at UNC combined with a student counseling job preceded a brief 1959 stint as a foreign-policy assistant to Senator Hubert Humphrey. All along the way he was developing the assets that would thrust him forward in the decade to come. One of the chief amongst them was the breadth of his connections. Even back then, he was the hub of a network involving figures everywhere, many of whom were startlingly prestigious, others entirely unknown. He had at least one story to tell about each of them.

I can remember traveling to Berkeley with Allard one night in 1965. Someone had loaned him a Ford Mustang, and I drove while he rode shotgun with his elbow out the window. As he did whenever possible, Allard had stripped his upper body down to a skintight T-shirt. His dress shirt, tie, and sport coat were all draped over a pile of *New York Times*'s in the backseat. The wind blowing by made his hair even more scattered than usual.

"Have I ever told you about when Mrs. Roosevelt met Jack Kennedy at the 1960 convention?" he asked out of nowhere.

"No," I answered, "you haven't." Newspaper pages were hurtling around in the back.

Allard's hands leaped off his lap. "I haven't?" he exclaimed. "I can't believe it. I was sure I must have told it to you already. It's a great story."

I listened, feeling it was somehow my fault he hadn't recounted it before.

At the time the story took place, Allard was an alternate delegate to the convention, and Mrs. Roosevelt had come pledged to Stevenson. Lowenstein was often described then as one of her protégés. When it was apparent Kennedy would win the nomination, Allard thought it important that he do so with Eleanor Roosevelt's blessing, so he arranged for the two to meet. Allard told Kennedy that Mrs. Roosevelt was disposed to like him but had reservations about the family connection to Joseph McCarthy first made by Jack's father. Allard, 31, advised the soon-to-be President, 42, to confess his own immaturity, say supporting McCarthy had been his father's influence, and be sure to tell her how evil he thought McCarthy's red baiting had been. According to Allard, John Kennedy listened carefully and then entered the room where the grande dame of the Democratic party was waiting. Only after the door had closed behind him did Allard remember that he had forgotten to mention the most important thing of all.

Allard paused to make sure I was listening.

When I looked across the front seat at him, he was poised exuberantly on the story's first punch line.

"Mrs. Roosevelt," he blurted, "was deaf in her left ear. I had forgotten to tell Jack to sit on her right side." Laughter suddenly rose in spasms out of Lowenstein's thick chest.

When Mrs. Roosevelt emerged from the room 40 minutes later, he finally continued, she was shaking her head. Allard walked her to the elevator. "I don't think I could support that man," she told her protégé. "He still thinks he was right about Joe McCarthy." As soon as he could disengage himself from his mentor, he rushed back to the Kennedy suite to find out what had happened. As he told the story, Allard's own appreciative laughter began to rise again, signaling the last punch line.

"Jack had done everything I'd told him to," he explained, "but he sat on the wrong side. Mrs. Roosevelt didn't hear a word he'd said."

This time Allard slapped my shoulder while in his chuckling fit.

I was 19 years old then and he was the first person I'd ever known who called the late martyred president Jack. I would remember feeling indebted to him for sharing the intimacies of life in high places. I was still trying to get my own legs under me and such special treatment by such a special person was what I needed. I would also remember how he spoke of Mrs. Roosevelt in a worshipful tone.

In 1962, not long before her death, Eleanor Roosevelt wrote the page-and-a-half foreword to Lowenstein's book, *Brutal Mandate*. "I have known Mr. Lowenstein for many years," she wrote. "He is a person of unusual ability and complete integrity. I think he will always fight crusades because injustice fills him with a sense of rebellion. He wants to be of help."

The book itself recounted a trip to Southwest Africa organized by Allard in the summer of 1959 after the South African apartheid government had consistently refused to permit any outside investigation of conditions there. His unsanctioned and underground investigation was followed by testimony before the United Nations on behalf of the tribes he had visited.

I didn't hear of *Brutal Mandate* until one evening three years after it was published, when I was dropping Allard off at the airport not long after he told me the story about Mrs. Roosevelt and Jack Kennedy. His flight was to leave in ten minutes, and I was supposed to take the car back to the people he had borrowed it from. Then he mentioned that there was a box of books in the trunk. I was to take those and sell as many as I could for him. I started to say I didn't think I'd be able to do that, but he was running for the check-in counter. I kept those copies of *Brutal Mandate* until Allard finally reclaimed them, entirely unsold, two years later. By then, we were lined up on opposite sides, and he just took the books and left.

Only after Allard's death did I finally read the text in its entirety, and I was most struck by Allard's description of a white Anglican priest who was one of apartheid's leading opponents. In retrospect, it sounded as if it could have been Allard picturing himself from a vantage point across a room:

> He dashes about from meeting to meeting, invariably late,
> often lost, collecting and forgetting briefcases and documents
> and bits of paper with notes and addresses, doing alone the
> work that most men would shy from attempting with half a
> dozen. . . . He makes these causes his life, until it is easy to
> forget that he too must grow weary and discouraged, must on
> occasion wonder if [he will ever have] a time to rest. . . .
> Always there is the great patience-impatience, always the
> people pushing and pulling and seeking this and that.

Allard Lowenstein finished his manuscript shortly before arriving at Stanford. There, he eventually crossed paths with Dennis.

I think I can picture Dennis then, even though it would be another five years before we became friends. With one notable exception, his looks remained remarkably unchanged over the years. The hair was thick and somewhere between brown and blond, depending on the light. In 1961, Dennis combed it in a JFK wave across the front and left skin showing around his ears. His face was cherubic, his six-foot body fit. His jaw showed only shades of the fierce resolve that would eventually characterize it. His only disfigurement was a front tooth which had been damaged in a playground accident at the age of six and never repaired. To hide it, he smiled rarely and, when he did, it was often a somewhat embarrassed gesture. Even so, he is remembered as "appealing," "friendly," "intelligent," and "fetchingly shy." There was the hint of farm boy about his features, even though he'd been raised in the blue-collar suburbs of Portland, Oregon. His eyes were more visibly nervous than the rest of his appearance. They were blue, respectful, and betrayed pain if you looked at them long enough.

Dennis Sweeney arrived at Stanford as something of an anomaly and was bothered by it. The great majority of Stanford students were WASP, upper crust, children of professionals, secure in comfortable two-parent, two-and-a-half-sibling families. Except for looking the WASP part, Dennis Sweeney was the odd man out.

Dennis was without a father until his early teens, when his mother married a printing-plant shop steward. According to a published account of his early life, Dennis "did not much like [his stepfather], Jerry Sweeney, a perfectionist who demanded that the hair in his household be combed and the ashtrays emptied." Dennis was nonetheless adopted and given no choice about assuming his stepfather's name. The loss of that last link to his real father apparently rankled for a long time, but at least from the outside in, the most immediate result of the change appeared to be an upturn in Dennis's life.

A friend from his days at Clackamas High School remembers him as a 14-year-old on the edge of the greased-duck-tail set who blossomed into an honors student and campus leader. Dennis was friendly and outgoing, "someone with a great deal of potential who would go a long way." He played varsity basketball, ran unsuccessfully for student body president, and served on the yearbook staff. When the class of 1961 graduated, Dennis Sweeney was its graduation day speaker. He had won a scholarship to Stanford University and was universally regarded by those who heard him as a young man with high prospects.

Only a small portion of that Clackamas prestige translated into confidence in the face of Stanford the following fall. It was immediately apparent to Sweeney that he was facing a social stratum different from the one he had experienced in his working-class adolescence. He was intimidated. Even when that intimidation disappeared, he would never quite escape the self-consciousness that came with it.

D avid Harris is the third character in this story, and in 1961, when it began, I was starting my junior year at Fresno High School. Located at the heart of California's principal inland farming valley, Fresno had been home to parts of my family for three generations. My childhood had few, if any, twists and turns. My maternal grandmother was a member of the DAR, my father an attorney who had enlisted in the Army before World War II and was discharged as an officer when it was over. My older brother was an All–Central California baseball player who would eventually serve as a captain and flight surgeon with the Eighty-second Airborne Division. I would later be selected my high school's Boy of the Year. In the fifth grade, my goal in life was to attend West Point and become a career infantry officer. In the eighth grade, I wanted to be an FBI agent.

About the time Dennis Sweeney and Allard Lowenstein were arriving at Stanford, I was a substitute center on the high school's Warrior football varsity, waiting in a locker room before our game with the Tigers from the all-black high school on Fresno's west side. The floor had noises all over it from the nervous scraping of our cleats, and, like most substitutes, I was toward the back of the crowd listening to one of the coaches giving final instructions. His red hair stood straight up on top like bristles on a hog's neck and then swept back on the sides in two Brylcreem wings. He used the last few minutes before game time to remind us that it wasn't Tigers but "jungle bunnies" and "jigaboos" we would be pitted against. His admonitions included a number of stereotypes typical of Fresno's white population at the time. We believed you had to jump the niggers early, and get them on the run. If we didn't, they would dance the boogaloo all over our faces, all night long. Just the mention of that prospect was intended to be humiliating. Real white men, it was assumed, would never let that happen.

Far-off Warrior cheers drifted in through the overhead window facing the stadium.

"You got to be mean," the coach roared.

"Be mean," we roared back.

In Fresno, times still showed few, if any, signs of changing.

Stanford wasn't all that far along itself. At the freshman convocation kicking off the 1961–62 school year, most of the young men's hair was flat on top, cropped to the skin before reaching the ear. The young women's was mostly puffy hairdos done up like hair-spray helmets. A few bold ones among them expressed themselves by subscribing to the *Reporter* and displaying copies of Kahlil Gibran. The convocation was held in an amphitheater, and the day was sunny, the setting green and confident. Many of those wearing jeans had the cuffs rolled up so their white socks showed. The university president gave a speech in which he bragged that this class had been selected from the "top one percent" of the nation's high school students and urged the freshmen to "keep your faces into the wind, your feet on the ground, and your eyes on the stars." He got a big round of applause.

I have searched all the back issues of the *Stanford Daily* published during those first fall months of 1961, looking for signs presaging future turmoil, but there are few. One was a "staff opinion" editorial entitled "Freedom Riders OK." The author concluded that the stirrings of southern black people were "pro-American" and "indicative of a new spirit in American youth." The spirit was identified as "spontaneity." Most of the remaining copy spoke more to where everyone was coming from rather than where they were going. The "peacetime" draft had been in place since 1948, but attending Stanford was then seen as ample insurance against ever being subject to it. The hottest issue of the time was whether "domestic Reds" ought to be forced to register as agents of the Soviet Union. Nearby Sunnyvale, California, had commenced a study on how to keep Communists out of civic buildings, and the state Board of Education was introducing a mandatory high school course in the evils of international Marxism.

Another brief glimmer of the future was reflected in the campus paper on October 12, 1961. That morning, the *Daily* reported that President John F. Kennedy had ordered General Maxwell Taylor to the Far East to help draft defense plans for meeting the increased "red threat" to a place called the Republic of Vietnam.

There is a case to be made, in retrospect at least, that Allard Lowenstein's arrival hinted at more of what was to come at Stanford than any other event of 1961.

Thirty-two years old, he had been hired on a one-year contract to serve as an assistant dean of men and director of Stern Hall, a men's dormitory complex run by the dean's office. He would also teach "Politics of Sub-Saharan Africa" for the Political Science Department during winter quarter and "Constitutional Law" during the spring. It is doubtful Allard would have been hired had not the Stanford administration had a pressing problem it thought perhaps only he could solve. He had few of the traditional qualities expected of assistant deans. He dominated conversations, invariably believing he knew best, and, never really comfortable working for anyone but himself, he was not much of a company man.

The problem that provoked Lowenstein's hiring was Stern Hall. During the previous decade, the administration had launched an intensive campaign to transform Stanford from a finishing school for the Pacific rich into the "Harvard of the West." The Stanford so envisioned would be renowned for providing "the Stanford experience," a richly intellectual environment usually pictured by administration planners as a small group of handsome young fair-headed men and women sitting around in a relaxed and convivial setting with one of the great minds of the day, sharpening their understanding of eighteenth-century Austria or the Greek notion of *patria* as reflected in the writings of Thucydides. In that scenario, Stern Hall, the eight two- and three-storied concrete blockhouse-type structures, was an embarrassment at best. To live there was to be considered a "dork" and consigned to social isolation. Faculty members fled from invitations to dine there. The dean of men who hired Lowenstein reportedly bragged to one of his colleagues that if Allard couldn't "liven Stern up," then "it just isn't possible."

"Livening things up" was second nature for Lowenstein. Energy suffused his presence. Each of the different things he devoted himself to was always treated as a pressing question of emergency proportions upon which something deep and important depended. Such intensity set him in sharp contrast to his blasé surroundings and acted like a beacon to kids looking to apply themselves to something more than just advancing their prospective careers. Word of the Stern director's virtues began spreading soon after he assumed his post. Dean Lowenstein was impressively intelligent and quick on his feet. Dean Lowenstein possessed worldly experience and was willing to share it. Dean Lowenstein got phone calls from Ralph Bunche and Adlai Stevenson, once addressed the UN, liked to be called "Al," and was willing to talk to students as if he were one of them.

Lowenstein actively enjoyed the company of young men fifteen or more years his junior throughout his life. He had a knack of evoking an immediate sense of intimacy and was comfortable talking about everything from the most personal subjects to the world at its most large. "Guidance" was a Lowenstein specialty. He loved being confided in and felt entirely at ease telling his juniors what they ought to do. Most commonly attired in khakis, T-shirt, and Yale jacket, Allard's informality put them at ease. On what he deemed formal occasions, he would extract a shirt and tie from where they were stashed in a corner under last Sunday's *New York Times*. His door was always open. Single and unencumbered by demanding peer relationships, he tried to make time for all those people who sought him out. Much of the talk was about "making the world better for all mankind." Those politics, Allard always pointed out, were his real boss and ought to be everyone else's as well.

In his politics during his year as an assistant dean of men, the issues singled out by Allard for special emphasis fell into two general categories. In the first were Lowenstein's regulars—including opposition to Fascist Spain and South African apartheid, and concern for equality under the law in all its forms. The logic he used to tie them together would remain basically unchanged for the next 20 years. Injustice was a blight, he argued, and if the advocates of democracy ignored or reinforced it, then those who wanted to free themselves would have no recourse except for politics further to the left and hence much more dangerous. "Students in the free world and the Communist world are competing," he explained at one of his numerous campus speaking appearances, "and the free world is losing."

In the second category were those issues of the moment in which Lowenstein perceived important principles manifesting themselves in local ways. Two such issues stood out in the 1961–62 Stanford school year.

The first was his attempt to persuade Stanford students to reaffiliate their student body with the National Student Association. Allard had been NSA president 10 years earlier and was always an NSA partisan. Over three decades he rarely missed an annual National Student Association congress. Stanford's membership in the organization had been terminated by a succession of fraternity-dominated student governments in the late 1950s, and Lowenstein urged rejoining the organization in a campuswide meeting at which he was the featured speaker. As reported by the *Daily*, he stressed NSA's "international work" and called it "the only effective counter to an intensive worldwide Communist student movement."

By 1967, that long-standing connection between Allard Lowenstein and the National Student Association would take on a nefarious cast, at least in the eyes of Dennis and myself. In 1961, it registered as no more than idealism on a international scale.

The second and by far most important local issue of Lowenstein's assistant deanship was the invigoration of Stern Hall. There, his mere presence brought immediate improvements. The director's apartment soon became a place where students from all over campus congregated to discuss subjects that were "relevant" and "meant something" in the world at large. Stern residents began talking to each other, and professors began accepting their invitations to give after-dinner speeches. Lowenstein drew his charges out and prodded their awakening at every turn.

To institutionalize that stimulus, Allard also began to pursue a longer-range strategy. At that time, all freshmen males were required to live on campus, and although a few lived at Stern, 98 percent resided in Wilbur Hall, the all-freshman dormitory 50 yards away. Once their first year at Stanford was over, those men were free to choose any "living option" they wished. Fraternities were by far the most prestigious of those options in 1961 and Stern by far the least. If Stern was ever to escape its outcast reputation, Allard knew he would have to recruit actively, something Stern had never done before.

Typically, Lowenstein announced his intentions to compete directly with the fraternities during a speech at the Sigma Nu fraternity house. The social stigma against men who weren't accepted into a fraternity shouldn't exist, he said, and the young men usually considered "fraternity material" should not feel obligated to join. In the interests of creating a "true option," he intended to bring "the best of the freshman class" to Stern.

As he had promised, while the fraternities were holding "rush parties" during spring quarter, Lowenstein hosted a string of receptions at his dormitory. The Stern gatherings were much less raucous than the fraternity bashes, but people didn't come there for raucousness. Allard was looking for young men who wanted to take their "responsibilities" seriously. The idea, as he explained it, was that such people had an obligation to create better options than simply the frivolity of fraternities. They ought to come and live with him at Stern and help turn it into a model community for the exploration of values and the cultivation of responsible citizenship. That was a task worthy of "the best."

Dennis Sweeney, 18 years old and already respected by his classmates for his integrity, came to one of Lowenstein's receptions at the urging of a friend. His self-consciousness about his own background automatically disposed Dennis to shy away from the snobbishness of fraternities. The idea behind Lowenstein's Stern attracted him, as did Allard himself.

Dennis Sweeney was ripe for such a figure in his life, a classic case of the earnestness of the times and a particular young man with a need.

Sweeney was an eager and intelligent student, intent on taking the Oregon sheen off of his thinking. Even before he met Allard, the intellectual circles he drifted toward were dominated by political scientists and theologians exploring the relationship between mass behavior and morality. Dennis Sweeney took it all seriously. He was quiet, polite, and, as his high school yearbook had described him, "a gentleman through and through." Intellectual life inspired him, but he was still tentative, ready to chase his vision but unclear exactly what it was or how to achieve it. In need of breaking out, Dennis Sweeney was not yet prepared to do so on his own.

Location on that particular psychological continuum was one of the qualities Allard Lowenstein looked for and recognized in young men. To him, it was a sign of sensitivity, awakening talent, and the desire to learn. Over the years Allard took a thousand similarly positioned young men under his wing. They, like Dennis Sweeney and David Harris, became his protégés. The role itself was fluid, of varying duration, and based on mutual attraction. Protégés revered Allard and accompanied him on his various errands for change. They waited for him to arrive, drove him around, and were generally available to be thrown into some pressing political breech, the true significance of which Allard would be able to expound upon with absolute authority. The relationship was as much that of bishop and novitiate as it was the best-friend tone Allard gave it, but such latent inequality often went unnoticed in Lowenstein's eschewal of any of dominance's formalities.

In return for indenturing himself to Allard's frenetic quest, the protégé was given a safe pass to pursue his developing urge for commitment and clarity. Lowenstein supplied adult approval, a program that could be carried out immediately, and a model to shape oneself after. In the spring of 1962 Allard Lowenstein was the first activist, an older man of the world already deeply involved in devoting his life to causes that meant something. To a concerned, earnest young man like Dennis Sweeney, who for all intents and purposes never had a father in his formative years, the prospect of protégéhood must have been enthralling.

Lowenstein's goal in his Stern recruiting was to locate 16 young men with "leadership potential" prepared to act as the infrastructure of Allard's strategy, two for each of Stern's eight buildings. They were later to become known as the Original Sixteen, an important early fragment in Lowenstein's Stanford legend. Soon after Lowenstein and Sweeney met, Allard told Dennis he was just the kind of "talented leadership material" he was looking for. Sweeney in turn became one of the first of Allard's sixteen recruits.

As the Sixties picked up steam, the conclusion that established hierarchical institutions inevitably victimized their constituents would become a truism among the young, and most were led to that conclusion by their experience as college students. Two events at Stanford in the spring of 1962 seem to have set that loss of faith in motion for Dennis Sweeney. In both, it would be obvious to him that, whatever its representatives might spout in the way of professed ideals, in practice the university was narrow, undemocratic, and unjust.

The first was an example of the Stanford administration at its most paternalistic. Not long after he decided to cast his lot with Allard at Stern in the coming fall, Dennis and his girlfriend of the time attended an off-campus party whose refreshments consisted of an unidentified vodka punch. Neither Sweeney nor his girlfriend had had much experience with alcohol, and at 4:30 A.M. the next morning, the Palo Alto Police found them both passed out on a nearby lawn. Both were brought up in front of the administration-controlled student judicial system.

Dennis was arraigned by the men's council and charged with the lesser offense of having passed out on a lawn in Palo Alto. He was suspended for a quarter, and the suspension was itself suspended so that the judgment amounted to no more than a formal notation on his record.

Sweeney's girlfriend was arraigned by the women's council and charged with the much more serious offense of "leaving herself defenseless in the presence of a male." She was sentenced to suspension for two quarters, and the suspension was enforced.

The second of those formative experiences was what the *Stanford Daily* described as Allard Lowenstein's being "edged out" of the dean's office. To Dennis and students like him, it was proof positive that the administration would go to any lengths to stifle the student awareness that Allard's presence had come to symbolize.

In retrospect, the termination of Lowenstein's assistant deanship seems to have been inevitable. Although enormously popular with students, both his message and style soon earned him a host of critics among his employers in the administration and the political science department. Lowenstein's principal political science critic derided him as wanting to be "the first Jewish President of the United States"; that spring, the department indicated that it had no post for Lowenstein during the coming school year, even though the courses he had taught during winter and spring quarters had been well attended. Lowenstein's critics in the administration were upset at his championing of student activism and argued that university policy toward the student body had to be unified, an impossibility as long as adventurous free-lancers like Lowenstein remained on the staff. Apparently the only defender Allard had in the administration was the dean of men who had hired him in the first place.

The event precipitating Allard's departure was the resignation of this lone defender. Lowenstein's own resignation followed shortly. He apparently reasoned that if the dean who had brought him to Stanford was gone, it meant the approach Allard had been hired to enact was gone as well. Resignation or not, it is extremely doubtful his contract would have been renewed. The students in his circle first learned of the power play when several overheard him talking on the phone in his Stern Hall apartment, telling the caller he would be going someplace else next year. Allard's notions of loyalty even in the face of rejection kept him from ever publicly commenting on his departure but did not prevent him from actively "getting the truth out" through surrogates.

Dennis Sweeney was certainly at least somewhat involved in this effort. Most progressive students experienced a sense of outrage at the loss of Lowenstein, and Dennis was not only progressive but also on the verge of protégéhood. Being sent to man the ramparts when Allard was under some "unwarranted" and "vicious personal attack" smack-ing of "betrayal" was always a central protégé function. In the spring of 1962, the strategy took form in a series of open letters in the *Daily* from an assortment of student collections and groups, designed to answer all of the administration's behind-the-scenes criticism. Allard knew of the letters' planning stages and, in some cases, reviewed the final wording.

One letter, signed by 29 students, accused the university of indifference to "student needs and opinions" and of giving "its answer in the none too mysterious resignation of Dean Lowenstein," a man "courageous, energetic, and deeply interested in student problems," who had "won . . . respect and admiration." Another letter signed by the Stern Hall president's council called the resignation "recent and sudden" and claimed, "Mr. Lowenstein has given us excellent guidance and incentive to help ourselves on issues of concern both to ourselves and the campus." Eight honors students in political science credited Lowenstein with "an ability to effectively communicate that has seldom been equaled in our experience . . . and the desire and ability to share . . . with all who make themselves available, no matter how humble their credentials." His courses were described as "extremely meaningful."

None of the protests had any visible impact, and Lowenstein's resignation was accepted with alacrity.

To someone in Dennis's position, it must have seemed that a significant part of the world he had found for himself was being snatched out from under him before he had even had a chance to explore it. Allard, however, reassured his Stanford friends that this did not mean they would lose touch. Lowenstein would be going to Europe in the first months of summer to monitor the World Youth Festival, a triannual international student conference scheduled for Helsinki, Finland, and visit his anti-Fascist contacts in Spain. The next fall, he would be teaching in the political science department at North Carolina State College in Durham, North Carolina, but that, he promised, would not preclude his coming West to check on Stanford's progress personally. He did not intend to abandon what they had begun there.

No doubt heartened by that reassurance, Dennis Sweeney returned to Portland and found a summer job.

I remember the adolescent summer-job routine well. David Harris was hooked into it just like Dennis Sweeney.

During the summer of 1962, I finally found employment at a peach-packing shed in Pinedale, California. The shed operated seven days a week, at least twelve, usually sixteen, hours a day, and my post was the last on the packing line. As the packed flats reached me, I fed them one at a time under an eight-foot-tall hydraulic press, jerked my hand back, and the press slammed down, driving 16 nails through the top. Both the person who ran the nailing machine before me and the one who did it after I left had their hands accidentally nailed to a box when they were too slow. I was paid $1.20 an hour.

Eventually, my terror of the nailing machine became extreme enough that I stopped going to work. By then, all of Fresno's other summer jobs were filled and I was left to mark time with two of my similarly unemployed friends. In Fresno, that meant cruising in whatever automobile was available, getting 11 miles per gallon and watching everyone else doing the same thing.

Along the way we managed to catch that summer's big political event in Fresno, a visit by President John F. Kennedy to the Fresno Air Terminal. By that time the Kennedy aura had enveloped the nation: Harvard student, war hero, Congressman, Senator, the first Catholic ever in the White House and the first of World War II's junior officer corps to assume national leadership, founder of both the Green Berets and the Peace Corps when there still seemed to be no contradiction between the two.

The President walked briskly from the plane to a spot where microphones had been erected on the tarmac, smiled, and began by making a joke about not having brought his wife along. The rest was all language about fulfilling America's unfulfilled promises. There were things left to do and he wanted to lead the nation to do them, a particular note of hope for three 16-year-olds oppressed by the boredom of summer in the long hot valley. After his remarks, Kennedy approached the crowd behind the short airport fence and began shaking the first layer of hands. I remember pressing forward to get a look before he left in a caravan of limos and police cars.

At that moment, it was hard not to believe that vigor and good intentions were in and of themselves invincible. No one's days seemed the least bit numbered.

Certainly not Allard's and Dennis's. Despite the distance enforced on it by Lowenstein's move away from Stanford, their relationship thrived during the 1962–63 school year, just as Allard had promised.

At North Carolina Allard threw himself into the antisegregation movement then in full swing around the Raleigh-Durham area. Allard's role in the "disturbances" was significant enough to cause the presiding officer of the North Carolina State Senate to denounce it publicly as "disgraceful" for the state of North Carolina to pay this man $7,500 a year at the same time that he was "messing around" with Raleigh's "racial harmony." When the reporters called Lowenstein for comment, he said, yes, it was disgraceful. Seven thousand and five hundred dollars a year was much too little for the service he provided. At North Carolina State, as at Stanford, a furor was also aroused by administration plans not to reappoint him. In North Carolina, Allard was to win and, having made his point, resign to pursue a fresh challenge.

Even with the intensity of that North Carolina involvement, he managed to keep active connections to Stanford and a number of other campuses around the country, which were sustained by phone calls or postcards and cemented by periodic two-day flying visits to make a speech and meet with everyone possible. Often these visits were announced to the campus's resident protégé with a phone call from Allard saying his plane would arrive at midnight. The protégé's function was to drop whatever else he was doing and help make the visit as "productive" as possible. At first it felt like an honor to be asked. Dennis Sweeney performed that role and enjoyed doing so.

The "intimidation" ascribed to Sweeney as a freshman had by now disappeared entirely. He had earned a reputation as a "deep" thinker who, in seminars, often raised questions that had escaped the attention of his classmates. Despite being intense, his intellectualism was neither cold nor distant. He was articulate, personable, easy to get along with, and unpretentious. In all his endeavors he evidenced an overriding concern with ethical questions. Sweeney's favorite professor taught religion and was a campus voice for the new theology of social responsibility. Dennis read Martin Buber, Deitrich Bonhoeffer, Ignazio Silone, Max Weber, and Albert Camus with an interest that far transcended class requirements. Though no longer intimidated, he still saw himself as somehow outside the Stanford mainstream. His working-class background continued to set him apart from his classmates, and Dennis continued to be conscious of his differentness. He was turned off by the process by which most Stanford undergraduates locked themselves into preprofessional training before ever exploring what life was all about. Sweeney himself seems to have had no clear post-graduate aspirations; at one point he mentioned vaguely the possibility of attending a seminary in preparation for the ministry of some undefined Protestant denomination.

For Dennis, Allard's visits seemed like bursts of relevance that must have been highly valued for their serious purpose. They coincided with all his own best instincts. Sweeney would borrow a car and drive the visiting Lowenstein around, complete with the *New York Times* all over the backseat and a tie stuffed into an overnight bag. In between Allard's visits, Dennis also acted as a Stanford outpost for his mentor's program. The causes they pursued together would later be summarized by Dennis as "my efforts to end social injustice" at Stanford.

In the course of Dennis's sophomore year, campus tides shifted noticeably in the direction first staked out by Lowenstein. The principal sign of this was the outcome of the student body president elections held at the end of the previous school year. In them, an irreverent graduate student named Armin Rosencranz had succeeded in breaking the fraternity stranglehold on the office. Though not a member of the largely undergraduate Lowenstein circle, Rosencranz was a partisan of the same politics. Not long after assuming office, he was approached on the subject of NSA reaffiliation by a Lowenstein protégé who was a friend of Dennis's. With the student body president's support, a campuswide referendum returned Stanford to the list of NSA member institutions by a slim margin. Dennis Sweeney devoted long hours to the effort.

The Lowenstein influence was also felt in that year's hottest campus dispute. The conflict was set off when Rosencranz sent a letter to the Federal Communications Commission on the stationery of the organization representing the student body, Associated Students. This letter supported the license renewal of a local subscriber-owned radio station then under attack by Bay Area conservatives as Communist. The president of the university responded to Rosencranz's move by issuing a public letter to the effect that henceforth students would not be permitted to comment on issues outside the confines of the university itself. As in the case of the "edging out" of Lowenstein during the previous year, the subsequent campaign against the ban took the form of a public dialogue on the pages of the Stanford Daily and the surrounding San Francisco and suburban newspapers. Allard was involved in the campaign, passing on advice about strategy over the phone from North Carolina. One of those he passed it to was Dennis Sweeney. As a member of Stern Hall's Original Sixteen, Dennis's campus stature was such that he was included in the group of a hundred or so students who composed Armin Rosencranz's informal "kitchen cabinet," a breeding place for much of the antiban strategy.

By spring quarter, the president of the university offered a compromise proposal: The student body would officially create a mechanism, to be called the Stanford Student Congress, in which all student political clubs and factions could propose and debate resolutions on the issues of the day, as was traditionally done at England's Oxford and Cambridge universities. Although the offer failed to grant their right to unfettered political activity, the student activists pushing the fight decided to accept the compromise and run with it. The Student Congress, headed by an elected "speaker," would go into effect starting with the new academic year in the fall.

As it turned out, its first speaker and presiding officer was Dennis Sweeney. In the capacities of his office, the first outside "lecturer" Sweeney invited to address the body was former assistant dean of men, Allard Lowenstein. But by then, the administration's compromise had been virtually swept away by a wave of student political activity that preempted further administration attempts to restrict student activism.

But before all this, Dennis Sweeney returned to Portland for what he expected would be another dull summer of wage earning. He was by then one of Allard's most trusted lieutenants. An honors student, he was also one of the two dozen upper classmen selected to act as counselors to the males in the next year's freshman class. His jawline was firm, his words came quickly, and his glance was direct. Allard, in a number of conversations during his 1962 and 1963 visits to Stanford, held Dennis up as an example for other students to emulate, and his contemporaries remember that Sweeney responded with devotion and increased attempts to excel.

During July 1963, a month after Sweeney's return to Portland for vacation, Lowenstein called his protégé from Mississippi. He'd gone there, he said, to "assist" the local black struggle for civil rights and wanted Dennis to come join him in Jackson until school started. The period now remembered as the Sixties was about to begin in earnest.

When it did, Allard Lowenstein was, if not the father figure in Dennis Sweeney's life, certainly the next closest thing.

3

Allard Lowenstein drove a used car with North Carolina plates into Jackson, Mississippi, that July day in 1963. Before he even knew exactly what was going on there, he was convinced of the contribution he would make. Allard's belief in Allard was unswerving. It was the strength that underlay his impact and the weakness that undercut most of his victories as well. After his assassination, Lowenstein would be described as both the most "selfless" and "self-serving" of men—and both adjectives were, at times, deserved. Both would be widely circulated in the course of the struggle over the state he entered that July.

Going to Mississippi was apparently his own idea. On the face of it, there was little to recommend the state to civil rights advocates. Nowhere was more Dixie. Transgressors of segregation were dealt with in an unrestrained vigilante fashion. Nowhere were blacks a larger proportion of the population and nowhere were their rights more minimal. Only certifiable Caucasians held public office and, as a rule, the vote itself. In one Mississippi county, 112 percent of the resident whites were registered to vote—and less than 1 percent of the blacks. The arrangement was called "the Southern way of life" and was defended as "what God intended when He made the Negro kinky-headed, flat-nosed, thick-lipped, and black-skinned." Mississippi seemed the last place that would change.

It was exactly that seeming hopelessness that attracted Allard. He had a predilection for redeeming lost causes. They provided him with a challenge suitable to his sense of himself and an opportunity to exercise influence with no more credentials than those generated by the persuasiveness of his own presence. Lowenstein always sought out such critical situations, believing he was all that was needed to turn the tide, and he was always nagged by the sense that he got too little credit when he did. Mississippi would end up epitomizing those feelings.

He began his involvement there looking up the names he had listed in his head or scribbled on a wad of paper in his pocket. He knew some local civil rights figures through his days as Mrs. Roosevelt's protégé and had no qualms about introducing himself to others.

On July 4 Allard Lowenstein showed up at the home of Reverend Ed King, the white campus minister for black Tougaloo College. King had never heard of him before. Where he had gotten King's name, Allard didn't say, only that the minister was known to be one of a handful of Mississippi whites on public record as favoring black rights. Lowenstein told King he wanted "to help out" and identified himself as one of those who had "just finished integrating Raleigh, North Carolina," the year before. King provided an assessment of the local situation. The demonstrations in Jackson that spring had been the peak of the movement thus far. White response had been characteristic: The police chief had augmented his forces with a war-surplus armored car, over a thousand marchers had been arrested, and Medgar Evers, the best-known civil rights figure in the state, had been assassinated by vigilantes. By now, a known civil rights organizer could hardly venture into the streets without being pulled over by the police. King made a joke about how these days, three people in the same room constituted a rally.

Lowenstein laughed appreciatively and wanted to know what groups were still active.

Ed King told him that the statewide coalition was called the Council of Federated Organizations (COFO). It included the Mississippi chapters of the National Association for the Advancement of Colored People (NAACP), the Congress of Racial Equality (CORE), the Southern Christian Leadership Conference (SCLC), and the Student Nonviolent Coordinating Committee (SNCC). COFO was designed to demonstrate a united front, but, King said, the appearance tended to hide the real arrangement. Without SNCC (called "Snick" for short) there would be no Mississippi movement. Virtually all of those arrested that spring had been young people, inspired and aroused by SNCC. SNCC had begun a voter-registration program in 1961, when other national organizations had for all intents and purposes abandoned the state. It had recently opened an office in Jackson, but its state headquarters was in Greenwood. King advised Lowenstein to drive up and visit. He thought SNCC was full of "exceptional" people and recommended talking to Bob Moses, their Mississippi Project director.

Shortly afterward, Allard Lowenstein headed for Greenwood. He had originally intended to spend less than a week in Mississippi, just long enough to make a solid connection, and then return to New York City, where he had already committed himself to organizing a "Citizens for Ryan" campaign in the reelection effort of Manhattan Congressman William Fitz Ryan. That initial estimate was already changing. He sensed something with great potential was going on here, whatever its momentary weakness, and Lowenstein responded electrically. He was already sure Mississippi could be the cutting edge of the American black uprising. His excitement bubbled out in his singing snatches of Gilbert and Sullivan tunes to himself as he drove.

At Greenwood, Lowenstein introduced himself at SNCC head-quarters with the seeming embarrassment he always manifested on first contact. Bob Moses, the man he asked for, was not around. SNCC was in the midst of a prolonged strategy discussion, looking for a way out of the corner the spring demonstrations seemed to have left them in, and Moses had gone to Jackson to talk with people there. Lowenstein proceeded to engage several others at the Greenwood office in conversation. The innocuousness of the occasion gave little hint of just how momentous the moment really was. More than any other entity, SNCC shaped the Mississippi stage upon which Lowen-stein, Dennis Sweeney, and the rest of the Sixties played out the first act in their mutual drama.

Allard and SNCC were initially attracted to each other for a variety of reasons, but neither party would ever be more than barely comfort-able with the ongoing alliance, and a good number of the internal tensions of the Mississippi movement's next year would end up focused on tensions between them. Their mutual suspicions were similar to those that would frame the divergence of Allard and Dennis as well.

Once back in Jackson, Lowenstein immersed himself in the Mississippi Project's pursuit of strategy. To many SNCC members, Allard just seemed to materialize out of thin air at those discussions. Only a few had heard of him before. A typical introduction occurred early in July at SNCC's Jackson office on Lynch Street. Five SNCC staffers were sitting around in a room there, chewing over the same old question. There was almost universal bemoaning of how thoroughly the movement was stymied. Further work would be impossible unless some means of deflecting redneck reaction was found. At that moment, the door opened and Allard Lowenstein walked in.

"Hi," he said, somewhat sheepishly. "I'm Al Lowenstein." With-out hesitation, he moved to an empty chair. "Go on with what you were saying."

No one in the room had any idea who this Jewish-looking white dude was, but they continued talking. Within five minutes Lowenstein had begun offering his opinion.

Had Lowenstein not arrived in Mississippi at a moment of intense ambivalence and indecision, it is doubtful he and SNCC would have ever made common cause at all. If ever two styles of thought were destined to reach disagreement, they were Allard's and SNCC's. Allard was a take-charge kind of guy who expected quick decisions made by leaders with the authority to speak for everyone else. SNCC as an organization was long since wedded to participatory democracy in substance as well as form. Everyone had an equal voice, and decisions were made only after a consensus acceptable to everyone had been reached. Charismatic oratory was enormously suspect. Allard overflowed with it. SNCC distrusted the liberal wing of the national Democratic party, and Lowenstein saw himself as the champion of that same wing's best instincts.

Half of the leverage Allard exercised that summer of 1963 was a function of his faith. He had no trouble believing great things were still possible, lending energy to a dynamic that was battered, flagging, and waiting somewhat desperately to catch its second wind. The other half of Lowenstein's leverage grew from the fact that once they'd met, Bob Moses took what he said seriously. Without that, Allard's impact would have been minimal. Everyone in SNCC listened to Bob.

In July of 1961, Robert Moses, a 26-year-old black with a Masters in Philosophy from Harvard, had first entered southwest Mississippi and begun holding voter education classes under the auspices of SNCC's Mississippi Project. Since then, he had been arrested, beaten, chased, shot at, and machine-gunned. In the days when Allard finally made contact with him, Moses was often seen carrying a volume of Camus in his back pocket. Initially, Bob and Allard were impressed with each other.

Fourteen years later, long after the Mississippi alliance had disintegrated in much bitterness, Lowenstein taped an oral history interview with a Stanford professor in which he described Moses as brilliant, gentle, serene, and infinitely patient. "Moses had," Allard claimed,

> . . . an almost inhuman quality. I mean inhuman in the sense
> of angelic. He had such goodness as a person. . . . He
> reminded me of Frank Graham. . . . He had an extraordinary
> intellect, capable of grasping people's sensibilities and then
> becoming them. [He was] a real figure of strength. . . . You
> always felt when you were with him that you were in the
> presence of someone better. . . . As a person, Bob Moses was
> not only indispensable but unparalleled.

There were few arguments between the two men that summer, and Bob's respect made Lowenstein credible.

At one of the Jackson discussions, word having gotten around that Allard had been in South Africa, he was asked what blacks there did on election day. Allard answered that blacks in South Africa held a day of mourning and went on to speculate that maybe Mississippians should do something similar. "But then," as he would later say, "I thought that wasn't right. In South Africa, black voting was constitutionally prohibited. In the United States, the Constitution supported black voting, only Mississippi did not. It shouldn't be a day of mourning. It must be a day of voting instead." Lowenstein would repeat the story of that response in the years that followed, offering it as solid proof that the 1963 Freedom Vote had been his idea.

SNCC veterans of the same discussions vehemently dispute Lowenstein's claim and point out that before Lowenstein even arrived in Mississippi, Bob Moses had asked the SNCC legal staff to research possible ways of somehow taking part in the upcoming 1963 gubernatorial elections. The subsequent report pointed out that an obscure Mississippi statute provided that anyone who felt they had been unfairly denied the vote could go to the polls and cast a ballot "under protest." Not long after Allard's South African comments, Bob Moses formally recommended that the Mississippi Project utilize those "protest ballot" provisions during the August primary election. The strategy would allow them to maintain their focus on voting rights without having to rely on the large demonstrations that had been effectively stamped out that spring. Lowenstein argued for the proposal enthusiastically, and Jackson and Greenwood were targeted for this first experiment at casting protest votes.

That decision gave the Mississippi Project an immediate focus but, in and of itself, did not resolve the movement's largest dilemma. Because of the continued lack of visibility of the struggle going on in the state, to the nation and world at large, official Mississippi lost nothing in exercising repression of the most brutal sort against blacks. Federal intervention was needed, but by now, most SNCC members had somewhat bitterly reached the conclusion that Washington, D.C., would ignore whatever happened in Mississippi until it happened to someone white. That imbalance of national perception was referred to frequently in the protest-ballot discussions.

Allard Lowenstein immediately spoke up for using this imbalance to their own advantage. Recruit white young volunteers to supplement those few already on SNCC's staff, he argued. The idea was one Moses himself had been toying with since January. Lowenstein's presence bolstered the notion and made it seem possible. Allard claimed to be able to recruit as many "good" northern white college volunteers as SNCC wanted. The Mississippi Project eventually decided to give the idea a trial run by having him bring several northern white students down to help with the protest-ballot effort in the August primary.

Dennis Sweeney was one of those Allard called.

D ennis took a Greyhound from Oregon to Memphis, Tennessee, and by the beginning of August was at the SNCC office on Lynch Street in Jackson.

Now that the Sixties are over, the mind tends to assume they were inevitable and, in so doing, obscures just how extraordinary Dennis's presence in Jackson during that summer actually was. Young Northern whites' risking their lives south of the Mason-Dixon Line was unheard of back then, and Dennis was among no more than a handful of his peers. Although Allard Lowenstein had provided the specific opportunity, it was Dennis's own mind that led him there. The previous two years of intellectual exploration had made him a gifted student of social thought, with both a knack for conceptualization and a firm belief that such abstractions had to be incorporated into daily behavior. He had few doubts that intellectual conclusions bred practical obligations in whose fulfillment every person's true moral identity was to be found. Dennis believed in "All men are created equal," "Black and white together, hand in hand," and "As long as one man is in chains, no one is free." He went to Mississippi to give those ethics substance. Dennis was still a young man, it was still a young decade, and he was, by all standards, ahead of his time.

There is no surviving record of how his first glimpse of Jim Crow affected Sweeney, but the impact can hardly have been other than stunning. Dennis had never before seen bathrooms designated "white" and "colored." He had never seen separate drinking fountains, separate restaurants, or separate laws. He had never had much contact with black people or ever known anyone who picked cotton for a living.

A number of SNCC's Mississippi staffers remember Sweeney from that first summer he was in the state, but none of these memories have the clarity of those from the year after that. In August 1963 he seemed little more than a fair-haired blur at Allard Lowenstein's elbow, and most SNCC members just accounted him as part of his mentor's pattern. As one put it, "Ever time you'd see Lowenstein, he'd always have some young Waspy-lookin' white boy with him." Another, who would become a close friend of Dennis's during the next year, described Sweeney in 1963 as "following Lowenstein around like a little puppy dog." Dennis's official role apparently amounted to filling in at the Jackson office so that someone else could go out and organize.

Though limited in its scope, the August protest-ballot strategy was deemed successful enough that talk about extending the model filled the last two weeks of the month. Once again, Lowenstein argued for it vehemently. Dennis Sweeney probably listened to some of the discussions but said nothing. By September, the strategy had evolved into a mock election called the Freedom Vote. To demonstrate to the nation the extent to which their rights to the franchise had been denied, the Mississippi Project would organize a parallel election in which blacks would cast ballots for their own slate of candidates. Bob Moses took the idea to the SNCC national executive committee meeting in Atlanta and asked them to make Mississippi and the Freedom Vote the organization's principal fall focus.

Around the same time that Moses was making his Atlanta proposal, Dennis Sweeney was saying good-bye to Allard and leaving for California and his approaching junior year at Stanford. Sweeney was scheduled to be one of the upperclassman counselors for the incoming freshmen as well as speaker of the new Stanford Student Congress. Lowenstein was about to hop a plane to New York to try and raise some outside support for the fall effort. Allard told Dennis he would see him soon.

I was a member of the freshman class Dennis Sweeney returned to Stanford to welcome to Wilbur Hall, the dorm for freshman males. Wilbur was of the same concrete-blockhouse design as Stern, painted to look like sandstone from a distance and topped with a red-tiled Spanish roof. Each of its eight houses had an upperclassman counselor living on each of its three floors. These counselors were called sponsors. Dennis Sweeney was a sponsor in one building, I a freshman in another. We never met while at Wilbur, but I heard of Dennis Sweeney soon and remembered his name.

I was, according to several of my classmates, friendly, with "a knack for saying funny things at the right time." The previous spring I had been selected Fresno High School's "Boy of the Year," but Fresno was looked upon as the backwoods by most, and I was excited to be away from there and in the big leagues at last. I seemed "confident" and quickly became a "noticeable" personality, but underneath all that I felt at loose ends about who to be in this new environment. I wanted great things to come my way, but where to look for them was not at all clear.

Like the rest of my class, I attended the annual freshman convocation. The visuals of the afternoon assembly in the amphitheater were somewhat different from those of Dennis Sweeney's two years earlier. No one rolled up the cuffs of their Levis anymore, and saddle oxfords had virtually disappeared. Kahlil Gibran was still displayed, but so was Allen Ginsberg. Flat-tops no longer dominated male hairstyles, but women continued to use large quantities of hair spray, especially those from Texas. Much of the president's speech was quite similar to what had been said to Dennis and his class the year they and Allard Lowenstein had arrived. The setting was still green and quite confident. The phrase "the pursuit of intelligence" was repeated, and so was "the responsibility to seek a better life through the development of the mind." "Keep your faces into the wind," the president closed, "your feet on the ground, and your eyes on the stars." For the third year running, the line got a big round of applause.

More than 2,000 miles away, the Mississippi Project was on the verge of officially launching its slate for the 1963 freedom vote. Aaron Henry, a black pharmacist, Clarksdale, Mississippi NAACP leader, and national board member of Martin Luther King's Southern Christian Leadership Conference (SCLC) was running for governor. Allard had known Henry for several years prior to coming South. The nominee for lieutenant governor was Reverend Ed King, the man Lowenstein had looked up in Jackson on the Fourth of July. Robert P. Moses was named campaign manager. Allard K. Lowenstein was named "chairman of the campaign advisory committee." The Council of Federated Organizations (COFO) was the sponsoring body of record.

The difference that would eventually split the Mississippi Project into fragments was already a crack running through COFO's base. SNCC was on one side of it and the NAACP on the other. The N-double-A was older and more established, but 85 percent of COFO's field force owed its allegiance to SNCC, and since policy is often defined by its enactment, SNCC's dominance in the field only heightened the NAACP's suspicions of young SNCC's confrontation tactics and incipient radicalism. SNCC's suspicions of the NAACP had been solidified in 1962 when Bob Moses asked Roy Wilkins, the N-double-

A's national chairman, for backing in an aggressive Mississippi voter-registration push. Wilkins had answered that Mississippi was a hopeless cause, the last place that would change. By the fall of 1963, most of SNCC perceived the N-double-A as "accommodationist."

Since he had become close to several of Mississippi's NAACP leaders and, at that time, still had Moses's ear, Lowenstein tried to act as the self-appointed white bridge between the two largely black camps. On the one hand he made a point of nagging Moses to talk with the people in the NAACP. On the other, he soothed the N-double-A's resentments as best he could. It is a testament to Lowenstein's self-confidence that he insisted on explaining one group to the other, whether asked to or not.

Lowenstein gravitated to that bridge role over and over again throughout his life. Being the broker of political coalition was among the most powerful possible ways for a single individual to affect any situation quickly. The role's power was matched by an inherent vulnerability as well. The risks of either being caught in the middle or playing one side against the other and thereby isolating himself were both ever present in such posturing. At least the part about being caught in the middle would happen to Lowenstein over and over again in the decade to come, sometimes as a direct function of his own behavior and sometimes not.

The pattern was already in place. One of the first signs was Allard's growing impatience with SNCC's cumbersome participatory process. He wanted to be able to get Moses and Aaron Henry to agree on something and then have it happen. SNCC insisted that everyone talk it out first, and Lowenstein thought all the talk was "wasting valuable time."

One of the issues Allard grumbled about most was the continued failure of SNCC to decide whether to use Northern white students for the Freedom Vote. SNCC's reluctance to do so was based on several members' feelings that white outsiders tended to incite rednecks to further violence, not less. Most of that violence still fell on the Mississippi blacks, who could not leave when the vote was over. Lowenstein down played the risk and said it was worth taking.

SNCC was not to agree with him until less than a month before the Freedom Vote was to be held. Then Bob Moses sat down in the Lynch Street headquarters and wrote a five-page appeal for assistance on a dime-store writing tablet, each sheet a different color.

Allard Lowenstein immediately took the letter and flew North to begin raising troops.

Before this, however, Allard flew out to Stanford, where his protégé, Dennis Sweeney, speaker of the Stanford Student Congress, had invited him to address the group. I did not attend, but the speech was covered in the October 3, 1963, edition of the *Stanford Daily*. The headline "Lowenstein Describes Negro Oppression in South" ran in a banner across the top of the front page.

Lowenstein was identified as a "former Stanford assistant dean of men" who was a "legal advisor" to the Mississippi civil rights movement. "Mississippi," he said,

> is a place where America is at its worse and also where anyone who is an American can see himself at his worst. . . . One should feel an involvement in Mississippi, not because of the harm it does to American prestige or a guilty conscience because injustice exists somewhere, but because it is one of the most flagrant and egregious parts of America. . . . Voter registration is dependent upon [the] risk of lives, and other forms of protest are equally foreclosed.

"Mississippi is not a foreign country in our midst," he closed, "it's a foreign part of all of us in our midst." Several people who attended later told me it was one of the most moving presentations they ever heard.

A smaller article in the same *Daily* was headlined, "Student Congress Collects Over $400 for 'Mock Vote.'" It described a discussion of the Freedom Vote in which both Lowenstein and Dennis Sweeney participated. Both were characterized as recounting their "personal experiences in the South this summer." Allard told about how young blacks, cut off from marching downtown by Jackson police with rifles, had yelled, "Shoot us, shoot us," until restrained by "older Negroes." Dennis told how anyone attempting to register to vote had his name published in the paper for two weeks, making the listed blacks an open target to every white who could read. The meeting was informational and designed to raise money. There was not yet any open recruiting.

Privately, Allard let it be known that SNCC was still chewing over the idea of using outside white students but predicted that they would end up wanting volunteers. Dennis was told to keep himself prepared to act quickly, and Allard flew back to Jackson for more meetings.

On October 16, 1963, Allard Lowenstein arrived at Yale University with Bob Moses's letter in hand. Allard still had connections there dating from his own law school days. In the Collegiate Press Service coverage of his campuswide meeting, Lowenstein was identified as "former president of the United States National Student Association, former Yale law student, and professor on leave from the University of North Carolina." He began by reading Moses's letter. It was addressed to Lowenstein himself and amounted to a charter to recruit. For many years Allard would keep the original document among the cluttered files and innumerable back issues of the *New York Times* he stored in his brother's New York City basement. "The Freedom Ballot," Moses wrote, "will show that if Negroes had the right to vote without fear of physical violence and other reprisals, they would do so. . . . The need is . . . desperate and we would be deeply grateful for any help you may be able to get for us." By October 21, the first contingent of more than two dozen Yale students reported to SNCC headquarters on Lynch Street for assignment to COFO's outlying Freedom Vote projects.

Around the same time, Allard Lowenstein phoned Dennis Sweeney. Volunteers were needed quickly, and Allard had personally selected Stanford and Yale as the places to provide them. Yale, he said, was already on its way.

Stanford followed with alacrity, in great part because of Sweeney's efforts.

That October, Dennis Sweeney began his emergence as Stanford's foremost civil rights hero with a speech to a campuswide volunteers' meeting held in a lounge at Wilbur Hall. I did not attend, but echoes of it reached me shortly. As news of the Mississippi adventure spread, groups of 17- and 18-year-olds began to congregate in the hallway, feverishly discussing whether to go or not. Twenty-year-old Dennis Sweeney's name was mentioned a lot, more even than 34-year-old Allard Lowenstein's. It took me half an hour to decide I was going, and another half hour in the line at the phone booth downstairs was spent waiting to call home and deliver the news. "Freeing the Negroes of Mississippi" seemed an admirable cause and fit easily into my search for "great things" to do, now that I was out on my own. Age 17, I had been away at college for little more than a month.

My father responded in the voice that always signaled me that he was pissed off, saying I should stick to studying and make sure I got to my job waiting on tables in the dining hall punctually. He hoped Mississippi Negroes got to vote, but he was not about to pay Stanford tuition in order to supply them with a campaign worker. I went back upstairs and unpacked my bag.

In the end, 13 Stanford students drove South. The first four left on Sunday evening, October 27. Dennis Sweeney, the sponsor whose name I'd heard so often, was among that contingent. The following Monday's *Stanford Daily* carried his name and a long statement from Allard Lowenstein, the man who had summoned him South.

"What is going on in the state of Mississippi in October 1963," Allard wrote,

> is astonishing to an American citizen not experienced in the ways of this state. . . . It could not survive the test of a free election. That is why these people will not allow a free election to be held. . . . The atmosphere of this campaign suggests more nearly what a campaign might be like in the Soviet Union or Cuba . . . than in the United States. . . . The courage of the people who are continuing their efforts in the campaign cannot fail to impress and move those of us who have arrived from other parts of the United States.
>
> We shall tell what we have found in Mississippi wherever we go when we leave here and we shall not leave here until we have seen through the rest of this dismal affair. We shall submit evidence of what we have found to . . . the Congress of the United States in the faith that the American people, once they know the facts, will not be willing to allow tyranny to wrap itself in the American flag. . . . It is of course a pity that it should be necessary for people to make such sacrifices in our country at this late date, but it is wonderful to know that there are many prepared to do so as long as it may be necessary.

The same day that statement ran in California, one of the recently arrived Yale volunteers encountered the former assistant dean of men in the SNCC headquarters in Jackson.

"We're all in luck," Allard blurted. "There's a great group on the way from Stanford." He then proceeded to name names.

Dennis Sweeney was at the top of the list.

Just as SNCC—with a measure of bitterness—had predicted earlier that fall, visibility arrived in Mississippi with the Yale and Stanford students and escalated as the story of the white boys' experience broke in the press.

Six of the Yalies were arrested within 36 hours of reaching the state. One, driving through Natchez in an out-of-date car with a black SNCC worker, was followed by two Mississippi vehicles and a police car until he stopped at a gas station. There the trailing rednecks beat the Yale man's head against the ethyl pump while the cop watched. Another Yale man was arrested for alleged reckless driving and beaten up by one of the policemen in Clarksdale. Two others tried to hail a black cab in downtown Hattiesburg, but the cabbie refused when he saw a police car watching. The Yale students then walked across to the white cab company's office. When their ride finally came, the redneck driver beat the two students up. The cop then arrested the Yale men for assault and battery. Back in Natchez, a Yale student was chased through the dark in automobiles at high speed. It was the tenth time the SNCC worker riding with the Yalie had been fired upon and the first time the Justice Department saw fit to investigate.

Stanford's saga ended up reading much like Yale's. Dennis Sweeney and a Stanford sophomore were sent out to work in Tougaloo. They were soon arrested on charges of being "suspicious characters," taken to Oxford, Mississippi, and released. The Stanford student already in Oxford was arrested on similar charges. One of several Stanford students in Jackson was ordered out of a black café by a white police officer saying, "You can live with niggers if you want to, but not in Mississippi." According to the *Daily*, Stanford and Yale students were ordered out of more than a dozen towns and commonly "driven from Negro doors at gun point by white citizens." An Aaron Henry for Governor rally held on the evening of November 1 in one of Bulovie, Mississippi's black churches was attacked by a mob of whites while the local police watched and ran their sirens. Jackson's white newspapers reported the incident as "Mixed Church Affair Sparks Battle," one of over 200 assaults in two weeks. "Jackson," campaign advisory chairman Allard Lowenstein told California reporters, "is in a state of siege."

Following events in the *Stanford Daily*, one had the impression that Lowenstein was the entire Mississippi civil rights movement. One day it was a headline, "Lowenstein: 'We Will Win.'" On another, his comments were displayed in a box with heavy black borders on the front page: "BULLETIN. Allard Lowenstein called as the *Daily* went to press last night and stated: 'The campaign is a much greater success than we ever dreamed possible. There is no question that Stanford and Yale have changed the nature of the campaign in Mississippi. . . . This is what can stop the intimidation, the force of someone from outside.'"

In the eyes of most SNCC members, Lowenstein's importance was exaggerated in the process. Allard was "a resource" who "offered his help and was accepted on it," they admonish, but nothing more. He didn't "make decisions."

The discomfort that had begun to surround the Lowenstein-SNCC relationship was exemplified by an incident that happened the week Dennis arrived, when Lowenstein was in the headquarters, taking a turn on the bank of phones used to communicate with the state's various projects. At one point he answered a call from the Yazoo City Project. The caller had reports of some arrests made by the local police. After getting the details, Lowenstein told Yazoo City that there was no option but to challenge the authorities.

"Fill the jails," he instructed them.

Yazoo City hung up. Within five minutes, the SNCC Yazoo City Project director was on the line again, demanding to talk to someone from SNCC.

"Look," he finally screamed at the fellow staffer who was fetched, "I don't know who Al Lowenstein is, but if he ever orders anybody in Yazoo City or elsewhere to 'fill the jails' again I'm gonna come up to Jackson and personally break his goddamn jaw. Where does he get off telling people what to do?"

To say the least, SNCC did not do things Allard's way.

Despite differences in approach, Lowenstein continued like a dervish, making flying visits out of the state to recruit "name" support, spending hours on the phone with Northern reporters, and filling political breeches around Jackson.

On one such Jackson occasion, he was followed for twenty minutes by city police and then arrested for running a stoplight at an intersection that had no traffic signals whatsoever. On another, he and two young men from Yale were arrested as "suspicious characters." After several hours in jail, the three "nigger lovers" were released with a $16 fine. On yet another, Lowenstein was in the Lynch Street office late at night with Bob Moses and several others when someone noticed that the block was being steadily circled by white people in slow-moving cars. The silhouettes made it obvious they were carrying rifles. Someone in the office immediately switched all the lights off, and everyone crouched below window level to avoid becoming targets. The circling outside continued for hours. Finally at 2 A.M. Allard got on the phone, called a Justice Department lawyer he knew in Washington, and got the man out of bed. Lowenstein told him the SNCC office was surrounded and they stood "a fifty-fifty chance of surviving the night." The lawyer responded that there was nothing he could do.

The headquarters and Lowenstein survived nonetheless. The image of him there is a blur, moving from phone to desk to phone, counseling here, cajoling there, always insisting on something, obsessed with the details of language and strategy. His public statements continued to appear regularly in the *Stanford Daily*, often along with those of his protégé, Dennis Sweeney. "Please," Dennis said, "communicate to Stanford students how much [their] support has meant to us."

Over the next few days, Stanford students and faculty responded by donating more than $8,000 to the effort. Dennis Sweeney and Stanford's twelve other volunteers stayed until election eve, a total of six days in Mississippi.

The last event many of the Stanford volunteers and their Yale counterparts participated in was the Aaron Henry for Governor rally in Jackson on November 4.

The crowd was large, 95 percent black, and the white Jackson police were drawn up on the street outside in force. The candidate for governor was nowhere to be seen. Eventually an organizer appeared at the podium and announced that Mr. Henry was coming and no one should go away. A long, nervous silence followed. Then Lowenstein appeared in a rumpled coat with equally rumpled tie askew at his neck. He told one of the COFO people at the edge of the stage to find Henry and get him here. Allard himself would hold the crowd.

One of the Yale volunteers would later write about Allard's speech:

> I can't remember his precise words, but I do remember his drift and tone. He talked about the Constitution and the rights of man. He recounted the history of Aaron Henry, the druggist from Clarksdale who had worked long and hard for the rights of Negro Americans. He talked about the thousands of voters. . . . The whole nation was watching, the day was fast coming when the vote would be theirs as a natural right.

Then Lowenstein started to talk about the whites in
Mississippi, the scared folks who crept around at night in
white bedsheets and ganged up twenty to one before they
dared beat up a Negro boy. . . . I wish I could remember how
he did it, but Lowenstein got the audience to laugh, and then
he got them to cheer, and then he got them laughing and
cheering and whistling and he kept it up, never breaking
stride, for the better part of an hour until Aaron Henry finally
arrived, swept up onto the stage by a wave of cheers and
yells and hallelujahs.

Dennis Sweeney mentioned Lowenstein's performance in his last
interview from Mississippi later that evening. According to the *Daily*,
"Sweeney reported . . . that Lowenstein's speech to the crowd created
a highly dynamic atmosphere. . . . Sweeney said the mock vote . . .
convinced him that 'the Negroes here really want to vote, but we must
give them moral support.'"

After Dennis and the other Stanford men had left for California,
Allard himself placed a postmidnight call to the campus paper. "It has
been important," he said, "to know what Mississippi will do to keep
people down. The very fact of Negroes wearing campaign buttons for
the first time . . . has been a great educational experience for the state.
The psychological impact upon Negroes of outside support, the
growing awareness of whites of what is coming, succeeded in doing
something in Mississippi far beyond our expectations. . . . We have
finally promised these people something," Allard admonished in
closing, "and hopefully [we] won't stop now."

Dennis Sweeney, then speeding West to return to school, would
soon take Allard's admonition to heart more than any of his Stanford
peers.

J ust what shape the continuing commitment of Dennis,
Allard, and the others ought to take had become a subject of
much discussion even before the Freedom Vote was held. As usual,
Lowenstein was in the middle of it. During his visit to Stanford in
October, he had hinted at the idea of "a mass assistance campaign from
outside Mississippi next summer," but offered no firmer definition. A
concrete plan was a long time in coming but eventually emerged as the
1964 Mississippi Summer Project, another strategy Allard later claimed
credit for thinking up.

"In the beginning," he later told one interviewer, "I was the only one proposing [the Summer Project] and ended up selling it to everyone else. . . . Moses was enthusiastic, but other parts of SNCC were not. . . . My role was getting the idea approved. . . . They [COFO] ended up offering me whatever position [in the Summer Project] I wanted, but I thought it would be better to give the visibility to blacks."

SNCC veterans later vehemently disputed Lowenstein's claim, calling it "incredibly self-serving" and "hopelessly distorted." They denied that Lowenstein was ever offered any post and asserted that the 1964 Mississippi Summer Project had been discussed by SNCC before Allard even showed up. What Lowenstein did provide, they pointed out, was a great deal of advice to direct the summer's work toward the Democratic party and its national convention, scheduled for the end of the 1964 summer in Atlantic City, New Jersey. He was also "extremely useful" in recruiting white outside students and the white liberal support the white students attracted. Such mutual need kept Lowenstein and SNCC working together until late spring 1964, but SNCC's suspicions of him grew steadily, until many in SNCC eventually came to consider Lowenstein the personification of manipulation.

One of Lowenstein's principal detractors was James Forman, SNCC's national secretary. Forman and Lowenstein had first crossed paths at the 1956 National Student Association congress, where Forman was trying to get the students to adopt a resolution calling for the end of Rule 22, the filibuster provisions in the operating code of the United States Senate that had, in effect, given the Deep South veto power over national civil rights legislation.

Forman later claimed:

> People told us we were fighting an uphill battle because
> Allard Lowenstein opposed us. Lowenstein . . . was indeed a
> powerful fellow, a past president of NSA . . . one who had
> addressed the convention earlier and received a tremendous
> response. Lowenstein . . . led the fight against us not from
> the floor but by assisting those . . . who wanted us to leave
> the business of the Senate to Senators. . . . Finally Lowenstein
> . . . got the student body president from the City College of
> New York, a Negro, to stand up and argue against us. The
> moment this young Uncle Tom rose to speak, I was on the
> floor and saw with my own eyes how Allard Lowenstein
> shoved him, literally pushed him, toward the microphone,
> saying, "Go now. Speak now." . . . To this day I remember
> the expression on the face of Allard Lowenstein as he pushed
> the black cat down the aisle. This was a young white who
> would later build a big liberal image. . . .

The Freedom Vote . . . contained an omen, a warning, which we did not fully recognize as such at the time. That omen took the form of Allard Lowenstein's presence in Mississippi. . . . Seven years had passed since I had seen him in action at the NSA conference. . . . I was disturbed to see him in Mississippi now and very briefly mentioned to Bob Moses that I had reservations about Lowenstein. I did not press them because . . . Lowenstein's presence was a *fait accompli.* In any case, it soon became clear that Moses was developing his own reservations about Lowenstein. . . .

Allard also served as SNCC's symbol for a host of new elements that showed up in Mississippi after the Freedom Vote. "We would," Forman claimed, "discover that he represented a whole body of influential forces seeking to prevent SNCC from becoming too radical and bring it under . . . control." The United Auto Workers, the NAACP, and the National Council of Churches were all now prepared to back COFO's work during the coming summer. On paper the alliance seemed simple. The liberals would provide money and volunteers, largely white ministers and college students. Those volunteers would be hooked into SNCC's existing network of native black Mississippians and the entire force channeled into two principal activities under the aegis of COFO: the freedom schools, providing a summer alternative to the stultified black Mississippi educational system, and the Freedom Democratic party, another parallel electoral gambit. The Freedom Democratic party would select a delegation, proceed to the Democratic National Convention, and demand that Mississippi's regular Jim Crow Democrats be denied recognition in favor of themselves. For the liberals, such an effort was a means of changing the Democratic party to more closely fit their own national civil rights agenda. For SNCC, it was the promise of abundant resources to enhance their local base. The seam where the two pictures joined would never be very stable. Again, Allard tried to act as the bridge among all the major players.

He had little success. The coalition would last only to the 1964 Democratic National Convention in Atlantic City and no further. The relationship between SNCC and Allard would disintegrate even before that.

None of those coming differences were yet visible at Stanford.

Upon their return to campus on November 7, Dennis Sweeney and the other Mississippi volunteers were greeted as heroes who had risked great personal harm for the sake of something undeniably good.

Politics of any more sophistication than that was certainly beyond me at the moment. My personal Boola-Boola was not yet dead, despite my urge to charge off to the Freedom Vote. It was, however, on its last legs.

My final episode of it began on Thursday evening, November 21. The experience was known as the 1963 freshman bonfire, a lesser part of the cross-Bay football game with the University of California, Stanford's biggest Boola-Boola of the school year. It was the responsibility of the freshmen to build an immense construction out of scrap lumber on an exposed lake bottom that would be incinerated at the Friday night pregame rally. The freshmen worried that some Cal student might sneak down and light the bonfire ahead of time, and so the wooden heap was guarded constantly. That Thursday I was recruited to stand around in ankle-deep slop and darkness, holding down one stretch of the Bonfire's perimeter among the rampant frog calls of the lake bottom. At 5 A.M. I finally returned to Wilbur Hall and bed.

It was 12 noon November 22 when I awoke to my clock radio. The announcer was talking about "other Presidents who have died in office." I reached over and turned the volume up. I could hear shouting in the courtyard outside my window, and someone was running down the concrete hall. The announcer repeated his bulletin. John Fitzgerald Kennedy, thirty-fifth President of the United States, had been shot in the head while riding in a motorcade through Dallas, Texas. Lyndon Baines Johnson was now President of the United States.

Stanford's classes were immediately suspended and the approaching big game postponed. University policy left it up to each living group to decide what to do about their planned festivities for the now punctured big game weekend.

My house at Wilbur stood to lose a significant deposit on an off-campus hall rented for our party and decided to have it anyway. I suppose the evening that followed can be accounted for as the confluence of pubescent repression, collective grief, and alcohol all at the same place. The times were such that youth could still be used as an excuse.

Certainly excuses were needed. That Saturday evening, some 60 or 70 Stanford freshmen and their "dates" went berserk celebrating a football game that had never happened, consumed immense amounts of beer, and ransacked the Palo Alto hall where the party was held. Eighteen-year-olds were staggering around the surrounding neighborhood, vomiting on sidewalks and pissing on trees until quite early in the morning. I was in the back seat of a Plymouth down the block with my date, a former cheerleader from Fresno who was now a Berkeley sorority member. I was much drunker than she and attempting to get my hands under her dress. She told me we had to wait until we got married.

I woke up the next morning ashamed of the whole scene and soon began to flee Boola-Boola with a passion. I never saw my cheerleader from Berkeley again. As it turned out, my life was being slowly tugged into the same current that was already impelling Allard Lowenstein and Dennis Sweeney into the decade neither would ever completely escape.

No single event marked the course of that decade more fully than the 1964 Mississippi Summer Project, and no two white men epitomized that Summer Project more than Allard and Dennis. When preliminary recruiting began that January, Lowenstein continued to dash in and out of Stanford regularly, and Sweeney drove him around. When Stanford compatriots said later that Dennis "worshipped Al," this was the period to which many referred. By all outward signs, Allard Lowenstein and Dennis Sweeney thrived on each other.

In this case, all outward signs momentarily hid the secret confusion that had begun to infect Dennis's attitude toward his mentor. It dated from something that happened one night when Dennis was driving Allard around the landscape from one political meeting to another. It was very late, the car was borrowed, and Allard said they were both too tired to get anything else accomplished until morning. Dennis agreed and Allard told him to pull into the next motel. When they stopped, Lowenstein went by himself to the motel office.

When Allard returned from registering, he told Sweeney that the place only had one room left, and that room only had one bed. Allard said he thought it best to take what was available.

Dennis accepted the arrangement as a movement privation and nothing more. Such small discomforts were dwarfed by the cause.

Both men stripped to their underwear, got into their respective half beds, and turned out the lights. Soon thereafter, Lowenstein left his side of the mattress for Dennis's and began to embrace his protégé, offering no explanation of his intentions. Sweeney took the approach as a sexual advance. Nothing like it had ever happened to Dennis before. When Lowenstein finally asked if what he was doing made him uncomfortable, Sweeney said yes.

Allard stopped immediately and was asleep in 15 minutes. Apparently nothing more was ever said between them about it.

The subject does not seem to have been so easily dismissed from Dennis's mind. Any explanation of him or Allard or their relationship would be flawed without an account of it. I later found five people to whom Dennis told the story of Allard's attempt to add a physical dimension to their closeness, and all of them agreed about its importance. In effect, this seems likely to have torn Sweeney between his admiration for Lowenstein as role model on the one hand and the spectre of imagined incest with his father figure on the other. When Sweeney later described the event, he claimed that, for the first time, it had made him feel "manipulated" by Lowenstein: it made him feel Allard was "more than he seemed" and possessed of a "hidden agenda."

A decade and a half later, those same suspicions would be caught in galloping madness and twisted into something homicidal. At the time it occurred, the incident only bred unarticulated confusion, and there was no visible rift between them yet. When the rift eventually did open up, politics was the most immediate reason.

In January of 1964, such political differences still seemed exceedingly remote, if not impossible. Sweeney still cited Lowenstein as the ultimate authority on a wide variety of subjects, and virtually all *Daily* stories about the civil rights movement referred to Sweeney in one way or another. One of the first of the year ran on Friday morning, January 31, under the headline, "Panel Advises Forethought in Civil Rights Campaign." The accompanying photo showed four people sitting behind a table with a microphone on it. Three of them were faculty members in suits and ties. The fourth was Dennis Sweeney. He was wearing a sweater, and his hair, although it stopped well above his ears, was longer than any of the professors'. The caption identified him as speaker of the Student Congress, introducing the topic, "Civil Rights and Student Workers in the South." Dennis was making a point, his left hand lifted off the table, palm up, with all his fingers separated and extended their full length in the direction of the audience.

I came across the photo among the *Daily* office's back issues two months after Dennis Sweeney finally cornered Allard Lowenstein in his Manhattan office and shot half his heart and lungs away. The photo struck me as odd, but at first I couldn't figure out precisely what bothered me about it. Finally I noticed that in it, Dennis Sweeney was wearing spectacles. It was the only time I ever saw or heard of him wearing glasses and looked closer. The pair Dennis was wearing had heavy plastic rims and tended to slip forward a little on his nose. Combined with the hand gesture, they made him look like a young Allard Lowenstein.

In the course of the January panel discussion that Dennis moderated for the Stanford Student Congress, one of the professors touched briefly on the friction underlying the approaching Mississippi Summer Project's facade of solidarity, warning that there was "warfare" among the various civil rights groups. The comment marked the first mention of internal movement strife in the pages of the *Stanford Daily*. Such division among the forces of good was still largely an abstraction to the student audience.

The principal sign of it was simply increased direct contact between students and SNCC itself. The fall effort had left SNCC with contacts on a number of Northern campuses. At Stanford, the student they knew best was Dennis Sweeney, and they now sought to cut out the liberal middlemen linking them to young outside whites. One of the motivating factors was the organization's increasing distrust of Allard Lowenstein.

Though tied strongly to Lowenstein, Sweeney admired his SNCC acquaintances, and when they began sending staffers on speaking tours through Northern college campuses, Sweeney arranged for a hall at Stanford. He also called the campuswide meeting to order and introduced the visiting SNCC field secretary.

The field secretary's speech was blunt and challenging. "We need our best people in Mississippi," he told the Stanford students, "but don't come down with any high-minded notions. SNCC has no place for white liberals. When you come, come to help yourself, not the Negro. This [commitment to the Summer Project] is a pact between your conscience and yourself. This is a chance for you to find yourself, to learn what the problem really is."

After the speech, Dennis Sweeney returned to the microphone and attempted to duplicate the Mississippi freedom meetings he'd seen by leading the student audience in singing. Fifteen clumsy minutes spent finding a song were followed by a chorus that was embarrassed and hesitant.

"If my freedom depended on your singing," the field secretary quipped, "we'd be back in chains."

Dennis Sweeney laughed apologetically.

Within a month of that visit, Stanford had formed a Campus Civil Rights Secretariat, hooked directly into the SNCC-manned COFO headquarters in Jackson, to coordinate preparations for the Summer Project. One of the Secretariat's three principal organizers was Dennis Sweeney, although certainly his politics had not yet become SNCC's.

The presence of Stanford students in Mississippi, Sweeney told the *Daily*, "has a positive psychological value that transcends the limitations of specific achievement. . . . Anything we can do to create contact between the intelligent Northern white and the Mississippi Negro raises their expectations immeasurably and puts a mark of hope into their lives."

Closer to the hub of the 1964 Mississippi Summer Project, Allard Lowenstein was now so frustrated with SNCC's consensus procedures that he had begun insisting that the Summer Project's national headquarters ought to be moved from Jackson to New York City, out of SNCC's backyard and into his own. At one point, he even attempted to do so unilaterally. Since Allard's problems with SNCC were those of quite a few Northern liberals, many parts of the newly constructed liberal support network lent him a sympathetic ear.

The discomfort within the alliance came to a head in a controversy remembered as "the National Lawyers Guild question." In the course of the dispute, Allard Lowenstein was central in both pulling the SNCC-liberal coalition apart and patching it back together at what seemed the last possible moment.

Initially, that meant dropping his role as self-appointed bridge to SNCC and becoming one of SNCC's leading adversaries. The precipitating event was SNCC's inclusion of the National Lawyers Guild in the Summer Project. In liberal circles, the Guild was considered "notoriously leftwing" and was said to include "known Communists." Such terms meant little to SNCC. SNCC's standard of judgment was whether someone was willing "to put their body on the line," and they consequently accepted the offer of a volunteer NLG legal team in late 1963. By the spring of 1964, the out-of-state liberals were clamoring for that decision to be rescinded.

Lowenstein quickly surfaced as one of the Guild's harshest critics. When making his case, he usually opened with an "attorney's response" to the simple issue of "legal competency." Although hardly an experienced legal practitioner himself, Allard had "severe questions" about how the particular lawyers in question had conducted themselves in pursuit of their duties as counsel. Many of the NLG briefs, he claimed, were full of sloppy work, and their lawyers' courtroom antics reprehensible. Lowenstein often repeated the story of how one Guild lawyer had supposedly arrived in front of a Mississippi judge wearing a sweat shirt and two days' growth of beard. "The movement kids loved it," Allard complained, but it only made "the defendant's chances much worse." In that particular case, Allard alleged, a sympathetic appeals judge had voted to reverse the civil rights worker's conviction on grounds that the defendant had been "deprived of responsible counsel." In telling the story, Allard always laughed out loud at the "sheer craziness" of such behavior.

Then he launched on a "much more serious" tack. There was, Lowenstein noted, the question of "Stalinism" tied up in the NLG issue as well.

The political trait that emerged in Allard with this line of argument left a number of people with bitter memories of Lowenstein's "red-baiting." He insisted that the Guild had Communist connections and said he was prepared to name names. "We had to fight those people once," Lowenstein pointed out on one occasion, "and we will again." It would be a "serious mistake" to "take them for allies." Everyone who did so was sooner or later "betrayed." They had "hidden agendas" and were interested only in "their own version of revolution."

Allard's SNCC opposition responded that Allard was the one with a "hidden agenda" and held his argument up as a classic example of New York liberals' trying to force Mississippi blacks to accept the liberal version of political priorities. Lowenstein in turn called them "extremists" and railed that "America cannot tolerate a presence as far left as SNCC." They had, he said, strayed into "very dangerous territory."

At least partly as a consequence of Allard's vehemence against SNCC, there were growing signs that the larger alliance would collapse into feuding factions before the summer even started.

A t that point, Allard switched roles and suddenly took it upon himself to repair the equally damaged relations between SNCC and the rest of the liberal camp. It had become apparent to him, as he later explained, that "the Summer Project had to be saved" and if he didn't do it, no one else would.

That mission took him to Yale in late March, where Frank Graham was giving a speech. The NLG issue was now out of control. Roy Wilkins, national chairman of the NAACP, was, according to Allard, about to issue a public statement denouncing SNCC as under "Communist influence." If Wilkins did so, the Mississippi Summer Project coalition would crash down around everyone's heads. Allard planned to solicit Graham's help in heading Wilkins off when the two men

drove back from New Haven to New York City. To free himself of the
actual driving, Lowenstein recruited one of his Yale protégés.

The trip that followed was a classic example of Allard's political
technique. His specialty was language crafting. Since SNCC would
clearly not reverse itself on the NLG issue, he needed to find words
that would allow Wilkins to rationalize accepting the Guild in Mississippi, however distasteful that might be. Allard told the old man he
called "Dr. Frank" that he "didn't know what to do," but as their
conversation progressed, that claim proved less than accurate. Lowenstein had in fact formulated an approach, only he explained it as verbal
speculation rather than as an outright proposal. Allard didn't see why
Roy Wilkins couldn't cite every American's right to choose his own
attorney. Such a precedent was just the kind of liberal principle that
could lift Wilkins off the hook, and Lowenstein convinced Dr. Frank to
make that argument to Wilkins. Graham agreed to approach A. Phillip
Randolph of the sleeping car porters union the next day and accompany Randolph to Wilkins immediately thereafter.

Allard's strategy apparently succeeded. Wilkins never issued his
statement, the alliance was patched back together, and the Summer
Project was stabilized. Lowenstein's intervention did nothing,
however, for his own relations with SNCC.

A llard predicted as much the night he talked to Dr. Frank.
Lowenstein and his Yale protégé drove on from Graham's
to Allard's West Eighty-second Street apartment. It was close to 4 A.M.
Allard appeared exhausted and momentarily low. He stripped down to
his T-shirt, took his glasses off, and rubbed his eyes. They were
underlined with deep black smudges of fatigue. For once, the effort
seemed to have taken its toll.

"You know," Allard told his protégé, "even if this works out, it
will just be two or three weeks before it all happens again." He bent
forward so his thick arms rested on his knees. "It's been like this ever
since Mrs. Roosevelt died. She was the last person with all the
credentials to call everyone in a room together and keep them there
until they talked out their differences. Mrs. Roosevelt would have
handled all this with ease." Allard seemed to think about his own
unworthiness for a moment. "It won't be like that again," he added.

His Yale protégé immediately wanted to comfort and reassure
Allard.

The protégé noticed, as I myself had, that if Allard Lowenstein
ever wanted to be someone else, that person was Eleanor Roosevelt.

D ennis Sweeney still wanted to be Allard Lowenstein, or so it seemed.

The SNCC-Lowenstein friction seemed to mean little to Sweeney in April. He was a known student leader whose opinion was sought on anything to do with civil rights, and he never mentioned such a split to anyone. In addition to his Summer Project duties, he continued to feel a deep responsibility for the fate of the campus agenda Lowenstein himself had initiated.

An annual item in that agenda was the spring student body elections. The group of campus liberals Dennis belonged to had controlled the student body presidency for two years. Facing stiff fraternity opposition, they were now putting forward an undergraduate who, along with Sweeney, had been one of Allard Lowenstein's Original Sixteen at Stern Hall. An incident in the course of Dennis's involvement in that April election gave indications that behind his calm self-confidence and quiet stature lurked an uneasiness with himself that was, at times, frenzied.

Late at night, Dennis Sweeney phoned the liberal candidate for student body president. Though they were friends, there was a certain stiffness in Dennis's manner. Sweeney was convening a "small meeting" that "couldn't wait," so the candidate got out of bed, dressed, and walked over to Dennis's room.

Sweeney was waiting with two other students: one was the liberal lame-duck president; the other, like both Sweeney and the candidate, was a member of Allard's Original Sixteen. Sweeney, the convener, made a short presentation in the manner of someone with a painful task to perform. He said it was clear to him that if steps weren't immediately taken to rectify the situation, the election would be lost. With the vote little more than two weeks away, it was apparent that his friend, the liberal candidate, was "unelectable." The candidate, he said, had not identified himself with the liberal cause "clearly enough," allowing the distinctions between the progressive and fraternity candidates to become blurred. He wanted his friend to withdraw from the race and let the other member of the Original Sixteen whom Dennis had invited to the meeting run in his place. Sweeney said the fate of what they all—including Allard—had been building at Stanford was at stake.

The candidate, clearly undercut, said he would think it over.

He was apparently still thinking it over the next day when he encountered Armin Rosencranz, the graduate student who in 1962–63 had been the first progressive president of the student body. The candidate told him about Dennis Sweeney's midnight intervention and said he might very well withdraw.

Rosencranz told the candidate to do no such thing. Sweeney's actions were, he said, nonsensical, a classic case of lost perspective. Rosencranz then walked over to Wilbur Hall and found Sweeney in the dining hall. Rosencranz was still worked up about what Dennis had done and told him that it was absurd to cut across a friendship on the basis of some imagined gain in student politics. Rosencranz said he was amazed at how thoroughly Dennis had lost sight of the relative value of things.

As Rosencranz was speaking, the blood drained from Dennis's face; he sagged in his chair and for a moment just sat there somewhat deflated. When he finally answered, he didn't attempt to defend his action of the night before.

"I see the point you're making completely," Sweeney said. His expression was downcast, and he had an air of having been found out. "You don't know this, but it applies to other parts of my life too."

Rosencranz was surprised by the weight of guilt and vulnerability embedded in the statement.

Dennis then gushed forth a confession about how he had recently thrown over his girlfriend, the same one who had been suspended after passing out with him on a lawn. He had pursued his "own interests in utter disregard" for someone else, he said. "What do you think of someone who would not only betray his friend," Sweeney asked, "but could also betray a woman whom he's been deeply involved with for two years?"

Rosencranz was taken aback at how instantaneously Sweeney had turned on himself and now counseled Dennis not to be so hard. Recognize your previous behavior as mistaken, Rosencranz told him, but don't go overboard. It was sufficient to amend the situation and pay closer attention the next time.

Dennis Sweeney said he would find his friend, the candidate, and retract last night's ultimatum. First he thanked Rosencranz for bringing him to "a new recognition" of himself.

The former student body president found that response excessive as well.

Sweeney met with the candidate that afternoon, reaffirmed his backing, and attempted to return their relationship to its previous footing. His friend lost nonetheless. Dennis then devoted himself to his Campus Civil Rights Secretariat work for the rest of the spring quarter and continued to earn high esteem in the eyes of his peers.

Dennis's recruiting efforts for the 1964 Mississippi Summer Project culminated with a visit to Stanford by Bob Moses.

Not yet a "student activist," I attended Moses's speech but would not be part of the Summer Project itself. I was still "discovering myself." I wrote poems that reeked of adolescence undergoing its first exposure to Ingmar Bergman movies, I owned a $29 phonograph, listened to Bob Dylan and Joan Baez records, and had begun to "experiment" with marijuana. I was just 18 and had registered for the draft only the month before Moses's visit.

In their coverage, the *Daily* identified Moses as "chairman" of COFO, "head" of SNCC, and the recipient of a M.A. in philosophy from Harvard. I can still remember snatches of that Friday night in April. Every seat in the auditorium was taken. From the balcony, Bob Moses looked frail, generating an immense, almost Zen presence as he talked. He made no attempt to work anyone up. Each word had clearly been considered and was said with the rhythms of a man crossing a stream, hopping from rock to rock. The audience grew increasingly intent as Moses proceeded.

"It's a question," he said, "of whether in this country we can find people who are committed, who care, who will sacrifice and who are willing to do their share."

When Moses finished, the hall was absolutely quiet for almost a minute as more than 400 students continued to listen. Then a five-minute standing ovation began.

Everyone I talked to afterward was taken with the "saintly" Bob Moses and wanted to follow him to Mississippi. My fantasies kept pace with the rest, but I had few illusions of actually being able to participate in the Summer Project. I was still chained to finding a job, while Dennis and the others made a frontal assault on the Old South.

As the crowd filed out of the balcony, I stopped at the rail. Down below, Moses had stepped off the stage and was standing with a circle pressing in around him. Dennis Sweeney was at Moses's elbow. From the look on his face, he was clearly as enthralled with the SNCC man as anyone there.

Within a year, Dennis concluded that Bob Moses was the best human being he'd ever met. By then, he had also concluded that Allard Lowenstein was Moses's antithesis.

With the advent of May, the beginnings of a rift finally surfaced between the protégé and his mentor, provoked by another sudden reversal of course in Allard's maneuverings with SNCC and the Summer Project.

Lowenstein now claimed that SNCC had been telling "all kinds of lies" and trying to sabotage his standing with the rest of the Project. As Allard later explained it, it wasn't just that they were doing it to him that mattered. The point was that such behavior was "overwhelming" evidence of SNCC's "irresponsibility" and "radicalism." Impelled by that conclusion, Lowenstein suddenly withdrew from the Summer Project completely, explaining this as a "personal" decision and making no attempt to pull the major liberal organizations out with him. He did, however, expect his protégés to follow his lead. That expectation was communicated in a rapid-fire series of phone calls in May.

Dennis Sweeney got his early in the month, and Lowenstein apparently asked him point-blank to withdraw from the Summer Project.

Sweeney's subsequent dilemma was immense. His devotion to Lowenstein was still largely intact, despite the confusion provoked by what had happened that night at the motel, and there was no one to whom Sweeney felt more attached or obliged. On the other hand, Mississippi Summer was by then the most important thing in his life, transcending any "personal" considerations. He had been committed to going since it was first announced. Whichever choice Sweeney made, it still echoed "betrayal." Several SNCC members remember subsequent conversations with Dennis in which he referred to having been under "tremendous pressure" from Lowenstein that May.

If he was, the pressure was probably applied indirectly. Certainly, Dennis would have been told that the final decision was his alone and that he should do what he thought was right, whatever Allard himself did. Just as certainly, Allard would have made no secret of the fact that he would be "disappointed" if Dennis ignored his recommendation. Allard just "hoped" he could "count on" Dennis's "backing," now that he "needed" it. That theme of victimization of someone close to him must have in turn unleashed a heavy load of Dennis's guilt.

It did not, however, lead him to agree. Saying no to Allard was hard, but whatever was going on between Lowenstein and SNCC, Sweeney felt his own body belonged "on the line." He thought his mentor was significantly wrong and told him so. Come June, Dennis would go South, whatever Allard said.

As the Summer Project commenced, Allard Lowenstein at first kept to his last-minute strategy and stayed away from Mississippi, coming west to California to visit friends and catch up on a few other political odds and ends. He explained his decision to boycott as something his "conscience" demanded. He was not going to help SNCC do things he "disagreed with." Better to start over again, he claimed. The decision was "irrevocable."

His obstinacy began to reverse itself shortly. On Sunday, June 21, Andrew Goodman, a 20-year-old white college student from New York City who had arrived in Mississippi the day before, Mickey Schwerner, a 24-year-old white CORE staff member and Mississippi veteran also originally from New York City, and James Chaney, 19, a black civil rights worker from Meridian, Mississippi, drove from Meridian to Philadelphia, Mississippi, to inspect the charred ruins of the Mount Zion Baptist Church, attacked by white arsonists the week before. The Summer Project trio was stopped and arrested on their way out of Philadelphia. After being detained until after dark, they were released. Schwerner, Chaney, and Goodman then disappeared and were never seen alive again. Two months later, the three young men's bodies were found buried in the base of a remote earth-fill dam. Within 24 hours of their disappearance, it was already being assumed that they were dead.

In Mississippi, the news galvanized the Summer Project.

In California, it provoked Allard Lowenstein into revoking the "irrevocable." Under this kind of attack, Allard told his friends, everyone had to band together, whatever their differences. Lowenstein left for Mississippi immediately and would spend the summer there in a relatively inconspicuous position with the liberals' legal assistance team.

The month of June had been officially designated "hospitality month" by the Mississippi state government. In Jackson, white men fired into black Henderson's Cafe, wounding one Negro in the head. In Clinton, the black Church of the Holy Ghost was burned to the ground. In Hattiesburg, two cars belonging to civil rights workers were shot full of holes. In Hinds County, three civil rights workers were arrested and beaten by their jailers.

Dennis Sweeney was already in Jackson, preparing to accompany a select SNCC-led task force into McComb.

The selection of Dennis Sweeney for McComb was testimony to the high regard in which he was held by SNCC, whatever his relationship with the suspect Lowenstein. SNCC's personnel rule was, the more volatile the place, the better the people who ought to be sent; under that logic, assignment to McComb was the highest rating a volunteer could have. McComb had the reputation of a rabid dog. Before the summer was over, two-thirds of the state's 70-odd racial bombings would happen within a half hour's drive of the place.

Located in Pike County, southwest of Jackson, the town was the trading and cultural center for surrounding Amite and Walthall counties as well. Large parts of the white population gave at least perfunctory obeisance to either the Ku Klux Klan, the White Citizens Council, or the Citizens for the Preservation of the White Race. "God wanted white people to live alone," one local Citizens Council tract explained. "Negroes use their own bathrooms, the Negro has his own part of town to live in. This is called our Southern Way of Life. God had made us different and God knows best. . . . ONE DROP of Negro blood in your family could push it backward three thousand years in history." Of some 15,000 voting-age blacks in Pike County, only 200 had been permitted to register to vote; in Amite County, of 5,000 blacks, only one was registered. Among Walthall's 3,000 blacks, not even one could vote. In January, white night riders had swept through black McComb, firing into six houses and wounding a young boy. Jackson might be the state capital, but if Mississippi ever had a heart, it was McComb.

McComb was also at the root of SNCC's own history. When Bob Moses began the Mississippi Project in 1961, he opened his first black-voter-education school in McComb. Within three months, he and the rest of the SNCC staff had been arrested, beaten, and were serving 90 days in the jail in Magnolia, Mississippi, Pike County's seat. One of their local black supporters had been shot dead on the street by a white state legislator. When they finished their jail terms, the Project had decided to move out of Pike County to the Delta, which was said to be somewhat less brutal. The seven-person contingent, including Dennis Sweeney, would be the first civil rights workers in McComb in over two years.

When they were briefed in Jackson, the potential danger was emphasized. Anyone who wished could request a different assignment without stigma. "Anyone who goes in," Bob Moses warned, "faces a high probability of death." No minds changed. Both the McComb houses where the volunteers had first been scheduled to live had been dynamited two weeks earlier. In Magnolia, armed whites had begun practicing military drill in the courthouse square every Thursday night. The SNCC people would be on their own with nothing but their visibility to protect them. Once again, the opportunity to withdraw was offered. Once again, no one took it.

Young Dennis Sweeney's heart must have been in his throat. His compatriots from that summer remember Sweeney as "straightforward" and "enormously sincere." He never complained and only showed his fear in the way he sometimes pressed his lips together.

He and the others opened the McComb Project during the first week of July, living in a rented freedom house on Wall Street in black McComb.

On the evening of July 8, white McComb officially welcomed the "race mixers" who had just arrived in its midst. Dennis Sweeney and his fellow civil rights workers were all asleep. The air was hot and soggy, and the night outside the Wall Street house seemed to lurk. Dennis was curled up in the living room on the bed closest to the front door. He didn't hear the car screech to a halt in the driveway with its motor running. The first sounds he was conscious of were the clunk of a package being flung at the porch and then the squeal of the car's getaway. Before his head cleared, eight sticks of dynamite exploded barely 10 feet away, tearing up a section of the driveway and collapsing the house's front wall. Dennis was lifted up by the blast and dumped over with his mattress and bedboard on top of him. At first he couldn't hear anything, but he saw shards of glass all over the floor and smelled cordite fumes. Once he extricated himself, he had to agree that they had been lucky. No one had been killed, and Dennis, the most seriously injured, had nothing more than a pair of badly concussed eardrums.

The next issue of the McComb *Enterprise Journal* carried a picture of Sweeney. In it, the handsome, 21-year-old integrationist invader from Oregon via California stood in front of the remains of the Wall Street freedom house, smiling grimly and with great resolve.

Two McComb policemen came over to investigate on the morning of July 9. A Northern newspaper reporter arrived as well. While the three of them were examining the damage, one of the cops reportedly grinned and shook his head.

"Looks like termites to me," he said.

Mississippi was in a state of war. The same week McComb's freedom house was bombed, a COFO rabbi in Clarksdale was bludgeoned with steel bars. A car full of whites fired guns into a black church in Moss Point, wounding a 19-year-old girl. The blacks who chased after the assailants were arrested and charged with assault. In Browning, the Pleasant Plan Missionary Baptist Church was burned to the ground. So were the Jerusalem Baptist and Bethel Methodist churches in Natchez. Two blacks trying to use the white window at a drive-in in Laurel were stabbed. In Kingston, three more black churches were torched.

In McComb, one of the Mississippi Summer Project's first goals was to try to ease white paranoia by making contact with the "responsible" elements in the white community. Dennis Sweeney was one of the volunteers assigned to that effort; they immediately encountered a belligerent white common front, intent on enforcing its own solidarity. Sweeney would end up an eyewitness to a classic example of what could happen to local whites who got out of line. It was a family named Heffner.

Red Heffner was an amiable and good-natured white insurance agent, active with his wife, Malva, in the local Episcopalian Church. Malva's daughter by a previous marriage was the reigning state beauty queen, Miss Mississippi. The couple's younger daughter was away for a summer of school in New York City. Sweeney got drawn into the Heffners' lives when they received a phone call one Sunday from a young outside white minister with McComb's Summer Project. The civil rights workers, he explained, were trying to open a "dialogue" with the white community and were looking for someone who would act as intermediary in setting up a meeting with McComb's mayor and chief of police. Red allowed as how he believed in people talking to each other and invited the minister to come over to his house in the nicer, all-white Caroll Oaks section of McComb. The minister then asked Red whether he could bring someone else with him, a student from Stanford named Dennis Sweeney.

At the Heffners' house, Sweeney and the minister made small talk and snacked on tamales for almost an hour, until they were interrupted by the Heffners' younger daughter's weekly phone call from New York. Malva mentioned to her that the minister was there, along with a young man named Dennis Sweeney. After the family phone conversation was done, the civil rights workers and Heffner got down to the subject at hand. Ten minutes later, they were interrupted by another phone call.

Malva answered, and an unidentified woman asked to speak to Dennis Sweeney. Thinking it must be someone from the civil rights office, Mrs. Heffner handed Dennis the phone. Sweeney did not recognize the female voice on the line. She asked him how his civil rights work was coming along.

"Pretty well, I guess," Dennis answered, still trying to think who the caller might be. The voice next asked if Sweeney was a friend of the Heffners. Dennis had only known Red and Malva for an hour, so his answer was tentative. "I guess so," he said. "Who is this?" The woman immediately hung up.

A third call followed shortly. This time it was for Red, from a vice president of Help, Inc., McComb's white "early-warning system," which had been set up to counter the invasion of young Northern race mixers. He said people were "upset" at the strange car parked in front of the Heffners' house. Red told him whom it belonged to and what they were doing there. By the time the caller rang off, cars driven by local whites were cruising back and forth in front of the Heffners' house. Sweeney and the minister were apprehensive and suggested that it was probably best to continue the conversation another time. When Red agreed, the civil rights workers thanked Malva for the food and stepped out onto the Heffner front porch, Dennis in the lead.

Halfway to the car, the surrounding darkness erupted in a sudden glare. The Heffners' corner was ringed with autos whose headlights all came on at the same time. For a moment, Dennis Sweeney froze in his tracks.

Fighting back his panic, Dennis resumed walking calmly toward the car with the minister. He started the engine, and as he headed back toward headquarters, each of the waiting autos wheeled into a caravan behind him. Sweeney immediately got on the two-way radio to the freedom house, a caravan of civil rights vehicles was dispatched, and when the cars met up with Sweeney's, the whites pursuing him wheeled around and headed back to cruise around the Heffners' house again.

Within two months of his visit from Sweeney and the minister, Red Heffner's house insurance business was in a shambles, his wife and children had been harassed, his pet dog poisoned. The family had little choice but to leave Mississippi. Dennis Sweeney felt close to them and was present at their last act in the state.

U nderstandably, black fear was the McComb Project's major problem. The only local black institutions with any independent resources—such as a meeting hall—were the churches, and when the summer began, McComb's black churches remained unwilling to run the risks inherent in open support. As a consequence, the first organizational meeting of the local Freedom Democratic party was held in a café run by a Mrs. Alvene Quin. Some 200 local blacks attended.

Church assistance finally came when the pastor of Pike County's Mount Zion Hill Baptist Church agreed to make some of his McComb church's facilities available for the freedom school. Using a set of Berlitz records, Dennis Sweeney was the school's French teacher. The church was also used for a community meeting one evening in July. Dennis Sweeney was in the crowd.

The gathering was opened by COFO's McComb Project director, who thanked Mount Zion Hill Baptist's pastor for the use of the building. "A lot of people," he continued, "came here tonight to find out what's goin' on."

"That's right, that's right," someone in the crowd answered.

"I guess you can understand how the mayor, the sheriff, the police chief all got elected. It boils down to the fact that a minority of the peoples in McComb voted them in there, because you didn't vote."

"True, true."

"That's why us workers come to McComb."

"Amen."

"But we don't do no good cooped up in a corner down there at the freedom house."

"No sir."

"We get lonely."

The crowd laughed.

"We can't make progress unless you try to vote. As long as they can keep you from the courthouse, you're gonna stay up at night with a shotgun lookin' for bombs. But I don't live here. Someday," the project director continued, with a motion of his hand toward Sweeney and the other civil rights workers in the crowd, "we'll be gone. Who's gonna keep the sheriff under control then? You're gonna have to do it so you might as well start."

The black crowd responded enthusiastically. A number of people joined the Freedom Democratic party, and others pledged themselves to go down to the Magnolia Courthouse and try to register to vote. In the discussions that followed, it was agreed that a big railroad worker said it best.

"We have to stop talking about Mr. Charley," he offered, "and start talkin' to him and start actin'."

"Boy that's right."

"We sing, 'Before I'll be a slave, I'd be buried in my grave and go home to my Lord and be free.' Now if you don't mean it, don't sing it."

"Yes, sir."

"Let's get on the bandwagon and let's ride it till the wheels fall off. If there's nothin' to COFO, there's nothin' to you, me, or anything else."

"Amen, brother, amen."

Next came more freedom songs, flooding through the church and into the crawling night outside. Dennis Sweeney clapped his hands and followed along in his loudest voice.

"The freedom train is coming, coming, coming," Dennis sang. "The freedom train is coming and we'll all get aboard."

Within a week, the Mount Zion Hill Baptist Church was burned to the ground by night riders.

McComb was like that all summer long. Five more black churches were attacked with explosives; the grocery store across from the freedom school was blown up, as was the barber shop of a local NAACP leader. Three visiting Northern journalists were dragged from their rented car and thrashed. COFO supporters were threatened, and some were fired from their jobs. COFO cars were regularly chased. Armed rednecks still drilled in Magnolia on Thursdays, and every evening, like clockwork, one of McComb's Ku Klux Klan leaders, an oil dealer with a third-grade education, circled the freedom house in his Cadillac.

It was, as the McComb volunteers told each other, "crazy not to be paranoid."

Allard and others would later blame the pressure of living in McComb, unarmed and constantly on the edge of death, for what Dennis Sweeney became, but there was nothing diseased about him while he was there. A number of the students he knew at the freedom school still remember him as "genuine" and "concerned." Paradoxically, the immediate effect of the attacks was to reinforce and draw all the young civil rights workers into a tight circle. Dennis thrived on the community.

The project had grown from the original seven workers to more than 20 by the end of July, living in three residences near each other on Wall and Dinwittie streets. The Sixties would be epitomized by various communal clusterings of the young, and Mississippi's freedom houses were the first in the genre. Theoretically, the COFO males and females lived in separate buildings, but early on the practice was discarded. All the civil rights workers met each morning over breakfast to discuss the day's activities and divide up household tasks. Days were spent with the freedom school or canvassing for the Mississippi Freedom Democratic party. Early evenings were consumed with community meetings and late evenings with more freedom-house discussions, at which the day's activities were evaluated.

The pace was frantic and adrenaline leaked into all aspects of freedom-house life. Among other things, being on the battlefront together led to a level of heterosexual experimentation unavailable in the more regulated college circles from which the COFO workers hailed. Dennis Sweeney slept with several different women that summer—no more than average. The coupling was considered not so much license as one more small expression of a liberation that was taking place on all fronts.

After a month in McComb, Sweeney still cited his mentor, Allard Lowenstein, as an authority, but it was with the tone of an adult referring to an equal. Allard stopped in McComb at least once that summer, and the meeting was apparently friendly. Dennis's closest sidekick on the McComb Project, a white volunteer from Cambridge, Massachusetts, named J.D., remembered that Dennis talked about Lowenstein a lot, but since J.D. hadn't heard of Lowenstein before, he paid little attention. J.D. had run a sandal shop in Harvard Square before coming South, and his precocious hipness contrasted sharply with the Sunday-school air that still clung to Dennis. Both dressed in Levis and work shirts. Dennis's looked new and J.D.'s were faded. Dennis was quiet, "straight," and serious, but J.D. was raucous and told funny stories. Like everything else that summer, J.D. widened Dennis's horizons.

One such widening came when the two friends and several other McComb workers drove to a statewide COFO meeting at Tougaloo College. At one point J.D., Dennis, and another white volunteer went outside and stood around in a dark parking lot, where J.D. rolled a joint and got his friend Dennis Sweeney high on marijuana for the first time. The three passed the weed among them until it was reduced to a nub.

The Summer Project had been an overwhelming success thus far. In June, just the prospect of it had pushed Congress into passing a Civil Rights Act. Some 80,000 Mississippi blacks had signed up with the Mississippi Freedom Democratic party (MFDP) by August, and over 30 freedom schools had been opened. Increasingly, COFO attention focused on Atlantic City, New Jersey, where the Democratic National Convention was to be held at the end of the summer. The organization spent late July and early August in county MFDP caucuses, choosing a delegation to send North and force the Democrats to repudiate Jim Crow. Sweeney's intensity attached itself to that goal without hesitation. He saw it as only a symbol of the amelioration of how blacks in Mississippi were forced to live, but it was an important symbol nonetheless. If nothing else, repudiation of Jim Crow politics would signify that the country at large was worthy of the sacrifices blacks and civil rights workers were making in its name. Sweeney submerged himself in the effort and played an important role.

The first critical contest at Atlantic City was in front of the convention's credentials committee. Sweeney's home state, Oregon, was one of that committee's key delegations. Dennis was assigned to concentrate all his efforts on influencing Oregon's stance, and in the middle of August, he left Mississippi for the first time in two months and flew to Portland. There, he momentarily discarded his jeans and work shirt for a tie and sport coat, looking every inch the Stanford honors student. By the time Sweeney left Portland with the Oregon delegates headed for Atlantic City, he was on a first-name basis with Senator Wayne Morse and Congresswoman Edith Green, the state's two leading Democratic politicians.

The approaching Democratic convention was to be a Sixties landmark. For Dennis and Allard, it would also be their last joint political endeavor. Afterward, the coalition would wrench itself apart, taking them in different directions.

A llard Lowenstein also had an important role to play in Atlantic City.

Despite his difficulties with SNCC, Lowenstein was, for the MFDP, one of the few resources available to whom the quadrennial Democratic National Convention was familiar turf. Allard thought of his effort there as the last act of the solidarity to which he had pledged himself after the deaths in Philadelphia, Mississippi, the previous June. He left the South during the second week of August, headed for the National Student Association congress in Minneapolis and then on to Atlantic City itself.

From Minneapolis Lowenstein drove East with a Harvard protégé. Somewhere in western Pennsylvania he had the protégé stop at a phone booth, and he called ahead to the convention. Whoever Lowenstein talked to told him he was needed immediately. Instead of driving farther, Allard had the Harvard student rush him to the nearest airport and told him they would meet up in Atlantic City.

B y then, it had long since been apparent that the Democratic party was divided over the MFDP challenge. Some nine state delegations and 25 incumbent congressmen had gone on record as supporting the Mississippi Freedom Democrats, but the governor of Mississippi had informed the Jim Crow delegation that President Lyndon Johnson had personally assured him that the MFDP would not be seated. On August 19, Johnson invited a group of civil rights leaders to the White House but bluntly refused even to discuss the approaching convention. In the meantime, LBJ had ordered the Federal Bureau of Investigation to establish surveillance of the MFDP convention forces, and when the 68-person contingent, Dennis Sweeney included, set up headquarters in Atlantic City's Gem Hotel, their phone lines were already tapped.

For its part, the Mississippi Freedom Democratic party came north with the certitude of moral shock troops. Their attitude toward the convention was rooted in what they had been through to get there. On July 25, a Molotov cocktail had been thrown at the house of two Hattiesburg MFDP leaders. On July 28, the Holly Springs police had surrounded a school where an MFDP precinct meeting was being held and had threatened to burn the building down with the MFDP members inside if the meeting took place. On August 11 in Ruleville, an MFDP leader had been arrested and beaten. On August 12, three carloads of masked men with rifles had broken down the doors of several MFDP supporters' houses in Oak Ridge, firing as they came. The MFDP and its young COFO organizers reached Atlantic City in a mood to settle for nothing less than full recognition.

Allard Lowenstein had trepidations about their chances, and private differences with their attitude as well. His yardstick of success was much closer to that of an experienced Democratic party operative than an inspired victim of Jim Crow. Where SNCC saw political action as an embodiment of principle, Allard instead saw it as an incremental means of realizing a principle, an important and immense difference. Incumbent presidents are hard to buck, and walking in with an unwillingness to maneuver would, Allard argued, only tie their hands.

Lowenstein's official position was as a lawyer on the five-man legal team acting as the MFDP's counsel to the credentials committee, but his

real role was that of a lobbyist. Though virtually unknown to the
general public, Lowenstein had connections throughout the main
elements of the Democratic party, a young New York mover and shaker
with a surprising breadth of influence. Those connections were both
the reason the MFDP needed Allard and the reason they would end up
accusing him of betrayal.

W hen they eventually rendezvoused, the Harvard student
who had started out with Allard in Minneapolis got a
glimpse of just how well connected Lowenstein was. During a brief
break from the convention, the two men walked along the boardwalk.
Everything, Lowenstein pointed out, was focused on the report by the
credentials committee. Thus far, the Administration forces were advancing to the line that, Jim Crow or not, Mississippi's regular
delegation had to be seated in order to keep the South "solid." The
MFDP argued in return that the Mississippi regulars only had their
seats by virtue of the grossest kind of suppression and immorality, had
publicly supported the Republican nominee in 1960, and showed every
sign of doing so again. Allard noted that a number of SNCC people
objected to even arguing party disloyalty, saying that immorality was
argument enough and that arguing lesser grounds was demeaning to
those who had suffered at the regulars' hands. Lowenstein thought
them stupid for feeling that way. The point, he said, was to win seats,
whatever argument it took.

When Lowenstein talked he was relatively oblivious to everything
else. The protégé happened to notice a crowd approaching from the
opposite direction. Drawing closer, the crowd turned out to be one of
the familiar clusters of press people and gawkers that marked the
approach of one of the party's major celebrities. The swarm veered
toward Lowenstein, parted, and out stepped Adlai Stevenson. The
Democratic party legend and two-time candidate for President of the
United States had gone out of his way to say hello.

"Hi, Al," he said.

"Adlai," Allard blurted, "you look great."

The two men made small talk for several minutes, and then Allard
and his protégé headed back to the convention.

S ixteen years later I was able to find no one who had seen
Dennis and Allard together in Atlantic City, but I have little
doubt that their paths must have crossed. Lowenstein was enmeshed

in the credentials fight and so was Sweeney. At the level where Sweeney was working, the strategy was simple. His job was to put Oregon Democrats into face-to-face contact with the MFDP delegates, and old friends who saw Dennis in action were impressed with his surprisingly smooth and skillful political mingling. He introduced MFDP sharecroppers to his home-state delegation, remembering everyone's name and nurturing conversation between very dissimilar people.

During the convention preliminaries, the MFDP cause captured the nation's attention and aroused enormous sympathy. The television networks covered the credentials hearings live, and the most compelling testimony came from Mrs. Fannie Lou Hamer, a sharecropper representing Sunflower County. Though she was uneducated, her testimony was enormously articulate. She told how she had been arrested for trying to register to vote and, once she was in jail, had been beaten. "I was beat," she claimed, "until I was exhausted. . . . I began to scream, and one white man got up and began to beat me on the head and tell me to hush. . . . All of this on account we want to register, to become first-class citizens. If the Freedom Democratic party is not seated now, I question America." Telegrams supportive of the MFDP flooded into the various state delegations that evening.

At the same time, the liberals who had backed the MFDP all summer were becoming openly uneasy about the uncompromising tone the black rookie politicians from Mississippi had begun to adopt. The NAACP's Roy Wilkins reportedly suggested to Mrs. Hamer that she and the others from Mississippi had made their "point" and now ought to "go home" and leave politics to those who "knew how to do it." Fannie Lou Hamer's indignant response did little to dispel the NAACP's trepidations.

Neither would the MFDP's response to the Atlantic City compromise, Lyndon Johnson's eventual attempt to strike a bargain. By the time it was put forward, the MFDP was attempting to bypass their credentials committee opposition by getting a minority report that could be brought up in front of the full convention. The Atlantic City compromise was designed to head off that move, and it put a good number of liberals in an enormous quandary. The President offered the MFDP two "at large" seats while reserving all of Mississippi's for Jim Crow, and made promises to support a provision prohibiting any segregated delegation from being seated at the next convention, four years away. Johnson also insisted that the only MFDP people who could assume the two seats were Aaron Henry and Ed

King, the candidates for governor and lieutenant governor in the previous fall's freedom vote.

The hook for the liberals lay in who was made responsible for putting the offer across. The task of selling the Atlantic City compromise had been assigned to Hubert Humphrey, Senator from Minnesota. If he succeeded, Humphrey would be LBJ's choice for Vice President. If he didn't, Johnson's people alleged, he wouldn't be chosen. Hubert Humphrey had been the reigning left Democratic hero since he first championed civil rights at the 1948 convention, and to many liberals his advancement was of greater importance than the MFDP itself. All the principal outside liberal players in the summer coalition were touched by that dilemma. When they began putting extensive pressure on the MFDP to accept the compromise, the summer coalition began coming apart at the seams.

The possibility of Hubert Humphrey's becoming Vice President meant nothing special to the MFDP. As far as they knew, the Senator from Minnesota had never even been to Mississippi. The delegation first caucused on the compromise the same evening the offer arrived. Dennis Sweeney was in attendance. The Freedom Democrats were addressed by several Northern black congressmen, who argued for acceptance. This was politics, the congressmen pointed out, and you couldn't get everything the first time out. When they were done, a Mississippi woman responded. This compromise would "let Jim Crow be," she objected. "Ain't no Democratic party worth that. We been treated like beasts in Mississippi. They shot us down like animals. We risk our lives comin' here. . . . Politics must be corrupt if it don't care none about people down there." While the speeches ran on, the MFDP headquarters back in Tupelo was burned to the ground by white men with jerry cans of gasoline. The delegates took no votes on Johnson's offer that evening, but sentiment was obviously running against it.

Allard Lowenstein was one of the few among the liberals who didn't agree with the impulse to pressure the MFDP. Allard's initial position was that some compromise would have to be accepted in the end, but this one wasn't good enough. He did not intend to be stampeded. The way Allard saw it, Johnson would pick Humphrey for Vice President if that was who he wanted, whatever happened with the MFDP. This talk his people were spreading was just the Texan's way of getting the maximum mileage out of his choice.

Lowenstein's reasoning seemed to sway none of his traditional allies. Instead, the liberals argued for the compromise and, coupled with heavy presidential arm twisting, caused the MFDP's support on the credentials committee to begin to slip seriously. After the MFDP's first discussion of the offer, Humphrey himself met with Bob Moses and pleaded with the SNCC hero to accept the compromise. Moses noted that the decision was not his but the MFDP's. That evening, the black Mississippi delegation voted unanimously to refuse.

Such defiance did nothing to quell the tide that had turned drastically against them. Within a day, the last MFDP supporters on the credentials committee went over to the compromise and the compromise was in turn accepted by the convention as a whole. There was disagreement later about just what role Allard played in all that. Several SNCC members remembered, with great accumulated bitterness, actually watching Lowenstein lobby against the MFDP position. Other Mississippi veterans and Allard himself later claimed that he did no such thing. In either case, by that evening the choice facing the MFDP had narrowed to one between the Atlantic City compromise or nothing at all.

For all intents and purposes, in less than 12 hours the 1964 Mississippi Summer Project alliance would come irretrievably apart.

At the insistence of the liberals, the MFDP delegation met in an Atlantic City church at 10 A.M. the next day to reconsider its previous rejection. Everyone there knew that this was the showdown.

Aaron Henry, chairman of the delegation, called the meeting to order. The speakers list was heavily weighted to the liberals. The staff director of the National Council of Churches described the compromise as "the greatest thing since the Emancipation Proclamation." A well-known national civil rights leader urged, "We must think of our friends in labor. . . . If we reject this compromise, we would be saying to them that we didn't want their help."

At this point, a young white SNCC member couldn't take it any longer. "You're a traitor," he yelled. "You've sold us out." It took several minutes to reestablish order and get on with business.

Next, Martin Luther King, the nation's most celebrated civil rights leader, spoke, saying that he had talked to Hubert Humphrey himself and had been promised that "there would be a new day in Mississippi if you accept this proposal." Joseph Rauh, a United Auto Workers lawyer, called the previous rejection "hasty." The list went on and on, and somewhere in its course Allard Lowenstein popped up. There is no surviving record of exactly what he said. As is true with almost all of Allard's dealings around the question of Mississippi, there are two different memories of the position he took.

The SNCC version was that Lowenstein came out foursquare in

favor of accepting the compromise. Allard claimed that he had opposed it for being still too little, arguing only that compromise in general was a good thing and that just because this one stunk, the MFDP should not lose sight of how the American system worked. Whatever was actually said, there can be little doubt that Lowenstein's distinction between generals and specifics was lost on the bulk of his audience. He would be tarred with the same brush as the other liberals when the coalition disintegrated. That day in the church, accusations of "sellout" and "snake in the grass" were already flying around the crowd.

The opposition part of the speaker's list was led by Bob Moses, James Forman, and Fannie Lou Hamer. Mrs. Hamer put it most succinctly. "We didn't come all this way for no two seats," she said.

When the vote was finally taken, the Mississippi Freedom Democratic party rejected the Atlantic City compromise unanimously.

Afterwards, Rauh went to the microphone again and attempted to evoke a note of solidarity. "Whatever our differences," he said, "we are still united in our cause."

The attempt didn't wash. Oregon's Congresswoman Edith Green, the MFDP's last diehard on the credentials committee, challenged him from the audience immediately.

"How can you say that?" she shouted. "You know that just isn't true."

Something in the tone of Green's statement captured Allard Lowenstein's ear. Green, Allard would later say, sounded like she really did know something.

Her comment haunted him until he learned two months later that the night before the meeting in the church, Walter Reuther, who was Joseph Rauh's boss, had secretly flown into Atlantic City for a stormy meeting with Aaron Henry and Ed King, the two men LBJ had designated to represent the MFDP. Reuther had become furious and reportedly promised that if the MFDP rejected the compromise again the next day, he would pull all the UAW's money out of Mississippi, which would turn many of the summer's programs into a shambles. The meeting with Reuther was never mentioned anywhere in the public discussion, but somehow Green knew of it. Her knowledge impelled her outburst that day.

Lowenstein was one of the last people to leave the church when the meeting was over. His Harvard protégé found him inside, drained by what had gone on.

"It's all over," Allard told him. "Now the whole thing's going to fall apart."

In his memoirs, Lyndon Baines Johnson did not even mention the Freedom Democrats. Instead, he called the Atlantic City convention "a place of happy, surging crowds and thundering cheers." After the MFDP voted against his compromise for the final time, the Democrats proceeded to other business, and Dennis Sweeney and the COFO troops began straggling back to Mississippi to lick their wounds.

Allard Lowenstein stayed in Atlantic City until the last gavel fell. By then, he had agreed to campaign for the Johnson-Humphrey ticket on campuses that fall.

The next morning Allard slept late in his motel room. When his Harvard protégé found him there, Lowenstein expressed an immense sense of release at escaping the political straitjacket his summer's "solidarity" had enforced upon him. While in the shower, Allard made up a song to the tune of "Hello Dolly." As part of an orchestrated celebration of Lyndon Johnson's birthday, the Democrats had sung a version that went, "Hello Lyndon." Allard's version substituted "Hubert" for "Lyndon."

"Hellooo, Hubert," Lowenstein sang, "it's so great to have you up where you belong."

His verse went on to speculate in rhyme about the possibility of Lyndon Johnson's having a heart attack. Allard sang it through several times and broke up laughing each time.

Dennis Sweeney's disillusionment following Atlantic City was difficult for me to reconstruct once the fresh impressions as to what had provoked it had been succeeded by so many others. The task was doubly difficult since the edge of Sweeney's disillusionment was obscured by his own close-mouthed style. "Alienation" was suddenly manifesting itself among members of our generation, and Sweeney's reaction during the aftermath to Atlantic City was a classic example.

Despite Dennis's relatively experienced stature in the civil rights movement, his political perspective had heretofore rested on a faith in the process of power that was no longer credible after Atlantic City. The MFDP had gone North with right clearly on their side and had been turned away. Sweeney felt betrayed both by his previous faith and by those who had engendered it in him. The immediate issue in the postconvention civil rights movement was whether Atlantic City had been a "defeat" or a "victory," and Sweeney soon joined the "defeat" camp, ascribing the failure to having placed trust in people more interested in using the power process to preserve themselves than to change things for the better. Allard Lowenstein, on the other hand, was among those claiming victory most loudly.

Sweeney's pain and sense of betrayal were only heightened by his return to Mississippi. Immediately upon arrival in Jackson, he learned that the Heffners, from McComb, were in town. Red and Malva told Dennis they had decided that they couldn't live with the harassment directed at them any longer. The next morning they were driving North to a new life in suburban Washington, D.C. For Dennis, what the Heffners were now suffering reinforced all of Atlantic City's lessons. Intensely conscious of the fact that their hospitality to him was directly responsible for their plight, he hastily made the arrangements for a press conference at which Malva Heffner would tell reporters how her family had been run out of the state.

The press conference was something of a disaster. Most of the national press had left Mississippi for the convention and had not returned. The white Mississippi press consequently took after Mrs. Heffner like sharks after a leg of lamb. They listened to her story, but they were more interested in who this man Sweeney was who had put the press conference together. Was Mrs. Heffner being used by Communists? Was their relationship "degenerate"? Had he poisoned her dog? Most of the time, Sweeney stood silently against the wall. When it was all over, both he and Malva Heffner were reportedly close to tears.

The Harvard student who had driven Allard Lowenstein from Minneapolis toward Atlantic City saw Dennis several hours later. In Atlantic City the Harvard man had connected with a mutual friend of Dennis's from Stanford, and the two of them had driven South to visit the movement. Sweeney's attitude was serious and bittersweet. He said he was not yet sure whether to return to Stanford for his senior year when school started or to stay in Mississippi. Either way, he had no doubts about what he'd been doing. "It's the most right thing I've ever done," Dennis claimed.

When the Harvard man asked about Sweeney's view of Lowenstein, he just bunched his shoulders in response. The voice Dennis adopted was full of resignation.

"Al has his way . . ." he said.

That Sweeney's way was different was articulated with nothing more than an accompanying shrug.

Back in New York after Atlantic City, Lowenstein attended several rump meetings of liberals to discuss the convention. The most memorable of those was held on September 18 at the behest of the National Council of Churches. Aside from Lowenstein, representatives of the Council of Churches, SCLC, the NAACP, CORE, and the UAW and several individual liberal sympathizers were present. SNCC sent two observers, one of whom took notes. At issue for the liberals was how decisions about Mississippi were to be made now that the Summer Project was over; it quickly became clear that most had no intention of accepting a backseat position any longer.

The Council of Churches staff member who opened the gathering phrased its purpose as discussing "ways of cooperating in Mississippi in the future. If possible," he admonished, "let us try to avoid raking the coals of the past."

The admonition fell by the wayside almost immediately. The next speaker was from the NAACP. "I have questions about SNCC," he opened. The discussion moved around the circle to several others, and when it returned to the N-double-A man, he continued where he'd left off. "I also have questions about the MFDP. Wherever they are, there are suspicious characters. . . ."

The CORE representatives noted that they had to "agree on a decision-making structure."

"We also have to make the right decision," the NAACP representative continued. ". . . The problem is that Bob Moses and SNCC feel—perhaps because of their youth, frustration, indignation, and bitterness—the need for a single-minded approach. They need an understanding of strategic complexity that they don't yet have. . . ."

By now, the SNCC observers were fed up with what was going on. "Accusations are being made," one of them complained, "but nobody has even asked the people in COFO just how decisions *are* made. . . . Our present structure is made up of the people of Mississippi and those who must face the consequences of any action taken. . . ."

Then Allard Lowenstein spoke up for the first time. "The past is done," he said. "Now the question is how to maximize cooperation and not drive anyone out."

"But," Joseph Rauh interrupted, "I would like to drive out the Lawyers Guild. I think it is immoral to take help from Communists."

"I agree with you," Allard continued, "but we must maximize cooperation. . . . We need more structure. . . . Right now, decision making is metaphysical. . . . It is true that SNCC was once the main source of funds and resources. . . . Now students, labor, and other groups are, so they must have a say. . . . We need the commitment of people here to the formation of a new central body . . . broadened in its base from how decisions are presently made. . . . We need structural democracy, not amorphous democracy."

Lowenstein's proposal for "structural democracy" funneled the remaining discussion. The SNCC observers considered it a liberal attempt to seize control of the Mississippi Project but said nothing. The rest of the meeting amounted to arguments in favor of Allard's proposal.

"We must consider our national responsibilities," the NAACP man reiterated. "No matter how democratic, if decisions are made injurious to our national interests, we must have a way out of them."

"In practice," Allard added, "we are bound by the decisions as they are now made. We can't leave Mississippi, though we might talk about the possibility."

"Precisely the point. We're caught."

"Unless," Allard broke back in, "we write off Mississippi or engage in an open clash, then we must take this action I propose."

"I have been listening to the crying of people in Mississippi for seventeen years," one of the other liberals complained. "I don't want to have to listen to Steptoe anymore. [Steptoe was a poor, uneducated black farmer and MFDP leader in Amite County whom SNCC revered.] We need high-level meetings so we can cut away all this under-brush. . . ."

"At some point," Allard interjected, "we also need to think of the volunteers, who are not being represented."

"We have the experience," another liberal continued, "to know the problems. We don't have to caucus with the Negroes in Mis-sissippi. . . ."

The representative of the NAACP then summarized things before adjournment. "The Mississippi Project must be continued in 1965 under a new coordinating agency," he said. "These are realistic problems and we can't just listen to the grass roots. . . . We will have to decide . . . at the top level . . ."

When a transcript of the meeting was subsequently circulated through SNCC circles, it was treated as concrete proof of what they had long suspected. The story of how the liberals had called Mr. Steptoe "underbrush" was greeted with outrage. The liberals wanted to strip the people of Mississippi of what little power they had won, just to make them pawns in another white man's game. Allard Lowenstein was given credit for having put them up to it. Both he and Rauh visited Mississippi shortly after the New York meeting. Allard gave several radio interviews in the course of the visit, claiming that Atlantic City was a "victory" and that the Summer Project had originally been his idea. He would be openly greeted by SNCC as an enemy.

Dennis Sweeney at first refused to believe what his colleagues were saying about Allard, but that changed rapidly.

In the meantime, SNCC offered Dennis Sweeney a $10-a-month staff position and he took it. It was to be an entire year before he returned to Stanford, and even then, he would never again identify himself as a "student." From September 1964 until the Sixties were almost over, Sweeney was an organizer first and foremost. That September, there was no sense that he would end up lost in the process. Staying only made Dennis more of a hero than ever in the eyes of Stanford. He was the only one of the University's summer volunteers to do so.

The convention, whether "victory" or "defeat," seemed to have changed nothing in McComb. A fresh wave of white assaults began on the night of September 6, with the demolition at midnight of the black Bogue Chitte Billiard Parlor. The next evening, the Chison Methodist Church, Mrs. Coney's Barbeque Pit, a home on Beech Street, and Booker T. Gutter's Grocery in outlying Ruth, Mississippi, were all bombed as well. On September 9, an explosion rocked the home of a black McComb minister. McComb's SNCC project director appealed directly to the Justice Department for increased protection, but the only response was a 70 percent reduction of the number of Federal agents assigned to Pike County.

The McComb bombings resumed on September 20. The first target was Mrs. Alvene Quin, a local black who ran a club and fast-food joint where Sweeney and his sidekick, J.D., often finished the day with a beer. After the earlier bombings, the McComb Project had organized a network to guard the homes of local civil rights figures, including Mrs. Quin's, but late Sunday night her guard was away from his post; a white man drove up, ran to her porch with a package, ran back to his car, and sped off. A young neighborhood black ran over to Mrs. Quin's and kicked the package off the porch. It then exploded, collapsing part of Mrs. Quin's roof down onto the heads of her three sleeping children. Neither she, her children, nor the young neighbor were injured. Thirty minutes later, another bomb destroyed the Society Hill Missionary Baptist Church. It was the eighth dynamite assault in less than three weeks.

Dennis Sweeney wrote an account of the bombing of Mrs. Quin's, which appeared a month later without a byline in the *Stanford Daily*:

> The first bombing comes at 10:50. Most of the Negroes of McComb are in bed—but only some are sleeping. These days most Negro adults don't fall asleep until the wee hours of morning. Then the blast. That sickening, anguishing sound

that Negroes in McComb have come to know so well. . . .
This night . . . the sound is more anguishing—for the pain
grow worse with each bombing. . . . And then the moments
of torment that follow—whose house, who is dead? It's not
mine. Then who?

Who? And one's stomach aches with pain and the pain
seeps up into the chest and the head and comes out of every
pore. Who? Is someone dead? The fear and the suspense
grow—the anguish becomes unbearable. People grab
whatever clothing they can find and run out into the streets.
People quickly learn the news—it's Mama Quin's house. It
couldn't be worse. Everyone loves Mama Quin. She owns a
popular café. She is kind and good to everyone. . . . She is a
towering figure of strength. She can't be intimidated. . . . The
house is almost demolished. They weren't out to frighten
tonight. Mama Quin was to be killed.

"How much," Dennis beseeched, "can a human being take?"

Within an hour of the bombing of Mrs. Quin's, a crowd of several
hundred gathered in the streets on the black side of McComb, shouting
at the police cruisers drawn by the explosions. Dennis Sweeney was
there, urging people to refrain from violence.

Two nights later, September 22, two more bombs were lobbed at
black McComb homes, and the crowd that subsequently gathered in
the streets began slinging rocks, bricks, and bottles at a patrol car. Soon
black McComb was surrounded with local police, sheriffs, and Mississippi state patrolmen. Dennis Sweeney was once again in the
middle, trying to get people to stop throwing things. He and 19 local
blacks were arrested before the evening was over. The blacks were
charged with "criminal syndicalism," a violation of a new state law
prohibiting "unlawful" acts "in effecting any political or social
change." Sweeney was charged with being "an accessory after the fact"
and held for several days while the police tried to intimidate the
arrested blacks into naming him as the bomber of Mrs. Quin's. When
they were unsuccessful, everyone was released from custody.

Eventually, nine local whites were charged and convicted of the
September bombings. The judge sentenced each to five years and
immediately suspended the penalties, arguing that they "were just
getting started in life," "came from good families," and "were unduly
provoked by outside agitators, some of whom are of low moral
character, some of whom are unhygienic."

The running conflict with the liberals left the Mississippi Project short of resources, and the only statewide strategy planned for the fall of 1964 was a rerun of the Freedom Vote. Compared to the summer or even the previous fall, it got little publicity and enjoyed even less organizational fervor. A number of elements internal to SNCC had different directions they wanted to pursue; as a system of management, consensus was proving only barely operative. Once again, Aaron Henry and Ed King were the Freedom Vote candidates, and once again, the call for outside volunteers went out late. Until then I was sure I had already missed out on the noblest adventure of my generation.

I was a sophomore, renting a room in an old army barracks two miles from campus and feeling dreadfully out of place at Stanford. I was attached to my girlfriend, Rose, but everything else was out of sync.

Rose brought me the news of the Freedom Vote on October 15, 1964, after a campuswide meeting about Mississippi. She said a carload of volunteers was going South the next day. I immediately decided to go, and we walked to the fraternity house where Morse, the senior who owned the car, lived. I claimed the one remaining empty seat.

I still don't altogether understand why, out of nowhere, I jumped at that opportunity. Part of it must have been an urge to adventure, to be tested. Part of it was being bored with life at the university. I had little notion of anything that had gone on in Mississippi over the summer, except for the killings of Chaney, Schwerner, and Goodman. I just wanted to be sure to get there before it was all over. That it was far more important than anything else I might do was obvious to me.

The car left that night at 11 P.M. Morse, the senior fraternity man, was driving. Two other sophomore men were in the backseat with the journey's one woman. A senior, she and Dennis Sweeney had been going together when school ended the previous June, and she had only received letters from him since. She was headed for McComb to see him and find out what was left of their relationship.

Riding South with his Stanford girlfriend was as close as I got to Dennis that trip. I would meet neither him nor Allard Lowenstein while in Mississippi, but the fact that I had been there would provide an immediate contact with each of them when our paths eventually crossed.

Our small band of Freedom Vote volunteers arrived at the Jackson SNCC headquarters on Lynch Street early Sunday morning, October 18.

Our fright was still hidden by sophomoric bravado. Both Morse and I requested an assignment to McComb, where Dennis Sweeney was, because it was the "most dangerous" place in the state. The SNCC woman charged with assigning us smiled indulgently. We were told that only the most experienced people were being sent to McComb because of the danger. Morse complained that the woman who had traveled South with us was going there, but that, we were told, was because she was a friend of Dennis Sweeney's and her presence in McComb was "personal," not "organization-related." We would have to settle for Marks in Quitman County, the heart of the Delta. There were, the SNCC woman assured us, plenty of risks in Quitman County as well.

Morse and I reached Marks Monday afternoon. COFO headquarters there were on the second floor of a black Masonic hall. The project amounted to a total of three full-time workers and ourselves. Tuesday morning we began canvassing for the Freedom Vote. At the request of the *Stanford Daily*, I also compiled a "documented economic profile of a Negro family in rural Quitman County," later run in the same edition as Dennis Sweeney's unattributed description of the attack on Mrs. Quin's.

"I cannot cease to be amazed that these people bear up so well under the circumstances," I wrote with great naiveté.

Once the cotton has been picked and chopped, the residents
of Quitman County are liable to starve. The family I
studied is presently afflicted with a case of goiters due to
malnutrition. . . . Some of the people here have houses that
sit in the middle of large pools of excrement. . . . We don't
need to send Peace Corps all the way to Africa to find
subhuman living conditions. . . . The father is a farm laborer,
chopping and picking cotton. The children also pick
cotton. . . . The father has two years of school, the mother,
three. The children attend classes from time to time. For
breakfast yesterday the family ate biscuits and fatback. . . .
The family had no lunch and had only turnip greens for
dinner. . . . The wife has had eight pregnancies, five of her
children have died. . . . They are such good people. . . . I
wish I could take every adolescent cuddling in the warm

intellectual womb of Stanford and show them what needs to
be done.

The day after I wrote that, I got my first sample of the risks to
which the SNCC woman in Jackson had referred.

Morse, I, and two others had all gone to the small town of Lambert
to do more canvassing. After several hours we returned to Morse's car,
parked on the main street of Lambert's black side. Morse had a letter he
wanted to mail, and he and the others then walked over to the post
office two blocks away. I stayed with the car. Five minutes after they
left, a pickup carrying two rednecks pulled in next to me and the driver
got out, carrying a shotgun. His friend had a revolver stuffed into the
waistband of his pants. The driver raised his shotgun so it pointed at
my chin.

"Nigger lover," he said, "we're givin' you five minutes to get out
of town."

I shifted my feet and scrambled around in my head trying to figure
out how I was supposed to respond. I decided to try being legal and
asked him what authority he had to order me around.

The redneck said nothing and just looked at his weapon.

I started to argue, but he interrupted.

"Nigger lover," he repeated, "I said five minutes."

At the same time, Morse and the others returned, took one look at
what was going on, and we sped out of Lambert immediately.

That night I spoke long distance to the *Stanford Daily* and recounted
what had happened. When the interview was over, I asked if they had
had any word from the others with whom Morse and I had driven
South. They knew only that everyone had reached their assigned
project. Sweeney's girlfriend was in McComb and reported that things
there were intense, but that Dennis was all right.

I never learned many details about what went on between
them, but in McComb, things weren't working out well
between Dennis Sweeney and his old Stanford girlfriend. She stayed in
a local motel, and he visited with her when he wasn't consumed with
his SNCC duties, but he had switched worlds and had few emotional
ties left to the campus she represented. Sweeney was out on his own,
devoted to his new life, and breaking with her was only one small
consequence.

As a four-month veteran of Mississippi's foremost combat zone,
Dennis was widely known and respected throughout COFO. His voice

was prominent in McComb freedom-house discussions, and his opinions were sought out in Jackson as well. His primary sidekick was still J.D., the Cambridge sandal maker, and the two men often spent their $10 salaries Friday nights down on the local black juke-joint dance floor. Dennis danced a roosterlike strut and women were attracted to him. Every now and then, he, J.D., and others went out back to smoke weed. Always in danger, he lived a fast life, leagues apart from his days as a student, no longer able to pretend that anything was the same as before.

I was getting a strong dose of that same feeling back in Marks. On the evening of Wednesday, October 21, Morse and I and the rest of the Marks Project workers were hanging out in the lodge-hall headquarters where we slept. Morse was writing another letter, and when he was finished, he wanted to go out to find a mailbox. Everyone reminded him that COFO rules forbade any workers from going out alone at night, but he sloughed it off, saying he'd be back in five minutes. In fact, he disappeared for an hour.

While cruising in search of a mailbox, his car was forced off the road by four whites in a truck who then beat, kicked, and urinated on him. Morse finally made his way back to the headquarters, explained what had happened, and we reported the incident to the Jackson COFO office and the *Daily*.

When reports of the beating ran in the California newspapers, two FBI agents were dispatched to Marks to investigate. It was my first encounter with federal agents.

When I answered the door, the agent showed me his badge and identified himself. Then he commenced his investigation.

"Well, nigger lover," he began in a heavy drawl, "what seems to be the problem?"

Within 24 hours of the federal visit, I received a phone call from the sheriff of Quitman County informing me that I was under suspicion in the beating of Morse. This was too much for us. Twenty minutes later, Morse and I fled across the state to the town of Columbus, rendezvoused with the two other Stanford sophomores, and headed back to school the next morning.

We stopped in Jackson to pick up Dennis Sweeney's girlfriend, but she had left a message there saying Dennis was "in trouble," and whatever was going on between them, she couldn't leave yet.

At 1:30 P.M. on the day Morse and I left Marks, police entered the McComb freedom house and arrested three people on charges of "operating a food-handling establishment without a county health certificate." At 7:45 P.M., they returned and arrested 10 more people, including Sweeney, on the same charge. According to McComb's police chief, the "overcrowding" of the freedom house created a "boardinghouse" situation and a county permit was required. Sweeney, the *Stanford Daily* was told, had been arrested on county food-code violations because he "hadn't taken a bath in 90 days." The McComb jailer explained it as a consequence of "living with niggers." Dennis, the "niggers," and the other "nigger lovers" were held over the weekend in the basement of the McComb jail with nothing to sleep on except cement.

Word of Sweeney's arrest spread across the Stanford campus while we traveled West, and more than $1,800 was collected for a McComb bail fund. When we arrived back at Stanford Monday morning, October 26, the lead *Daily* headline was "Sweeney Out on Bail After McComb Arrest." In an interview, Dennis claimed that the 13 arrests "were calculated to force the canceling of the Project's Freedom Day," a mass attempt to register voters at the Pike County courthouse scheduled for that same Monday. Dennis "expressed fear" that "more harassment and arrests" were imminent. "We're headed into the most difficult week yet," he said.

As I read the story, 29 more "Negroes and civil rights workers" were being arrested in front of the Pike County courthouse. All 29 were charged with trespassing and were held in the McComb jail. On October 27, 18 more were arrested. Dennis Sweeney was among this second group. All 18 refused any bail and stated that they intended to stay incarcerated until "the federal government intervenes." Fearful of federal intervention, the local authorities released all the 47 Freedom Day arrestees after a night in custody.

On Thursday, October 29, the *Daily* headline was "Sweeney Released." The campus paper noted:

> The release came suddenly yesterday morning after the group had spent a grueling night in the Pike County jail during which five of the arrestees were beaten and kicked by a jail attendant. . . . Sweeney was not beaten, but his wallet was taken from him and its contents (including addresses and phone numbers) were removed. When he asked for its return upon his release, he was summarily shoved out the door. . . .

Another one of the arrested, Mrs. Quin, a McComb Negro, sustained serious injury when the jailer slammed a cell door on her arm. She was taken to the hospital after her release. Mrs. Quin was a victim of a bombing incident last September 20. . . . Nine whites convicted of the bombing were given suspended sentences in a Pike County court. . . . Since the release of the nine, harassment of the Project workers and central office has increased measurably, Sweeney reported. Sweeney expects more arrests, and possibly violence, as election day nears. "There are," Sweeney claimed, "no brakes at all on this community any longer."

Dennis Sweeney's October 28 trepidations would prove exaggerated. In fact, this flurry of arrests was the crest of the rednecks' fall onslaught. Within weeks, McComb's solid white front broke, when 50 prominent white Pike County businessmen signed a public appeal for an end to "the violence." After that, vigilantism would steadily recede—so much so, that by December Sweeney would come to think of Pike County as "tame."

On the evening of October 28, I received my second visit from the FBI.

I had commented on the behavior of the Mississippi FBI for the local papers, and the arrival of two Palo Alto-based agents served as a sudden reminder that such talk had consequences.

I was in bed with Rose; I stumbled into a bathrobe and cracked the door open.

The big man closest to me flashed his badge. "Federal Bureau of Investigation," he said. "Are you David Victor Harris?"

"I am," I admitted.

"We'd like you to come down to our office and answer a few questions."

I did not yet know I had the right to say no.

When I had dressed, they walked on either side of me out to their car. Once at the Bureau's Palo Alto office, the agent in charge turned the desk lamp on and pointed it into my face. The other agent turned the overhead light off and the two of them stood behind the glare, where I could barely see them.

Their questioning was eventually summarized in a memo to "Director, FBI" from "SAC, San Francisco (157-380)" on the subject of "MISSISSIPPI SUMMER PROJECT . . . DAVID VICTOR HARRIS . . .

RACIAL MATTER." According to the field agents, I told them about the incident in Lambert, Morse's beating, and my encounter with the Mississippi FBI. They asked a number of questions about the newspaper reports that had been printed, and I observed that "the basic truth" was in all of them.

The last inclusion in my file referring to Mississippi was a memorandum from "Rosen" to someone named Belmont filed at FBI national headquarters three weeks later. "Morse and Harris," it alleged, "are immature, unreliable and obnoxious individuals. . . . This whole matter arose as a result of an insidious effort on the part of these individuals to create a situation designed to harass and embarrass the agents who were conscientiously engaged in their duties." I sensed the Bureau's dislike immediately.

It took me several hours of lying in bed with Rose afterwards before my fear eased.

Rose soon threw me over, and, after that, my life fell off to the isolated nadir of my college career. My brief Mississippi adventure had flooded my life with new and unsettling information and provoked an irresolution that would plague me for several more months. I was no longer sure how I felt about the country I lived in. I still wanted to pursue something "meaningful" and "worthwhile," but nothing of that order seemed even remotely within reach. That feeling wouldn't change until I finally met Allard Lowenstein early in 1965.

On October 30, 1964, the *Daily* announced that Lowenstein would be on campus that weekend to give two speeches. I didn't attend either. One was sponsored by the Young Democrats on behalf of the vice-presidential campaign of Hubert Humphrey. The other concerned itself with Mississippi. "Lowenstein," the *Daily* explained, "has long been involved with the Mississippi Freedom Project"; he was credited with being "instrumental in Stanford's involvement." He was also inaccurately credited with having been "floor manager for the Mississippi Freedom Democratic party delegation to the Democratic National Convention." He would be coming to Stanford straight from Mississippi, "where," according to the *Daily*, he would "talk with Dennis Sweeney . . . and other COFO workers in McComb."

No record of that October 30, 1964, visit between Allard and his onetime protégé has survived, but it can be reconstructed approximately from similar encounters that would follow over the next six months. They were now on opposite sides.

Dennis Sweeney, fresh from Pike County jail, was in no mood to hear Allard talk of Atlantic City as a "victory." What victory, he asked. Mrs. Quin was being thrown in jail and the people who blew her house up were walking the streets. What had changed? All Atlantic City had proved was whose side the Democrats were on. Given a choice between their agenda for power and the suffering of black Mississippi, they had chosen themselves. They were part of the problem, not the solution. The feeling that Allard might be, too, was only lurking in the back of Dennis's eyes, but Allard saw it.

Lowenstein said Sweeney was losing his perspective. A year ago, a Civil Rights Act had seemed the wildest fantasy, but they had won that much with just the threat of the Mississippi Summer Project. Atlantic City had been invaluable in bringing the case of Mississippi to the country at large. They had forced an incumbent President who was a Southerner to recognize blacks as a political force. Nothing would stay the same after that, and if people like Dennis didn't give up on it, the strategy would succeed. "There are some doors open now," Allard said. "The question is whether you go through them or not." He was sure federal protection for the right to vote would be won shortly.

Dennis responded by repeating a saying that was being heard regularly in SNCC circles those days. "The best way to keep someone a slave," Sweeney said, "is to give him the vote and call him free." Freedom was a lot more than getting to choose between racists to live under. The Democrats hadn't yielded to the MFDP because it was poor and black. If the Democrats let those kinds of people get control over their own lives, MFDP wouldn't need the Democrats anymore. A new structure had to be built from the ground up.

Lowenstein expressed disbelief that Sweeney was saying all this. He ought to know better. Allard had been a champion of the electoral process throughout his life and had little tolerance for those who did not share his faith. Dennis was sounding like SNCC, he said, and making a great mistake. The system worked.

The system only worked for those on top of it, Sweeney answered. All that worked for those on the bottom was themselves.

Lowenstein reached Stanford on Sunday fresh from that discussion and chose to spend his second speech praising what had gone on in Mississippi during the previous year, keeping most of his trepidations about the present state of affairs to his private conversations. On this informal level, he talked about a "distortion" that had come over "a lot of the SNCC people." It was an analysis he would often apply to those who were young, to his left, and critical of him. Mississippi, he observed, had been an "incredibly intense experience" and inevitably some had become "warped" along the way.

Lowenstein did not go so far as to classify Sweeney among them, but when he spoke of Dennis, it was clear he now thought the issue was up for grabs.

What Dennis Sweeney eventually did to his former mentor would make many look back and try to locate a time and place when some kind of definitive "break" happened between them, but "break" is much too clean and quick to what happened. Their differences were an issue between them for another eight months, and they did not stop talking to each other until they had simply run out of things to say. That Allard took the disintegration very personally is a matter of record.

While taping an oral history interview in 1977, some 13 years later, Lowenstein brought up Dennis Sweeney as an object lesson of the civil rights movement. He called their parting of the ways "one of the most bitter experiences I had in Mississippi, in personal terms." He described Dennis as "one of the individuals I'd brought down to Mississippi as a result of my efforts at Stanford." It was, Allard said, "a very illustrative story in terms of autobiography. The basic point of it was that . . . [Dennis] got there and became very radicalized. He was sent to McComb and was in great danger physically. . . . In the course of that he decided that . . . I and other figures involved in what he viewed as reformist politics were the enemy much more than the white power structure. . . . Since Dennis and I had been close friends, it became a very bitter thing.

"We were good friends," Allard repeated, "[but] we met under very ugly kinds of circumstances where he would attack me from a very personal feeling."

It was all over between Allard Lowenstein and Dennis Sweeney by election day, 1964, but by no means yet done.

Just when Dennis Sweeney threw himself irretrievably into the Southern movement, that movement began to disintegrate around him. SNCC was now strung between two poles of thought and was having increasing difficulties coming to terms with itself. One side wanted to concentrate its energies on building a pyramidical structure all of whose members pursued a common program. The other thought the organization should be a loose association of free-lance political samurai, working under the instructions of whatever community they sought to help. The unresolved dichotomy effectively turned everyone in SNCC loose to do what he or she thought best.

In McComb, that drift was coupled with a noticeable reduction in redneck vigilante activity, and, without the immediate threat to cinch it together, the freedom-house community began dispersing. Irritation crept into relationships, and, to Dennis Sweeney, the McComb Project felt increasingly confining for his expectations. In the words of Sweeney's friend, J.D., "The McComb scene had pretty much burned out by December," and he and Dennis began to look around for a fresh mission to pursue.

Adding to that impulse to move on was an intense broadening of the movement's horizons. The change it wanted, once minimal, now seemed deep and massive. New issues and approaches abounded. Malcolm X, the Black Muslim leader, paid a visit to McComb that fall and said blacks should arm themselves. In Berkeley, California, students calling themselves the Free Speech Movement shut down the university. The war in Vietnam had begun as well—23,000 Americans were now fighting there—and Sweeney was already saying that stopping it might very well be the most important cause of all.

Another question Sweeney wrestled with was the role to be played henceforth in Mississippi by outside whites. The paramount need, as most black SNCC members saw it, was to develop black identity. The experience of white volunteers that summer had demonstrated that native blacks tended to defer to them both because of their greater organizational skills and their color, an arrangement in which black identities would always be compromised.

Dennis sought to resolve this dilemma with a fresh approach to his own organizing. He thought the whole country needed an awakening to itself and its own liberation, like the one already experienced by Mississippi blacks and people such as himself. In his epistemology, it was the organizer's responsibility to transmit those experiences. What he needed was a vehicle. After much discussion, he and J.D. hit upon the idea of making a film about Mississippi. Anyone who saw such a visual record of liberation, he theorized, couldn't help but be moved and drawn to duplicate Mississippi elsewhere. Neither had any experience with filmmaking, but J.D.'s neighbor in Cambridge, Ed Pincus, was a filmmaker. J.D. was sure they could convince him to do the shooting.

In December, Sweeney and his friend J.D. left for Cambridge to see Pincus and begin trying to raise the money needed to capture liberation on celluloid.

A s with Dennis, the war in Vietnam was becoming an issue in Allard Lowenstein's life. After Lyndon Johnson and Hubert Humphrey had been swept into office by a huge margin, Allard had a long conversation on the subject of the war in the lobby of New York City's Algonquin Hotel with an American economist who had just returned from Saigon. At the time, Lowenstein struck the economist as still knowing very little about Vietnam, and the two hours they spent together in effect became a briefing. Allard listened intently.

The economist described at length how American aid was fashioning the infrastructure of a police state. The South Vietnamese government had no popular support. Without Americans to prop it up, it would fall in a matter of days. Saigon was beset by huge antigovernment demonstrations. Instead of being "phased out" as promised, American presence was burgeoning. Simply put, he said, we were on the wrong side. The countryside belonged to the National Liberation Front, and the Saigon government controlled little of anything after dark. Only the Americans could keep them in power, and the Americans were systematically doing exactly that.

The involvement was being justified by the Gulf of Tonkin Resolution passed by Congress in the weeks before the Atlantic City convention. The resolution had been described as a response to an alleged assault on two American destroyers by a North Vietnamese torpedo boat, but the economist had his doubts about whether the precipitating attack had even happened. Instead, he maintained, the Tonkin mandate, endorsing "whatever measures" the President considered "necessary to repel attacks on American forces" and "prevent further aggression," served as a de facto declaration of war. The policy was already a disaster with the potential to do little but lead to a worsening of the situation.

Allard asked perceptive questions but was not yet ready to make the war more than just one among the flock of political concerns that kept him running around the country, lecturing at every opportunity.

In Cambridge, Dennis and J.D. approached Ed Pincus, the filmmaker. Dennis did most of the talking. As he put it, the McComb Project was "behind" them, and they wanted to film the next scene of action as it happened. He said the most logical target was nearby Amite County and Natchez, its major city. The civil rights movement there was led by SNCC's hero, Mr. Steptoe, and to excite Pincus, Dennis described how they took teenagers from McComb's freedom school out to Amite to see Steptoe and how the kids had been almost immediately moved to intense activism. They wanted to capture this "human blooming" on film. If Pincus would do the filming, Dennis and J.D. would raise the money and arrange things in Amite.

Pincus's take on Sweeney was mixed. Dennis's style was nonassertive, after the manner of Bob Moses, but the filmmaker saw much of it as repressed anger. Both Sweeney and J.D. had the somewhat disdainful attitude of veterans under fire talking to people who had never been there. Dennis especially was consumed by his politics. Everything for him was a public act. Pincus thought the film idea was good and drew his partner, David Newman, into the discussion.

Newman was struck by Sweeney's boy-scout manner. Despite all his battle-veteran accoutrements, he sensed something irreversibly Sunday-schoolish about Dennis. According to Newman, he was "a real crusader, an idealist." Newman was impressed, too, with Dennis's connections. A number of known national civil rights names were among his acquaintances and friends.

The two filmmakers estimated that it would take $10,000 to make the documentary. They agreed to it after Dennis assured them that Eastern liberals were "uptight" about the increasingly vocal opposition to the war and were prepared to donate heavily to civil rights activity in hopes of deflecting the antiwar movement.

In fact, Sweeney's fund raising efforts in the East were completely unsuccessful, and he only raised enough to get himself and J.D. to Oregon, where he was sure the pickings would be better. He raised that small sum from a leading social critic who knew Dennis by reputation as one of the best young men in SNCC. Sweeney told him a story about having to get back down to Mississippi immediately, and when Dennis finally allowed the older man to hold his hand as they rode together in a taxi, the man bought him a plane ticket to New Orleans.

Sweeney promptly cashed the ticket in, and he and J.D. had traveling money for Oregon.

First, they purchased a lid of marijuana, then they headed West in an enormous drive-away Cadillac they had contracted to deliver in San Francisco. Later, J.D. described the journey as like being in "some kind of space capsule." They kept the windows up, smoked joint after joint, and stayed tuned to whatever rock 'n roll station was within their reach. Several times they absentmindedly ran out of gas and had to hitchhike to the nearest filling station.

In Chicago they stopped to pick up a motorcycle J.D. had left there the year before. They dismantled the machine and piled it on canvas in the Cadillac's backseat. When they reached California, they left the cycle in Palo Alto and turned in the drive-away. After reassembling the bike, they motored 100 miles toward Portland before a fierce rainstorm drove them back to Palo Alto. For their second try, they sold the cycle and lined up another drive-away to the Northwest.

The Portland press had followed Sweeney's Mississippi tribulations avidly, and he and J.D. encountered the consequences of that soon after they reached town. They had gone out to a club on the black side of Willamette River to drink beer. At the time, both were what J.D. called "freedom-burned" and dazed from the pace at which their lives had been changing. They just wanted to get a little drunk and unwind. The floor show at the club featured one Cocoa Brown, wearing a G-string and pasties, strutting her stuff on a raised stage, and bending so her cleavage wobbled.

When Cocoa's first set was over, the emcee made an announcement. One of the club's employees had recognized Sweeney from his picture in the paper and passed the word on.

"Ladies and gentlemen," the emcee said, "we have the distinct pleasure of having a celebrity with us tonight. Portland's own civil rights hero is sitting right down here. Dennis Sweeney."

With that, the spotlight whipped across the dark room to the table where Dennis Sweeney and J.D. were nursing beers and talking about Cocoa Brown's tits. The spot caught them in a freeze frame, like two bugs nailed to a board. The crowd clapped. Dennis Sweeney made a slight nod of his head and wave of his hand. His expression was both confused and embarrassed.

Public recognition would eventually become an issue among the young during the Sixties, and this was as close to being a celebrity as Dennis would get that decade. Despite his pioneering role, he would be remembered as no more than a bit player when it was over.

Fund raising was indeed easier in Portland. One of Sweeney's strongest local supporters was a Presbyterian minister, and he assisted in setting up a number of speaking appearances where the civil rights workers could solicit contributions. Dennis did most of the talking.

Having decided along with J.D. that money for the film project was best raised by treading lightly, he kept the political conclusions to a minimum as he spoke of the Mississippi experience. Sweeney was his most eloquent when describing the freedom schools. He had personally witnessed, he said, "children blossoming in their first realization of racial equality."

Once, in front of a largely black church congregation, he dispensed with his customary text and launched into the war. He said Vietnam was as wrong as anything in Mississippi, maybe even more so, and that the government was lying to call such suppression a protection of democracy. In a way, talking about the war was a daring move. In another way, it was a serious miscalculation of his audience. The Portland supporters of civil rights were not ready for any across-the-board indictment of American power. Their perspective at the time was no wider than that of ensuring Mississippi blacks the right to vote, and Dennis's exposition backfired somewhat.

When he took questions from the audience, the first came from a local NAACP member, and he was furious. He had come to hear about the aspirations of Negroes in Mississippi and instead he'd heard nothing but a bunch of "radicals" running down "our country." He and a number of others then walked out. Afterward, Sweeney laughed it off with more cynicism about liberals.

Despite that incident, Sweeney raised close to $4,000 in his hometown, and later he and J.D. headed for Natchez to make preparations for filming once summer arrived.

I first met Allard Lowenstein not long after Dennis and J.D. left Portland. I had just turned 19, and although our relationship would have neither the length nor intensity of his involvement with Dennis, I would, for a brief period, be Lowenstein's principal protégé at one of his favorite college campuses.

Our initial encounter took place at a cabin in the foothills behind campus where two upperclassmen lived. Lowenstein was visiting them, and that Saturday morning he was having what was presented to me as a "bull session." I was persuaded to come by a friend who had himself been one of Allard's Stern Hall Original Sixteen. My friend thought I was too isolated and said I would like Allard a lot.

At the time, Lowenstein was working under a Ford Foundation grant to research the state of higher education. The study had been inspired by the recent revolt in Berkeley, and he was traveling around the country to talk with students and to "assess their concerns." When I arrived, some four or five young men were listening with great deference. Several issues of the *New York Times* were strewn around the room, and Allard was in a skintight T-shirt that displayed his weightlifter's arms. His tie and coat were slung over the back of the couch. The discussion was interrupted for a moment when I was introduced. He told me to find a place to get comfortable and began again where he had been interrupted.

The day's discussion proceeded in a variety of ways. Sometimes Allard just expounded on a particular subject. Sometimes he was asked a question, which he then answered. At other times, he asked someone else a question, let them provide a short answer, and then provided a longer one himself. He spoke at length of the intricacies of the student coalition at Berkeley and the antiapartheid one at the UN. He knew all the latest details on Mississippi and mentioned Adlai Stevenson, Hubert Humphrey, and Martin Luther King by their first names. I found that impressive, but I wasn't entranced until he struck the theme his life would eventually be said to have epitomized.

He argued that one person can make an immense difference and that the course of history itself could be shaped by a single decision. Especially in a democracy, every person had a terribly important contribution to make. Everyone should take his life seriously, he urged, and devote it to worthy efforts.

My own adolescent sense of worthlessness was rampant enough so that to hear that I mattered was a need as great as any I then possessed. Allard hooked onto it right away. He himself seemed proof that you could devote yourself to something noble and prosper. I was soon listening as avidly as the rest.

After several hours, Lowenstein finally suggested we take a break. All this mental activity was tiring him out, he joked. He suggested we wrestle instead.

No one took him up on the suggestion right away.

Allard didn't drop it. "Come on," he goaded, "I'm an old man. One of you should be able to take me."

Still, no one responded.

"How about you?" Allard asked, looking at me.

"Me?" I was six feet two inches, he about five feet ten.

"Sure, you. Someone told me you used to play football."

"No thanks," I said, somewhat embarrassed.

Allard asked several others until he found a taker. Then everyone cleared to the edges of the room and the two of them assumed the starting position on all fours on the floor. At a shouted command of "go," they commenced. Right away it was obvious Allard was going to win. He quickly reversed into the top position and got his opponent in some sort of arm lock. When he wriggled out of that, Allard wrapped his body in another grip and began slowly forcing the student's shoulders to the floor. Both of them were grunting mightily and sweat was breaking through Allard's T-shirt. Finally, with a surge of leverage from his upper body, accompanied by a tremendous exhale of wind, Allard got the pin.

The small crowd of men cheered.

Lowenstein looked up. "Who's next?" he said.

After the session in the cabin finally broke up, I prepared to leave in the car I had borrowed for the day and asked whether anyone needed a ride. Allard spoke up. He said he had to get to Berkeley and asked whether I would take him. I was already late on my promise to return the car and this would make me even later, but I agreed. I wanted more contact.

During our drive, his curiosity about me was apparent as well. He asked about who I was and what mattered to me. I told him about being from Fresno and what I'd done in Mississippi. Then I told him about Rose and how devastated I was when she dumped me. I told him classes were boring and I wasn't sure where I belonged.

Allard counseled me as he would hundreds of others, but it never felt like a routine. He talked as though we were best friends. He seemed to understand my own secret feelings about wanting to be someone special. Allard said that on the basis of what little he knew about me, it was obvious I was bright and talented. He said I shouldn't let school scare me but neither should I underestimate its importance. It was important to be a good student and I could easily be one. I should just stop wallowing in my alienation. There were plenty of things to do. It was dark now and lights were stabbing around us on the freeway.

He then returned to the comments I had made about Rose. He said he knew how painful love could be and told me that for several years he had been engaged to the daughter of the Democratic whip in the House of Representatives. Breaking it off had really torn him up, he said, but he'd finally done so because it was clear to him that she wouldn't be able to accept the demands his commitment to politics would make on anyone connected to his life. Sometimes, Allard claimed, he still wondered whether he'd done the right thing.

I was 19 years old and Allard was 36. It was 1965, and elders did not deal easily or on such intimate terms with their juniors. Allard seemed one of a kind.

When we reached Berkeley, he tried to involve me in the discussion there, but I said I had to return my borrowed car. He suggested I sleep here on the floor where he was going to sleep and then drive him to Sacramento. I begged off, but when his expression made his disappointment clear, I offered to come back the next morning and drive him through the day.

He gave me an address to find him at 10 A.M.

The address was the residence of the chancellor of the University of California. I waited for 15 minutes until Lowenstein finally came out of the door, wearing his coat and tie, carrying an overnight bag and a thick pile of *New York Times*'s. In the car, he explained that he had been there all morning, trying to work out a formula for "resolving" the situation brought about by the Free Speech Movement. On our way to Sacramento, he spent the first half hour describing the current Berkeley impasse. He had never met the chancellor before and knew few, if any, of the students' principal leaders; nonetheless, he had, he said, offered himself as a bridge between the two camps. Nothing, as it later turned out, would ever come of the offer. The problem, he said, was keeping the "radicals" from "going off half cocked." When we were 20 minutes from Sacramento, he told me to wake him in 15 and went to sleep almost immediately.

In Sacramento, a meeting of Young Democrats was addressed, and then we headed south again and Allard returned to the subject of what I ought to do with myself. He said I was too isolated. Living where I did, he noted, I hardly even participated in normal student life. That, he said, was a shame for someone who was so clearly "leadership material." I blushed at the endorsement, having no such notion of myself. He said I should move to Stern Hall, where he had once been director.

Back at Stanford, I drove Lowenstein to a faculty residence where a dozen people had been waiting two hours to have dinner with him. He had another ride arranged to the airport, but I hung around anyway. Almost immediately, a discussion about Mississippi broke out. Allard launched into SNCC with a string of negatives.

Somewhere in the course of it, someone asked him about Dennis.

Lowenstein's mood sank visibly when Sweeney's name came up. He shook his head. Dennis, Allard claimed, had thrown in with his enemies. Everyone asked why, and as he explained about SNCC and Atlantic City, it struck me that Dennis's reaction was something of an obsession with Allard. It had somehow breached his self-confidence and brought a note of pain into his voice.

Not long after the discussion had moved on from the question of Dennis, I got up to leave. Allard thanked me and said he would be coming back soon, and he'd let me know when.

A week later I got a postcard from him. It was one of Allard's traditional vehicles of communication. The only thing unusual about my first one was how soon it came. Often Allard wrote and then hauled the postcard around for months before mailing it. Mine must have been mailed almost immediately.

"Move to Stern," it said.

D ennis Sweeney was back in Mississippi, hanging around and "getting things ready" for the summer. It was a searching time for Dennis, full of talk with his SNCC peers about where the movement was headed.

SNCC held two staff conferences that spring that had a deep effect on Sweeney. The first, in early March, was at a seminary in Atlanta.

What to do now was, as usual, the central question. The war was discussed a lot, but as an organization SNCC continued to abstain from taking a public position on it. The momentous part of the Atlanta meeting centered around Bob Moses. Moses had already resigned as Mississippi Project director in late 1964, tortured by the question of the proper model for leadership. His position, he explained, had become "too strong, too central, so that people who did not need to began to lean on me, to use me as a crutch." Led by his study of Camus, Moses had come to see the exercise of personal influence over others as overwhelmingly manipulative. People's desire to follow him was itself a political obstruction, he said. It would strip them of their true power. He could lead no one into the Promised Land. To escape that expectation, Bob Moses announced in Atlanta, he was changing his last name to Parris, his previous middle name; afterwards, he broke most of his contact with SNCC.

The reactions to Moses's move fell into two general categories. One group thought it made little sense for Bob to leave when people needed him more than ever. The other considered it brilliant and appropriate. Dennis Sweeney fell into the second group.

By now, Sweeney's own respect for Moses was immense. He was obsessed with making his personal behavior consistent with his moral abstracts, and their similar intellectual bents had always made it easy for Bob and Dennis to relate. Throughout Dennis's life, Moses's example remained as a model of honest dedication in the face of the temptations of power. In Atlanta, Sweeney argued that Moses was just defending the integrity of his "work," something all of them had to do, each in the way he thought best.

Dennis talked a lot about "work" in those days. It was not "work" in the sense of "job," but work in the sense of "mission" and "calling." He apparently felt that the internal tensions increasingly consuming SNCC's energies were making staying much longer in Mississippi impossible and began to fantasize about other options once the Natchez film was finished. One such fantasy was joining the Peace Corps. Sweeney apparently checked the possibility out with a Peace Corps recruiter and was told he would be sent to the Dominican Republic should he enlist.

The Peace Corps fantasy was abandoned in April when the United States Marines invaded the island to which he would have been assigned. Dennis later said it was foolish of him to think the government wanted peace in any form.

By the time Allard Lowenstein returned to Stanford in April for a two-day visit, I had taken his advice and moved to Stern Hall. He was pleased. He had borrowed someone's Mustang convertible this time and wanted me to drive him. The Ford Foundation project was apparently not yet finished, but he also had a new effort he was putting together. He had recently been named director for that summer's Encampment for Citizenship in New York City and was recruiting participants.

He described the Encampment as a six-week series of seminars sponsored by the Ethical Culture Society, involving a wide mix of young people from all over the country, living together in a private school in New York City. He himself had attended the one held in 1948. In Lowenstein's mind, it was the perfect opportunity for young people to reflect on all the changes that were going on around them in the company of the best of their generation. The country's world view was shifting, he said, in everything from art to sexual mores to politics, and all of that shift would be the Encampment's curriculum. In effect, it was Allard's own summer university, full of the "relevancy" students complained was lacking elsewhere. The participants would include "the leaders of a generation," and he claimed I belonged among them.

I felt honored in the selection, but it cost $600 to attend the Encampment and I didn't have the money. Allard said some of the participants would be given scholarships that covered everything except transportation to New York. I said I would have to see.

Most of Allard's two-day visit was spent with similar recruiting, and while I drove him, he told stories about Frank Graham, Norman Thomas, and Mrs. Roosevelt. The only other thing on his agenda that trip was his continuing campaign to disseminate his version of what had gone on in Mississippi the year before.

A great deal of that effort went into getting his argument into the pages of the *Daily*. Lowenstein met for several hours during both this trip and the next with the woman who was then editor. After being interviewed, he read her drafts and suggested revisions. Since he would never get around to putting his version of the Mississippi controversy on paper himself, the subsequent *Daily* story remains the closest he came to outright authorship. The headline read, "SNCC: New Directions, New Problems." The text began:

> A year and a half ago, in November of 1963, Bob Moses of SNCC. . . spoke in praise of Professor Allard Lowenstein and the contribution he had made to the civil rights struggle in Mississippi. "He's a man who transcends a lot of situations," Moses said. "He was very deeply [involved] in this campaign, and while he wasn't sufficient, he was certainly necessary to bring it off. Without him it would never have come off as it did."
>
> Several months ago, words of praise were once again raised for Lowenstein ("who has as much claim as anyone to be called the founder of the Mississippi Freedom Democratic Party") but this time not by Moses of SNCC but by Norman Thomas—speaking in angry defense of Lowenstein against SNCC and its supporters who, in some strange migration of attitude and logic, have come to regard not only Lowenstein but the whole spectrum of "Liberals" as "sellouts" and "traitors."
>
> In fact, there has been no "treason," no "sellout," by

Lowenstein or any other of the accused "Establishment
Liberals," but, rather, merely a perseverance in the attitudes
and aims which had once been SNCC's own and are no more.

Aside from Moses, the only voice cited as representing SNCC was
that of Dennis Sweeney.

> "Does voting made a man free?" SNCC staff member (and
> former Stanford student) Dennis Sweeney asks. "Clearly it
> doesn't," he answers . . . [but] not too many years ago . . .
> the idea of true "majority rule" for Mississippi looked like
> Utopia. "When I first got to Mississippi [in July of 1963],"
> Lowenstein remembered, "everything was
> finished." . . . When all seemed hopeless, Lowenstein came
> up with the idea for a Mock Vote drive . . . an idea that
> proved to be the progenitor of both the Mississippi Summer
> Project and the Mississippi Freedom Democratic Party. That is
> what Norman Thomas and others mean when they say that
> Lowenstein has as good a claim as any to be called the
> founder of the M.F.D.P.

The story covered two inside pages. In speaking of the Atlantic
City rift, Lowenstein said in the article, "The SNCC people. . . acted as
if they should have a monopoly on decision-making." "SNCC," the
article claimed, "had come to regard the Atlantic City convention as a
time of great disillusionment—proof, in the words of Dennis Sweeney,
that Democratic 'politics isn't all it's cracked up to be.'

"Far from being a 'betrayal' or a 'defeat,'" the article quoted
Lowenstein:

> Atlantic City was one of the greatest proofs of the vitality of
> American democracy—when the President of the United
> States at the height of his power was forced—forced by the
> aroused conscience of the nation—to move, to compromise.
> "The true hope for change," [Lowenstein concluded in
> the article] "is not in ideological purity, but in coalition. . . . I
> see a great opportunity for . . . a vast coalition of
> conscience. . . . We won't get everything we want all at once,
> . . . but we're not in a revolutionary situation. . . . There are
> pockets of injustice that can, and must, be wiped out. . . .
> What we're going to have to learn now is to work out our
> problems with a sense of mutual respect. . . . If finding
> common ground is betrayal of principles, then we certainly
> don't want to ask them [SNCC] to betray their principles.

By the time the article appeared, SNCC had stopped paying much attention to Lowenstein. SNCC members' resentment of him was irreversible. A decade and a half later, SNCC veterans would still epitomize him as someone who "needed to control and take credit for everything."

Dennis Sweeney agreed.

D ennis also shared much of SNCC's urge to push the war in Vietnam as an issue. He was among the delegation that traveled to Washington, D.C., that April to participate in the nation's first large-scale march against the war. Some 20,000 people attended. Bob Moses (now Parris) was one of the featured speakers.

Moses saw the war as a direct expression of the same mentality that had terrorized Mississippi for a century. A nation that allowed vigilantes to run amok, free to murder the most defenseless of black people, he said, was bound to "plan and execute murders elsewhere in the world."

At the time, opposition to the war was enough to get a person branded as "Communist" even by many supporters of civil rights. Americans considered it an article of faith to "support their President" at time of war. Many liberals openly worried that public criticism of Vietnam by civil rights advocates would undercut all the previous gains in civil rights. Within days of that Washington march, a number of prominent political figures began denouncing SNCC for Moses's statements.

The furor was one more sign that Vietnam policy was losing its remoteness. The First Marine Division had recently landed there in force and the 173rd Airborne was on its way. Since March, the intense bombardment of North Vietnam by American air and naval forces had been in full swing.

F rom Washington, D.C., Dennis Sweeney traveled north to Cambridge for more film preparations, staying in the Northeast for at least a week. In New Haven he crossed paths with Lowenstein, and the two of them had their last extensive argument.

The encounter took place in a room in Stiles College at Yale. The room was assigned to Allard by virtue of his six-month designation as Stiles College's "writer-in-residence," a post he held despite not being in residence very often and having written only one not very successful book.

As usual, the argument was about SNCC. At issue specifically was how blacks and whites could best "work." SNCC had by then reached the conclusion that outside whites ought to return to their own communities and organize there. Sweeney agreed and saw his own film efforts as a step in that direction. From personal experience, he thought SNCC was right to point out how intimidating white workers could be to the identity of blacks. You can't give anyone their freedom, Dennis said. People have to acquire it themselves. It wasn't so simple as black and white together anymore. First, black people had to figure themselves out and recover their sense of worth and dignity. Their history of subjugation and whites' history of dominance made that doubly difficult in each other's presence. On top of that, Mississippi wasn't the only problem. Whites from California and New York ought to be dealing with their own oppression rather than traveling two thousand miles to deal with someone else's.

Of course there were problems all over, Allard responded. That had nothing to do with whether they ought to be approached by blacks and whites together or apart. Mississippi had been chosen to concentrate on because it was the worst, where blacks had been systematically excluded to the highest degree, but the object, whether in Mississippi or California, was to build an interracial society. The kind of racial separation and exclusion SNCC was now talking about was "racist."

The answer infuriated Dennis. The real racism was in not letting people control their own lives, he argued. If blacks wanted time to themselves, who were white people to refuse them that right? Anything else was just another white man telling them how they had to behave.

Allard threw up his arms and shook his head. What black people was Dennis talking about? It was SNCC's imaginary notion of black people, that's all. One more part of this vague "revolution" Moses and the others kept talking about. Dennis ought to know better than that. Was he still saying black people in Mississippi didn't want to vote?

There was more to freedom than the vote, Dennis answered.

But, Allard interrupted, the vote is what lets them get the rest.

Like at Atlantic City? Dennis interrupted back.

They went on like that for hours. At some point in the discussion, they were joined by one of Lowenstein's Yale protégés. The protégé had been a 1963 Freedom Vote volunteer, and though he was not as critical of SNCC as Allard, he was uncomfortable with recent developments in the organization. The phrase "black power" was coming into circulation then, and to the Yale man that meant SNCC was drifting away from participatory democracy as a goal—and he disapproved. The argument continued. The protégé could tell that Dennis was "clearly Allard's friend" but was "terribly angry" at him. He thought Dennis was being "ideological" and "irrational" and "rigid."

Eventually the argument moved from Lowenstein's room to the home of a faculty member who had been instrumental in Mississippi Summer Project's freedom-school network. Both Allard and Dennis claimed to respect the man, but he refused to come down on either side. The protégé then introduced the question of how badly SNCC had maligned Allard and tried to convince the faculty member to intervene with SNCC to try and straighten things out. He refused to do that as well. After several hours of beating around that bush, Dennis, Allard, and the Yale protégé returned to Allard's. When the protégé finally left at 2 A.M., the two were still going at it.

There is no surviving record of how much longer the conversation went on, but at some point that night, Lowenstein made one more unsolicited attempt to alter Sweeney's direction. He told Dennis that the film idea was a waste of his talents and he should get out of Mississippi. He noted that the triannual World Youth Festival, last held in Helsinki in 1962, was scheduled this summer for Algiers, and he said he could get Dennis on the delegation. He gave him the name of a man who was in charge of providing money for those who needed financial assistance.

Sweeney took the man's name but ignored the advice and returned to Mississippi.

There, a number of things were going on. Probably the most important of them to Dennis was a conference planned for Waveland, Mississippi, where the future directions SNCC might take would be discussed in detail, but he had something personal to take care of first. It had to do with his teeth.

Along with building a political infrastructure, COFO had also built a volunteer-staffed network of free medical and dental services. After returning from the Northeast, Sweeney approached one of the volunteer dentists to see if he could get something done with the upper teeth in the front of his mouth. One was obviously damaged and he apparently considered the others too far apart, too small, not quite straight, and ugly.

The dentist made a replacement bridge, normally a purely cosmetic procedure, apparently figuring that if anyone had earned new teeth, it was someone who had been in McComb as long as Dennis.

The existing teeth were filed down and new dentures crafted and then wired onto the old stubs. The new ones looked perfect, and the arrangement was of course designed to be permanent. Within ten years, Dennis Sweeney would tear those dentures out with his own frenzied hands. He tried to hide the gap that was left by keeping his upper lip pulled down like a window shade.

The SNCC gathering in Waveland from May 10 to 15 was billed as a "retreat" to consider "options." These options were laid out in 37 mimeographed position papers, all of which were discussed. According to one historian of SNCC, the papers "revealed a pervasive concern about SNCC's loss of a common sense of purpose and its resulting failure to act decisively and effectively after the [1964] Summer." They also "suggested the general outlines of the subsequent development of American radicalism in the 1960s," providing "a seedbed for the resurgence of the moribund American traditions of Afro-American separatism, feminism, and participatory democracy."

It was, interestingly enough, the issue of feminism that had the greatest impact for Dennis during his days at Waveland. SNCC's women staff members were sufficiently apprehensive about retaliatory "insinuations, ridicule, [and] over-exaggerated compensations," that the authors of the paper on women's issues decided to remain formally anonymous. The paper argued that "assumptions of male superiority are as widespread and deep-rooted and every inch as crippling to women as the assumptions of white supremacy are to the Negro." SNCC should "force the rest of the movement to stop the discrimination and start the slow process of changing values and ideas so that this is no more a man's world than it is a white world." Many male SNCC staffers responded rudely to the paper and with arch insensitivity, but Dennis Sweeney was not among them. He sympathized completely. He had also become increasingly drawn toward Mary King, one of the paper's "anonymous" authors.

King, the daughter of a white minister in suburban Virginia, had been in the South with SNCC since the organization's beginnings in 1961. At the time of Waveland, she was SNCC's assistant press secretary, working out of national headquarters in Atlanta, Georgia. Dennis Sweeney's name had come to her attention several times, but they first met face to face during those five days in May 1965. She too was up in the air about what to do next, and they spent a lot of time at the conference together. Mary appreciated Dennis's sensitivity and he appreciated her strength. By the time the Waveland retreat concluded, they were "involved."

Afterwards, Dennis stayed in touch with her by phone, and eventually Mary agreed to come and join him in Natchez once things had gotten under way there.

A round the same time, Lowenstein returned again to Stanford to give a speech and solidify commitments to that summer's Encampment for Citizenship.

By then, his notion of me as a potential "leader" among my peers was coming true, although on a small scale. I was one of 15 sophomores named to honors in Social Thought and Institutions, the same interdisciplinary social sciences program Dennis Sweeney had been enrolled in before he left school. I was also one of two members of my class named a Wilbur Sponsor, again treading in Dennis's footsteps. Both were highly prized achievements.

Allard said he was proud of me. He was also pleased when I told him that I had secured my parents' permission to attend the coming Encampment. His visit this time lasted three nights and two days, and again I drove him around in his borrowed Mustang to Sacramento, Berkeley, San Francisco, and back to Palo Alto.

Around 10 P.M. on Saturday, Lowenstein's last night in town, he had me stop at a phone booth, conducted a fifteen minute conversation with someone, and then returned to the car. Instead of returning to Stanford for the night, he said, he had to get to Big Sur Hot Springs, two hours further south, where he was to meet up with "a number" of student "leaders" from Berkeley. Getting together with them was crucial.

The change in plans put me in a quandary. I had a Sunday morning job waiting on tables.

Allard said I could get someone to cover for me.

I was hesitant because I'd had people covering for me at work ever since he'd come to town. On top of that I was getting tired of driving. But unable to say all that, I just got flustered and said I didn't know whether I could or not.

"Sure you can," Allard insisted. This was very important. He had to see these people, and all of his work at Berkeley was coming to a head. "Call someone," he said, handing me a dime.

When we reached Big Sur Hot Springs well after midnight, Allard checked into the office and then returned to the car. The Berkeley people had not shown up, he said. He'd called them on the phone inside and they weren't coming. There was nothing to do about it now, he said, so he went back into the office to get us a place to stay. He returned, this time saying there was only one vacant room and he had gone ahead and rented it. The room only had one bed, he explained, but it was the best we could do.

I was uneasy with the arrangement, but I thought I would demean myself by complaining about something Allard treated as no more than one of the rigors inherent in trying to change the country for the better.

In the tiny room, we stripped down to our underwear and got in our respective sides of the double bed. I faced away from Allard and kept to the edge of the mattress. After five minutes, Lowenstein left his side and, without a word, began hugging me from behind.

I was 19, it was 1965, and men who hugged other men in bed were only a rumor in my circles. The move terrorized me, but I had little idea of what to say or do. Allard kept hugging me for several minutes, pressing his chest against my back, and then finally asked if what he was doing made me uncomfortable.

I said yes.

He immediately pulled back, said nothing more, and was asleep in minutes.

Sixteen years later, I am still unsure as to what Allard had in mind or what, if anything, he would have done if I had been comfortable with his approach. I eventually talked to a number of other people, Dennis Sweeney included, whom Allard had maneuvered into similar "one room, one bed" circumstances and then suddenly begun to hug. None of them were sure how to define the hugging either. Some unequivocally described it as a form of "homosexual" contact. Several, however, said they had responded to Allard by saying that "homosexuality" wasn't their preference and that Allard had in turn challenged this interpretation, saying homosexuality was "anal or oral intercourse" and that was not what his attentions were about. He left these men with the sense that his impulse wasn't so much genital as a desire to hold and be held. The distinctions between that and something more, though apparently carefully drawn in Allard's own head, were, however, largely nonexistent in the thinking of the young men subjected to the experience.

For myself, I cowered as far from Allard as I could and didn't sleep at all. My perception of Lowenstein was in tumult.

On the one hand, I felt totally used and my hero worship had ended on the spot. I thought I had been manipulated into the situation under false premises, and to this day I have doubts as to whether anyone from Berkeley was ever supposed to meet us in Big Sur. Looking back on it now and wanting to give Allard whatever benefits hindsight provides, I suppose in some vaguely preconscious way these late-night encounters were his own confused, if habitual, device for making a kind of human contact he needed and had no other way of making. I don't resent the need, but it is nonetheless still hard not to hold the manipulation in his pursuit of it against him.

On the other hand, his maneuver did not lead to any immediate breaking off of our relationship. His hugging possessed a childlike desperation that I had never seen in him before. It was one of the few, if any, moments between mentor and protégé, according to all those I have discussed it with, when Allard fronted his own needs, undeflected by the excuse of politics. There was a torment in it that showed not so much in what he said, as in the fact that Allard, the most verbal of men, said nothing at all. Ironically, the torment created enormous sympathy in the beholder. As I lay awake trying to figure out what had happened, my only clear, unconfused response was that I did not want to hurt him.

When morning came, Lowenstein made no mention of the night before. We drove north, and after several hours I delivered him to the San Francisco Airport. He said he would see me in June at the Encampment and then mentioned the 40 copies of *Brutal Mandate* he had put in the trunk of the car. He said I should sell them for him.

In June, Dennis Sweeney, Ed Pincus, the filmmaker, and David Newman, his partner, J.D., and J.D.'s girlfriend all set up shop in Natchez. Several SNCC staff members and a half dozen summer volunteers opened a freedom house there as well. Sweeney and the film people rented a separate house of their own.

Dennis seemed to have lost much of his previous passion for the film enterprise, and he spent most of his time before Mary arrived in SNCC discussions, groping for a role. When Pincus and his partner finally edited the summer's footage into a highly respected documentary called *Black Natchez*, Dennis Sweeney would be given a subsidiary credit as a "field assistant." His contributions were more episodic than continuous. On one occasion, he complained to Pincus that there was as yet no freedom-school footage. Pincus found the complaint irritating and pointed out to Dennis that there was no local freedom school for them to film. In a brief flurry of organizing, Sweeney put one together, and among the *Black Natchez* outtakes are scenes of him teaching a group of six or seven black adolescents about the war in Vietnam.

Dennis's teaching technique was to ask the question, "Why are we in Vietnam?" and then work with the answers, trying to connect the war to the kids' innate knowledge of their immediate Amite County circumstances. It was a hard connection for 13-year-olds to make, but they struggled with the notion under Dennis's tutelage. Finally one just said that it didn't matter anyway. He had just one voice and it would be ignored whatever he thought.

Dennis responded by saying all those single voices could be put together into one big voice that couldn't be ignored. "Finding a voice" soon became a theme in Dennis's attempts to articulate his own political location as well.

Fifteen years later, when the cacophony of voices in his own head had driven him to assassination, the theme seemed ironic.

The war was also on the curriculum at Lowenstein's Encampment for Citizenship at Fieldston School in New York City. There, the discussion, at least as advanced by the speakers arranged by Allard, centered around the disagreement that had been raging among liberal Democrats ever since Lyndon Johnson had commenced bombing North Vietnam. Both those who supported the war policy and those in opposition cited "the national interest" as the basis of their reasoning, and the debate amounted to slinging the phrase back and forth between them. Although he gave no speeches of his own, Allard obviously sided with the critics.

To liberal opponents, the war jeopardized both the nation's international standing and its domestic priorities. "Search and destroy," the nation's ground strategy in South Vietnam, was little more than a running body count, they argued, and was having next to no success against the guerilla opposition. The costs of waging the conflict were already cutting into the liberals' desire to erect a second domestic New Deal; the fact that the poor and minorities were bearing a disproportionate share of the casualties contradicted their attempts to destratify society as well. Although no doubt possessed of a number of private trepidations about the morality of the effort, they were careful to phrase their arguments against Vietnam policy in terms of politics rather than morality, emphasizing that opposition within the United States had to be "effective"; "effective" generally meant concerned with persuading Congress to cut off Johnson's war appropriations.

An even larger group of liberals considered it a given that the President had to be accorded bipartisan backing at time of war. Opposition to Johnson on international policy, they thought, might very well jeopardize all the gains of the civil rights movement and cut off left Democrats as a whole from the centers of influence. The procession of generals ruling with increasing corruption in Saigon was something of an embarrassment, but the President's liberal supporters made noises of belief when the Defense Department talked about "the light at the end of the tunnel." The Americans, these liberals argued, would humanize the military regime, and, in any case, defying the President would only nourish political elements of which they were intensely suspicious. In expressing that suspicion, the liberals who supported the war pointed past the other liberal camp to a third more "radical" position.

Although this third position was not part of the Encampment's program, it was represented on most of the nation's campuses, simplistically called "the New Left" in the national press. One of its first expressions had been the march in Washington that Dennis had attended in April. The members of the New Left, almost exclusively young, sought to galvanize a moral outrage that would give Johnson no choice but withdrawal of troops from Vietnam. The war was a crime against everything the nation was supposed to be. Inspired by SNCC, but largely an unorganized network of activists, the "radicals" didn't mind offending those to their right and thought demonstrations were far more important than currying favor with Congress through the Democratic party.

I was already flirting with this third camp. At the Encampment's discussion of Vietnam, I maintained that the most important question was whether the war was wrong. If it was, it had to be denounced, pure and simple. The national interest, I argued, always ought to be the truth. I had little sympathy for the supposed necessity of couching my arguments in "acceptable" terms. Vietnam was the war my generation had to fight, and, from the beginning, being used that way felt like a personal affront.

Not long after the day we spent discussing the war, the Encampment witnessed one of the last acts in Lowenstein's Mississippi drama. In response to a personal request from Allard, Bob Moses came to speak. We all sat out on the lawn and Lowenstein handled the introductions. It was obvious there had once been something close between the two men that had since turned painful for both of them. Allard said he was proud to introduce Bob Moses or Parris or "whatever he was calling himself now" and pretty much butchered his introduction, praising the SNCC hero so heavily that it was clear he was masking his own ambivalence.

Moses was even quieter than he had been the one time I'd seen him before. Mostly he answered questions. He listened intently, and he never spoke without sorting through his thoughts for several moments. His words carried an air of integrity and self-control, as though much rested on being as honest as possible. The tone and mannerisms were all traits I would eventually see reflected in Dennis Sweeney.

I remember only a few of the themes Moses hit upon that day. It was not just who wielded power that mattered, he said, but the shape of the power they exercised. Domination remained substantially the same, no matter who exercised it. There was a need for people to construct a new society from the ground up. The changes incumbent on us were impossible through the old notions of liberal democracy.

Bob Moses sat on the grass talking like that for two hours and then left. Allard held his tongue throughout.

Mary King joined Dennis Sweeney in Natchez around the same time, and for the rest of the summer their relationship dominated his life. They talked a lot, either alone in their room in the communal house or on long walks in the surrounding countryside. It was Dennis who eventually raised the question of marriage. Typical of him, he deflected his emotions into the realm of abstractions. Marriage was an "issue" approached as a quasi-theological expression of their "commitment" to mutual work and its shared pursuit. Mary at first responded that living together was sufficient, but Dennis insisted on formalizing their attachment. In retrospect, it seems he needed something to invest himself in now that SNCC was dispersing. For Mary, equally confused by the movement's accelerating collapse, getting married was the line of least resistance. Before accepting Dennis's idea, she insisted that she would keep her own name, and Dennis agreed. Having lost his own real father's name, he was automatically sympathetic.

Dennis also hung out with J.D. and the Natchez Project's staffers and summer volunteers. They all talked about how the movement's momentum seemed to have disappeared and why they weren't working much anymore. At one of those discussions, a SNCC staffer, himself a three-year Mississippi veteran, had a simple explanation.

"My truck broke down," he said, meaning the pickup that was his only means of transportation.

Dennis seized on the statement as a metaphor for the situation. "Our truck broke down," he explained. "Don't you see, all of our trucks broke down." It became his symbol for the summer.

"How ya doin'?" someone would ask him.

"My truck broke down," Dennis would answer.

The image of an old Ford in the weeds off to the side of a country road, its hood raised and one wheel up on blocks, would cling to Dennis Sweeney for much of the coming year.

Though not apparent to Sweeney yet, the first signs of his next vehicle began to emerge that same summer. Fittingly, they came out of McComb.

When five black Pike County servicemen were killed in Vietnam during a single week in July, a group of the dead soldiers' friends distributed a leaflet.

"No Mississippi Negroes," it read,

> should be fighting in Vietnam for the White Man's freedom
> until all the Negro People are free in Mississippi. Negro boys
> should not honor the draft here in Mississippi. Mothers
> should encourage their sons not to go. We will gain respect
> and dignity as a race only by forcing the United States
> Government and the Mississippi Government to come with
> guns, dogs and trucks to take our sons away to fight and be
> killed protecting Mississippi, Alabama, Georgia, and
> Louisiana. No one has a right to ask us to risk our lives and
> kill other Colored People . . . so that the White American can
> get richer. We will be looked upon as traitors by all the
> Colored People of the world if the Negro people continue to
> fight and die without a cause.

The leaflet was reprinted in the Mississippi Freedom Democratic party's statewide newsletter and was immediately denounced by two Northern black congressmen, Aaron Henry, and the Mississippi NAACP.

Dennis Sweeney endorsed the leaflet's sentiment, though he was not yet ready to commit himself to its tactic. When he did move in that direction, he and I would meet.

As near as I can tell, Dennis Sweeney and Allard Lowenstein had their last face-to-face encounter for almost ten years late in July. It was on the final weekend before the Encampment ended. Lowenstein, I, and a carload of other students drove down to

Washington, D.C., for a gathering called the Congress of Unrepre-
sented Peoples, a "radical" event that Allard and the rest of us went to
observe. The idea behind the congress was to join the emerging set of
New Left concerns into a single unified agenda. The day before had
featured a march to the White House protesting the war. The day we
were there, the assemblage was divided into workshops around the
slope at the foot of Washington Monument. I and several others drifted
off one way and Allard and several more another.

When I later saw one of the young men who had left with
Lowenstein, he told me that Allard had run into Dennis Sweeney. He
mentioned it because he knew Dennis and I were both from Stanford.

"Where'd that happen?" I asked. The image of Allard and Dennis
talking to each other surprised me.

"Right at the foot of the monument," he answered. "Sweeney was
standing there with a woman named Mary something."

"What'd they say?"

"Hello."

"What else?"

"That's it," he reported. "Just hello."

M y own relationship with Lowenstein began dropping off
not long thereafter. In the wake of the Encampment I hung
around New York, staying with friends and getting by as I could. The
first week I saw Allard regularly, and my attitude irritated him. Most of
the other Encampment protégés had made plans to spend the rest of
their summer "constructively," and Allard ragged on me to do
something "useful" instead of just hanging around doing nothing. He
was going to be leaving for a trip through the South, he said, and if I
wanted his help finding work, I had better ask for it soon. One
evening, he finally cajoled me into driving him around.

The last stop on our agenda was a coffee klatch for West
Manhattan Congressman William Fitz Ryan, then a candidate for
mayor. Ryan was an outside bet at best in the election, and around the
Encampment Allard's support for him was always explained as a
function of the fact that Allard wanted to run for the House seat Ryan
would vacate. After the coffee klatch, Allard and I returned with
sandwiches to his apartment. There I asked him about the Congress
rumor, and he confessed to ambivalence over running. He said he had
always pictured himself as someone who operated outside of established power, organizing influence. Still, he couldn't rule it out.
Running for office, he went on, was the kind of thing his father had

always wanted him to do, and now that his father was dead, Allard found his desire to live up to his expectations even stronger. If Allard did run for Congress, he said, the saddest part would be that his father would never get to see him do it.

The sadness of that subject soon drifted into another as Allard began talking about how unfair life was to ugly people. Despite an overwhelming number of examples of his own attractiveness, Lowenstein always considered himself one of the ugly. Next came the subject of how lonely life was for anyone who wanted something other than predictable stereotypes for himself. It was, he said, the immense price paid by all of us who cared about things. Allard confessed he often felt that pain. I confessed that I did as well.

We talked about such things until 3 A.M., when the question of getting some rest finally arose. Allard said I should sleep in his bed and he would sleep on the living room couch. After considering that arrangement for a moment, I said no, I'd take the couch.

Within several days, Lowenstein commenced his planned trip through the South, accompanied by the same Harvard protégé who had driven him toward Atlantic City the summer before. The trip seemed to provoke Lowenstein's memories, and he talked of Dennis Sweeney often. On several occasions, Allard mentioned that he wanted to write a book about his relationship with Dennis.

According to Lowenstein, Sweeney had been embittered by what had happened to the movement in Mississippi; he thought it had been turned into a political opportunity by national groups rather than remaining an effort totally to transform Mississippi society. Now Dennis pictured Mississippi as no more than a stark picture of the way America was everywhere. He had lost all faith in established institutions.

Allard said the story he wanted to tell was about the two different directions their lives had taken. He wanted to show what Mississippi had done to a "good" person who was "caring, concerned and talented," who had "leadership" qualities and was "respected" on the Stanford campus. Dennis, Allard claimed, had become "bitter," "angry," and "alienated." The book Lowenstein planned to write would tell how that effort to change had "transformed" and "warped" Dennis's life in ways that were "tragic." The battle "to keep Dennis involved," Allard said, "had been lost." For the first time, Lowenstein referred to Sweeney as a "victim."

When it surfaced years later, many of Sweeney's Mississippi contemporaries would dispute parts of Allard's 1965 characterization of Dennis vehemently. Perhaps its most obvious shortcoming was its apparent assumption that the story of Dennis Sweeney and Allard Lowenstein had already played itself out. If that was true, this book would never have been written and Allard might eventually have found time to write his own.

The three of us existed on separate planes for most of the next year.

Dennis Sweeney and Mary King were married in late September near her parents' home in Virginia on a grassy knoll under a huge oak tree. They wrote the ceremony themselves. There were no promises "to obey," but there was much talk of "mutual respect" and "common work." The words were recited while the couple sat in a circle with a half dozen of their friends. Among those friends was Bob Moses and his wife, Dona Richards. The example of Moses's and Richards's married relationship had been one of the factors that made Mary receptive to Dennis's proposal. Dona Richards had not been subsumed under her husband, and Mary King had no inclination to be either.

Not long after the wedding, Dona Richards, Bob Moses, Mary King, and Dennis Sweeney all attended a meeting at the Institute for Policy Studies in Washington, D.C. The subject was how to link the civil rights and peace movements, but no link came out of it. However stimulating the discussion, the participants seemed stuck in a pattern of dispersal rather than combination. Moses and Richards were soon to leave the United States for several years in East Africa, and Sweeney and King would lose touch with them.

Dennis's own thoughts about the future increasingly focused on returning to Stanford. By now he had an idealized memory of the university, remembering the prelude to the 1964 Summer Project, when Stanford's sense of social responsibility was increasing rapidly. Dennis told Mary that it would be a receptive climate for his kind of organizing and that "something" would "work out." In the absence of any clearer option, Mary King eventually agreed to the Stanford plan, and they moved to Palo Alto in November.

My protégéhood to Allard Lowenstein dwindled to something of an end not long after school resumed.

Early in October, Allard telephoned me. It was after midnight. He said he was coming through Stanford in two days. He was enormously excited about something new he was setting out to do, called ARFEP. He said he would explain it all when I picked him up at the airport.

I balked at the task. I felt as though I was coming into my own now and did not relish disrupting my life to serve as Allard's gofer. I didn't need the bolstering anymore. What I needed was room to maneuver on my own terms. I told him I had other things to do.

Allard's voice changed immediately. "Okay," he said. He sounded both hurt and distant but didn't try to talk me into it.

I didn't know it at the time, but my refusal pushed me across one of protégéhood's boundaries. Allard did not waste time on young men who did not "appreciate" the opportunity, and "appreciation" was always demonstrated in willingness to subordinate all else to Allard's pressing task of the moment. The work he had to do couldn't be done without people he could "count on." Turning Allard down when he asked for help automatically made the protégé "unreliable," and I now entered that category. Allard and I still professed friendship, but it wasn't the same, and henceforth I saw little of him—not as a result of any animosity, as in the case of Dennis Sweeney, but simply because we both thought we had better things to do.

During his stop at Stanford two days later, he visited my room at Wilbur Hall for 15 minutes with the young man driving him around. It would be almost ten months until I saw him again. He asked how many copies of *Brutal Mandate* I had sold, and when I told him none, he shook his head as though the information was unfortunately consistent with the rest of my behavior. He would obviously have to proceed on his mission without me.

I didn't press him on it or try to change his mind. I didn't even bother to ask him what ARFEP was.

The acronym stood for Americans for Reappraisal of Far Eastern Policy, Lowenstein's first public thrust into Vietnam policy. To split the support of the Senate away from the President, Allard maintained that the issue had to be refocused to give the Senators room to maneuver. He proposed to do so by raising the question of Asian policy in its entirety and "reopening the China Question." In light of a large national necessity to reformulate our Far East relations, Vietnam would be seen as an obstruction, thereby establishing a patriotic framework for opposition and further undercutting Lyndon Johnson's support.

ARFEP was never very influential, but it stands out in retrospect as a classic example of Lowenstein's technique. First, a front group was created, composed of as many "responsible" names and titles as Allard could muster; his student network was then plugged in, supplying the evidence of a "broad base" among the nation's young as well. All of it generated publicity that allowed Allard to wield the impression of power as leverage on those political outposts he was aiming to influence.

Aside from Allard himself, ARFEP's operational structure amounted to a number of "campus representatives." Had the strategy commenced six months earlier, I might have been Stanford's ARFEP rep. "The job," the man who had held that position at Yale later told me, "was basically to answer the phone, and when a reporter called, to tell him that there was indeed a thriving ARFEP chapter at Yale. Allard did the rest."

On October 22, the *New York Times* carried an announcement of ARFEP's founding toward the end of a three-column story summing up the status of dissent against the war.

The story led with the news that three Protestant religious leaders expressed "strong sympathy" with "student demonstrations against United States policy in Vietnam" and had called for "an end" to the bombing of North Vietnam. Next, the article noted that students at the University of Chicago had voted 2846 to 981 against censuring the government for its war policy. At Yale, 500 had signed a petition saying, "A position of protest justifies no one in an attempt . . . to undermine morale abroad and to encourage our generation to repudiate its military duties." The Selective Service claimed that there had been "no significant increase in the number of youths attempting to evade the draft," but an Army spokesman nonetheless said it would put new emphasis on "indoctrination" of recruits.

Then came Allard. The *Times* continued:

> Meanwhile, a new national organization to urge a
> reevaluation of American policy in the Far East was
> announced yesterday. The group, Americans for Reappraisal
> of Far Eastern Policy, will open its campaign by sponsoring
> meetings Sunday on at least 30 campuses. "The question of
> Vietnam can only be solved in the context of China and the
> entire Far East," Allard K. Lowenstein, a New York lawyer
> who is a member of the group's national committee, said
> yesterday He was a foreign policy aide to Vice President
> Humphrey when Mr. Humphrey was a Senator. "We want to
> encourage a wider debate on the deadest limb of the tree of
> our foreign policy, which is our China policy," Mr.

Lowenstein said. "It is wrong to let groups only concerned with Vietnam monopolize the discussion."

The *Times* coverage ended with a paragraph explaining that the group was "basically educational and disavowed civil disobedience and draft dodging as effective ways of discussing foreign policy."

Even had I been offered the opportunity to join ARFEP, I doubt if I would have taken it. My mind and Allard's seemed to be headed in opposite directions. He, 36, was busy compounding complex strategies, rearranging language, looking for the precise formula to unlock the war policy's hold on the government. I, within months of turning 20, was distilling simple truths to construct my life around and was in no mood for such technical intricacies. Simply put, I identified with the "draft dodgers."

I participated in my first antiwar march that fall. It was still very much a "radical" thing to do. The identification made me skittish at first, but I went anyway. The announced theme of the procession was "Get Out of Vietnam": no formula, no legislative maneuvers, just a demand. In all, some six or seven thousand people walked five miles between Berkeley and a park in Oakland. The Stanford contingent numbered a little more than a hundred. I drove up with Jeffrey, my best friend of the time and a fellow Wilbur sponsor, in his Volkswagen van. Jeffrey was already classified as a conscientious objector, 1-O, by the Selective Service. I was classified 2-S, the standard student deferment. Around us, people carried signs quoting Thomas Jefferson. Plainclothes police were photographing the crowd.

At the park, there were several hours of speeches. The only one I remember concerned the 1954 Geneva Accords. The United States, the speaker said, had walked all over the international agreements assuring the decolonization, independence, and unification of Vietnam. The Administration's pretense of "legality" was a "sham." We were fighting in violation of both our own principles and system of law.

More reasons why the war was wrong floated by, but my head was full. I imagined myself up on the stage behind the microphone, rousing the crowd, but I didn't know quite what I would say.

As yet, I had no words for what I felt.

That condition was changing rapidly. It was breakout time and I wasn't alone. Late at night, the circle I ran with usually showed up at Jeffrey's room to smoke dope and listen to Bob Dylan, the Beatles, Joan Baez, and the Rolling Stones on his stereo. We all wrote poetry and read Nietzsche, Camus, Gandhi, and Hemingway. Our exuberance bordered on possession. We treated all our thoughts as discoveries of immense magnitude. Late at night at Jeffrey's, we all felt we had the bull by the horns.

Distancing myself from it now, I can see that, at least implicitly, we all subscribed in varying degrees to a world view: people, we agreed, were no more and no less than what they acted out. Explanations were bullshit. What mattered was what you did. Means and ends were the same thing. You either embodied your values fully in the present, or you didn't have any. Hypocrisy, we agreed, was pernicious and everywhere, disguised as the ethic of deferred gratification and the politics of compromise.

Whenever we wanted an example to prove the point, we had to look no further than the war, steadily grinding up Southeast Asia, using the best of words to describe the worst of realities. Such was the stuff from which national policy was being made in the winter of 1965.

When Dennis Sweeney and Mary King reached Stanford late in November, they rented an apartment on the second floor of a small three-unit stucco building in East Palo Alto, a black suburban enclave between the freeway and the bay. Mary found a job with the local War on Poverty office. Dennis, now 23, reenrolled at the university and reclaimed the scholarship he had left the year before. He also got part-time work driving a truck for the Stanford libraries. An old friend who saw Dennis then described him as "totally exhausted" and "lost." The connection Sweeney had expected to be waiting for him was not there, despite his being a hero to campus activists. Politics was at a momentary low ebb as the fledgling antiwar movement struggled to get on its feet, and Sweeney took little part in campus activities.

He and Mary moved in a very small circle of friends and tried hard to adjust to being out of the South. Their closest friends were another married couple involved in "radical" campus politics. Sometimes the four of them sat around at Dennis and Mary's drinking cheap wine and talking. Whenever Lowenstein's name came up, Sweeney dismissed him with a bittersweet laugh. Lowenstein didn't want real change, he said. He, like the rest of the liberals, just wanted power.

Allard's name did not, however, come up a lot. Dennis now considered him irrelevant. The topics he and his friends most often talked about were how wrong the war was and how hard it was to leave Mississippi. Deflecting his own pain with a flickering smile and a few boyishly solemn words, Sweeney was also open about feeling at loose ends. He was looking for another mission, but it had not yet appeared. "Struggle" was a word he used frequently in personal terms, and "the movement" were the words he most often used when discussing politics. His difficulties often depressed him, and eventually he had several appointments with a psychiatrist.

There was nothing openly sick or disturbed about Dennis Sweeney at that point. He was simply a sensitive and very political young man in the throes of a deep life change, a condition he shared to varying degrees with everyone who had been South even for much briefer and less intense spans than he.

During one of their meetings, the psychiatrist asked Dennis to name some of the things he "hated." Dennis could come up with only one. "People who abuse their authority," he said.

S hortly after 1966 began, I walked my first picket line against the war. The picketing was preceded by a campuswide rally at which Stokley Carmichael, the new national chairman of SNCC, spoke. He had arrived in Palo Alto the previous evening and spent the night at the apartment of his old friends, Dennis Sweeney and Mary King. Through the SNCC leader, Dennis and Mary caught up on all the latest news out of Mississippi. "Black power" had become a dominant theme in SNCC with the advent of Carmichael's chairmanship, but that didn't prevent them all from enjoying each other's company.

At the rally, Carmichael denounced the war. There was, he said, a direct connection between lynching black sharecroppers in Alabama and blowing yellow peasants to shreds in the Mekong Delta. The position was one that had first been pushed in SNCC by a group that included Dennis and Mary. Afterward, about 50 of us traveled 40 miles south to the town of Coyote, where a plant manufacturing napalm for the war effort was located. Dennis did not come along.

Jeffrey and I did. Napalm was manufactured by combining huge quantities of jellied gasoline with lesser quantities of plastic. Delivered in canisters from a swooping airplane, the gasoline burst into an immense wave of flame and the plastic ensured that the flame stuck to what or whomever it splattered upon, leaving both civilian and military survivors with parts of their bodies melted into each other. The local plant manufacturing it was an adjunct of a rocket-engine research facility isolated in the middle of the countryside. From the front gate, all that was visible was a dirt road mounting a hill and dropping over the other side. County sheriffs and private security police prevented our little demonstration from going any farther. We broke into two lines, walking back and forth on either side of the road. By now, rain was falling in sheets.

When the plant's shift changed, a succession of pickup trucks and cars began passing between our lines. Several swerved to the side, scattering pickets, and roared off.

For a while, I carried someone's sign. It read, "HOW CAN YOU DO THIS?"

A t about the same time, Allard confirmed rumors that he was seeking the joint Manhattan Reform Democratic Club's nomination to challenge Nineteenth Congressional District incumbent Leonard Farbstein in the June 21 Democratic primary for the 1966 congressional election. So were three others: a radio station president, a city councilman, and a former New York County Democratic party official. Lowenstein was identified by the *New York Times* as a "lawyer and college teacher," and the Nineteenth was the first of five New York congressional districts in which he would eventually run. The incumbent Farbstein had been in office for five terms, sat on the House Foreign Affairs Committee, and had survived Reform Democrat attempts to unseat him in both 1962 and 1964.

Lowenstein said he was "certain" that the Vietnam War would be the "principal issue." All of the four potential liberal challengers criticized Farbstein heavily for showing a "lack of leadership" and "failing to encourage discussion and debate on the conflict." But since all of them also agreed that the bombing of North Vietnam should be halted, a cease-fire called, and an international conference convened to settle hostilities, their Vietnam exchanges centered on fine print and verbal vehemence more than policy. The group debated in front of nine different Reform gatherings and on one live local television show before the campaign was over. At each stop, the crowds wanted to hear about the war, whether the four men agreed with one another or not, and all the latest developments were analyzed over and over again. The most significant of those was that Robert F. Kennedy, now the Senator from New York, had tentatively called for offering the Viet Cong "a share of power" in Vietnam. According to the *Times*, "Mr. Lowenstein said he was grateful to Mr. Kennedy for helping make clear that any interim regime, pending Vietnam elections, could not simply be the current regime of Premier Nguyen Cao Ky. Mr. Lowenstein suggested . . . a coalition including the Viet Cong or some sort of international trusteeship."

The candidates' disagreements focused on who had the best Reform Democratic credentials. Allard emphasized his "commitment to the liberal principles which have motivated the Reform movement." He also pledged himself to fight for the "dispossessed," not only in the Nineteenth District but "all over the world."

The *New York Times* judged the race "one of the best political shows in town" but made no endorsement.

Besides participating in those joint appearances and debates, Allard's principal campaign events were a series of coffee klatches and receptions. At those his friends noticed hints of an approaching change in Allard's life. Several young women acted as hostesses at the events, and one of them, Jennifer Lyman, 22, had clearly become very close to him. He pointed her out to a friend and assumed what his friend remembered as "a beatific expression."

"Isn't she extraordinary!" he exclaimed.

Later, the two men talked more about the relationship. Allard said he was thinking of marrying her. He had no doubts about whether he loved "Jenny" but said he had trepidations about whether any woman could adjust to his kind of life. His experience with his one previous broken engagement had made him pessimistic. But, he said, letting some time pass with Jenny would answer that question.

On March 10, the debates over, the Reform Democrats conducted a joint balloting by the Nineteenth District's 11 Reform Clubs. The lowest finisher was dropped after each vote tally, and his votes were redistributed on the basis of indicated alternate choices. In the first count, the radio station president received 681, the city councilman 598, Allard 575, and the New York County Democratic Committee official 191. In the second count, the radio station president polled 736, the City Councilman 650, and Allard 637. The final count threw the election to the City Councilman 1008 to 966. Like all the other defeated candidates, Lowenstein pledged a solid Reform Democratic Front for the Farbstein primary.

Not long after his 1966 campaign in the Nineteenth was over, Allard was contacted by Robert Kennedy, a connection which would inspire and haunt him much of the remainder of his life. Kennedy had accepted an invitation to visit South Africa to address the student body at the all-white University of Capetown and wanted to make an important statement. As he explained it to Allard, he had been told by a lot of people that Lowenstein was the man to talk to about what to say.

Allard had looked upon Bobby Kennedy with a certain amount of suspicion until then, but, as one lifelong friend of Allard's would tell me much later, "Nothing could change Allard's impression of someone quicker than if that someone demonstrated an appreciation of Allard himself." It was, by both Lowenstein's own and a number of other standards, a positive sign that Kennedy would look to him for guidance on South Africa; Allard told several friends in New York that spring that Kennedy had mellowed and matured.

Their relationship began with Allard's reviewing the tentative draft of Bobby's address. Lowenstein criticized it as too tame. In the words of one Kennedy intimate, he advised going "full tilt." There was much unarticulated antiapartheid sentiment among the white students who would be Kennedy's audience, and Allard argued that Bobby had to appeal to that sentiment, and position himself as the spokesman of the idealism it embodied. Eventually, Lowenstein wrote additions to the draft before it was polished by Bobby's principal speech writer. When eventually delivered by Kennedy, certain passages still echoed Allard's authorship.

Kennedy warned the standing-room-only crowd in Capetown against submitting to

> the belief there is nothing one man or one woman can do against the enormous array of the world's ills. . . . Many of the world's great movements . . . have flowed from the work of a single man. . . . Each of us can work to change a small portion of events, and in the total of all those acts will be written the history of this generation. . . . Each time a man stands up for an ideal, or acts to improve the lot of others, or strikes out against injustice, he sends forth a tiny ripple of hope, and crossing each other from a million different centers of energy and daring, those ripples build a current which can sweep down the mightiest walls of oppression and resistance.

The ovation that followed was enormous.

The sentiments Kennedy enunciated in Capetown drew applause in a number of domestic circles as well. Each of those circles, however, had differing notions of just what phrases like "acts of courage and belief," "standing up for an ideal," "striking out against injustice," and "sweeping down the mightiest walls of oppression" meant in actual practice. Among the young, the compass of such phrases tended to be all-inclusive, reflecting not just a thirst for a new national agenda but for a new culture to feed it as well.

Changes in personal appearances were the most obvious facet of that thirst. Under its influence, I let my hair grow toward my collar, groomed a moustache, and began wearing rimless glasses. Looking that way was a "radical" thing to do at Stanford, but it paled in comparison with the colony of young people who had begun congregating in the Haight-Ashbury district of San Francisco. Eventually dubbed "hippies," some had hair down to their waists, lived communally, and smoked dope on the streets. Their gatherings in Golden Gate Park were called "be-ins," and the title captured the overriding logic of Haight-Ashbury succinctly. Change, it postulated, came through being changed yourself. In differentness was revolt.

The press would later call this way of life the counterculture, but it was, in fact, more the lead edge of an urge to get out from under than a culture; as such, Haight-Ashbury marked one end of a continuum that stretched deep into a generation. Being "human" or "real" was rapidly becoming synonymous with being conspicuously at odds with the norm.

Despite his in many ways deserved reputation as the decade's foremost and, at times, seemingly only bridge between youth and the hierarchy of their elders, Allard Lowenstein neither identified with that urge nor participated in any activity expressive of it. Throughout his life, his hair remained short. The only drugs he ever used were aspirins. He never willingly listened to rock 'n roll. He is never known to have worn a pair of Levis, faded, patched, or otherwise, and had no use for expressions like "blow your mind" or "far out." He absolutely never said "fuck" in public.

David Harris, on the other hand, had enough of the hippie in him at least to identify with Haight-Ashbury from 30 miles to the south, in the academic suburbs.

So did Dennis Sweeney.

Early in 1966 Dennis and Mary moved out of their apartment in East Palo Alto and into a two-story house on Channing Street in Palo Alto, which they shared with a couple who were close friends. The other husband was one of the organizers of a campus "We Won't Go" petition, pledging its signers to refusal to serve in Vietnam if drafted. Dennis Sweeney signed it and so did I, but it was something of an abstract threat, especially for Dennis. He was classified 4-C, or some such number that translated as "only surviving son of a deceased veteran, killed in the line of duty," which completely exempted him from induction.

That March, David Newman, Ed Pincus's partner in the previous summer's film effort, visited Sweeney. Newman had brought along some footage to screen in an effort to raise enough money to complete the cutting. Little new funding was collected, but Newman wasn't especially put out by the failure. He had never been to California before and was excited just to be out West. He had heard about Haight-Ashbury while in Cambridge, and Dennis talked about the place a lot. It appeared to Newman that what was going on there acted as a salve for Dennis's painful transition and relieved some of his internal pressure. Sweeney raved that Newman had to see the Fillmore Auditorium, the Haight's cultural heart, and one evening he finally took him there.

The band was on a stage at one end of a cavernous room, almost obscured by a spotlight connected to an opaque projector. The projector was fitted with a glass dish into which the operator added colored oils and water, creating an endless mingling of giant amoeba on the wall. There were no overhead lights, but stroboscopic spots were mounted in two corners. Around the edge some of the room's scruffiest creatures were approaching the less hip with offers of "hash, grass, acid," "Panama red," or "good shit, real cheap." The smell of marijuana was everywhere, as was that of patchoulie oil.

All in all, the Fillmore Auditorium was an environment stripped of stable reference points, so full of stimuli that it was devoid of any focus except the participants' own nerve endings. Time was distorted, space either pitch-black or primary-colored. The favorite local bands were the Jefferson Airplane and the Grateful Dead; they kept their speakers turned up loud enough to vibrate the floorboards. Otherwise shy, Dennis had no qualms about getting out with the dancers. He did his McComb rooster strut, took a joint passed to him by someone he had never seen before, and boogied until his shirt stuck to his back.

It was easy for David Newman to see the Haight as a place

"movement burnouts could get into." Sweeney was, to all appearances, less political and more frantically personal than he had been when they'd last seen each other in Natchez. On the drive back to Palo Alto, Dennis told Newman that he had "taken acid" and it had "totally changed" his perceptions. Even so, Newman still recognized the same naive idealism he'd noted the first time he and Sweeney had met, only now it was tied to words like "love," "community," "consciousness," and a lot of other words that at that time went down in streetwise Cambridge as "Sunday-school shit."

Despite his identification with hippies, Sweeney never did look like one. His hair was now long enough to touch his ears, but it was still neatly trimmed. His clothes were always clean, and he still thought of himself as an organizer between gigs, looking for "work."

Allard Lowenstein's life never seemed to have that kind of slack in it. While Sweeney was experimenting at the Fillmore, Allard was hip-deep in another foreign-policy effort. This one was called the Committee on Free Elections in the Dominican Republic.

Although Lowenstein had been independently connected to Dominican politics since the late 1950s through several anti-Trujillo exile efforts based in New York, his involvement in the 1966 Committee for Free Elections was at least formally an offshoot of his relationship with his hero, Norman Thomas. Thomas had for a number of years headed an organization known as the Institute of International Labor Research (IILR). The IILR had been involved in Dominican Republic politics since 1959, when, as part of an effort to create "Social Democratic options," it had begun channeling funds from the American J. M. Kaplan Fund—the private foundation of an American sugar millionaire—to the organization of Juan Bosch, the leading opponent to Dominican dictator Rafael Trujillo. He was then in Costa Rican exile. Like Thomas, Bosch's Partido Revolucionario Dominicano belonged to the Socialist International, and the two men were friends.

In 1962, when the generals who inherited the Dominican government after Trujillo's assassination yielded to pressure from the Kennedy Administration to hold free elections, Bosch returned to the island, and the IILR's secretary-treasurer, a naturalized American born in Romania, accompanied him as his chief political strategist. Bosch carried 60 percent of the vote and was the president of the Republic for the next nine months. For eight of them, the IILR continued to support him with J. M. Kaplan Fund grants. Then, in August 1963, the Kaplan Fund charged that Bosch's government was "infiltrated with Communists" and withdrew all funding. In September, a military junta seized power and Bosch fled to Puerto Rico. Throughout his exile there, Bosch and Thomas remained on close personal terms.

The base for Lowenstein's 1966 involvement began being laid in the spring of 1965, when the exiled opposition invaded their homeland in an attempt to reinstate the 1962 constitution by force. After three days of fighting, it appeared the opposition was on the verge of a complete military victory, but when Bosch sought to personally join them for the final push, he was prevented from leaving Puerto Rico by the American government. The next day, United States Marines landed, reinforced the military junta's troops, and occupied the Dominican Republic. "Our goal," Lyndon Johnson explained, "in keeping with the great principles of the inter-American system, is to help prevent another Communist state in this hemisphere." The State Department also reassured the New York Times that "free elections" would be held within "six to nine months."

These promised "free elections" were essential to Johnson's "democratic" rationale for the invasion, but from the beginning, the promise looked impossible to fulfill. No election without Bosch would have any credibility, and now Bosch refused to participate, saying it was impossible to hold a free election in a country still occupied by foreign troops who had been dispatched there specifically to keep one of the contending parties from coming to power. It fell to Allard's hero, Norman Thomas, to convince Bosch otherwise.

Thomas argued to his friend that only through elections and the subsequent establishment of a "stable government" would the occupying Marines be withdrawn. In September 1965 Bosch finally agreed to participate, and elections were scheduled for June 1966. Thomas promised Bosch that he and other leading American Social Democrats would organize an effort to ensure a fair election, eventually called the Committee on Free Elections in the Dominican Republic. The Committee would send a team of "independent unofficial observers" to watch the elections and lessen potential fraud and coercion. That team of "independent unofficial observers" used to convince Bosch was where Allard Lowenstein came in. Recruiting them was his principal responsibility, and once involved, Allard, as always, became a dominant influence.

In March 1966, Lowenstein contacted a former Stanford protégé who was familiar with Latin America and asked him to go immediately to Santo Domingo, the Dominican capital, set up a preliminary local headquarters, and prepare things for a late April visit by Allard and other committee members to kick off the oversight campaign. Allard gave him the names of three people to contact there. One was the IILR's secretary-treasurer, who had been such a key force in Bosch's 1962 victory and was now an unofficial member of the Committee on Free Elections. Once in Santo Domingo, however, the former protégé found that the IILR man had left after reaching a private agreement with the State Department to stay off the island during the election.

When Allard's committee of American liberals arrived, several members noted an "atmosphere of fear." They found Bosch resigned to losing. Afraid of assassination, he ended up spending the entire campaign in a heavily guarded house on the outskirts of the capital.

Allard and the committee toured for three days and then returned to the United States. In June, led by Allard and Norman Thomas, they would be back in Santo Domingo for their second and final visit.

In the meantime, Allard recruited Americans as poll watchers. Acting as observers was, he argued, a way to get direct citizen intervention against the American invasion without simply resorting to protest. They could actually make good the Johnson Administration's mistake, he said, and ensure that the elections would be "truly free."

That same April, I was about to embark on an electoral venture that would change my life, elevating me to a political visibility that would in turn nurture all my impulses to do something exemplary. It began by accident.

By spring 1966, I had clearly come a long way from the troubled sophomore Allard Lowenstein had "discovered" a year earlier. I was confident, relatively well liked, and had developed a reputation as both articulate and radical. Some of my peers considered me brash. Those traits had made me a central figure in several political battles between the Wilbur sponsors and the university administration over the running of Wilbur Hall; in late March I was visited by a senior I knew through antiwar marches. He was the informal leader of the relatively tiny radical caucus in the student legislature. He said he had heard what I'd been saying to the administration over here at Wilbur and thought the campus at large ought to hear the message. He wanted me to run for student body president in the upcoming student elections.

I had never had anything to do with official student government. "You've got to be kidding," I said. "I don't want to be student body president."

"It'll just be an educational campaign," he assured me. "It only lasts a month. You just give a few speeches and that's it. You don't stand a chance of winning. This is Stanford. We just want to raise some issues."

"You sure?" I asked.

"You'll be lucky to get 200 votes," he said.

The assumption that a candidacy such as mine stood no chance was commonplace. Despite its early involvement in Mississippi, Stanford was considered the outpost of student conservatism compared to neighboring Berkeley—and even there, fraternity men still held the student body president's office. Nor did I seem to be making much effort to change Stanford's traditional electoral bent. While the six other candidates wore suits and ties, constructed elaborate campaign organizations, and cast themselves in the style of future congressmen and senators, complete with whistlestop dormitory tours and handshaking expeditions, I campaigned leisurely. I gave one speech a day and had no real campaign organization. On top of everything else, I looked like no one who had ever run for student body president before. In the words of the *Stanford Daily*, [Harris] "wears a wrinkled white shirt, open wide at the neck, underneath a blue sports coat, tan moccasins without socks, blue jeans, and gold wire-rimmed prescription spectacles. His hair, beatnik style and straw-colored, crowns his neck, and he has a moustache. . . ." The *Daily* assessed me as the campaign's "ideological dark horse."

My platform called for elimination of the board of trustees, student control of student regulations, equal policies for men and women, the option to take classes on a pass-or-fail basis, legalization of marijuana, and the end of all university cooperation with the conduct of the War in Vietnam. When asked if I was a radical, my answer was that "radical" meant "to get to the root of things," and I certainly meant to do just that.

Against all odds, I was a hit. When all seven candidates debated each other, I expounded on the similarity between Mississippi and Stanford. "Students are the niggers here," I offered. I expected to be reviled but got the largest ovation instead. The fact that I obviously cared nothing for the office itself only added to my credibility. The designation as "dark horse" soon disappeared from the *Daily*'s references.

In the primary, I finished first with 26 percent of the vote. A runoff election between myself and the fraternity man in second place was scheduled for a week later.

A note of panic entered my attitude with that primary victory. I

had joined the race under the absolute premise that I stood no chance
of winning and that premise was now a shambles. I felt trapped and set
out to try and lose the final election before it was too late to escape. My
strategy was to emphasize those of my beliefs that I thought would give
the allegedly conservative Stanford student body both compelling
reasons and a special incentive to turn out and vote against me.

I talked about the war and how wrong it was. I argued that the two
qualities essential for education were "equality based on a pure
democratic model" and "freedom bordering on anarchy." On several
occasions, I hinted that I had once been interrogated by the FBI without
mentioning why. While my opponent spent the last day before the
election in an 18-hour effort to turn out his vote, the Harris campaign
sponsored only two events. The first was an hour of music on White
Plaza by Stanford's one and only blues band, most of whose members
ranked among the scruffier of the campus LSD set and were personal
friends. To get amplifiers, the lead guitarist and I had gone up to the
Jefferson Airplane's house in the Haight and traded a lid of weed for
the rental of theirs.

The second event was my appearance in front of the Interfraternity
Council. It was the only fraternity crowd I spoke to during the election.

"What's your attitude toward fraternities?" they immediately
asked.

"I think fraternities are a crock of shit," I answered.

The next day, David Harris carried 56 percent of the vote in
the largest turnout in student-body election history. "The
President Elect," the *Daily* subhead read, "Voice of Radicalism."

I was later told by the president of the university that my election
had cost Stanford "several million dollars" in alumni contributions.
"Stanford Students Pick a Revolutionary," "Ex-Football Player Turned
Marxist Elected at Stanford," and "Stanford's New Left Victory" were
just a few of the national headlines flowing into the university clipping
service. Copies of press stories were also being filed with the Federal
Bureau of Investigation by its Palo Alto office under HARRIS, DAVID
VICTOR, #230 829 G. "David Victor Harris," the *Daily* faithfully
explained to its readers, "personifies the campus radical of his day."

My life would never be the same. In an age when students were on
everyone's mind, I had been suddenly transformed into California's
most notorious student-body president. Although I would never
amount to more than a minor celebrity and that for only about as long
as the decade lasted, anonymity henceforth disappeared as one of my

immediate dilemmas. Eventually I would take what prominence I had and run with it, but at first I was stunned by the weight it had added to my life. When that began to wear off, I felt inspired. I pictured myself as the messenger for a whole list of truths, and by embodying them I hoped to act as the vehicle through which they gained ascendancy. The role, partly selfless, partly not, came easily to me.

The decision to pursue such a role was still, like the times themselves, an innocent response. I was somewhat fresh to missions in the spring of 1966 and as yet had no idea how they compound themselves endlessly through time, but I would learn. Before this one was done, I would become the only Stanford alumnus in the maximum-security cell block at the La Tuna Federal Correctional Institution, ten miles outside of El Paso, Texas, a mile from the New Mexico border.

Fittingly, the first campus controversy to arise after my election concerned the draft.

The steady escalation of the number of American soldiers in combat had forced a corresponding inflation of monthly inductions, and the Selective Service responded by tightening up its deferment structure, intent on drafting the stragglers. Married status now conferred automatic exemption only if it was accompanied by fatherhood. Registration at a university was no longer considered sufficient proof of studenthood. Instead, the Selective Service scheduled its own "Selective Service qualification tests" to ascertain that everyone holding a 2-S was indeed "making reasonable progress toward a degree." A Selective Service spokesman told the *Daily* that draft boards would be scrutinizing freshmen in the bottom half of their class, sophomores in the bottom third, and juniors in the bottom quarter. Seniors had to graduate. Once they did, they had to find a new deferment, enlist, or go 1-A and take their chances. It was hard to find a man on campus who wasn't thinking about the draft that spring.

I certainly was no exception, but unlike most of my peers, I had qualms about students being deferred at all. My position on the student deferment had been one of the most controversial of my campaign. I said I thought no one should be drafted, but if they were, then no one should be allowed to remain exempt. All student deferments meant in practice was that the poor served while everyone else watched. American wars weren't supposed to be fought that way.

At the same time I carried a 2-S card just like everyone else, and the inconsistency rubbed. The first obstacle my uneasiness encountered after my election was the Selective Service qualification tests. To take the May test, it was first necessary to sign up during April. As yet unable to confront the issue directly, I just let the sign-up day slide by with no thought to consequences.

A small group of students went several steps beyond that on the day the tests were held. The Selective Service's planned presence on campus had been an issue among student and faculty antiwar caucuses all spring, and on the day the tests were scheduled, a protest rally of some three hundred people was held at noon on White Plaza. Afterward most of the crowd walked down to the university president's office, where approximately two dozen students occupied the waiting room and refused to leave. It was Stanford's first sit-in.

I was at the rally and walked down to the president's office too, but I didn't join the occupation. I was not yet ready to break the law.

The university let the protesters stay overnight. Apparently the administrators figured that, the next day being Saturday, the crowd outside and its attendant reporters would disperse, and then they would offer the sit-in the option of leaving or facing arrest. In the meantime, people were allowed to come and go from the waiting room all night long. After spending the early evening studying for finals, Jeffrey and I bought a pile of takeout pizzas and delivered them there. Dennis Sweeney was among the visitors already mingling in the waiting room when we arrived. The scene had the air of a social occasion.

Dressed in his customary work shirt and Levis, Dennis soon came over to where I was and introduced himself. The smile was genuine but embarrassed in a self-conscious kind of way. "I'm Dennis Sweeney," he said, extending his hand.

I said I knew who he was.

Sweeney grinned again. "I like the work you're doing," he said. The tone of his voice was familiar "organizer to organizer."

I prized the compliment. Dennis Sweeney was the biggest hero Stanford had produced.

Dennis said he and his wife, Mary, were living with some other people on Channing Street. We ought to get together, he said, and we arranged to do so once finals were over.

In the meantime, Allard Lowenstein, former mentor to both of us, was on his way back to the Dominican Republic for the Committee for Free Elections. It was, at least in the abstract, a representative Lowenstein strategy. In an international era dominated by revolution, civil war, and American intervention, he would often propose the "free election" supervised by "genuinely neutral" observers as both an alternative and antidote to violence.

At least as played out in the Dominican Republic, the model had two major flaws. The first was in the mechanics of observation. Most of the observers arrived just two days before the election and, never having been in the country before, had little basis upon which to judge intimidation other than the grossest kinds of violations. For their presence to carry weight, the observers' impartiality also had to be trusted by the Dominicans, a difficult if not impossible trick for Americans, unknown to the populace, to pull off in a country occupied by American Marines.

Allard certainly recognized the difficulties, but in his usual indefatigable manner, he set out to surmount them. He hit Santo Domingo in a last-minute whirlwind, shuttling among various Dominican politicians and briefing the volunteer observers who were now flowing into the country.

Allard also took private steps to, in his terms, "neutralize" the possible reactions of his own government. On election eve, he had the former Stanford protégé in charge of the Santo Domingo office drive him to the Hotel Ambajador, a relatively modern American-owned facility just inside the cordon of U.S. Marines that bisected metropolitan Santo Domingo. The hotel was the headquarters of the Organization of American States' mission charged with "solving" the Dominican crisis. The director of that mission was the United States Ambassador to the OAS, Ellsworth Bunker, with whom Lowenstein was acquainted through their mutual involvement in New York political circles. Though both considered themselves liberals, Bunker wanted the candidate favored by the Dominican military, Joaquin Balaguer, to win, and Lowenstein favored Bosch. The protégé had openly driven Lowenstein to meet with Bunker at the Ambajador on several occasions before, but this time Allard cautioned him to secrecy. Lowenstein and Bunker met in private.

When Allard returned to the car where the Stanford man was waiting, he again pledged the former protégé to secrecy before telling him what had gone on inside. According to Allard, he and Bunker had been searching for common ground upon which an understanding could be reached; the common ground they had was their desire to avoid a civil war. Both agreed it could only be avoided if the election results were allowed to stand, one way or another. Otherwise, the democratic process itself would be discredited and the country plunged into "chaos." Accordingly, Bunker agreed to give Bosch the immediate and full public support of the United States government if he won. In return, Lowenstein pledged that if Balaguer won, he would use all his own considerable influence on the Committee for Free Elections and among stateside liberals to gain acceptance of the results.

Taken aback, the former protégé voiced surprise. Allard had no right to make secret deals behind everyone's back, he said. There were 70 poll watchers and hundreds if not hundreds of thousands of Dominicans who had a stake in this. It wasn't right.

Lowenstein responded with exasperation at the former protégé's "lack of sophistication." The object was to get democracy installed in the Dominican Republic, he argued. If the elections were challenged, civil war would very likely ensue. In real-life politics, there were times when agreements had to be made and secrecy invoked. The point, he reminded the Stanford man, was not to get one party or the other elected; it was to install the electoral process so that Dominicans didn't have to shoot each other to resolve their differences. Unabashed, he suggested his former protégé get his priorities straight.

The Dominican elections were held over two days, but from the beginning, it was obvious Balaguer was going to win. According to several international observers, illegalities were rife and largely one-sided. Soldiers lounged fully armed near the polls, and army officers stood by the ballot boxes. Bosch, fearing assassination, had never left Santo Domingo to campaign in the countryside, and on the first day of voting, his campaign workers fled to the capital from all over the island, seeking protection.

By the end of the second day, before observer reports from the countryside were in, Norman Thomas and Allard Lowenstein boarded a commercial flight to New York at the Santo Domingo Airport without issuing a public statement. Thomas, a known and respected figure to Dominicans by virtue of his involvement with Bosch and the Socialist International, had been the source of much of the committee's credibility, but, nearly blind and plagued by accelerating deafness, he had been largely dependent on Allard during his inspection tour. During the flight back to the United States, he and Lowenstein discussed what had gone on. At the New York airport when they landed, Thomas was besieged by press demands for a comment about the authenticity of the Dominican Republic's "free elections."

"There has been no violence," Thomas said, "and no obvious evidence of fraud during the polling process."

Run on the front page of every Dominican newspaper the next day, Thomas's premature statement infuriated the Dominicans who had supported the committee, most of whom were Bosch partisans. A number of volunteer observers were critical as well. The former Stanford protégé who had driven Allard to the Hotel Ambajador was one of them. He felt there had been a clear understanding that no statements would be issued until all the observer reports had been collected. Two days after the election, ditched ballot boxes were beginning to float up on Dominican beaches and tales of murder and extortion in the countryside multiplied.

Soon after returning to New York, Lowenstein convened a meeting, in response to the criticism, with Thomas and Mrs. Juan Bosch, who was in the city at the time the Dominican elections were held. The object of the gathering was to draft another statement for Thomas that would be acceptable to the Bosch partisans. Señora Bosch was reportedly incensed and, like most of the committee's critics, directed much of her ire at Allard. She wanted a denunciation of Balaguer and the Army goon squads. Allard's position was that there had been irregularities, but the people had voted in a democratic process and the statement ought to say just that. The meeting lasted for hours, but the supplementary statement Thomas eventually issued did nothing more than voice his and the committee's confidence that any claims of election fraud would be investigated by the new government.

Lowenstein's former Stanford protégé dropped by Allard's West Eighty-second Street apartment shortly after his return to New York from Santo Domingo and found a number of people there waiting to meet with Allard about a number of different projects. Lowenstein knew of the protégé's criticisms and was distant. He introduced the former protégé to a third man who, upon learning the protégé was "also involved in Latin America," began to recount stories about his own involvements there.

Lowenstein overheard and turned back to the protégé's conversation. "Don't tell him about that," Allard snapped at the third man. "He's on the other side now."

Such suspicions would reach epidemic proportions before the decade was over. Paranoia was a constant hazard among the politically involved, and it made all of us frantic whenever it gained the upper hand.

One such frantic incident happened to Allard that summer after the Dominican elections. He was now spending most of his time in either Washington, D.C., or New York. While in the nation's capital, he stayed at the apartment of Armin Rosencranz, the former Stanford student body president. Rosencranz was working as an aide in the office of Senator Robert F. Kennedy. Besides Stanford, Lowenstein and Rosencranz also had South Africa in common. Rosencranz had traveled in the region extensively the year before, visiting a number of people Allard had recommended, including Helen Suzman, the white woman legislator who was the only antiapartheid official in the country. One morning in D.C., Lowenstein mentioned that Suzman was in town. He was having breakfast with her and invited Rosencranz to come along.

After breakfast was over, the three of them discovered they were all headed for the same place. Rosencranz had to get to work at Kennedy's office, and both Allard and Suzman were headed there too. "I've arranged for her to meet with Bobby," Allard explained. On the way across town in a shared cab, Lowenstein fed Suzman a steady stream of advice about what to say.

"Enough, Allard," she finally snapped. "I can talk for myself."

It was a quick exchange, not an indication at the time of lasting animosity, but later, the woman legislator would use it to pinpoint the moment she had finally "had it" with Lowenstein.

The three waited together in the sitting room outside of Bobby's inner office. When the door opened and Kennedy looked out, Suzman stepped away from the others, crossed the office threshold, and turned back to Lowenstein. "I'll see you in half an hour, Al," she said, "when this is over." Kennedy smiled again and closed the door behind them.

Allard was beside himself. "You have no idea what just happened," he blurted out.

"What?" Rosencranz asked.

"She has just betrayed the whole colored population of South Africa. Why else did she go in there alone?"

"Come on, Al," Rosencranz countered. "There could be a thousand explanations. Her own vanity to begin with. She may also believe she can get more accomplished one on one."

Lowenstein wouldn't buy the objections. "Absolutely not," he insisted. "You don't understand. The only possible reason she doesn't want me involved in that conversation that's going on in there is that she doesn't want me to know what she's doing, and there's only one thing she could be that afraid of me knowing."

Lowenstein seemed so upset that Rosencranz postponed going to work and took him down the hall for a cup of coffee. Allard stuck to his opinion for the next half hour, punctuating his conversation with words like "betrayal" and "duplicitousness."

Nonetheless, Lowenstein was waiting for Suzman when she emerged from Bobby's. The two of them then walked back out into the Washington summer together and caught a cab to their next meeting.

I still remember the summer of 1966 in California. It was a final
interlude of garrulous self-discovery, after which the battle
would begin in earnest. It was also the summer my life first became
entangled with Dennis Sweeney's.

By virtue of being the new student body president, I had a summer
job in Stanford's Office of Undergraduate Education and didn't have to
go back to Fresno. Nor did I have to live in a dormitory. Jeffrey and I
rented a ramshackle eight-room house on the other side of the freeway
in East Palo Alto, on Cooley Street, for $125 a month. The backyard was
overgrown and dominated by a 40-foot tree that had toppled over on its
side several years earlier and was sprawled across the width of the
property. Seven of us lived there together. We painted the kitchen a
combination of bright yellow, fire-engine red, and an almost turquoise
blue.

It is hard for me to describe us and what we were about that
summer without lapsing into what now sounds trite. The intervening
decade and a half has reduced much of the language we then used to
describe ourselves into a rubble of jargon that, however I try to arrange
it, now reads like parody. We were all still students. We were all still
confident in the way only people who think they have their whole lives
ahead of them can be. We all wanted to become "human," "aware,"
"honest," and "true to our beliefs," traits few of our elders seemed to
possess. We all believed the war mirrored everything wrong with
America. We all, to one degree or another, found a discredited America
impossible to reconcile with who we wanted to be. It was a sign of the
times that, without hesitation, we all assumed we could resolve that
discrepancy in our favor. The society we were expected to adhere to
had been so thoroughly compromised, we said, that it now demanded
an entirely new formulation. We believed we were laying the foundations of a New Age. Being hopelessly outnumbered only added to the
adventure. We weren't a parody, whatever has since become of our
words. We were the "real thing." As far as we were concerned, no one
had ever done what we were doing.

Fifteen years later, I have no choice but to look back at us across
much accumulated cynicism, both my own and the country's. Nothing
is simple anymore, so it is hard not to be embarrassed by how simple it
all seemed then. Such embarrassment is a disservice to the memory.
Not because we weren't occasionally clumsy in our definitions and
even simplistic, but because, even so, things were indeed simpler. Life
and death were obviously at issue, and we were obviously surrounded
by a nation with oatmeal in its heart. At the time, complexity was most

often used as an excuse for ignoring what was actually happening to people. It was a sign of character, if not wisdom, that we latched onto the simple truths no one else wanted to see and rode them until their wheels fell off. I, for one, thrived during that summer spent with six other young men perched together on what felt like the front bumper of reality.

There was no trench warfare yet, and the ground we broke out over was flat and in bloom.

With school out, most of the scene we belonged to was set around Cooley Street and several other houses off campus, one the two-story wood-frame house on Channing Street where the Mississippi hero Dennis Sweeney, his wife, and close friends lived. Soon after moving to East Palo Alto, I and several of my housemates went over to Dennis's for dinner. Everyone liked one another. We talked about Mississippi, Stanford, the Fillmore Auditorium, music, the war, and getting out from under.

Though slightly older, Sweeney usually followed the conversation rather than leading it. Mary King was much more assertive in manner than he. Dennis's self-consciousness created an air of undefined pain about him and induced sympathy. "The movement" was everything to him still, but he wasn't even sure of what it now was. The question of "what to do next" was discussed endlessly. Dennis's style was gentle, and he listened intently to everyone. On all things to do with organizing, he was widely deferred to.

That night back at Cooley Street, after dinner at Dennis's finally broke up, I sat in my room and wrote a poem about him:

> *Blue boy bored,*
> *I spy you*
> *In the traces of the cloud.*
> *Panting the sweat of your countless mothers,*
> *Your long lost gone.*
> *Blue boy bored,*
> *Tied to a cloud with thongs*
> *Of wet leather.*

The poem was thrown into a box in the closet where I kept my writings. There, a succession of cats would eventually invade it in pissing expeditions. When I finally left Cooley Street, I would haul the rank and yellowed package with me, storing it in the succession of garages or storerooms my life went on to include. I reopened it fourteen years later. By then, Dennis Sweeney would be incarcerated by the State of New York, charged with homicide in the second degree, and I was one of those assigned by the *New York Times* to try and explain how he and his former mentor came to such an end.

M ost of the madness that summer in 1966 was confined to self-inflicted recreation. Every week or ten days, several people from among Cooley Street and its friends would take LSD together, a necessary step, we thought, toward having a mind of your own. Two of the fairly regular participants in the ritual were myself and Dennis Sweeney.

I can remember one Saturday when everyone at Cooley Street took some acid and decided to drive over to Dennis's. There, we discovered he and several others had also spent the morning getting stoned and joined forces. Mary was not part of the group. She did not share Sweeney's enthusiasm for getting high, and although it was not a conflict between them at the time, it was one of the first signs of the erosion of the bond they had pledged themselves to the previous November. That Saturday, all of us who had taken acid sat together in Dennis's favorite room, a small low-ceilinged place at the top of the stairs with bay windows opening out onto the roof. When the tight room got to be too much, we stepped out the bay windows and sat on top of the house, watching Palo Alto change colors. Eventually the downstairs phone rang until Mary answered it. She called up to Dennis and said it was for him. We wished him good luck at dealing with the telephone.

When he got back to the roof, Sweeney's face was somewhat crestfallen. "I think I fucked up," he said.

"What happened?" I asked.

Dennis explained that the call had been from a nationally syndicated columnist whom he had known in Mississippi. The columnist was in town for part of a day doing a story about former Mississippi Project activists and wanted very badly to talk to Sweeney.

"What did you tell him?"

"I didn't know how to say no."

"What do you mean?"

"He's coming over in half an hour," Dennis answered.

Everyone laughed.

Several of us were nonetheless down in the front room of the house a half an hour later watching Sweeney being interviewed by the columnist. For most, the room appeared to be melting at the corners. I kept my sunglasses on, tried to look like I wasn't wired, and didn't introduce myself. Dennis looked at his hands and feet a lot, answered all questions in three sentences or less, and didn't expand on his answers. His voice was so quiet the columnist had to ask him to repeat himself several times. In response to the standard question trying to assess the latest state of "alienation" among the young, Dennis said it was "growing" and left it at that. When asked why, he said "the war." When the columnist asked how Dennis was finding the adjustment out of the South, Sweeney said "hard." It took several questions to extract the statement that "things were real intense down there" and that things "here" felt consequently "less real." At that answer, one of the more stoned observers almost chuckled but managed, with some difficulty, to control his impulse.

The interview went on like that until Dennis finally told the man that he just didn't feel like talking anymore. When the columnist left, the whole room broke out laughing, several people so hard they fell out of their chairs.

Dennis grinned.

"What a trip," he said.

In July, Mendy Samstein, a white former SNCC staffer Dennis had worked with in McComb, visited him and Mary for a week. Samstein had been traveling around the country talking with "movement people" about what to do now. Eight of us gathered in the tiny room at the top of the Channing Street house's stairs.

Mendy's starting point was the tail end of the Mississippi Project. Like Dennis, he agreed with SNCC's decision to urge whites to return to their own communities to organize "against their own oppression" there. Also, as for Dennis, just what that meant for him was still up in the air. The most likely options were the war and the draft. The "We Won't Go" petitions had been a step in the right direction, but the government could easily dismiss the threat of students protected by deferments. The rest of his talk was mostly questions. What if white students organized on a wholesale basis and refused their privilege, forcing the government to draft the middle class just like everyone else? If those draftees also refused to be inducted, wouldn't the government be forced to incarcerate thousands or be discredited? Politically, might that not be more than Vietnam policy could bear? The first draft-card burnings had already taken place at several demonstrations in New York. Why not extend that civil disobedience on a broad scale?

The discussion that followed was somber, even frightening. The first thing on everyone's mind was the penalties involved. The Selective Service Act of 1948 called for up to five years in prison for simply not having a draft card in your possession. Induction refusal carried a five-year maximum as well. "Conspiracy to obstruct or violate" carried five years for each count. Pursuing that line of action meant increasing the stakes geometrically. It would also, Dennis offered, be the first step in creating a new "white SNCC," a "net to pull through the campuses of the country and collect the people you really wanted to work with." Although the action might conceivably reach a size where prosecution of everyone was impossible, the organizers would have to proceed under the assumption of eventually receiving a prison sentence. Upping the ante seemed appropriate to both our mood and the circumstances, but no one was yet ready to commit himself to those consequences, and the meeting with Mendy Samstein at Dennis's led to nothing concrete. His visit did, however, plant a seed, and its germination would provide the grist for my relationship with Dennis Sweeney.

Afterward, Sweeney accompanied his friend from Mississippi up to Oregon, where they participated in a series of similar meetings, but the response was disappointing and Dennis remained in his political holding pattern. "I was sure I was going to do it," he would remember two years later, "but I was sure I wasn't going to do it by myself, because I believed that to have an impact, to have some kind of political effect, it had to be a number of people doing it together."

The more we learned about the war, the worse it seemed. Late in July, Cooley Street attended a lecture by a Canadian journalist who had just returned from North Vietnam. Dennis and the Channing Street group were at the lecture as well.

With what amounted to only a fledgling air defense system, explained the journalist, North Vietnam had no hope of turning the American Air Force back. Theoretically, strategic air power destroys the enemy's industrial, logistic, and transportation systems, but North Vietnam possessed little centralized industry and only a rudimentary transportation system. Consequently, the target increasingly became the population itself. The American strategy's starting point was a calculation by Defense Department planners that it took only two Vietnamese to deal with one of their dead countrymen, but one wounded required five. Mass woundings, it was assumed, would tie the enemy's hands, and the American arsenal had developed wounding devices in great variety.

The CBU 46 was a small explosive package stuffed with hundreds of one-inch steel darts, each shaped with fins, designed to "peel off" the outer flesh, make "enlarged wounds," and "shred body organs" before "lodging in the blood vessels." They were dropped a thousand at a time from 30,000 feet. The BLU 52 was 270 pounds of "riot control" chemical that induced vomiting, nausea, and muscle spasms, occasionally fatal to old people and children. The M-36 was an 800-pound casing containing 182 separate "incendiary bomblets," the most horrendous of which were manufactured from phosphorus, commonly lodging in the flesh and continuing to burn for as long as fifteen days, causing its victims' wounds to glow with an eerie green light.

The two antipersonnel weapons then in most common use were versions of the BLU 24/26. The "pineapple bomb" was the earliest model. A yellow cylinder, it contained 250 steel ball-bearing pellets packed around an explosive charge. On impact, its pellets fired out horizontally. A batch of a thousand pineapples would cover an area the size of four football fields, leaving anything above ground level a casualty. The "guava bomb" was the pineapple's successor. Gray and round, it doubled the number of pellets and had a fuse that let it either explode at a set altitude or on impact. Since it fired its pellets diagonally instead of on the horizontal, the Guava also fired into the holes where people might be hiding.

After the program was over, we all decided to proceed to a place we called End of the World Beach. It was the edge of a causeway supporting the eastern approach to the Dunbarton Bridge, where beer bottles, old tires, two-by-fours, tennis shoes, condoms, dead fish, and seaweed were strung out for half a mile. It captured the devastation still haunting everyone's thinking. At one point, Dennis and I stood next to each other, staring across the refuse at the blinking lights of civilization on the other side of the bay.

Without looking at Dennis, I spoke up.

"You know," I said, "those bastards have got to be stopped."

When I turned to Sweeney, he was nodding his head like he knew exactly what I meant.

Three weeks later I sat at my typewriter and wrote local Draft Board 71 in Fresno, California, a letter "To whom it may concern." I enclosed a Selective Service classification card indicating that the bearer, David Victor Harris, possessed a student deferment. The letter informed my draft board that I could no longer in good conscience carry the enclosed document or accept the deferment it signified. It was a privilege I found unwarranted for any student. It also signified tacit assent on my part for both the task the Selective Service System was performing and the power it had assumed over my life. Being even implicitly a party to the destruction of Indochina was not part of my plans. If they ordered me for induction, I warned them, I would refuse to comply.

I feel as though I have explained that act of defiance a million times in the intervening years without ever quite capturing it. The repetition eventually burdened my explanation with a shell of distance and matter-of-factness that distorts what I did. It was an act of wonderment and impulse, taken in the calmest and most practical frame of mind. I was prepared to abandon what seemed a promising future and pit myself against the war one on one, believing I would redeem my country and realize myself in the process. It seemed that to do anything else would have dishonored both. There was nothing matter-of-fact or distant about it that August. I took my life in my hands and it was the bravest I have ever been. It was also, I think, the most right. That I have never doubted. Times change and I am no longer the same person, but my past and I are still directly related.

I remember mailing that letter at the mailbox next to the neighborhood store, scuffing along in the dust at the road edge, wearing Levis, moccasins, and a brown khaki work shirt. My moustache had become a full beard and my hair covered the top of my ears. I was both frightened and exhilarated. The last barrier was down. Henceforth, I was my own soldier advancing in my own kind of war.

My adrenaline didn't diminish until long after midnight. Lying in my bed, I pictured the penitentiary as a very cold and lonely place that I planned to endure for the sake of us all.

7

The first battle in "my own kind of war" was fought at the National Student Association Congress held later in August at the University of Illinois. The principal skirmish was between myself and Allard Lowenstein.

Founded in 1947 by a group of 24 young Americans convinced of the necessity of a national organization to speak for American students, close to 400 American colleges and universities were affiliated with NSA. By 1966, its annual budget was three-quarters of a million dollars, raised principally through foundation grants and dispensed, in theory at least, in pursuit of a program approved by the annual congress.

Lowenstein was at the 1966 congress as a matter of both personal habit and political agenda. He had attended every such congress for the previous decade and a half. In later publicity about NSA, one New York writer would call him the organization's "father," a status that had continued without the benefit of any official position since his own presidency of the organization during the years 1950 and 1951. A succession of young men under his influence had held NSA offices and staff positions, and his protégés dotted the floor during the congress's debates. The principal mechanism of Lowenstein's influence was "the liberal caucus," an informal gathering of student delegates who took positions on issues and campaigned for them during activity on the congress floor. Every year the liberal caucus invited Allard to address its members, and such was Lowenstein's consistent eloquence that he customarily carried the caucus to whatever positions or candidates he supported. The summer of 1966 was no exception.

As incoming student body president, I headed the Stanford delegation. It included several veterans of our visionary Palo Alto summer, and we saw ourselves as representatives of a wholly different campus tradition than the "politicos" who customarily dominated NSA. In the parlance of the time, we were activists who scorned officialdom in most of its forms, wore Levis and work shirts, and were often labeled "unkempt" or "hip."

After being assigned rooms in the giant dormitory, we set up a tape recorder and began playing tapes of the Jefferson Airplane at top volume. Eventually word got around that we had arrived and the room began to fill. The people who had arrived the day before said the scene here revolved around the congress floor and the cafeteria downstairs. Right now, everyone was in the cafeteria looking everyone else over.

"Well," I said getting up off the bunk, "let's go blow a few minds."

A number of heads turned when the scruffy-looking Stanford delegation entered that University of Illinois cafeteria for the first time. The high we had been riding on all summer made us anxious to press the attack, but we nevertheless arrived without a single plan. Our subsequent strategy was completely off the cuff.

It would later be remembered by the then editor of the UCLA *Daily Bruin* as the "real-life argument." NSA had an immense agenda covering dozens of issues, but since students had no real power over their respective institutions, we considered the congress a mock exercise and hence meaningless. What students ought to address themselves to was the life-or-death questions that events like congresses often ignored in favor of parliamentary exercise. What kind of lives were we going to have? How could we rebuild the culture around us? What were we as individuals going to do if drafted? To contrast ourselves to the liberals, the radicals formed a caucus in which Stanford was joined by activists from Michigan, UCLA, Columbia, Barnard, Brown, University of Pennsylvania, and several black colleges in the South.

When *Time* magazine later wrote up the radical rising at NSA, I was identified as its "leader" and accorded an accompanying photograph taken in a concrete stairwell at the close of a debate that had lasted all night. With scraggly hair that had not been cut all summer, a thick beard, and heavy shadows under my eyes, I came out looking like one of Henry Luce's nightmares. No doubt I was, although no one ever took me for personally "dangerous." According to several people who met me for the first time at NSA, I was unassuming, loose, and "a very charismatic speaker." I postured myself as "just another student" and did not seem terribly impressed with my sudden stature. The caucus I spearheaded took a concerted position only on the issue of conscription.

There were three resolutions on the subject awaiting action at that congress. The conservative resolution treated the draft as a necessary fact. The liberal resolution criticized conscription's unfairness and the foreign policy it was being used to wage, but called for no more than a formalization of the criticism. The radical offering described Selective

Service and its function as "unconscionable" and committed NSA to organizing widespread "noncooperation" and "civil disobedience" among the student population.

When the question was finally called on the congress floor, a coalition of liberals and conservatives defeated the radical resolution by one vote.

As the leader of the defeated contender, I was surprised we had even come that close, as were a lot of others. Using a spontaneous, unorchestrated strategy, the radicals had, out of nowhere, made themselves a force to contend with. Shortly after the vote on the draft, what amounted to official recognition of our status came my way. A debate had been planned between Allard Lowenstein and Stokely Carmichael, but Carmichael had canceled. I was asked to take the SNCC leader's place.

Several hours later, the UCLA *Daily Bruin* editor ran into me in the cafeteria. I had a solemn look on my face.

"What's up?" he said.

"I'm going to debate Allard Lowenstein," I answered.

The *Bruin* editor remembers that I treated the face-off as the most significant event of the congress, and that memory jibes with my own. Challenging my former mentor was an essential part of coming into my own, especially since by now our political paths had diverged sharply, making debate appropriate.

The debate was held in the afternoon. The room was packed wall to wall, and more students were jammed in the doorways and out into the hall. Word of my substitution had spread quickly, and, in the words of one liberal caucus member, the debate was considered "a classic match-up." "Allard," he would tell me years later, after Allard was dead, "deeply affected everyone he had contact with, and so did you." I was dressed in my usual well-worn work shirt, Levis, and rimless spectacles. He was in his usual rumpled short sleeves with a tie strapped loosely at the neck and plastic glasses slipping along his nose. The debate topic was strategies for change.

Allard spoke first.

He warmed up by saying the war was destroying the best of America. Students were right to oppose it, but in doing so, it would be a great mistake to "throw the baby out with the bath water." The system of electoral democracy already in place was our most precious possession. It was, he declared, capable of righting itself from Lyndon

Johnson's Asian misadventure. To urge people to step outside of that system was "irresponsible." It had worked in Mississippi, he pointed out, and it would work with the war. He could sympathize with our feelings of frustration, but taking them out by turning "radical" was not the way to get things done.

I responded by saying it was not just a question of systems working. What was at issue was behavior and personal morality, not just politics. As young people we had to decide how we were going to act in the face of something we all apparently agreed was wrong. With that as our objective, the system Allard was defending offered no recourse. It provided us only with the right to be drafted, not even to vote, and certainly not to make decisions. While we waited for the system to change itself, we would be forced to carry out the very crime we were trying to stop. Like "good Germans" in World War II, having had orders would be no excuse, nor would following proper procedure. Anything less than immediate resistance amounted to collaboration.

In the tangle of questions and exchanges that followed, we each assumed a respectful face toward the other. Allard noted what a fine person I was and then went after my comments in a manner one radical caucus member would recall as "cutthroat." Former protégé or not, I was the opposition. For my part, I was just as combative. I also thought, I said, that Allard was a fine person, but fine people often did less than fine things, the war being a case in point. Having summoned myself to confront my onetime mentor, I was determined not to back off.

He said the war was a tragic mistake. I said it was the logical conclusion of the values holding national sway. I said the war would never be ended in an election. He said it not only could, but would. He reminded people that he was no pacifist and had served as an enlisted man in the United States Army for two years. I said I wasn't sure if I was a pacifist or not, but that I was sure no one ever stopped a war by fighting in it. He said the point was "to be effective." I said the real point was "effective for what?" When asked what he would do if he were drafted, Allard said young people ought to find any deferment they could to stay out, but if they ended up being called, then they should go. I said massive civil disobedience was the most honorable strategic option we had and that I would personally refuse either to carry a draft card or be inducted.

The audience got the show it had come for. "All over the room," the *Daily Bruin* editor said years later, "there was a sense that people were listening hard" and that "minds were being made up." When the moderator finally called an end to the program so people could move on to other events, there was a common agreement that it had been "too short," and the outcome was considered a toss-up. Both of us were accorded standing ovations.

Afterward, we said nothing to each other. Allard Lowenstein and David Harris were on different sides now, and both of us had more loyalty to our respective politics than we did to each other.

For Allard, the confrontation at NSA coincided with the inception of a fresh tactic which would consume much of the autumn. It centered around organizing a succession of public letters addressed to the President of the United States.

The public letter was another regular Lowenstein technique, and Allard's use of it now was, in many ways, a response to the challenge he felt from young radicals, such as myself. He later explained, "The war protest was getting hooked on a very narrow radical base," and he wanted to help "rally moderate, reasonable student opinion." The form that took was gathering groups of certifiably distinguished undergraduates to sign open letters expressing their dismay at "the growing conflict between their own observations on the one hand, and statements by Administration leaders about the war on the other." Eventually, these would include one from student body presidents, another from editors of student newspapers, others from seminarians, more student body presidents, peace corps returnees, and Rhodes scholars.

The first letter to be put together was from the student body presidents. At a 2 A.M. meeting of the congress's liberal caucus the evening after the Lowenstein-Harris debate, a group of some two hundred delegates agreed to draft a letter, and $83 was collected to pay for mailing it to campus leaders for the purpose of gathering signatures. "The notion," the *New York Times* later reported, "was first put forward . . . by Allard K. Lowenstein, a former president of the association who is now a lawyer and active Reform Democrat in Manhattan." The next day, a Lowenstein protégé I knew from the Encampment approached me with the draft. I told him it was much too mild for me to sign. That fall, I would get several phone calls from the protégé reading me the latest version and requesting a signature, and each time I would refuse.

Aside from spurring a fresh tactic, the NSA confrontation seemed simply to add to Allard's backstage lamentations about the current plight of liberalism. An indication of that mood arose in a conversation with one of his Yale protégés shortly after the summer was over. Allard began by complaining about how few people there were left who were simply liberals, people who just believed in the Bill of Rights and the

Constitution, like Mrs. Roosevelt and Frank Graham. The drift of things these days seemed hopelessly left and exotic. It was, he said, at least partially the liberals' own fault. Why was it, Allard continued, that most people who thought as he and the protégé did had so little passion, so little energy and willingness to go out and really give of themselves?

"How many people do you know," he asked the protégé, "who are really willing to do that sort of thing who think as you and I do?"

The Yale protégé shared his mentor's momentary hopelessness. "I don't know," he answered with some intention of humor, "maybe five or six."

Lowenstein shook his head and laughed. "If we're lucky," he said.

M y sense of righteous battle was only reinforced when I returned to California and discovered what had gone on in my absence. Casualty reports of a sort were already flowing in. Jeffrey, one of the founders of Cooley Street, had gone to Mexico during the NSA congress, had been arrested at the border with a kilo of marijuana. He was out on bail, facing five years. One of the other veterans of our ecstatic summer, an English major who had taken the pseudonym Julian Burroughs, in homage to the junkie novelist William Burroughs, had been drafted and was now in boot camp at Fort Ord. Another friend had been forcibly committed to a midwestern mental hospital after confessing to his parents that he had taken LSD. All of those particular twists contributed to the atmosphere of escalating stakes.

I responded by accelerating the role I had carved out for myself in Illinois. My first official duty of the school year was to welcome the 1,300 members of Stanford's freshman class as part of their orientation.

According to the front-page *Daily* account, I "urged Stanford freshmen to 'build a University for people instead of people for a University.'"

Some of the freshmen cheered. Others didn't know what to think. I was not at all what they had expected when they had applied to Stanford the year before.

The *Daily* story ran with a small picture of me behind the podium. I was in the midst of making a point and had my left hand raised and two of its fingers extending upward. My work shirt hung loosely, and the lighting on the stage made the blond patches on my head and face shimmer, so that when the photo was printed, they came out looking more like some sort of clinging aura than hair. It was jokingly referred to as my "Moses" picture.

The Stanford fraternity housing a good portion of the football team posted that picture on its bulletin board, and they would gather in front of it several times a week during the next month, shouting imprecations and attempting to exorcise the hippie devil who had seized control of student politics.

During that first month of fall quarter, I devoted most of my energy to being president and was soon locked in a bureaucratic tussle with the administration over student regulations and decision making. I saw Dennis Sweeney a couple of times. Word was out among his friends that he and Mary were having a hard time, but I had little opportunity to pursue the subject.

Toward the end of October, all of that exorcism among the football team finally caught up with me. On my way to a speech I had agreed to give to a women's residence on fraternity row, I noticed a jock type waiting in front of my destination. He noticed me as well and approached.

"Mr. Harris?"

The politeness should have been a dead giveaway, but I was preoccupied. "Yes?"

"I need to talk to you for a second." Without waiting for an agreement, he gripped my arm and began walking with me along the sidewalk toward the vacant lot that bordered one side of the residence. At the boundary, I stopped and said for him to talk. I was in a hurry.

"Okay," he answered.

With that, four huge undergraduates wearing Halloween masks leapt from where they had been hiding, grabbed me by my arms and legs, and trotted back into the darkness of the vacant lot with me in their grip.

Some fifteen of their fraternity brothers were waiting, all similarly huge and dressed in Halloween masks. I was dumped on the dirt, pinned there by five sets of arms. Someone had run an extension cord out of one of the residence's windows and attached a pair of hair clippers. Exaggerated chuckling arose when my haircut began, but it died down shortly. In their later account of events, the fraternity men said they had expected me to beg and snivel and that some of the fun went out of things when I didn't. I just lay there. At one point, a flashbulb went off. Not long after that, a decision was reached among the masked men to forget about cutting my beard, and then the entire crowd ran off hooting toward the surrounding fraternity neighborhood.

Prints of the photograph that had been taken were delivered

anonymously to the *Stanford Daily* and the *San Francisco Chronicle* later
that evening. The right third of the photo was filled with the back of a
fraternity man, and my head was framed in the bottom half of the
picture. A dark lump of beard was apparent, as was the shine on my
now elongated forehead. The only feature that stood out was my eyes.
They were turned away from the camera so their whites looked the size
of saucers.

The fraternity men's apparent assumption was that the campus
would hail them for the humiliation they had inflicted on the "hippie"
in their midst, but the local newspapers said 90 percent of the students
interviewed the next morning expressed "admiration" for the way I
had dealt with the situation. Eventually, even the fraternity men
themselves voiced doubts about their assault. "Harris really showed a
lot of class," one told the *Daily*. "He made us feel sorry we did it." The
story of the incident, the response to it, and the accompanying
photograph all went out on the wire services. My visibility increased.
The David Harris presidency now had a slightly heroic tinge.

Frankly, it had also pretty much peaked. Dealing with the
university bureaucracy was like wrestling with a vat of jello, and my
"radical" proposals were all soon lost in a morass of committees and
commissions, being "studied" into oblivion.

A llard Lowenstein spent the fall in transit around the
country, giving speeches about the war and pushing his
public-letter campaign. Somewhere in all that rush, he also managed to
make the decision that had been brewing since his congressional coffee
klatches. Whatever doubts Allard had about marrying Jennifer Lyman
had disappeared.

The wedding took place at a rented hall just outside of Boston and
was preceded by a luncheon in the Lyman family house, a Boston
historical landmark. Allard had reportedly compiled a list of several
thousand guests he wanted to invite for "political reasons" but had
agreed to reduce the number by an order of magnitude to avoid
throwing the affair into a total numerical imbalance. Though much the
smaller, the bride's party included a lot of Massachusetts's purebred
upper crust, and it was not lost on several of them that Jennifer was
marrying a Jew who was 15 years older than her and didn't even have
an identifiable occupation. The groom's party was full of students,
Reform Democrats, journalists, civil rights veterans, and well-known
liberals, including Frank Graham and Norman Thomas. At the
luncheon, one of the bride's party gagged noticeably when the
octogenarian Socialist was pointed out to her.

Among the groom's party, there was widespread banter about whether Lowenstein would be late to his own wedding, but he arrived on time, dressed in a brown suit that was well pressed. He was ebullient, and it was clear to everyone there that the couple was very much in love.

Allard and Jenny's marriage lasted almost ten years and produced three children, Frank Graham Lowenstein, Thomas Kennedy Lowenstein, and Katherine Eleanor Lowenstein. The issues that would eventually separate the couple were always more questions of pace and life-style than affection. Jenny and the kids stood vigil in the hospital the night Allard died.

I n one of the ironic coincidences that marked their paths, Dennis Sweeney's marriage ended while Allard Lowenstein's commenced. The dissolution was initiated by Mary and was not so much acrimonious as resigned. Dennis seemed stuck in one spot, and Mary chafed at being stalled by his internal conflicts. She finally left the Channing Street house and moved East, stopping in Mexico to make the divorce official. The severance was complete. They never saw or talked to each other again.

With Mary gone, Dennis left Palo Alto for a while and returned to Oregon. There, he got some kind of job in a mill, lived in a small cabin near the ocean, and spent a lot of time, he would later remember, "reading, sitting by the fire, walking along the beach, doing a lot of thinking."

The most startling thing about Sweeney's attitude toward the abrupt termination of his marriage was how little he expressed about it. I didn't fully understand the uniqueness of that behavior until I myself had been married and divorced and had passed through the cycle of recrimination seemingly generic to the experience. None of that surfaced in Dennis. When he returned from Oregon, he said little or nothing about it. He didn't rail against his ex-wife. He didn't analyze it over and over again out loud. He just said it "didn't work." Whatever else he felt about that conclusion stayed stuffed somewhere beneath his surface.

I saw a lot more of Dennis as the fall wore on. Within several weeks after my hair had been reduced to stubble by the football team, word reached Cooley Street that Dennis was back and looking for a place to live, and we invited him to move in.

His room was distinctive for its spareness. He had a bed, a small table next to it with a lamp, a chair, and sometimes a book on the table or an open pack of cigarettes. The ashtray was usually empty, and when the bed wasn't in use it was always neatly made. There was no clothing scattered about other than a pair of Levis folded neatly over the back of his chair. There were no decorations on the wall. Aside from a diffuse working-man's air, the room was a blank: like a lodger's room, rented by the month with a shared bathroom down the hall.

Dennis Sweeney's life would eventually turn into a succession of such rooms, and, increasingly, each of them would echo.

It seemed no more than simplicity in 1966. Tidy, quiet, and congenial, Dennis fit right in at Cooley Street. We were all intensely political; coupled with our faintly "outlaw" notoriety on campus, it made a strong bond. Dennis responded to the familyness of it and his sense of drift began to disappear.

As the reinforcement of the group jelled something in Dennis, he did likewise for the group. Having him there made the house feel complete. He was a little older than the rest of us, widely respected for his role in Mississippi, and he seemed to add a stability. Shortly after he arrived, Cooley Street formalized its collective existence and began calling itself the "Peace and Liberation Commune," pooling all money with the exception of tuition fees in a common pot from which we all drew as we needed it. We were exuberant about the change and honestly thought we had invented the political unit of the coming new age. The Sixties were, among other things, a time of "experiments," and the Peace and Liberation Commune was ours.

It was to last not quite two years before collapsing in a shambles.

The Sixties were also a time of "revelations" and "exposés." Allard Lowenstein became enmeshed in one of those exposés when he attended a November meeting convened by a group of officers and staff from the National Student Association. They had, they said, a crisis on their hands. For at least the better part of this decade and the last, they confessed, the NSA's international arm had been secretly funded and at least partially directed by the Central Intelligence Agency. The officers were now somewhat desperately trying to find a way to break the connection without going belly-up.

Lowenstein treated the information as something he had long suspected but of which he'd had no proof. He would later tell reporters that he thought "the NSA kids" came to him because they knew he was "one of the few past officers who was not involved in or in favor of the CIA connection."

There were, the NSA people told Allard in November, strong and persistent rumors that the press had gotten wind of the arrangement and would soon go to print with their findings. Their fears of exposure were well founded, and, within four months, *Ramparts*, a leftish monthly based in San Francisco, would print a good portion of the story.

In its article, *Ramparts* was fuzzy on exactly when the relationship began, other than placing its beginnings in the early 1950s. Financial records prior to 1960 were incomplete, but in the fiscal year ending on September 30, 1964, the CIA had provided $370,000 of the NSA's $440,000 budget; in fiscal year 1965, $440,000 of $760,000; in 1966, $355,000 of $735,000, all earmarked for NSA's international programs and transmitted by the CIA through a series of cooperative or puppet foundations. In 1965, the agency had given NSA a fifteen-year rent-free lease on several buildings in Washington, D.C., which housed the NSA national headquarters.

Only the NSA president, the international vice president, and key staff members on the international side of the organization knew of the arrangement. Those who did were considered "witting," referred to the CIA as "the firm" and its operatives as "the fellas" or "the boys." Most face-to-face encounters were a function of the agency's Covert Action Division No. 5, and by the 1960s, all the agents the students dealt with were themselves former NSA officers. One international vice president later estimated that of the association's officers during the late 1950s and early 1960s, some 70 percent had ended up "in intelligence." Typically, the "witting" international staff members consulted with one of the "fellas" before formulating overseas programs and passed along reports about foreign student leaders. Their immense budget allowed youthful NSA officers and staff to conduct what amounted to full-scale international diplomacy while they were automatically deferred from conscription for work "affecting the national interest."

The CIA relationship had begun to disintegrate in the NSA year 1965–66 when that year's president had taken a friendly but reserved attitude to the connection and demanded full control of the international programs being funded. The result was a year of financial skirmishing: the CIA and its foundations applied heavy pressure, and attempts to raise the organization's budget elsewhere failed miserably.

Allard advised them to accelerate their severance, even at the risk of abandoning much of the organizational infrastructure the agency money had built. When word later got out, he would publicly criticize the CIA for "the secrecy of their relationship with NSA" and "the direct pressure" they had apparently put on the association's officers. If, he would note, the CIA had wanted simply "to give financial support," it could have "used its influence to channel money to the students . . . without involving the students in direct relations with CIA agents."

"I was," Allard told the student officers that November, "the one they kept it all secret from."

He repeated that explanation again and again during the next year, but even then, some people would refuse to believe it.

In December I returned to Fresno for Christmas vacation and found a communication from Selective Service Board 71 waiting for me. I was now, the letter announced, classified 1-A, part of the immediate manpower pool from which inductees were chosen. When I told my parents what I planned to do if called, my parents told me I would "ruin" my life by going to prison. I disagreed, and we suddenly had nothing to say to each other. I finally fled the tension on the day after Christmas. Back at the commune I told everyone about my 1-A status and tried to work off my anxieties about it in the general merriment of being 20 years old and on vacation from school.

On December 28, we all took some acid together and drove over the mountains to San Gregorio Beach. It was the next-to-last time I consumed any LSD. That night, the fog turned red and green and I felt like I had seen it all before. We got back to Cooley Street, no longer stoned, at 11 P.M.

There, we were hardly in the door when the phone rang. Dennis answered it, then cupped his hand over the receiver and looked in my direction with the trace of a chuckle in his voice. "It's for you," he said, "the *New York Times*."

I winced and got on the line.

"This is David Harris," I said.

The reporter wanted my comment about the letter I had signed.

I didn't know what he was talking about.

"The letter of one hundred student body presidents to President Johnson about the war," he explained. "You're listed as one of the signers."

I now remembered Allard's letter, which I had refused to endorse, paused, and let out a breath. While previously unwilling to put my name on the document, I was also unwilling now to blow it out of the water by raising questions about the validity of its signature. Fucking Lowenstein, I said to myself.

"You did sign it, didn't you?" the *Times* pressed.

"Sure," I lied.

"Do you want to make a comment?"

I confessed that it had been a while since I had seen the text, and he offered to read sections to me.

The letter was addressed to "Mr. President":

> We have been grateful for your concern and encouraged by your invitation to express some of our thoughts. . . . Growing numbers of our contemporaries are deeply troubled about the posture of their Government in Vietnam. . . . A great many . . . are torn by reluctance to participate in a war whose toll in property and life keeps escalating but about whose purpose and value to the United States they remain unclear. . . . Unless this conflict can be eased, the United States will find some of her most loyal and courageous young people choosing to go to jail rather than to bear their country's arms. . . . We hope you will find it possible to share your thoughts with us about these matters . . . and send our best wishes for the New Year.

"Well?" the reporter pushed. "What do you think?"

"It's too tame," I answered. "Frankly, I think it's much too respectful and doesn't go far enough. This dear Mr. President stuff is all bullshit."

On December 30, the *Times* ran a front-page account of the letter accompanied by the complete text. "Student Leaders Warn President of Doubts on War," the headlines explained. "100 at 100 Schools, Assert Some Loyal Youths May Prefer Jail to Fighting—U.S. GOALS QUES-TIONED—Collegians Write of Seeming 'Contradictions' Between State-ments and Actions." I was not quoted.

Several days later, I got a call from one of Allard's protégés. He said that "Johnson had taken the bait" and had agreed to have Dean Rusk, his Secretary of State, meet with a "small delegation" of the letter signers late in January. Since it was essential that such a delegation represent the "entire range of student opinion," I, the one "radical" out of the 100 student body presidents, had been selected to attend. This time, I agreed.

It would be my final involvement in any of Allard Lowenstein's stratagems.

In the meantime, Dennis Sweeney and I talked a lot about the draft. For both of us, the summer encounters with Mendy Samstein seemed to point the way. We were both convinced that, given an example to follow, thousands would willingly violate the Selective Service statutes.

Sweeney's faith in the notion was enormously reassuring, even though his approach to the draft had a very different starting place from my own. His classification was an exemption, not a deferment, and there was no possibility of his being drafted except for solely punitive reasons. For him, the question carried no immediate jeopardy, and his attraction to confronting Selective Service was as a way to recapture the "movement" he had been missing. Such a confrontation was real "work"; for both of us, conscription focused our urge to go whole hog.

My draft board soon responded as expected. On Thursday, January 12, 1967, they posted a notice to my parents' house, ordering me to report to the Fresno induction center for a preinduction physical examination.

The day the notice was mailed, I was the featured speaker at an antidraft rally on White Plaza in front of a low rock wall decorated with a sign saying "UNITE AND FIGHT THE DRAFT." About 400 students attended. I called on all of them to abandon their deferments: "You have no right to send others out to do your butchering." I also called on them to refuse to be drafted and "join me in jail." The time had come for "massive resistance." Dennis came up to me afterward. His hand was held out flat in front of him for me to slap.

The next day, Friday, January 13, my Selective Service orders arrived in the Fresno mail.

Nine days later, I took the bus to Fresno, stayed the night with my parents, and rose early to be at the induction center by the required 7 A.M. I can still remember how ominous that morning felt. It was foggy and cold, and I was frightened. A half block from my destination, I passed a dead dog. It was frozen stiff and lying with its legs straight up in the air.

At the induction center, all of us with physicals that morning were assembled in a large linoleum room with desks. First our names were called, and then we were each given medical forms to fill out. I finished mine quickly and looked around the room. There were farm boys there, greasers, junior college dropouts, and kids with nothing else to do, but I was the only Stanford student. I made no attempt to get acquainted with my fellow examinees.

Eventually, the sergeant in charge led us through a door and into another room the size of a small warehouse. It was lit with long racks of fluorescent bulbs and divided by partitions into a series of examination stations. Each station had a number, and the path we were to follow between them was marked by a line of luminescent footprints painted on the concrete floor. First, we stripped to our underwear.

Over the next six hours, I passed through every station without incident. The only thing at all different about my processing was the psychiatrist's office I was directed to after I put my clothes back on. Not everyone was sent there. The shrink was in uniform and his glasses were Army issue. His cubicle was the only one with a door. He told me to close it and then noted that I had answered the "use of drugs" question on my form by indicating I had smoked marijuana and ingested LSD.

"Yes, I have," I said.

He wanted to know if I thought that made me unfit to serve.

"No," I said, "I don't."

"Then why the hell did you write it down?" he snapped.

Without waiting for an answer, the psychiatrist stamped my examination papers and sent me on.

In the room where we had begun, the sergeant was standing behind a table near the street door, collecting our forms. He took mine and looked at the name.

"Harris?" he asked. "Ain't you the boy who's gonna refuse to go in the Army?"

I nodded silently and the sergeant began to chuckle.

"Well," he said, staring straight at the middle of my face, "we're gonna have to draft your ass into the Marines instead."

I swallowed hard. "In a million years," I answered through my beard.

The sergeant stopped smiling and handed me a form letter from Local Board 71 saying that I could expect to hear from them within a week. If found fit, I could plan on being inducted within the next three months.

Outside, the sun had come out, the dead dog had been carted off, and I felt as alone as I ever had.

In another week, I was in Washington, D.C.—courtesy of my former mentor, Allard Lowenstein—meeting with the Secretary of State, Dean Rusk.

I saw little of Lowenstein while there. Our only encounter was in a car with four other student body presidents on the way to Dean Rusk's. Allard produced a tie and insisted that I wear it, since I was the only president without one. At the State Department he said he would get back to us after the meeting was over, but that was the last I saw of him.

The student body presidents were taken up in the elevator to the sixth floor in groups of six, each group escorted by a uniformed security guard down a hallway carpeted with deep, blue pile and into a large, wood-paneled conference room. We waited the better part of an hour before Rusk appeared, preceded by a phalanx of eight plainclothes State Department security personnel. Four of them took up posts on either side of the Secretary's chair. The four others placed themselves in positions flanking the room's two doors. Then Dean Rusk walked in.

His ears were shaped like teacup handles, and he had age spots all over his head. When he talked, it was with an air of self-satisfaction.

Dean Rusk consumed most of the time allotted with a "briefing" on the "Vietnamese situation"; his manner showed that he clearly assumed this was something we should be grateful to get. The American effort had, he said, "turned the corner." Success against the "Communist infrastructure in South Vietnam" was proceeding, "stabilization of the countryside" was now "in sight." The recently resumed bombing of North Vietnam was yielding "great returns" in terms of "interdicted" logistics along "Communist supply lines." The "enemy," he assured us, was experiencing "great difficulties." It was, the Secretary said, only a matter of time before American presence would begin being curtailed. "The President," Rusk assured us, "has no desire to drag this out any longer than is absolutely necessary. He wants peace more than anyone else in the country."

All of this, Rusk pointed out with a biting look in our general direction, had been necessitated by "North Vietnamese aggression." It was the North Vietnamese who were "sending troops into their southern neighbors." It was, the Secretary continued with a motion of his hand on the tabletop to emphasize his point, the *North Vietnamese* who were supplying "tons of weapons and ammunition."

At this point, the Secretary of State paused to check his notes, and I interrupted. His hypocrisy incensed me.

"We aren't sending any weapons and ammunition there, are we?" I sniped. My sarcasm was pronounced.

Rusk looked up, snorted, and continued where he had left off. One of the security officers by the door came over to the wall behind my chair and stood there for the remainder of the Secretary's presentation. After fielding a few tame questions Dean Rusk rose and left the room, guards trailing after him.

Once the hallway was secure, we were all escorted out. I walked to the State Department steps with another president to smoke a cigarette while we waited for rides to the airport.

"What'd you think?" he asked.

"The man has no fucking shame," I said. "Only a whore would spout that kind of garbage."

Lowenstein stayed in D.C. for the remainder of that week. A meeting of antiwar clergy, theologians, and seminarians from around the country was scheduled for Washington, and Lowenstein made a two-hour presentation there.

Lowenstein began by pointing out the war's deficiencies as a purely practical venture. It was "unwinnable" as well as "unworthy" of the sacrifices being demanded. The government was "lying" about how well things were going, Allard argued. The "mainstream of America" wanted out of Vietnam; to substantiate this point, Lowenstein cited the recent letter by a hundred student body presidents to Lyndon Johnson and hinted that more such statements from "moderate and responsible Americans" were on their way.

The best option the peace movement had, he said, was at the ballot box. Given the right presidential election strategy, the Democratic party could be forced to repudiate the war. He claimed, "Lyndon Johnson himself could be defeated" and the country "rescued."

At the time, such a prediction seemed pure fantasy, and while the audience appreciated Lowenstein, few took his words seriously. For his part, their doubts only made Allard more sure. Within little more than a year, that belief would put a visible elbow in the course of history and, in the process, make him one of the more influential Democrats in the country, the political system's widely proclaimed "bridge" to the nation's "disaffected" youth, and ultimately a member of Congress from the State of New York.

A notice from Local Board 71 that I had been found physically fit to serve was waiting for me back in California.

Despite having expected the notification, it threw me into something of a panic. Fresh with visions of leading an antidraft uprising, I did not want my personal question to be put to me this soon, so I immediately appealed the classification to buy time and filed a form from a Stanford student health center physician saying I had a prostate infection. Local Board 71 wrote back within a week, reclassifying me as 1-Y, temporarily unfit, and putting me on notice that I would be scheduled for another preinduction physical after six months.

By now, Dennis Sweeney and I were having a discussion about the draft almost every day. I rationalized requesting a 1-Y, despite my professed "noncooperation," as a compromise that was necessary to ensure that I wouldn't be just an isolated personal witness. I wanted to use my act to build a movement, I said. Dennis reinforced my notion. I shouldn't worry about it, he said. Building a movement was of overriding importance. He was, Sweeney said, now prepared to join such an effort himself. He said that if I was ready to devote myself full time to organizing noncooperation with the Selective Service, he was too.

The only thing standing between me and that total devotion was the demand of my official duties as student body president, and I was now thinking seriously of resigning the office. The issues it encompassed were petty, I thought. Other men my age were dying in rice paddies 5,000 miles from home.

By the time I had leveraged my momentary reprieve out of Local Board 71, the story of NSA and the Central Intelligence Agency was on the newsstands, and the *New York Times*, the *Washington Post*, and the rest of the nation's dominant publications and news services had joined in the hunt for CIA revelations.

As it turned out, the agency had used the foundation gambit to funnel secret funds into a number of constituencies besides college students, including the American Newspaper Guild, the American Council for the International Commission of Jurists, the American Federation of State, County, and Municipal Employees, and the National Education Association.

With all the digging going on, the chronology of the NSA-CIA connection had also been clarified. According to a *Washington Post–L.A. Times* News Service story, the first known approach by the agency to anyone in the NSA hierarchy occurred before Allard Lowenstein had been elected NSA president, in the summer of 1950. It was allegedly made to one of the organization's senior staff at a time when NSA hoped to send delegations to world student conferences in Prague in August and another in Stockholm in December, but was having no success raising the necessary cash. A friend of the staff member called one day out of the blue and said some money "might be available." The friend and two other men subsequently drove the staffer for a ride on a lonely country road outside Madison, Wisconsin, where NSA's headquarters were then located. After being sworn to secrecy, the young NSA staffer was told that money enough to send the entire Prague delegation would be forthcoming from the CIA. "I was delighted," the staffer later told a reporter. "I thought it was a great coup." Few, if any, other people in the delegation knew the identity of the donor.

In the 1967 press investigation, one of the sources of information as to the presence of possibly tainted money around NSA at that time was Allard Lowenstein, who had been elected NSA president at the 1950 congress and then had led the international delegation to Stockholm that winter. On a New York City radio show in February 1967, Allard stated categorically that during his tenure, NSA "was not involved in any relationship with the CIA" and had "neither sought nor accepted any funds" from the agency or "any foundations." He himself had no knowledge of what was going on until consulted by a group of present NSA officers, "several months" prior to the *Ramparts* article.

Lowenstein then added that at one point in his NSA tenure, there had, however, been what seemed a "suspicious" offer. It came prior to the Stockholm conference, when, once again, NSA was short the necessary travel funds. At that point he was allegedly "told" that "money was available." Allard claimed that when he then asked where the funds would come from, he was told "Don't inquire." Lowenstein recalled that he rejected the offer and added that for all he knew, "It might have been [from] the Communist party." He had, Allard was careful to note, paid his own way to Stockholm.

Lowenstein did not mention that the speech he had subsequently given at the Stockholm Conference had drastically altered the format of international student politics. Up until then, the principal arena for student politicking had been the International Union of Students (IUS), a group NSA considered "Communist-dominated." At Stockholm, Lowenstein proposed abandoning the IUS and starting a new "International Students Organization" as an alternative body and met with considerable response.

Lowenstein's term as NSA president ended before the new body was formalized, but the students who took his idea and ran with it were quickly successful. The eventual organization was called the International Student Conference (ISC), and its rapid growth paralleled NSA's. Like NSA, in 1967 ISC was revealed to have taken immense contributions from alleged CIA foundations.

Lowenstein's speech in Stockholm, which eventually led to the creation of the CIA-tainted ISC, had become a hot issue among the delegates to the 1951 NSA congress. Allard said later, in an unpublished 1974 interview, that his proposal had so "outraged" the NSA's left, at the time largely composed of Henry Wallace Democrats and young Communist party types, that the leftists ran a student from Swarthmore as Lowenstein's successor who promised to ignore the previous president's Stockholm call for a new International Students Organization. Incumbents were not allowed to succeed themselves, so Allard threw his support behind one William T. "Bill" Dentzer, a fellow liberal. Dentzer was a friend, and Allard had even served as an usher at Dentzer's wedding.

When the press began unraveling NSA history, it was this William T. Dentzer who was identified as the first NSA president to formalize any relationship with the Central Intelligence Agency.

"Curiously enough," Allard would comment in 1974, "Dentzer never confided in me after his election."

Although Lowenstein never seemed to have any doubts that the CIA's penetration dated from the NSA tenure of his onetime friend, he never thought Dentzer initiated the connection. The man he would hold responsible for that was one Avrea Ingram, NSA's vice president for international affairs from 1951 to 1952 and again from 1952 to 1953. Allard always considered Ingram to have been the operative in the situation and remembered Ingram's election as one of the most "curious" he had ever experienced.

As Lowenstein recalled it, the popular choice of the congress for international vice president in 1951 was another person, a woman with whom Allard had once had what he described as "a romance." She arrived at the congress fresh from an international conference in Rio de Janeiro and delivered a very dramatic speech full of "lurid tales of Communist student terror in the streets," provoking a movement to draft her for the international affairs vice presidency. According to Allard, she had the support of 80 percent of the delegates and "could have easily been elected if she had wanted it." Instead, in a tearful scene at the microphone, she declined the nomination in favor of Ingram, a relative unknown in NSA who had not been, in Allard's description, a "student leader" and had "just appeared" at this congress. Several other people whose names were mentioned in opposition to Ingram's did the same thing, making Allard wonder if the real reason for her declining the nomination hadn't been the CIA's "preference for Ingram." He would also wonder whether, despite their intimacy, "she had kept her CIA contact from me." The one sure thing, Lowenstein said, was that Ingram himself could not possibly have been "the spontaneous choice of the congress voters."

In any case Ingram won and, along with Bill Dentzer, oversaw the first splices between the United States National Student Association and the CIA. Ingram stayed two years at NSA and then went on to work as the associate secretary of the coordinating secretariat of the International Student Conference, headquartered in Leyden, Holland, until October 1956, when he suddenly rushed to Vienna at the time of the Hungarian uprising and became an ISC "field worker," assigned to help the "student–freedom fighters" fleeing Hungary to resettle in the West. Bill Dentzer had also worked for ISC after NSA and had then gone on to United States Aid for International Development (USAID), for whom he was running a Peruvian mission at the time the NSA scandal broke. Lowenstein and his former friend, Dentzer, ran into each other in 1970 and had an exchange of questions and answers, in which, Allard claimed, Dentzer corroborated Allard's theory that Ingram was the man who initiated it all.

By then, of course, Avrea Ingram had long since ceased to be available for questioning. After his brief stint in Vienna, he had returned to New York City and begun working as a "research consultant" to the executive director of the Foundation for Youth and Student Affairs, one of NSA and ISC's principal financial backers. On February 5, 1957, ten years before the *Ramparts* article appeared, a maid found Ingram's nude body on the floor of his hotel room with a leather belt looped around his neck and tied to the knob of the desk drawer. According to the city medical examiner, the death was "asphyxia by hanging" with indications of suicide. Bill Dentzer was among those who attended Ingram's funeral in Anniston, Alabama; while he was there he allegedly told Ingram's father and uncle that he himself was a CIA agent and that the deceased Avrea had also "served his country in intelligence work."

When Bill Dentzer's friend and predecessor, Allard Lowenstein, was questioned in 1974 as to why, being as close as he was to some of the main players in the initial CIA liaison, he still had not been included in their plans, Allard would speculate that "they considered me uncontrollable" and hence "unreliable" to include in their secrets. By then, Lowenstein was used to being "smeared" with the NSA scandal and would quickly buttress his own innocence with an oft-recited string of evidence. He had, he would point out, never been asked to sit on any NSA boards or advisory committees after his own presidency, even those of the most honorary sort. He added that it was no secret to anyone familiar with NSA that, over the years, it was precisely those international types now known to have been CIA contacts who were most conspicuously "hostile" toward Allard's annual meddling in the organization.

No allegations of direct CIA involvement would ever be made about Allard Lowenstein in print, but despite that clean record, suspicions about Allard and "the fellas" remained a nagging question among the young people who knew or were influenced by him in the course of his life. Among the considerable number of those who ended up to Lowenstein's political left, "CIA" would be one of the principal epithets cast in his direction.

I can remember riding with Dennis Sweeney in my car shortly after the NSA story broke. He was smoking a cigarette and, after a while, noticed the copy of *Ramparts* on the seat between us. The cover announced "the truth about the CIA and the National Student Association." Dennis ground his teeth and snorted smoke through his nose.

"Lowenstein," he grunted, slapping the *Ramparts* with his hand.

The one-word statement came out with the air of something so obvious as to require no further explanation.

The NSA scandal dovetailed neatly with the paranoia of the age; deserved or not, the further collapse of Allard Lowenstein's reputation among those to his political left was a natural outgrowth of the process. It was, Allard claimed, a matter of "guilt by association."

Among former protégés, however, the inclination to suspect Allard was, ironically enough, abetted by their having known and once worshipped him. The image of Lowenstein implanted during protégé-hood did not jibe easily with his explanation of NSA events. This Lowenstein, though admittedly "suspicious" about NSA's financing, had supposedly for 15 years passively accepted being kept in the dark, despite being well positioned to pursue additional information. Further, his attachment to and involvement in the organization was one of the central facts about him, and it was hard to believe things went on there that he didn't know about.

For Dennis Sweeney, all of those generalized doubts were reinforced by his own history with Lowenstein:

• The year Dennis and Allard met as freshman and assistant dean of men, Lowenstein had campaigned for returning Stanford to NSA, praising the organization lavishly and even singling out NSA's "international work" as especially worthy, all at a time when he would later claim that the people in charge of that "international work" were at their most "hostile" to him.

• As a consequence of the efforts to return Stanford to NSA, several of the organization's officers had visited the campus during Allard's year as assistant dean of men. Among other things, they had recruited students to serve as delegates to the 1962 World Youth Festival in Helsinki. Held every three years, the festival was considered "Communist-dominated," and NSA was trying to make "the other side" heard. Allard recommended to those who sought his advice that they go. Those without the money for travel were offered grants from something called the Independent Research Service. Allard also recommended that students avail themselves of this assistance. In the spring of 1967, the *New York Times* revealed that the Independent Research Service had been a funnel for CIA funds.

• The SNCC people whom Dennis respected immensely had all long ago come to similar "intelligence" conclusions about Allard. Typically, James Forman wrote in his book, *The Making of Black Revolutionaries*, "Allard Lowenstein popped up while we were in Dar es Salaam, like a sudden nightmare. We assumed that he was there on behalf of the State Department or the Central Intelligence Agency."

• In Lowenstein's final attempt to win Dennis back from SNCC in 1965, he had urged his disillusioned protégé to cancel his planned movie venture in Natchez and attend the World Youth Festival in Algiers instead. Allard had given him the name of a man to contact about having his expenses covered; in 1967 that man turned out to be the Independent Research Service's director. When IRS collapsed in the wake of revelations, this director immediately went on to the USAID mission in Vietnam, a notorious outpost of agency types.

• Sweeney was also a friend of the former Stanford protégé who had run the Committee for Free Elections headquarters in Santo Domingo. By virtue of that connection, Dennis quite likely had heard of Lowenstein's deal with Ellsworth Bunker and also knew something about the Institute for International Labor Research's role in the Dominican Republic. Among the foundations now known to have been involved with the CIA was the IILR's principal funder, the J. M. Kaplan Fund. In this instance in particular, images of unknowing collaboration were hard for Dennis to accept. Unlike the rest of the CIA information, which didn't emerge until 1967, the news about the J. M. Kaplan Fund's connection had been accidentally released to the press in 1964 by a congressional investigation of tax-exempt foundations. Having seen Allard read each and every *New York Times* cover to cover, it was hard to believe he didn't know of the IILR's background when he joined up with its former members in the Committee for Free Elections in the Dominican Republic.

Viewed as courtroom evidence, Sweeney's suspicions were hardly the stuff from which an indictment, much less a conviction, could be fashioned, but they were sufficient for Dennis Sweeney. He would be convinced of Allard's connection to the CIA for the rest of his life. Eventually magnified by madness, this conclusion would help turn Dennis homicidal.

In 1967 as throughout his life, Lowenstein responded to such criticism from the left by labeling it the usual "distorted and dishonest rubbish" that was always slung at him from that direction. The New Left, he explained, needed to "villainize" him. They wanted young people to abandon the political system, and he was the strongest voice against such a move, the one liberal who could persuade students to save the system by using it to change things.

During the third week of February, while the NSA story was still hot, Hubert Humphrey, Vice President of the United States, visited Stanford and spoke at Memorial Auditorium. The event proved to be a landmark in Stanford students' expressions of disrespect for authority. Both Dennis and I were participants. The uproar began when a large antiwar crowd showed up, only to find that, whereas the administration had promised that seating at the event would be on a first-come-first-served basis, in fact half of the auditorium had been roped off for selected "dignitaries" from the faculty, administration, and alumni. As a consequence, several hundred of the antiwar crowd, myself and Dennis included, were forced to remain on the front steps while the campus's prowar element, who arrived after us, went inside. Broadcast speakers had been erected at both entrances to the building, so we waited on the steps and listened.

Humphrey's opening remarks ignored the war altogether. Instead, he said he wanted to address the "now generation" about "the Great Society and the role of students today." The Vice President vowed that people with the opportunity to wipe out poverty and hunger "could not and will not pause." Though, he admitted, there were those in government who did pause, "this is not a pause that refreshes, but the pause that retrenches." The joke drew scattered laughs and then fell flat. "There should be more change," the Vice President continued, but it should be "reasoned."

The questions from a faculty panel led to more of the same. When asked to characterize President Johnson's war policy, Humphrey said, "President Johnson is a man of restraint. He seeks to apply power to a limited objective."

Outside, the remark drew howls.

When asked about whether he, Humphrey, had rejected his liberal principles by supporting the administration policy, Humphrey denied the suggestion angrily.

Outside on the steps, people grumbled and made impolite gestures at the portable speakers.

Finally, in a long, convoluted question, someone asked the Vice President to explain the academic community's enchantment with John Kennedy, in sharp contrast to their disillusionment with Lyndon Johnson. Humphrey replied, "I never have found out." He added that if Jack Kennedy were alive today, he would be doing the same things in Vietnam as LBJ. At that point, some 250 people in the audience rose from their seats and silently walked out.

When the walkout faction joined the group on the steps outside where Dennis and I were, everybody broke up into spontaneous conversations about how to greet Humphrey's eventual exit. The Secret Service men on the steps were eyeing us nervously, and a detachment of county sheriffs was waiting in the lobby. As we saw it, Humphrey's limousine would have to be pulled up to one of two places. Both the front and back steps of the building opened onto streets. The only other exit was a huge sliding door designed for the movement of stage sets from the loading dock on the auditorium's south side. Beyond the loading dock was a vacant lot dotted with broad-leafed trees. Across it, sixty yards away, was a third street. The crowd split itself fairly evenly between the two sets of street doors. So did the Secret Service.

By a quarter to one, the speech was over. Dennis and I were outside the back door with about two hundred other students, but Humphrey was first sighted at an upstairs window on the opposite side of the building. The crowd there immediately surged toward the window shouting, "Shame, shame," and he disappeared. The rear auditorium doors then sprang open, a phalanx of sheriffs and Secret Servicemen charged out to seal off the walkway, and a limousine squealed up to the curb. The crowd pressed forward, but no one appeared. More than a minute was spent waiting before someone looked behind us in the vacant lot. There, halfway across the open space, was Hubert Humphrey, flanked by two security personnel and moving at a fast walk. Another limo was waiting on the street in that direction.

The crowd immediately began sprinting into the lot after him, Dennis Sweeney and David Harris included. Humphrey's convoy accelerated as best they were able, but the Vice President could only get his pace up to a wobbling trot and no faster. His head was tilted back so his jaw cleared his neck, and his arms jerked in circles next to his stomach. We gained on him rapidly. Dennis was at the front edge of the pack, a dozen yards ahead of me. When it became apparent we had a chance of catching Humphrey, I slowed, unwilling to risk that scene.

Sweeney and the others accelerated. Humphrey threw himself in the waiting car door, a Secret Service agent jumped in on top of him, and Dennis and three others caught the long black Cadillac just as it cleared the curb. As the automobile picked up speed, they ran along its rear fenders, shouting "murderer" and pounding on the trunk with their fists. Dennis Sweeney was the last to stop chasing when it finally pulled away. By then, he was laughing so hard his sides hurt.

Two days later, I resigned the presidency of the Associated Students of Stanford University in order to tackle the draft full time. I sat down at my typewriter and composed a letter dated February 22 and addressed to "the students of Stanford University." It read in part:

> I have done all I am capable of for the realization of education at Stanford. I feel my contribution in the context of the presidency has been made. A response to the questions I have raised over the length of my term remains in the hands of the community.
>
> David Harris

The letter caught everyone by surprise. The banner headline across the front page of the next morning's *Daily* declared, "Harris Resigns Presidency."

I still have a crumbling copy of that *Daily* issue. It is important to me that I won not just notoriety but respect as well. I suppose I saved that paper as proof. "Career of Commitment" one headline said. "He Broke Fresh Ground" another said. "He's been [President] long enough," the dean of the chapel commented, "for all of us to see his real stature, his authentic qualities of greatness. . . . All of us, and all of Stanford, and the whole college and university scene in America are better for having had him where he's been."

Those comments remain as flattering as any ever to appear about me in print. They were not, however, enough to make me regret resigning. I was glad to be rid of the mantle of student body president and anxious to join the ranks of free-lance "agitators" instead.

Six days later, I turned 21.

A week after my birthday, at 8 A.M. on a Saturday morning, Dennis Sweeney and I met at Cooley Street with two Berkeley students named Lenny and Steve. The idea we all discussed was clear-cut: set a date on which people all over the country would gather to publicly return their draft cards to the government and forswear all further cooperation. Such an action would call the question on the peace movement, forcing it to escalate its opposition and challenge the government's power in no uncertain terms. All that was needed was an organization to put the movement together.

The strategy we had hit upon was, oddly enough, laid out as a hypothetical circumstance in a *New York Times* column within a few weeks of our discussion. "If the Johnson Administration had to prosecute 100,000 Americans in order to maintain its authority," the column noted, "its real power to pursue the Vietnamese war or any other policy would be crippled if not destroyed. It would then be faced not with dissent but with civil disobedience on a scale amounting to revolt." The columnist went on to say that "given the difficulties of organization and the personal and social dangers to all involved," such a movement was "unlikely to develop at all."

We planned to prove his conclusion hasty, but at that moment in March we had little to show for our confidence except bravado. The name we chose for our newborn organization illustrated the attitude. Henceforth, our notion of revolt was formalized as "The Resistance." Even at its inception, when we were only four students in California with no resources, we spelled the name with a capital T.

The Resistance's first public attempt to expand itself was a leaflet distributed in April and headlined "We Refuse to Serve":

> We will renounce all deferments and refuse to cooperate
> with the draft in any manner, at any level. . . . The War in
> Vietnam is criminal and we must act together, at great
> individual risk, to stop it. Those involved must lead the
> American people, by their example, to understand the
> enormity of what their government is doing. . . . To cooperate
> with conscription is to perpetuate its existence, without which
> the government could not wage war. We have chosen to
> openly defy the draft and confront the government and its
> war directly.
> This is no small decision in a person's life. Each one
> realizes that refusing to cooperate with selective service may
> mean prison. . . . To do anything but this is to effectively abet
> the war. . . . We prefer to resist.

That March, the four of us pictured ourselves as shock troops. As Lenny from Berkeley put it, "Most people who claim to be in the opposition just aren't doing anything. Maybe handing out leaflets, maybe giving moral support . . . Well that simply isn't enough. The only way out is the hard way. That means incurring personal risks. That means attacking the machine with your minds, your bodies, and inevitably with your lives."

Each of us had reached that position along our own lines of reasoning.

Dennis Sweeney explained the politics behind his stand in a short statement written the following summer.

> Our lives and our politics will lead only to the despair, fear
> and impotence we see in the American mind unless we
> develop a resistance which takes into account the deep roots
> of authoritarianism and militarism in the institutions
> surrounding us. . . . I choose to refuse to cooperate with
> Selective Service because it is the only honest, whole, and
> human response I can make to the military institution which
> demands the allegiance of my life. . . . The price America
> exacts for refusing to cooperate is a maximum of five years in
> federal prison. But the price America exacts this instant in
> Vietnam from an uncooperative peasant is life itself. My
> sacrifice is very small in comparison.

The personal side of his decision was explained in much shorter bits and pieces. "I was looking for people I wanted to work with," Dennis told one friend, "and this seemed to be the issue where I could find them." For the person in him, The Resistance was a setting in which to belong, and in that, he had a lot of company. There was, as I would later explain to an inquiring historian, "a sense of intimacy between us [in The Resistance] which, whether we articulated it or not . . . was the basis of our organization. . . . Part of it was reinforcement of ourselves, and part of it was instinctively feeling that the closeness had to be there for the thing to function."

In March 1967, there was no sense that closeness would ever end. Sweeney was as important to that feeling as anyone. We all thought we were facing stiff consequences, and we all saw Dennis as the kind of person you could count on, however tight things got down the line. For a while, Dennis would flourish in the role, but that, like the rest of it, would not last.

Allard Lowenstein's act seemed to be wearing thin that Spring. He was now 38 years old, and other people his age or older were becoming much freer with their advice that he drop his role of vagabond organizer of good causes and "establish" himself.

One friend wrote later, "By April of 1967, very few people took Lowenstein seriously. His older friends like Norman Thomas . . . gave him Polonius-like lectures about getting a steady job, starting to wear a suit and tie, and stop hanging around with twenty-year-old students. When he tried to explain that he had this new project to deny the President renomination, they smiled and wished him good luck."

Around the same time, a New York–based journalist doing a story on Martin Luther King, Jr., had an interview with Lowenstein over lunch. The two men had first met ten years earlier, through a mutual friend. At that time, Lowenstein had been introduced as "(a) the oldest student leader in America and (b) someone who knows everyone in America." Lowenstein spent the entire time talking about "the role of the moderate left in trying to dominate the opposition to the war."

As a result of that interview, the journalist was invited over to Lowenstein's apartment on West Eighty-second Street later in the week. It was, he would later write, "an extraordinary evening. Norman Thomas, almost blind, is there, and so is Frank Graham, former North Carolina Senator who was successfully red-baited years ago. . . . Mrs. Lowenstein, young, quite pretty, quite confused, quite pregnant, is there, as well as about twenty students, none of whom know each other. It is the mark of a Lowenstein gathering that no one knows anyone else, but everyone knows Lowenstein; they all get together to share the common goal, which is whatever Lowenstein dictates."

Also typical of a Lowenstein evening, Allard himself was three hours late. When he finally arrived, he convinced everyone to accompany him to a West Side Reform Democratic meeting, where he was scheduled to speak. The topic was, of course, his new idea.

Though Lowenstein was impressively articulate, the journalist was anything but sold. "It seems very vague," he wrote, "and somehow Lowenstein is hard for me to take seriously; I have the same reservations about him that I have about Humphrey, that he is somehow intellectually promiscuous, that he jumps around from cause to cause, that all liberal causes are equal, that he is somehow the perpetual student leader, that there is a lack of toughness and discipline in him." Doubts, however, only seemed to egg Allard on.

Johnson will be beaten, he told Reform Democrats. The politicians were wrong about the situation. The presidential nomination is up in the air. Action now, at this critical time, could turn the tide.

When his speech was over, Lowenstein asked for volunteers. According to the journalist, "A few put their hands up."

8

To describe the notion of denying renomination to incumbent Lyndon Johnson as "Allard's idea" connotes exclusive authorship, which is less than accurate. In fact, the strategy first took root in a series of meetings in New York City that included a cross section of active liberals. But besides Allard, the only one of them who would end up having a major hand in bringing the idea to fruition was Curtis Gans, a friend of Lowenstein's from his graduate-student days at UNC in the late 1950s. He and Gans had met on opposite sides in a student political campaign then and joined forces in various local and national liberal enterprisès after it was over. At the time of the New York discussions, Gans was editing the house magazine of Americans for Democratic Action (ADA), the nation's dominant liberal organization.

Lowenstein initially advocated running civil rights leader Martin Luther King as a third-party candidate, while Gans argued for staying inside the Democratic party and challenging Johnson directly in the primaries. When it was learned that King would not be amenable to the third-party enterprise, Allard went over to Gans's position, though whatever stance he or the others assumed seemed of little larger consequence.

In the spring of 1977, Lyndon Johnson's presidential popularity was still at its highest level. Some 435,000 American soldiers were serving in the Vietnam theater, and, according to the government, light was visible at the tunnel's end. The war in Southeast Asia was going "well" and "according to plan." Though such "progress" was invisible on the home front, the popular urge to "support our boys" by expressing faith in both the President and his policy still seemed an irresistible political current.

That it was not irresistible would eventually be demonstrated by the idea incubating between Allard Lowenstein and Curtis Gans. When their scheme matured and went public, it was dubbed the "Dump Johnson" campaign. Lowenstein later claimed never to have liked the name.

"I considered it far too discourteous," he would explain. "'Stop Johnson' was as far as I ever went."

A day of peace marches in New York City and San Francisco on April 15 provided one of the first signals that antiwar sentiment might be broad enough eventually to wield electoral clout. In New York, more than 100,000 people participated, many of them noticeably "middle class and professional." San Francisco's march numbered over 75,000. The biggest single constituency at both, however, still remained people under 25. Dennis Sweeney, myself, a reporter from *Esquire* magazine doing a story about me, and the rest of the Peace and Liberation Commune all marched in San Francisco and distributed copies of *We Refuse to Serve*. By then, we had set October 16, 1967, as the date for our first national draft-card return.

The march's rallying point was San Francisco's Kezar Stadium, and I was one of the speakers. Seagulls were perched in the upper reaches of the stadium and fog was rolling in off the ocean. I told the crowd that talk was cheap. The time had come to put our lives where our mouths were. "We are mistaken if we call this war Johnson's war or Congress's war," I said. "This war is a logical extension of the way America has chosen to live. As young people facing that war, as people who are confronted with the choice of being in that war or not, we have an obligation to speak to this country, and that statement has to be made this way: that this war will not be made in our names, that this war will not be made with our hands, that we will not carry the rifles to butcher the Vietnamese people, and that the prisons of the United States will be full of young people who will not honor the orders of murder."

Afterward, all the commune marchers drove back to Cooley Street, high off having announced our existence. Out of that April march, The Resistance doubled its numbers and founded new chapters in both San Francisco and San Jose.

A llard Lowenstein did not participate in the April 15 marches, but two weeks later, a letter surfaced from 1,000 seminarians to the Secretary of Defense, asking, in the words of the *New York Times* headline, for an "Easing of Draft." Specifically, they asked for changing the conscription laws to permit "conscientious objection to a particular war." Such a change, they argued, would relieve the "dilemma" faced by "those law-abiding young Americans whose conscience would not permit them to fight in Vietnam."

In the course of putting this letter together, Lowenstein formalized an apparatus he called the Campus Coordinating Committee. It amounted to two seminarians with a WATS line and an office at Union Theological Seminary who agreed, once their own letter had been published, to do the work in putting together yet another. Allard, as the *Times* indicated, gave "advice on wording and suggestions about how to assemble signatures." At the same time, Allard and Gans were continuing to hatch Dump Johnson. The state of their thinking was reflected in an article ghostwritten by Gans that spring and later run in the July issue of ADA's magazine. The article said in part:

> Having largely failed in the attempt to give loyal counsel to a Democratic President, the liberal community's . . . strength to bring about a change in policies rests precisely on its ability to remain independent. . . . The most effective initial strategy must be for liberals to work within the Democratic Party . . . and organization should begin in preliminary form for a primary challenge to Johnson. Hopefully this can be accomplished by a national candidate of stature who might run in opposition to Johnson, but if not it could well be done through local candidates . . . willing to oppose him in the primary. . . .
>
> Most importantly, Liberals must begin to act now. For at stake are not only the present policies in Vietnam but the political future of the next decade. . . . If there is to be an end to the political polarization that threatens to strain the very foundations of American democracy, it is for the liberal movement to begin to pose another option.

That the "option" eventually posed would be overwhelmingly credited to Allard Lowenstein seems, in retrospect, almost preordained. His attributes meshed perfectly with the task. To pull it off would require a unique combination of widespread connections at the lower echelons of the Democratic Party where the President's influence would be least felt and a large student constituency to provide the credibility of youthful allegiance plus the foot soldiers to flesh out an electoral effort. At the same time, strong ties to the Party leadership were needed to be able to coax a major political figure into the arena against an incumbent President. Allard Lowenstein possessed all those resources and may very well have been the only single individual in the country who did.

On top of that, Lowenstein had the energy to keep all his resources in constant motion.

In May, Allard visited Stanford again and made two campus speaking appearances, neither of which Dennis Sweeney or I attended.

The first was headlined in the *Stanford Daily* as "Lowenstein Urges Viet War De-Escalation." According to the campus paper, Allard got his biggest laugh when he referred to Lyndon Johnson's public image as a "great gale of political halitosis coming out of the White House." In response to a question about the 1968 presidential elections, Lowenstein "expressed the hope" that "a Democrat other than Lyndon Johnson" might win, but gave no indications that he would be involved in that process himself.

The second appearance, a day later, was an "informal" debate between Lowenstein and a State Department official then serving as Stanford's "diplomat in residence." Allard claimed, "The United States does not want to negotiate an honorable peace."

"There are never any simple solutions," the diplomat responded.

Afterwards, Lowenstein left for Berkeley, where Martin Luther King was giving an address on Vietnam. He had the student driving him stop off at Cooley Street in East Palo Alto. Allard said hello in a bashful way and asked for his box of *Brutal Mandate* back. I fetched the books from a closet, and he left within two minutes of his arrival. It was three years before I saw him again.

In Berkeley, a crowd of some 5,000 students and faculty gathered for King's speech. Allard was among the people at the back of the crowd, many of whom were sitting in trees to get a better view. The journalist who had been at his apartment in March encountered him there and suggested they have dinner, but Lowenstein said he had to fly off to Oregon that afternoon for "meetings." Allard claimed he was just passing through "to give some focus to dissent on Vietnam."

"It's tough," Allard offered. "These kids. No one really knows how alienated they really are. Trying to keep them in the system is very, very hard. They're bitter and they're angry. They really resent this society. Of course," he added, "there are a lot of things in this society that are very resentable."

There can be little doubt that Dennis Sweeney, myself, and the remainder of the Peace and Liberation Commune were examples of Lowenstein's notion of "alienated kids." For our part, we saw ourselves as young heroes in open revolt, and it was, for all of us, an exhilarating experience.

That feeling was responsible for the growth of the commune in the first months of 1967 until it included a dozen people in three different houses, two in East Palo Alto and a third, half an hour away up the side of the nearby Santa Cruz mountains. The membership spanned the spectrum of interests rampant among our sort of young people that spring. At one end were aspiring Buddhists, with diets of brown rice, meditation as a regular ritual, and various other attempts to fine-tune their karma. On the other end were the organizers, consumed by politics and the expression of moral outrage on a grand scale. In 1967, both ends still got along.

The more political position was represented by the tiny two-bedroom cottage on East Palo Alto's Glen Way where Dennis and I now lived. The Resistance was everything to both of us then.

Strategically, I was the organization's principal source of visibility and we spent much of the spring trying to take advantage of it. We were the two parts to a political dog-and-pony show, traveling to all the university, college, and junior college campuses in northern California. I gave the speech and afterward, he and I huddled with anyone interested in discussing noncooperation and October 16 further.

According to a number of people who observed us in action that spring, we were remarkable for our "commitment" and seemed to feed on the intensity of the conflict we had marked out for ourselves.

"To choose Resistance," I told a crowd of about 300 in Berkeley shortly after Allard headed for the Northwest, "means that there are no longer simply issues, there are no longer simply problems to argue solutions to. Beyond innuendo and beyond observation and conclusion, there is an act with the totality of our lives against the machines of the state. The act begins with a refusal to cooperate with conscription. As long as America continues to mean oppression, the act has no end."

The immediate instrument I pictured as carrying on that endless struggle was, on the face of it, a fairly straggly-looking assemblage. Late that spring, the Peace and Liberation Commune arranged itself along the length of the immense fallen tree in the Cooley Street backyard for a group photograph: one black man, one Hawaiian, two Jews, and nine Wasps in a wide variety of styles, shapes, and sizes. At the time the picture was taken, we all expected to be arrested and imprisoned within the next year and a half.

I was seated in front of the tree in a wooden chair stolen from a Stanford lecture hall. By now, I had shaved my facial hair down to a moustache, and my hair itself was long enough to be swept back from my forehead. I was wearing dark aviator glasses, Levis, cowboy boots, and a khaki work shirt. One of the Commune dogs was sitting in my lap. On my right, Timmy had assumed the full lotus position on a rataan coffee table. He was dressed in Levis and a T-shirt with Hindu writing on it, and his hair flowed down his back. Stuart, a veteran of the 1966 NSA Congress, was leaning against the base of the trunk on my left. He wore Levis, a dark green janitor's shirt, and wire-rimmed glasses.

Dennis Sweeney sat on the upper portion of the collapsed tree, at the opposite end of the picture. Rodney, the one Commune black, who had once played bass in a rock 'n roll band while living in the Haight, was on his left. He had the nappy beginnings of an Afro and wore a loose velour musician's shirt with his Levis. On Sweeney's right was Robert, a former MIT student, wearing a cowboy hat, climbing boots, Levis, and a work shirt with blue pinstripes. Dennis himself was wearing his usual clean and faded Levis, Frye boots, a plaid Pendleton shirt, and a black velvet jacket styled long. His hair was cut in an early Beatle look with the top half of the ear covered and bangs combed straight down over the forehead. He was not smiling.

Nor were any of the rest of us. Instead, the group exhibited a grim pride in being the shock troops of the new age. All the mouths were set, and the stares were direct.

Fourteen years later, the thirteen men in the picture were to become a veterinary technician, a contractor, a preschool teacher, a journalist, an international expert on the soybean, a fundamentalist preacher, a chiropractor, a successful bookstore owner, a musician and bit actor in feature films, a factory worker, a printer, a nuclear research technician, and one free-lance carpenter so demented as to be homicidal.

Dennis's prized possession of the time was a Gibson guitar given to him by his old Mississippi friend J.D., the previous fall, and his attachment to it signaled a broadening of his self-image. Sweeney learned how to play the instrument with the help of several of the commune's more proficient guitarists and now fancied himself an aspiring musician as well as organizer. The internal issue facing Dennis Sweeney was always securing avenues of release, and his newfound immersion in music was as close to an outlet as he would ever manage. He wanted to be good and spent all his spare moments sitting in the Glen Way house, practicing chords over and over and over and over and over.

Sweeney had mastered several songs by the end of May. His

favorite was a folk number called "Joshua Gone Barbados," about a strike in the Caribbean by cane cutters whose principal organizer sold the strikers out for money and position. Dennis played it again and again for at least a month. When he finally sang it in front of others, his hands were slow on the neck of the guitar, and he often jumped between chords late and had to pause to let his instrument catch up with the verse he was singing.

When not chasing after music or serving as the backup man at my recruiting speeches, Dennis was in charge of *Resist*, our monthly Resistance newsletter. The first issue was mimeographed in April and included a picture of David Harris, the former Stanford student body president who had become a draft resister.

By May, The Resistance began receiving its first hate mail. The head of the Los Angeles region of Students for a Democratic Society, the nation's best-known "radical" organization, tore my picture out of the issue, drew bars across it, lettered the caption "jailbird" on the margin, and mailed it back. I was surprised to get that kind of response from SDS, but Dennis claimed not to be.

He said it figured that they would be threatened by our action. Their position in the vanguard of the movement, earned without engaging in personal risk, was being challenged by our upping the ante. We would, Sweeney predicted, see a shitload of such flak from that direction before October 16 came off.

Throughout The Resistance, Dennis Sweeney had something of a knack for predictions, and this was one of several that came true. We would have to argue with our fellow "radicals" all spring and summer long. They thought we were being "martyrs" and said The Resistance would end up doing nothing more than sending the people with the highest consciousness about the war to jail, where they would be "lost."

Having to run the gauntlet of your political "friends" before even engaging your "enemies" was fast becoming another characteristic of the Sixties. Allard Lowenstein and Curtis Gans went through the same thing, encountering stiff opposition immediately among their fellow ADA liberals, led by the United Auto Workers' chief counsel, Joseph Rauh, who had represented the Mississippi Freedom Democratic party's credentials committee challenge in Atlantic City.

This was an administration, Rauh argued, with whom liberals had great leverage. Assaulting the President would only squander that connection meaninglessly. Soon after the first Dump Johnson overtures, Rauh began circulating a memo inside ADA advising the party's peace activists to concentrate their activities on getting a "peace plank" adopted as part of the platform in 1968. At the same time, according to Allard, he began saying that Lowenstein was a "mad revolutionary" and "irresponsible."

Lowenstein, as usual, bridled at the "personal" attack and, after one particularly intense ADA meeting, reportedly confronted Rauh when the two of them were standing side by side at the urinals in the men's lavatory. Allard said that he could understand that they disagreed about the politics, but they ought to leave "personal attacks" out of the argument and drop all this "irresponsible" stuff. The lawyer reportedly refused.

Rauh's attitude did not seem to affect Lowenstein's growing personal stature. In June, the ADA announced that its national board had named a "New York attorney," Allard K. Lowenstein, a vice chairman. Lowenstein, the accompanying résumé noted, "has maintained close ties with students and youth and was partially responsible for the letters written to the President on Vietnam from a group of 100 student body presidents, 800 Peace Corps returnees, 1,000 seminarians, and 50 Rhodes scholars."

A long with the opposition of more established liberals, Dump Johnson's principal problem that June was the lack of a candidate to head their challenge. Allard inveighed against pessimism by saying that the political risks involved for any Democrat to run against his party's sitting President were such that the movement would have to entice someone into the race by demonstrating its own strength first.

There was, however, no doubt that Lowenstein was privately convinced Dump Johnson could have no better standard-bearer than Robert F. Kennedy; Kennedy was perhaps the only politician with the muscle to take on Johnson and come out on top. Bobby, however, did not seem eager for the role. On June 3, Kennedy introduced the President at a Democratic party fund-raising dinner in a Manhattan hotel while 1,500 war protesters picketed outside. The speech was later to be an embarrassment to him. Kennedy raved about Lyndon Johnson: "He has poured out his own strength to renew the strength of the country. . . . He has gained huge popularity, but never hesitated to spend it on what he thought important. . . . He has led us . . . to comfort the oppressed on a scale unmatched in history. . . ."

At the time, Lowenstein considered the remarks no more than a step in the necessary electoral dance and expected that Kennedy's attitude would change. Shortly after Bobby's speech, Allard traveled to Africa where he would spend a month shoring up his "Third World" political connections.

In the meantime, Dump Johnson lay somewhat dormant.

That same June, The Resistance went national. Lenny headed east of the Rockies, attempting to bring existing antidraft organizations over to The Resistance position, and Dennis and I took the area west of the Rockies, starting new Resistance chapters from scratch.

Our first foray into Los Angeles came the day after the local peace movement's first large demonstration. The occasion was an appearance by Lyndon Johnson at a Democratic fund-raising dinner at the Century Plaza Hotel, and the demonstration included about 10,000 people carrying signs and chanting slogans at the hotel's front entrance. The official security forces decided the gathering was a menace to the President's safety, and a line of Los Angeles police armed with billy clubs advanced into the crowd. The crowd panicked and began fleeing across the mall, colliding with late arrivals. Soon the whole mass was pinned against an automobile overpass and the police waded in swinging. A number of people were seriously beaten, at least one of whom was in a wheelchair.

When Sweeney and I reached town the next day, everyone we talked to was still blown out by what had happened. Through various contacts we had gotten the names of several people who, we thought, might be interested in noncooperation, and Dennis and I sat down with each one. We said we were looking for people to help us organize October 16. The Resistance had one rule for its organizers: no one got anybody to do anything he wasn't doing himself. Convincing people to risk long imprisonment was a heavy responsibility, and the only insurance against bullshit was to make everyone put his own life on the line first.

None of the original seven took us up on our offer, but after a week of searching we found three people at a UCLA peace group who were willing to disseminate information while they spent the summer making up their own minds. It was hardly an impressive beginning for a movement that pictured itself sweeping the country within the next five months.

Much of that week in Los Angeles was spent trying to pass time between appointments in a strange town. We located an older sympathizer who let us stay in the guest room of her house on the beach and hung out in there, gathering our strength and fighting discouragement. Sometimes I read while Dennis thumped on his guitar. Other times, we talked.

Fourteen years later, the remnants of those conversations have all blurred into one. It was a hot, smoggy afternoon. I was sitting on one of the beds, and he on the floor, smoking a cigarette and cradling his Gibson in his lap. Both of us were talking about how hard this search was; Sweeney said that it had felt that way lots of times in Mississippi too. Dennis paused to neatly stub his cigarette out in the ashtray. The subject of Mississippi seemed to bring back some memories, and he told me the story of the freedom house bombing in McComb. Afterwards, he lapsed into silence and fiddled with his guitar.

When Sweeney started talking again, he said it felt good to be back at it again. He was sure things would pick up. In any case, hard times would build community and that was the most important thing. After I agreed, Dennis said he didn't think his draft board would pay any attention to the return of his card, but he was sure that the Justice Department would go after October 16 organizers once our strategy had come off. They could send us away for an awfully long time if they chose. He gave me one of his embarrassed smiles. At least, he noted, we would all be there together.

Out on the beach, the middle of the day had turned flat and windless, the waves limp, and the heat intense. We stayed inside the guest room with the doors closed. We were due out in Westwood to see a guy at 4:30. Dennis had heard that he played the guitar, so he took his own along.

After L.A., we made a brief stop back at the commune to pick up Rodney and then drove on to Portland. Noncooperation was an option being openly discussed there even before we arrived, but it was still difficult to find anyone who would commit himself to joining the confrontation on October 16. We finally found someone at Portland State University and spent the last of our three days in town sitting around with him, playing music, and trying to encourage him to be the one-man Portland Resistance.

Back at the Commune again, we found two serious problems waiting for us.

The first was tactical. As news of October 16 spread, it became apparent that a potentially large group of people existed who were either not eligible for the draft or were unwilling to go that far, yet wanted to express their solidarity with our act. Just what to have them do had remained up in the air, although The Resistance had decided there should be a demonstration at the Oakland induction center. Our options were either to design the demonstration ourselves or simply throw the idea open to the hodgepodge of organizations that had expressed an initial interest. Dennis and I favored the former. If it was indeed going to be in support of our stance, we wanted to be sure it would reflect the spirit of our own undertaking. Steve, holding down the fort in Berkeley, favored the latter. Before leaving for the Northwest, we had agreed with him to postpone any decision until we returned.

Instead, he had ignored the agreement and had already held a first planning session that had been dominated by Berkeley SDS types, who badmouthed The Resistance as "sacrificial lambs" and "hopelessly middle class." They wanted to declare October 16 to 21 "Stop the Draft Week." Their plan included every day gathering a crowd in front of the induction centers, blocking traffic, and responding "spontaneously" to the cops. Sweeney and I were both furious when we found out. To us, the arrangement sounded like a way to put the entire demonstration at the mercy of its craziest participants. As a consequence of our objections, we would be involved in a further series of meetings about what to do at the Oakland induction center which spanned the summer and culminated in acrimony and factionalizing.

The other immediate problem was financial. We needed leaflets, posters, and printed literature desperately but could not afford them. As the organization's most visible representative, I had the responsibility for finding a donation large enough to rescue us, and I arranged to meet Joan Baez.

She had long since become the nation's leading folk singer, and listening to her records was one of the elementary steps toward joining the "counterculture." On the cover of *Time* magazine before she was 21, she had been elevated to the archetypal image of young, long-haired, bare-foot, guitar-toting hippie. Her pacifist politics were famous, and she was on public record as saying, in regard to the draft, that "girls should say yes to the boys who say no." I made an appointment to visit her in Carmel Valley, where she lived and supported her Institute for the Study of Nonviolence.

We met at her home on a hill overlooking the valley. Custom-designed and -built, it must have cost at least a quarter of a million dollars. There was a brand new Jaguar sedan in the driveway; she dressed expensively and displayed nothing of the scruffy quality attributed to her by the cartoonists of the day.

I told her what The Resistance had planned for October 16 and claimed that we were the most viable available representatives of her kind of politics. She agreed, but apparently was not all that impressed with me personally. She didn't like my clothes or all the hair on my face. She also thought I smoked too much and was too "impressed with myself."

For my part, I found her more than a little impressed with her own self and culturally distant as well. She didn't smoke dope or live close to the ground; more than that, she carried herself with a celebrity's air that made me uncomfortable. Seeing her fancy house confused me. At that point, I only knew it didn't jibe with her record covers.

Even so, she gave The Resistance a check for $3,000. It was the largest block of money I had ever seen. When I returned to the commune, everyone cheered and wanted to look at it.

Allard Lowenstein was barely off the plane from Africa when he convened a midnight meeting at his New York apartment with the two seminarians who had been running the Campus Coordinating Committee. Allard said he wanted to find out what had gone on in his absence, but he soon shifted into the first full-scale pitch for dumping Johnson the two students had heard. He admitted he was still pessimistic about getting a candidate but said their initial work would have to focus on persuading people to vote no in the upcoming presidential primaries, either by voting for symbolic local candidates or writing in other names. He said the early primaries had to be transformed into referendums on the war, candidate or not.

Stopping in New York City only long enough to collect clean clothes, Allard commenced an explosion of speeches around the country aimed at locating a base upon which opposition to Johnson could be built. Repeated endlessly, each time with a slight variation, his talk began by dealing with the war at its most practical, calling it a "diversion" of the country away from its proper "priorities." Sure, the government claimed it was about to turn the corner, but those were lies and phony optimism, he said, the grossest kind of subversion of the democratic process. Such "deception" was being used to promote a war that was going to "destroy the nation."

In all his speeches, Lowenstein used Rusk and Johnson as foils; he deflected questions as to specific "solutions" in favor of addressing himself to the political process itself. The only way to accomplish a change was to replace the people making the policy. That July, Allard talked convincingly of committees that were being formed around the country, dropped names, and made a point of demonstrating his personal knowledge of the workings of the Democratic party down at state and local levels.

Allard claimed he was making headway, but at first he and Curtis Gans were just about the only ones who could see it.

Lowenstein and what he was doing never came up in conversations around the Peace and Liberation Commune. During July, I continued to give speeches throughout the West, and Dennis oversaw the production of various printed materials on the used offset press we had bought with some of Joan Baez's donation. The only time Lowenstein's name came up was when Sweeney told me the story of what had happened between Allard and himself in the motel room more than three years earlier.

Dennis, Rodney, and I were in the front room at Cooley Street. Rodney noticed a copy of Lowenstein's *Brutal Mandate* in the bookshelf and pulled it out. This prompted a short discussion about the book's author.

"He's more than he seems," Sweeney offered, meaning CIA.

"In more ways than one," I added.

"What do you mean?" Dennis asked.

In response, I told the story of what had happened when Lowenstein had me drive him to Big Sur Hot Springs two years earlier. Dennis's mouth assumed a flabbergasted expression.

"Lowenstein did the same thing to me," he blurted. Sweeney then told an almost identical story about what had happened between himself and Allard a year and a half previous to my encounter. He was embarrassed and kept breaking out in nervous chuckles.

Other than that exchange, Lowenstein was ignored. His idea seemed irrelevant in the face of our own. Without conscripts, we pointed out, everyone would be a peace candidate.

That same July, Local Board 71 sent me orders to report for another preinduction physical. I ignored them.

On August 4, Allard Lowenstein boarded a plane for San Francisco, where he was to meet with Gerald Hill, a businessman and chairman of the California Democratic Council (CDC), a group of liberal Democrats who had already threatened to run a peace slate in the 1968 California presidential primary. As usual, Lowenstein flew coach.

Flying first class on the same plane was Robert Kennedy, on his way to a fund-raising dinner in honor of the speaker of California's assembly. When Kennedy learned Lowenstein was on the flight, his press secretary traded seats with Allard so he and the Senator could talk.

"Who's your candidate?" Bobby asked lightheartedly.

"You need a movement before you can get a candidate," Lowenstein answered, "but if you want to run, we'll let you."

That joking was apparently the closest thing to a direct approach made to Kennedy on behalf of Dump Johnson in the course of the flight. "I was aware that I was a flea and he was an elephant," Allard said later, "and that we had a lot more organizing to do before I could ask him. . . . I just explained to him what the Dump Johnson movement was really all about. . . . We were not kooks, or the New Left, or just the same old peace people. I explained that we were recruiting thousands of students and many regular Democrats. . . . I tried to convince him that his stereotype of these people was wrong and that we were committed to working inside the electoral system. . . . I told him we were going to defeat Lyndon Johnson for the party nomination in 1968. I told him that with him we could do it very much more easily, but that we were going to do it with him or without him."

Kennedy laughed. "He took it as seriously as the idea of a priest in Bogotá deposing the Pope," Allard later remembered. "I knew that his instinct was to run. But . . . I had no illusions at that time that he would ever risk it."

The two of them then discussed other possible candidates. Lowenstein mentioned General James Gavin, U.S. Army (ret.), the war's most prominent military critic. According to Lowenstein, Kennedy's reaction was, "If you get Gavin, you've got a new ball game."

Lowenstein also mentioned that he was headed for California to meet with some "CDC people." Kennedy reportedly "warned" him against them, saying they were "dangerous" and that Allard himself had "too good a future" in politics to get "mixed up with people like that."

"If you really think the CDC people are so bad," Lowenstein challenged, "why don't you say so to the reporters who meet us when the plane gets in?"

Lowenstein later watched Kennedy's encounter with the waiting California press. Finally thrown a question about what he thought of California's peace movement, Kennedy sidestepped. "That," Bobby said, "is a matter for the people of California to decide for themselves."

Allard viewed the otherwise wishy-washy answer as a sign that, though not yet willing to challenge Lyndon Johnson himself, neither was Kennedy willing to denounce the president's opposition.

The meeting with CDC's Gerald Hill that had drawn Lowenstein to California was, by all accounts, decisive in the course of Dump Johnson. Hill's organization had anticipated the strategy Lowenstein and Gans had just begun to articulate, and Allard found him a quick recruit. Hill pledged that CDC would raise money to carry the word to the Democratic parties of the other 48 states, and Allard pledged to match it with money from New York. In the middle of the night, Lowenstein called Curtis Gans to let him know.

"Well," Allard asked, "are you willing to put your body where your mouth is?"

Dump Johnson had begun.

Gans's house in Washington, D.C., became the national headquarters of the Dump Johnson campaign, and upon Lowenstein's return from the West Coast, the two friends sat in the middle of stacks of name cards and began dividing Dump Johnson's potential constituency into three primary categories: the politically respectable; activist types; and students. Each would have its own organization.

The "politically respectable" included politicians of any rank, party officials, and prominent or well-established political amateurs. Their organization would be the Conference of Concerned Democrats, co-chaired by Allard Lowenstein of New York, Gerald Hill of California, and a Democratic party leader from Wisconsin. Officially, Concerned Democrats constituted Dump Johnson's "leadership." Unofficially, it was the bait with which they hoped to lure a candidate.

The "activist types" included the young free-lance organizers who were a standard part of politics in the Sixties. To give them something to do while a base was built by "respectables," Lowenstein reached an agreement with another existing California-based organization called Dissenting Democrats, then collecting signatures for a series of ads calling on Johnson not to run for reelection. The free-lance activists would be given the Dissenting Democrats' petition to circulate, and the names would be passed on for possible use by the "respectables."

The "students" in Dump Johnson's terminology were of the "liberal" rather than "radical" stripe. They would be organized into the Alternative Candidates Task Force, Lowenstein's old Campus Coordinating Committee with a new name.

The technique for fleshing these organizations out was a joint Lowenstein-Gans effort. Typically, first Gans would enter a state, rent a motel room, and proceed to make phone calls. At least three meetings would be arranged, and then Allard would fly in to address them. After he left, Gans would organize the recruits into a functional structure. Over the next two months, he and Lowenstein covered 42 states, leaving Dump Johnson organizations behind in 40. Curtis Gans was the wiring that kept it all together, and Allard Lowenstein the jolt of energy that gave it all life.

On August 14, 1967, Allard addressed the NSA Congress in College Park, Maryland. It was the first congress since the organization's secret connections to the Central Intelligence Agency had been exposed, and there was much pressure among the NSA delegates to take a position as clearly separate from government policy as possible. Allard managed to attach the bulk of that sentiment to Dump Johnson by virtue of an exemplary speaking performance in front of an overflow crowd at the end of a hot, swampy day.

Allard was "spectacular," according to several members of the audience. He tore into the war and its architects. The only option was to stop Johnson. Change for the better, perhaps even the future of democracy itself, depended on it. "People say that we're trying to beat somebody with nobody, but it's not true," he laughed. "We're going to beat nobody with anybody. . . . This Congress," he said, "can be a launching pad for a decision to make 1968 the year when students help change a society almost everyone agrees is headed for destruction."

Afterwards, Allard was in a hurry to catch a plane back to New York, where his pregnant wife, Jenny, had been admitted to the hospital with her first labor pains. One of his Ivy League protégés was going to drive him to his flight, and the two headed for the parking lot outside the hall at a brisk walk.

"How was I?" Lowenstein asked his protégé.

The protégé considered his words carefully. He rejected "inspiring" and "overwhelming" as completely inadequate adjectives. "You were a spiritual transfusion," he finally answered.

Allard mulled the description over for a moment.

"Good," he said, "that's just what I wanted."

Lowenstein had hoped to stay in New York long enough to see the birth of his first child through, but it didn't work out that way. The next morning, the doctors said it promised to be a long labor and the baby wouldn't come for twelve hours at the earliest, so Allard vanished back in the direction of Maryland with Curtis Gans, telling Jenny he would return in plenty of time.

"We had to start with the students," Allard would later explain, "because we had no money and therefore no hope of getting anyone else to work for us." Accordingly, Gans and the two seminarians had arranged another meeting to take advantage of the enthusiasm Allard had aroused with his speech the day before. According to one participant, "The feeling at that meeting was that we had gone just as far as we could go through the normal procedures. They [politicians] had just acted as if we didn't exist and we weren't serious. And we didn't want to go into The Resistance, at least not yet. So we were ready to try what Al wanted. It was the last stop on the way."

Frank Graham Lowenstein was already several hours old when his father returned to New York. Allard was reportedly embarrassed at not having been there earlier.

For The Resistance, August was dominated by a tumultuous meeting in Berkeley about the upcoming October demonstrations. The Resistance was now one organization and Stop the Draft Week another; the latter had its own internal split between pacifists and SDS types. The Resistance, in whose support the action was planned, had trouble identifying with either faction.

The pacifist side wanted to emphasize Gandhian civil disobedience and organize people to sit in the induction center doorways, blockading the building and courting arrest. The SDS types' plan involved, as one local SDS leader later put it, "rejecting nonviolence [in order to] reach and forge cooperation with black militants . . . [and] working class youth." Black people, the SDS faction pointed out, had spent the summer in spontaneous riots that had had to be quelled by the National Guard and were not going to be impressed with a bunch of "middle-class garbage about civil disobedience and moral witness." The plan they put forward called for gathering as many people as possible in the street outside the induction center; when the police reacted, the response of the crowd would be left to what was called "spontaneity." Several advocates of the plan amplified their intentions by declaring that when "the shit comes down," no "pig" would ever get their hands on them without a fight. One claimed he planned to bring his "piece" to "defend" himself from "the Man."

All of that talk was duly noted by the Oakland Police Department informer in the room and reported immediately to his superiors.

The Resistance, for its part, argued that the SDS plan sounded like nothing more than a way to get a lot of unsuspecting people attacked by the police. The answer to that, we were told, was that the experience would "educate" its victims to "American realities" and "radicalize" them.

In Resistance terms, that kind of usurpation of an individual's right to decide his own course was considered manipulation, and both Dennis Sweeney and I denounced it as such. In addition, we labeled all the "working-class" jargon bullshit. Everyone involved in the discussion was white, middle class, and educated, I said, and trying to pretend they had to "impress" black people was just another version of "liberal guilt," a bunch of students trying to act like Black Panthers. The "middle class" might be a roadblock, but it was our roadblock, something we had to confront and change, not turn our backs on. That argument was hooted at from the SDS corner and answered with more talk about "kicking ass" in a revolutionary posture.

Finally, The Resistance walked out and withdrew from any formal involvement in the October Oakland demonstrations. Outside, I felt as furious as I ever had. Dennis was calmer, but his jaws were clamped together nonetheless.

Shortly thereafter, Sweeney left the country as part of a delegation from the American "movement," which was to meet with representatives of Vietnam's National Liberation Front in Bratislava, Czechoslovakia. Sweeney's name had been suggested to the organizers by several people who had known him in Mississippi, and he was chosen as much for his civil rights history as his current involvement in the fledgling Resistance.

Using a forged student identification card to fly discount as far as New York, Dennis bought a full-fare coach ticket on to Paris, where he was met by a young French woman designated as his contact. She took him to her flat, let him sleep with her that night, and then put him on the plane to Czechoslovakia the next day.

Sweeney told the commune all about the French woman when he returned. As an all-male household, we engaged in locker-room talk whenever we got laid. Most of us were usually falling in some form of love and raving about it, but Dennis rarely indulged in such romanticism, and his stories usually had a touch of misadventure to them as well. The one about the French woman fit with the pattern. He called her beautiful but dirty and said she smelled so strongly of garlic that he finally left her bed and slept on the couch.

The idea behind the Bratislava conference was to let Vietnamese insurgents and a cross section of the American movement get to know each other. The NLF representatives were led by the woman who would later become the organization's chief representative at the Paris Peace Talks. The chief North Vietnamese representative would later become his country's second-ranking representative at the same talks. "Our war is with the American government," they were all careful to say, "not with the American people. For the American people we have only respect and friendship."

Each conference day was structured around formal sessions where presentations were made. The Vietnamese talked about life under bombardment or the Saigon regime. A number were veteran guerillas, and several returned to combat after the conference was over. The Americans were moved as much by the quiet unpretentiousness of the Vietnamese as by their politics.

For their part, the Vietnamese found the Americans occasionally difficult to understand. The American presentation, made by selected delegates reporting on their own work, had no common thread to it, and the Vietnamese were dismayed at how little affinity the various groups in the American movement felt for each other.

Despite such occasional cultural discontinuities, a genuine camaraderie developed between the two groups of people by the time of the final banquet. One of the speeches that night was made by an American later tried as one of the Chicago Seven for "conspiring to disrupt" the 1968 Democratic National Convention. Talking about the NLF example, he became so moved that he burst out, "We're everywhere. We're all Viet Cong." His countrymen clapped.

Dennis Sweeney gave no speeches but shared much of the Chicago Seven man's enthusiasm for the Vietnamese he had met. He identified strongly with their absolute determination and the way they minimalized their personal identity and muted their presence. The cohesiveness of their community looked very much like the belonging Dennis had always wanted for himself but never quite pulled off.

When the American delegation left, each member was presented with a dull-gray, metal ring, fashioned, the Vietnamese claimed, from the fuselage of a downed U.S. Air Force bomber. Several delegates expressed qualms that their countrymen at home might interpret such an ornament as a celebration of the pilot's fate. The Vietnamese said that was not the spirit in which they were given, but some of the Americans nonetheless declined the present.

Dennis Sweeney was not among them. That ring became one of his favorite possessions. Until he lost it sometime in 1968, he wore the piece of dead airplane on his little finger at all times.

A llard Lowenstein paused briefly after his son's birth to do some more international traveling himself. To one journalist who knew him, it was another classic example of Lowenstein's capacity to pop up everywhere. The Republic of South Vietnam was holding its widely trumpeted "free elections," and the journalist had gone to Saigon to cover them. That Lowenstein would also see fit to put in an appearance might have been expected, but wasn't.

The journalist first learned of Allard's visit while sitting on the veranda of Saigon's Hotel Continental with a well-known television newsman, when the two men noticed they were being watched by a "very clean-cut" young American. He watched them for 20 minutes and then came over to the table, identified them both correctly, and asked "quite surreptitiously" whether they had seen Allard Lowenstein.

The journalist answered that he had seen Lowenstein in New York before he left.

The young man, a Lowenstein protégé, pointed out that Lowenstein was in Saigon and he was supposed to meet him here on the veranda.

"Sure enough," the journalist later wrote, "several hours later Lowenstein materializes; it is election time in Saigon and . . . Al has flown over, Air Lowenstein, to judge the elections since he intends to criticize Vietnamese politics in the year to come and he does not intend to be one-upped by people asking, Were you there? He is there, though of course observing a Vietnamese election is almost as futile as participating in one. Nevertheless, he seems to be known to everyone in Saigon, particularly underground politicians."

Once the vote was taken, Lowenstein issued a carefully worded statement that was run in the next day's *New York Times* as two paragraphs under the head, "New York Lawyer Questions Fairness of Vietnam Vote," dateline Saigon. "Allard K. Lowenstein," it read, "a vice chairman of Americans for Democratic Action, said today that the charges of fraud made by some of the losing candidates . . . should not be dismissed as the complaints of poor losers." Among his activities while in Saigon, Allard had met with the American ambassador, Ellsworth Bunker, the same man with whom he had negotiated a secret agreement about the Dominican Republic elections a year earlier. Lowenstein told the *Times* he "informed Mr. Bunker that many Americans in Vietnam, including government employees, do not share the euphoric reaction to the elections that has marked the public comments of many of the official American observers."

On the way back to the United States, Allard stopped for a day in New Delhi, India, and saw an American correspondent stationed there.

Allard told him that within a year Dump Johnson would have forced the incumbent President to pull his name out of the 1968 race for nomination.

The correspondent laughed. He thought Lowenstein was suffering from delusions of grandeur.

9

In the fall of 1967, established liberals still largely opposed Dump Johnson. The campaign still had no candidate, although by early September, Lowenstein had already made at least two unsuccessful attempts to recruit one.

The first, as he had discussed with Bobby Kennedy, was General James Gavin, U.S. Army (ret.). When Allard visited him, Gavin said he had indeed given the idea of running serious thought but felt it made more sense to do so as a Republican, his lifelong political affiliation. Lowenstein argued that that would be an impossible exercise, but Gavin said he would remain a Republican.

Next, Lowenstein had approached John Kenneth Galbraith, then president of ADA and the nation's most widely read economist. Galbraith had come around to Lowenstein's position over the summer, declaring that 1968 would be the year that "people were right and politicians wrong," and reportedly told Lowenstein that the only thing holding him back was the fact that he had been born in Canada. The Constitution specifically prohibited the "foreign born" from holding the presidency, but even if he could win a legal battle on the question, he said, the issue would so confuse things as to negate his candidacy. Accordingly, the economist refused Lowenstein's proposal.

On September 23, Lowenstein and Gans put forward a series of anti-Johnson resolutions at the ADA board meeting in Washington, D.C., but they lost them all by wide margins.

That evening, Allard attended a gathering at Hickory Hill, Robert Kennedy's house in suburban Virginia. Lowenstein had by now met with Bobby on several occasions, all of them "off the calendar," meaning they were never written into the Senator's schedule and, therefore, never officially existed.

Lowenstein and a journalist friend who would eventually be one of Kennedy's biographers arrived at Hickory Hill at around 10:30 P.M. One of the nation's most prominent historians and a man who had served under Jack Kennedy as ambassador to Peru were already there. Bobby was relaxed, wearing a sweater and a thin strand of "hippie love beads," but the mood was all business, and conversation quickly turned into a debate over the merits of a Kennedy challenge to Johnson for the presidential nomination, with Lowenstein and the biographer arguing in favor and the historian and former ambassador arguing against. Kennedy himself mostly listened, with what the biographer later called "a bemused smile on his face."

The historian said dumping Johnson would be impossible; 1968 would be a "Republican year." The war opposition was better off trying to get a peace plank into the party's platform, he argued. Kennedy was a "precious commodity" and would be wiser to wait until 1972 to run.

Lowenstein had kicked his shoes off and was sitting on a stuffed chair with his legs crossed, "college bull session–style." He dismissed the peace plank idea as insufficient to rally anyone, much less change actual policy. Then, ignoring presidential politics for a moment, he attacked the war directly and "emphasized the moral imperative of stopping the war by dislodging Johnson." Allard argued there was a strong possibility that Johnson would withdraw if beaten in the early primaries.

At that point, Bobby interrupted for the first time. "I think Al may be right," he said. "I think Johnson might quit the night before the convention opens. I think he's a coward."

The debate resumed and lasted almost two hours.

Finally Kennedy spoke up in a "slow, serious voice." "I would have a problem if I ran first against Johnson," he explained. "People would say that I was splitting the party out of ambition and envy. No one would believe that I was doing it because of how I felt about Vietnam and poor people. I think Al is doing the right thing, but I think that someone else will have to be the first one to run."

Bobby's answer was a disappointment, but Allard would not give up on him, even while intensifying his search for a candidate in other quarters.

By virtue of an article printed in *Esquire* magazine's back-to-school issue that September, I became, at least momentarily, the nation's most prominent draft resister. "The New Student President," it was titled, "David Harris of Stanford." The blurb read, "He preached peace, opposed the draft, tangled with fraternities, fought for educational reform and then quit." The premise of the story was that a whole new rebelliousness had grown up among student leaders, and my career at Stanford was put forward as the archetype. "Among these leaders," *Esquire* claimed, "David Harris is the one most cited by student editors and other presidents. He gathers disciples around him wherever he goes."

I was never much for predictions, but *Esquire* recorded one of the few I made. "Johnson is having a hard time holding the whole thing together," I claimed. "I think his next move will be a big escalation . . . and to do that he's going to have to double his manpower . . . and that's when the big climax is going to come, because all those people who are on student deferments are going to get called. . . . He's going to get this opposition from the youth and he'll try to clamp down. . . . They'll harass you and bust you . . . if you start getting people, and it's clear we're starting to get people."

At the time that issue of *Esquire* was on the stands, "starting to get people" meant that The Resistance had close to three dozen chapters nationwide, all building for October 16.

As it had turned out, the sixteenth kicked off an entire week of antiwar activity around the country. First came Oakland's Stop the Draft Week, the pacifists and SDS having reached a compromise whereby the morning of Monday the sixteenth would be given over to the pacifists' civil disobedience. Among those planning on being arrested was The Resistance's famous benefactor, Joan Baez. That same afternoon, we would turn our draft cards in in front of San Francisco's Federal Building. The "mill-ins" planned by the SDS faction would begin back in Oakland the next morning and last the rest of the week. On the weekend, a coalition called the Student Mobilization had scheduled a march on the Pentagon in Washington, D.C., which would attract tens of thousands of participants from around the country. To build for The Resistance's part in that overall push, Dennis and I set off in September for Oregon, where our chapter had scheduled several speeches for me.

We made the trip along with another veteran of the summer of 1966. Julian Burroughs, the pseudonymous Stanford undergraduate who fancied himself the spiritual heir to the nation's premier junkie novelist and had been drafted and vanished while I was at the 1966 NSA Congress, suddenly reappeared at the commune after a year's absence. Desertion from the military would reach immense proportions before the Sixties were over, and Julian's story seems, fourteen years later, like a paradigm of the age.

When his initial induction orders came, Julian had fled to Paris until his father, a wealthy California fruit grower, tracked him to there and begged him to go back home and into the Army. Broke and threatened with being cut off completely, Julian gave in. He was sent to Fort Ord for boot camp and then on to a Honolulu Signal Corps posting. His military service amounted to living on the islands and holding a job, but within six months, he bought a one-way ticket to San Francisco, abandoned his uniform in the airport restroom there, and fled to his old Stanford fraternity house where friends loaned him money with which he had flown to Salt Lake City. There he found work as a night watchman at a pipe factory and rented a one-room apartment on the seedier side of town.

The day before Sweeney and I were scheduled to leave for Oregon, Julian was awakened from his afternoon sleep in Utah by two policemen accompanied by his father. The policemen told Julian either they could arrest him as a deserter on the spot and hold him for the Army, or he could voluntarily return with his father to San Francisco and turn himself in. Julian chose his father. On the plane back to California, they had several drinks together, and Julian professed great shame at what he had done and great resolve to face the music. After arriving in San Francisco, Julian excused himself for a moment to use the lavatory, climbed through the window, dropped onto an outside parking lot, and fled.

He asked to go along with us to Oregon as a way of obscuring his trail.

In Oregon, our deserter friend always stayed at the back of crowds and only rejoined Dennis and myself when he was sure we weren't being watched. Sweeney and I were deep into our routine, and I gave what was becoming my standard rap all around Oregon.

Students kept talking about how they had no tools to stop war with, but I contended that that wasn't true. Your life is a tool, I told them. Without your allegiance, the government cannot, in fact, wage war. All the government needed from students was their willingness to play the game, holding deferments and making their separate peace with the selective service. With that cooperation, it then raised armies for Vietnam. We could not afford to be passive government property any longer. If jail was the price, then we would have to pay it. It was time we used our lives to grind the machine to a halt.

Every time I spoke, I tried to be my most inspiring. I wanted people to agree with me. I wanted them to duplicate my decision, and, though I refused to think it then, I now know that I wanted them to acclaim my leadership as well. In 1967, that impulse was confusing. Everyone in the movement was supposed to be his own leader, and so all leaders soon felt defensive about their role, myself included. I still have difficulty admitting I wanted to be important as well as right. Such feelings were not just ego. They were also a function of my own need to believe in what I was doing and my sense of responsibility for making it work. I took my leadership seriously. I said my best words and, while instigating others, exposed myself to great jeopardy. Each time I gave a speech, I violated the conspiracy provisions of the Selective Service Act, and each violation, should the government choose to prosecute, carried a maximum penalty of five years. I was ready to risk everything to prove myself.

At the end of each of our organizing days in the Northwest, Dennis and I and Julian would gather back at the house where we were staying, just hanging out with the recruits we had found. Sweeney had brought his guitar along and would sing his cane-cutter song. The chorus went:

> *Joshua gone Barbados,*
> *living in a big hotel;*
> *poor people on Saint Vincent,*
> *got many sad tale to tell . . .*
> *Joshua gone Barbados,*
> *just like he don't know;*
> *poor people on Saint Vincent,*
> *ain't got no place to go.*

Outside, it was raining, and no one in the room was sure just who the guy who had come with us from California was. Dennis had introduced him as "Maxwell Brown," but accidentally called him "Julian" several times in the course of the evenings.

By October, Lowenstein's quest for a candidate had taken him to Congressman Don Edwards of California and Senators Frank Church of Idaho, George McGovern of South Dakota, and Eugene McCarthy of Minnesota. Only McGovern and McCarthy hadn't turned him down flat.

McGovern had agreed about the need for someone to challenge Johnson but had serious doubts as to whether his base was secure enough to take on the President, in which case he would have no choice but to decline. He also recommended talking to Gene McCarthy.

McCarthy had been on the original list of potential candidates drawn up by Lowenstein and Curtis Gans, but Allard had been reluctant to approach him. The Minnesota Senator was something of an eccentric with a fondness for quoting poetry and a lackadaisical manner that made Lowenstein wonder whether he had the energy for a presidential campaign. Gans had heard rumors that McCarthy might be willing to run, but Lowenstein didn't follow up on them until Gans had scheduled an appointment to talk to McCarthy himself. At that point, Lowenstein called McCarthy's Washington office, got an appointment before Gans, and popped the question.

The Senator from Minnesota's first response was, according to Allard, that "Bobby should be running" instead. Lowenstein explained that Kennedy did not seem willing. Then McCarthy said he would have to think about it.

McCarthy's reaction seemed to typify the difficulties in finding a candidate that fall. Everyone in the Democratic party was waiting for Robert Kennedy, creating a log jam that prompted Lowenstein to make the closest thing to a public statement against Bobby as he would ever make. At a September 30 conference in Pittsburgh of an ad hoc group to draft Kennedy for President in 1968, Allard asked the group to "ditch Bobby." A powerful Dump Johnson movement would be easier, he argued, if "no candidate were put forward at this time." "Some people think we have to name a candidate now," Allard told the *New York Times*. "I believe there is much time to make a decision."

That remark was disingenuous. Behind the scenes, Lowenstein admitted that he needed a candidate soon if Dump Johnson was to stand a chance.

On October 11, Lowenstein, the biographer who had been at Hickory Hill in September, and one of the Ivy League students from the Alternative Candidates Task Force drove together to Philadelphia to appear on a midnight radio talk show. The biographer remembered: "There was a uniform tone to most of the questions we received: I don't like the war, I don't like Johnson, but you guys can't be real because you don't have a candidate." The three of them swam upstream against that argument all night.

Toward the end of the program, the biographer noticed that Lowenstein had doodled a newspaper headline on the piece of paper in front of him.

"McCarthy Wins Wisconsin Primary," it read, "Beats LBJ with 60 Percent of Vote."

On October 4, a letter arrived at the commune's Glen Way house from Local Board 71 notifying me that since I had failed to appear at my August preinduction physical, I was now reclassified "1-A, delinquent" and subject to immediate induction. A new draft card was enclosed. I would keep it in my possession less than 48 hours.

On October 16, the big fall peace week began with the pacifists' turn at the Oakland induction center. As promised, Joan Baez was one of the more than 200 arrestees, and wire service photos of her being taken into custody flashed around the United States and Europe.

At 1 in the afternoon, The Resistance turned in draft cards on the steps of San Francisco's Federal Building. Similar demonstrations were happening in 17 other cities, Chicago, New York, L.A., and Boston chief among them. Dennis and Rodney had spent the morning putting a sound system together, but by the time some 2,000 people had assembled the microphone still would not stop squawking and had to be abandoned. Shouting into a bullhorn, I announced that we were about to pass a basket out into the crowd, then The Resistance would take the cards upstairs to the federal attorney's office and give them all back to the government with the message that we would never carry another. We were in open violation of the Selective Service Act and would stay that way until the last American soldier was out of Vietnam. We weren't running, we weren't dodging, we were resisting. Given what the law was up to, we chose to be outlaws.

As the basket circulated, it was passed over the heads of the crowd. Hands holding cards popped up all around it. When it had reached almost out to the street and back, it was half full. Before we could do anything with the contents, shouts of "back here" broke out and more hands clutching draft cards sprang up, so the basket went back out. This time it returned three-quarters full. The third time the basket was summoned, it came back full to the brim. When sorted by the Federal Bureau of Investigation later that afternoon, it was found to contain some 400 certificates of registration and classification, several Social Security cards, a City College of San Francisco ID, a leaflet about Rosicrucianism, several dozen signed letters, a set of army discharge papers, and an envelope with the ashes of 67 draft cards publicly incinerated in Berkeley during the previous week to build momentum for the sixteenth.

A delegation delivered the basket to the federal attorney's office, both Dennis Sweeney and I among its members. The federal attorney's office was locked. We pounded on the door for several minutes and, when no one answered, left the basket crammed with draft cards sitting in front of the mail slot.

Once the crowd had dispersed, the basket was taken inside the locked office and examined, and each name on the cards was turned over to the FBI. The report pertaining to my own became part of field office file #SC25-834, SELECTIVE SERVICE ACT, 1948, PROTEST ACTIVITIES. "On Monday, October 16, 1967," it read, "U.S. Attorney CECIL F. POOLE, Northern District of California, made available to [name deleted] a wicker basket which contained a number of selective service registration and classification cards. . . . Among the items submitted was a registration certificate or classification card for DAVID V. HARRIS, Selective Service No. 4-71-46-104."

I drove back to East Palo Alto with Dennis and Rodney. The three of us were scheduled to fly to Washington, D.C., at the end of the week to represent The Resistance at the demonstrations there. Back at the commune, phone calls were coming in from all over the country. In total, The Resistance had returned more than 2,000 draft cards. Since we had expected to get 500 at the most, we were jubilant.

"Well," Dennis said, passing a joint on around the circle of some dozen young men in the room, "the shit's in the fan now."

Everyone there saw jail dead ahead, but, as it turned out, I would be the only one of us prosecuted.

I took my convict future out for a test drive much sooner than I had expected.

On Tuesday morning, the militant Stop the Draft Week "mill-in" commenced. Primed by their briefings full of "off the pig" quotes from the event's organizers, 200 police swept the streets of 3,000 largely unsuspecting demonstrators. They showed no mercy whatsoever. A group of high school students was trapped in the induction center doorway and several of the students had bones broken by police truncheons. Reporters trying to cover the event were manhandled as well.

That night, there was a Stop the Draft Week rally in Berkeley to discuss what to do next. I went to speak for a more nonviolent option.

When I got there, instead of pressing for confrontation, the Stop the Draft Week organizers were arguing for backing off from the induction center and picketing the administration building on the Berkeley campus. That made no sense to me, so I used my time on the speakers list to argue for going back to the induction center for a nonviolent, legal picket with optional civil disobedience. The motion I supported was carried, and I ended up in front of the Oakland induction center at 5:30 the next morning with about 400 others, 91 of whom spontaneously sat in the doorways and were arrested.

At approximately 8:30 A.M., I became Wednesday's ninety-second arrest. I was monitoring the picket line when several uniformed police arrested me on charges of disorderly conduct, disturbing the peace, and use of a bullhorn without a permit. On Thursday, I pleaded *nolo contendere* in exchange for a ten-day sentence and was hauled off to the county prison farm at Santa Rita.

Dennis and Rodney would have to go to Washington without me.

That same week, Allard Lowenstein and Robert Kennedy met in the Senator's East Forty-fifth Street office; according to one of Kennedy's later biographers, "This time Lowenstein directly asked Kennedy to become the official candidate of the Dump Johnson movement."

"Everything is falling into place," Allard told him. "We have local organizations in New Hampshire and Wisconsin, and the California Democratic Council is already committed to running an anti-Johnson candidate in the California primary. I've been across the country thirty times and I can tell we're going to win. . . . You have to get into it! . . . We are not the West Side Reform Democrats. We are grass-roots America. Johnson is finished."

Kennedy remained unconvinced.

Allard would recall a year later for an oral history of Robert Kennedy:

He said he would not run except under unforeseen circumstances. So I . . . said, "I'm an unforeseen circumstance." He recited all that business he used to recite in that period about why so-and-so said it couldn't be done. But you could see he wanted to do it. It made me very sad, but angry, too. I kept saying that if things were to be judged by traditional political standards, and by traditional politicians, by traditional judgments of what was possible, then of course nothing could be done. But that was the whole point! Nothing was the way it had been before and if he didn't know that, he wasn't anywhere near as smart as I thought he was; and furthermore, if he didn't try . . . it was hard to believe he cared as much as millions of people thought he did.

He said . . . "It can't be put together."

Then . . . I just glared at him, and said, "You understand, of course, that there are those of us who think the honor and direction of the country are at stake. I don't give a damn whether you think it can be put together or not. . . . We're going to do it without you, and that's too bad because you could have been President of the United States."

I turned and flew out. He came soaring out after me and in that familiar gesture, he turned me around with his hand on my shoulder. We both were standing there blowing our noses in this thick sense of emotion. It was really very unexpected. . . . He just said, "Well, I hope you understand that I can't do it, and that I know what you're doing should be done, but I just can't do it."

Not long thereafter, Lowenstein made arrangements to fly to Los Angeles, where Eugene McCarthy was scheduled to give a speech about Vietnam on Friday, October 20.

L ate Thursday evening, October 19, Dennis Sweeney had his own Stop the Draft Week encounter with the law.

There was no activity at the induction center that day, but another "mill-in" planned for Friday was expected to draw 5,000 people. That evening, Dennis, Rodney, and Julian Burroughs were in Berkeley running an errand. They had all been smoking some strong weed and were fairly wasted. Julian was driving, turned the wrong way up a one-way street, and was immediately pulled over by the police. Dennis, Rodney, and Julian were placed under arrest when a 35-millimeter film canister, full of "what appeared to be marijuana," was found under the piles of "Resist the Draft" literature in the backseat.

At the station house they were separated, run through a strip search, and then interrogated, one after the other. Sweeney told the police his name, his parents' names, his birth date, and his current address and listed his occupation as "political organizer and musician." Rodney did the same thing.

When it came to Julian's turn, he told the booking sergeant his father was William Burroughs, novelist, New York City. His mother had been killed in 1947, he said, when his father had accidentally shot her through the temple while trying to blast a wine glass off her head. His father, he claimed, had been strung out on heroin at the time. The desk sergeant wrote it all down without looking up from the page.

They were next locked up for overnight processing, Dennis and Rodney in one cell and Julian Burroughs in another. Julian, having apparently decided that the only hope of saving himself was to convince the police he was so weird he was harmless, took all his clothes off and spent the entire night engaged in robotlike Hindu chanting. "Ooommmm," the cell block echoed. "Oooommmmmm . . . ooooommmmmm."

Dennis just lay down on the upper bunk and lit a cigarette. He and Rodney talked and smoked until nearly 4 A.M. Sweeney was agitated. In the last few days, his opinion of Stop the Draft Week had changed, and he had been looking forward to being among the crowd confronting the police again on Friday morning. It pissed him off that he was missing out on everything because of a tiny canister of grass. Sweeney told Rodney that the whole country would be watching the streets of Oakland in a few hours. He now thought The Resistance's decision to boycott Stop the Draft Week had been a serious error, a lot of which he put off on my influence.

Several hours after he and Rodney finally fell asleep, an Oakland street full of at least 3,000 people engaged in an unprecedented peace movement action. This time when the police swept down, the crowd fought back. As one Stop the Draft Week organizer put it, "People were mad about Tuesday. . . . They went into the streets and built barricades from whatever they could find handy—benches, large potted trees, parking meters, garbage cans, and cars and trucks (these were placed in the middle of the streets and the air let out of their tires). People would run up behind buses and rip the ignition wires out or climb into trucks and steal the keys. . . . Then the National Guard was called so the people split."

When news of the clash filtered into the Berkeley jail, Sweeney's agitation only intensified. History was being made, he told Rodney.

It was 5 P.M. Friday before a lawyer got charges against the three dropped. Once released, Dennis and Rodney drove back to the commune, changed clothes, and then caught a plane for Washington, D.C. Julian Burroughs accompanied them as far as East Palo Alto, leaving there several days later for the anonymity of New York City. The day after his departure, FBI agents showed up at Cooley Street and were told no one there had seen a.k.a. Julian Burroughs in months, maybe years.

On Friday morning, while Sweeney was still at Berkeley police headquarters, Allard Lowenstein, Gerald Hill of CDC, and two others met with a confident and enthusiastic McCarthy over breakfast in the Senator's L.A. hotel suite. While they all ate, he made jokes and kidded, but also managed to ask where labor would stand on his candidacy and if there was any possibility of getting money and volunteers. The more they talked, the more jovial he reportedly became.

At 10:15, McCarthy addressed the reason for Lowenstein and Hill's visit directly.

"You fellows have been talking about three or four names," he smiled. "I guess," he added, "you can cut it down to one."

Allard got on the phone, informed Gans, and then headed East again.

It could not be announced until McCarthy himself made his public declaration in November, but Dump Johnson had a candidate at last.

Early Saturday morning, Dennis and Rodney joined at least 100,000 other people in the nation's capital.

Sweeney immediately hooked up with some old SNCC friends and Rodney didn't see him again until everything was over, despite the fact that they were supposed to meet at a demonstration in front of the Justice Department later in the day. Dennis was scheduled to be a speaker but never showed up, and instead Rodney read the international cable from the National Liberation Front in Paris that had arrived at Cooley Street addressed to The Resistance. It thanked us for our support of the Vietnamese people in commending noncooperation with the United States' military machine. "These are very brave acts," it said. The crowd cheered.

Just where Dennis was when he was supposed to be speaking at the Justice Department would never really be explained. He did show up later at the Pentagon demonstrations that consumed the rest of Saturday and parts of Sunday.

The government had refused a permit for the march on Defense Department headquarters, but thousands of people marched anyway. At the Pentagon, deputized marshals and paratroopers stopped the crowd halfway up a set of steps, and the two sides sat staring at each other for hours. "Suddenly, as the daylight died," a participant later remembered, "two or three tiny flames burst from different places in the crowd. There was only red in the west and the earth was black, when dozens of draft cards began to burn, held aloft, amid increasing cheers and applause. One by one, the lights flickered, burned and then went out. The burnings traveled to the other side of the Mall . . . and eventually down to the grassy plains below."

"We kept hearing news," another veteran of the Pentagon steps remembered, ". . . a soldier passed out cigarettes to three demonstrators down in the Mall and said, 'Keep up the good work.' This was greeted by cheers and [the] urgent chant of 'Join us! Join us!' In the brief silence that followed, the strained, high-pitched voice of a girl could be heard, 'We are brothers and sisters!' And again, absolutely spontaneously, a great chant, 'We love you! We love you! We love you!' It is impossible to convey the sound of this chant to those who did not hear it. . . . It was not a tactical maneuver. [It was] our sense of ourselves as a community—the community that could be, the one we felt had to be, and a deeply American one, at that. . . . There before us—one would say in panicked might—was the vast engine . . . destroying the modern world."

Early Sunday morning, when the crowd on the Pentagon steps had dwindled to 400 or 500, the order to advance was given to the troops and the steps were cleared.

Sweeney returned to California afterward. Another draft-card return had been scheduled for December 4, and while I was locked up, Dennis oversaw the commune's Resistance responsibilities.

Typical was an afternoon meeting in Berkeley at which a confrontation developed over the chapter's money. Aside from a proportion of the contributions I had been able to raise for the entire organization, the Berkeley Resistance's principal means of support were donations collected at their campus literature table. That fall, the take was anywhere from $20 to $50 a day. The resister in charge of the table was Milton, a young black from Oakland who had been one of Telegraph Avenue's regular "street people" before hooking up with October 16. The confrontation was over an accusation that Milton had been pocketing large amounts of the daily income for his own use. That kind of rip-off couldn't continue, Sweeney told Milton.

Milton immediately went into his outraged act and called Dennis "a jive honky."

"You ain't got no sweat down in Palo Alto," he raged. "All you white boys got money. I took what you owed me, sucker."

"You're full of shit," Dennis responded.

Milton jumped to his feet. "Well, then you can just git in my chest, motherfucker," he screamed, drawing his fists up to duke it out.

Dennis didn't rise from where he sat with his jaw clamped and his breathing audible. He just stared at Milton.

After the confrontation, Dennis and Rodney drove back down to Palo Alto together. The first subject of conversation was what an asshole Milton was.

"You know," Sweeney said, "in the South you meet a thousand motherfuckers like Milton." They were, Dennis said, mostly black preachers. He had come to hate few things, Dennis claimed, but black Southern preachers were one of them. In Mississippi, he said, they were all looking to fuck young white girls.

Eventually, the subject switched to The Resistance, and Dennis made it clear he thought the organization was going to have to shift its focus now. Friday in Oakland had a lot to teach us, he said. Sweeney also made it clear that he didn't think I felt the same way.

Although I was not privy to them at the time, other conversations of Dennis's after his return from Washington made it apparent that his enthusiasm for The Resistance strategy was waning. The idea, he said, had been to break the peace movement out of its passivity; now, however, getting people to send back draft cards was no longer an appropriate response to either the task or the opportunities of the moment. The entire course of the Sixties would be littered with strategies that had been given six months to succeed and then abandoned for something a notch more obstreperous, and this was such a moment of discard for Dennis Sweeney. He thought "the movement" had to escalate even further. At first, his feelings just led him to reduce his involvement. He continued to put out the newsletter and handle local business but spent increasing amounts of time playing the guitar. It would take me a while to realize it, but my relationship with Dennis Sweeney had peaked on October 16. Within nine months, we would have stopped talking to each other.

On the last day of October, I was released from jail and within days had left the Bay Area to swing through Los Angeles, Arizona, Oregon, and Colorado, giving speeches to build for December 4. Two occurrences during the next month ended up framing my separation from Dennis.

The first was a letter from the President of the United States. It was mimeographed. "Greetings," it began. The gist of it was that I was to report for induction into the armed forces of the United States at the Fresno, California, induction center on December 13. I immediately arranged to have the induction transferred to Oakland, which set the date back to January 17, 1968, but my latitude of movement with the Selective Service System was now exhausted, and the way I eventually chose to deal with my felony and its punishment would prove unacceptable to Dennis.

The second occurrence happened that November. The Resistance was broke again, and I went back to see Joan Baez. This time neither one of us was put off at all. She told stories about jail and said she was planning to go back to sit in again with another group of pacifists on December 18. I reported on the events of October 16, as well as on my coming confrontation with the law. I left with another check and the beginnings of an infatuation.

Within four months, that infatuation would blossom into romance, marriage, and status as prince consort to America's reigning female peace symbol until the Sixties were over. She was already an archetype of the decade, and I would be the man in the photo next to her for the coming year and a half. That change in circumstances convinced Dennis Sweeney that I had sold him and the rest of the commune out.

Allard Lowenstein kept McCarthy's decision to run secret throughout October, telling people not to worry about a candidate but to concentrate on laying an organizational base.

Nevertheless, rumors ran rampant—so much so that when Lowenstein and Gans called a Washington press conference to discuss Dump Johnson's status, the event was heavily attended by representatives of the national media. As usual, Lowenstein did all of the talking.

The reporters' questions largely zeroed in on just who was going to make the run. Lowenstein slid around them with a grin. "Who knows?" he said. "Senator McThis, Senator McThat. Someone will run."

Then one of the reporters asked Lowenstein who the person sitting next to him was, referring to Curtis Gans, his old friend and co-author of their strategy.

"Staff," Allard replied.

Among his critics, one of the things that was always said of Lowenstein was that he shared center stage either poorly or not at all. "Allard had two kinds of people in his life," said one man who knew him for 20 years. "There were his idols . . . and his followers. . . . In his own head, he had no peers. . . . He treated you as an equal until you then indeed became an equal, then he treated you as an underling or banished you to Siberia, froze you out. Public recognition was the key."

Such recognition had not been a major dimension to Allard's life prior to November 1967, but the acceleration of Dump Johnson began to change all that. Where once Lowenstein had made news as a relatively anonymous adjunct to an issue, for the first time the national press began treating him as a figure in his own right.

One of the first of those treatments ran in the *Wall Street Journal* on November 1, 1967, under the headline, "Liberal 'Shaker' Edges to Limelight":

> Allard Lowenstein is an activist who cannot tolerate injustice. When something disturbs him, he tries to do something about it. . . . His current enthusiasm is the "Dump Johnson" movement. . . . But being a professional liberal is what keeps him busiest, and although he isn't widely known to the general public, his reputation behind the scenes is considerable. In fact, he has been a "shaker" in almost every liberal cause extant. . . .
>
> Mr. Lowenstein is a trifle uncomfortable in the limelight. He says he prefers to operate independently and remain in the background . . . and wishes "some better-known figure" headed Dump Johnson. . . . "I feel like an understudy in a Broadway show," he says. "I know I can't sing and dance that well, but I have to go on just the same."

The attention coming Allard's way only intensified when, in the last week of November 1967, Eugene McCarthy announced that he would seek the Democratic nomination for the presidency of the United States. Most of the news accounts mentioned Lowenstein at length and often ran pictures of Allard as well.

McCarthy delivered the first speech of his campaign to a meeting of CCD (Conference of Concerned Democrats) at the Conrad Hilton Hotel in Chicago on December 2. Ten thousand people were crammed into the hall and another 2,000 waited on the steps outside.

Gerald Hill of California's CDC (California Democratic Council) had been scheduled to introduce the candidate, but that arrangement had bothered Allard. Hill, he told Gans and the seminarians running the Alternative Candidates Task Force, was not quite right for the job; he wouldn't give McCarthy enough of a "send-off." Finally, Lowenstein prevailed on Hill to stand down, and Allard took the Hilton's podium himself.

Lowenstein's "introduction" would be one of his most widely remembered performances. "It was Allard's oratorical genius in its highest expression," one protégé later claimed. "People were either on their feet or on the edge of their chairs." The reviews, however, were mixed. "It was Allard at his most demagogic," another old friend remembered. "He was supposed to be leading up to the candidate, but after a while it seemed like he had forgotten about Eugene McCarthy and thought he was the candidate himself." For over half an hour Allard managed to mention Eugene McCarthy, "our next President," about once every ten minutes, but only in passing.

Allard talked about the war and the deceit with which it was being pursued. Throughout the United States, citizens were tired of the lies, tired of misleading numbers, tired of public relations trickery and shallow promises. They were now, he claimed, standing up as was their democratic right and demanding an end to it. Johnson's war was not worth the price we had already paid.

All the while, Eugene McCarthy was standing offstage, waiting to go on. Curtis Gans was in the front row, trying to get Lowenstein's attention and signaling with a motion across his throat to "cut it off."

Allard later claimed he never saw Gans's gestures and thought McCarthy was still up in his suite. He pictured himself as filling a hole in the schedule, as he had for Aaron Henry in Jackson in 1963; he went on and on, all to cheers and interruptions for ovations.

Eugene McCarthy was, by now, stomping around the offstage area, kicking a crushed dixie cup, and muttering to himself. The Senator, who was not a rousing orator, was reportedly furious at being upstaged at his own send-off. Allard's introduction could only show him in the worst possible kind of contrast.

When word finally reached Lowenstein that McCarthy was waiting, he quickly brought McCarthy on, but the damage had been done. The candidate who was supposed to lead what Lowenstein's speech had given the aura of a sacred cavalry charge lectured at length about the Dreyfus case in nineteenth-century France and compared Vietnam to the Punic wars of the Roman Empire. According to one journalist, "After he had spoken for twenty minutes, some listeners were dozing."

McCarthy blamed much of the appearance's disaster on Lowenstein's introduction and later reportedly called it "amateurish." Afterward, Allard tried to get him to go out on the front steps to say something to the 2,000 people who had been waiting there, but McCarthy refused, reportedly with no small amount of anger, and retreated to his hotel suite.

Two days later, The Resistance held its second round of national draft-card returns. I was at the San Francisco demonstration on the steps of the Federal Building, but Dennis Sweeney was not.

According to Federal Bureau of Investigation field office file 25-68927 and headquarters file 25-562642, "There were several speakers . . . and one . . . was DAVID VICTOR HARRIS, identified as former student body president of the Stanford University, Palo Alto, California, through photographs of him . . . taken by [name deleted] utilizing a 35mm Topcon camera. . . ."

I began my speech by saying I had a letter from the President of the United States, as if it were somehow one of the standard communications read at rallies from people who could not attend. The crowd chuckled.

"Greetings," I read.

The crowd chuckled again.

When I had recited my entire induction notice into the microphone, I held the mimeographed document up for everyone to see and tore it into shreds.

"So much for the President of the United States," I said.

My approaching induction preoccupied me. It also marked my growing distance from Dennis Sweeney. Our fates were diverging and we both knew it. Sweeney's only-surviving-son exemption had not been revoked by his local board, just as he had predicted, and by December it was clear he would never be called to report. It was also soon apparent that if anyone from the commune would face any "conspiracy" prosecutions, he also would face them without Dennis. On December 13, two FBI agents visited me to talk about the violations of the conspiracy sections of the Selective Service Act of 1948.

I sat in their car for the interrogation. They immediately asked if I had ever counseled anyone to violate the rules and regulations of Selective Service, and I read to them from my date book a list of the dates and places, when and where I had violated the law. My attitude at the time was to turn the force used against me back on itself by accepting their persecution and transform it into symbolic political confrontation, a game I was convinced I would win rather than lose. I also had a seemingly endless faith in my own capacity to absorb punishment.

The agents' report on our interrogation was eventually filed under the caption "DAVID VICTOR HARRIS/SSN 4-71-46-104/SELECTIVE SERVICE ACT, 1948—SEDITION, COUNSELING EVASION." It went on for page after page. "HARRIS," the agents wrote,

> has urged, counseled, aided and abetted others in violating
> the Selective Service Act. In public addresses he . . . has
> urged those who are registered to refuse to cooperate with the
> Selective Service System and to return their Selective Service
> cards to the Selective Service boards with which they are
> registered. He has urged those who might be ordered for
> induction to refuse induction. . . . Noting that some of his
> speeches had been made under the auspices of The
> Resistance, he was questioned concerning this organization
> and he said . . . it is a loosely functioning organization with
> branches throughout the United States . . . connected in a
> common purpose. He said he is one of the four people who
> started the organization and that one of the other three is
> DENNIS SWEENEY but he would not name the other two
> individuals.

I raised Dennis's name as part of a prearranged strategy between us to try and widen the issue to include himself, but the agents expressed no interest in interrogating Sweeney and would not include him in their follow-up investigation. My interrogation was transcribed and forwarded on December 21 to Bureau headquarters.

Reading those documents thirteen years later was something of a surreal experience. "HARRIS," the opening synopsis warned in capital letters, "SHOULD BE CONSIDERED DANGEROUS DUE TO HIS CLAIMED USE OF MARIJUANA AND LSD AND IN VIEW OF HIS ARREST FOR DISTURBING THE PEACE."

The date of the next entry in the Federal Bureau of Investigation's log of my activities was December 18, when the pacifists returned to the Oakland induction center with Joan Baez. She and I had spent the previous evening running around San Francisco together. The infatuation had now become mutual, and I went over to the induction center the next morning to watch her and the others get arrested.

The two things I would remember about that day in December were that my felonhood was approaching rapidly and my infatuation with the woman who was to be my first wife was now intense. As a consequence of both conditions, I was living in a world of my own and withdrew somewhat from commune life, moving out of the house on Glen Way in East Palo Alto and occupying the commune's third house in the Santa Cruz mountains. There, I sat by myself and read a lot. I was about to pass through the eye of the needle and meet my future head on.

Yet another trait of the Sixties was that success often seemed only to compound dilemma.

In Lowenstein's case, the theme was exemplified by his relationship with Eugene McCarthy. On the verge of 1968, both men had immense suspicions of each other, often with good reason.

McCarthy suspected both Lowenstein's personal agenda and his loyalty. It was no secret that Allard preferred Bobby Kennedy, and McCarthy correctly assumed Allard continued to feel that way. Lowenstein's conversations with Bobby continued throughout the winter, but he maintained his public endorsement of McCarthy throughout the 1968 presidential drama.

For Allard's part, he was still suspicious of McCarthy's energy and campaign skills. The candidate's pace was slow and he was habitually late. Lowenstein fumed. McCarthy said he was "pacing himself" and Lowenstein said that if the "pacing" went on much longer, the movement would lose all the momentum it had gained. Behind the conflict were two different conceptions of the campaign. In those first two months, McCarthy did not yet believe he stood much chance of winning and pictured himself as furthering an issue he felt morally bound to raise. Lowenstein expected McCarthy to run to win and was inevitably disappointed. "I saw him as a candidate," he would later say. "He saw himself as a moral protester for a cause."

Negotiations to merge the Dump Johnson organizational framework with McCarthy's campaign began immediately after the Hilton Hotel speech, and McCarthy's suspicions ensured that Lowenstein was never named to any campaign post. There were two explanations offered for this. One was that Allard and McCarthy had never reached an agreement about an "appropriate" position for him, so Allard just filled in wherever he was needed. The other was that Lowenstein had begun negotiations by saying that he would accept no post except that of campaign manager; when that was not forthcoming, he abandoned to Curtis Gans the details of integrating the Dump Johnson and McCarthy organizations and made himself unavailable.

In either case, Allard was now attached to his candidate only by formalities.

By January 1968, Lowenstein was considering becoming a candidate from New York for the House or the Senate. He was apparently encouraged in his Senate aspirations by Robert Kennedy, the state's other Senator. "You running for Congress," Kennedy reportedly told Allard, "is like the Pope running for parish priest."

The impact of Kennedy's blessing on his confidence was sufficient for Allard to convene a private meeting in the middle of the month "to explore" his senatorial possibilities. He brought together selected personal friends whose frank advice he trusted, several people from the Conference of Concerned Democrats who were now with McCarthy for President, and several from Alternative Candidates Task Force, now with Students for McCarthy.

According to one of the meeting's participants, Allard wanted the group "to convince him" to run for the Senate. He said he was viewing such an effort as a way of "giving the McCarthy campaign in New York some focus." The McCarthy people reportedly responded that if Lowenstein wanted to run, he should do so without having to camouflage it as a McCarthy strategy.

The meeting led to neither a yes nor a no, and Allard continued to stew about his options through the winter.

My own options narrowed considerably on January 17, 1968. At 6 A.M. I reported to the offices of the San Mateo County Draft Board, where I and some 50 other inductees were loaded on a bus and driven to Oakland.

At the induction center, a crowd estimated as "approximately 150 to 200 people" by the FBI had already assembled to

> demonstrate sympathy and support for DAVID VICTOR HARRIS. . . . The inductees walked single file into the building, through the crowd. . . . When HARRIS stepped from the bus, he immediately left the line of inductees and walked directly to a group of assembled newsmen with microphones and news cameras. HARRIS spoke for approximately five minutes, stating that . . . he was pleased that he had finally been ordered to report because he now had the chance to set an example for other persons engaged in activities against the war in Vietnam and the Selective Service System. . . . Photographs were taken of HARRIS as he spoke. HARRIS then left with a large number of demonstrators and the crowd disbanded.

The "demonstrators" and I proceeded to a park in Berkeley where The Resistance was serving breakfast. The line I had crossed was invisible, and the experience left me feeling oddly disembodied. All the commune was in the park afterward.

"Well," I said to Dennis, "I'm on my way."

The remark bothered Dennis. "You know," he said, "you don't have to go to jail."

I thought he was joking and laughed.

Dennis dropped the subject.

Thirteen days later, after a flurry of memo exchanges among the FBI, Local Board 71, and several federal attorneys in different jurisdictions, a federal grand jury for the Northern District of California indicted me for "refusal to submit to a lawful order of induction." The trial date was eventually set for the last few days of May.

At least in my head, the next year and a half amount to no more than a momentary pause before incarceration. I was "in transit," always conscious of what was waiting for me down the line. In that frame of mind, I meant to make the most of the symbol I had turned myself into. I also wanted as many signs that I mattered as I could collect.

The most obvious expression of those needs came out in my relationship with Joan Baez. Confronted by what awaited me, I indulged my infatuation completely. She got out of jail several days after my induction refusal, and we spent the next few weeks largely together. Within ten days, we had announced that we would undertake a month-and-a-half-long speaking tour of college campuses in March. Within 60 days, we were married, a union that eventually lasted 38 months and produced one child. I spent 20 of those 38 months in prison. Of our remaining time, we rarely spent more than three continuous weeks together because of the intense demands of our different schedules. Between that January in 1968 and July 1969, when I was finally incarcerated, I gave over 500 speeches in 20 different states. Some of those I gave with her. Most I did by myself. It was a great blur in which what we believed thoroughly dominated who we were. Perhaps only a Sixties veteran who had intense politics and an intense relationship going at the same time can understand. There was an overwhelming urge to get all parts of my life stacked up on top of my political base. Somehow, anything less felt like abandoning the cause. It was a hard, if not impossible, balancing act to sustain. Ten years after it ended, David Harris's romance with Joan Baez is, for me, indistinguishable from the politics of the moment. We were public creatures. Sweet-voiced heroine of a generation joins with young knight advancing in the battle for peace in our time. Without the intoxication of those roles and the image they fostered, I doubt whether the relationship would ever have come off.

On a personal level, I began it heavily overmatched. Not quite 22 and still chasing visions of myself, I was tying my life to a woman five years older than I who had already made more of a name and fortune than I could hope to equal. I found the disproportion of that arrangement intensely frustrating and still hold it responsible for much of my private craziness over the remainder of the decade. During those first weeks of infatuation, the signs were visual. She didn't like my blue-jean look and ended up taking me around San Francisco and buying me new clothes. Late in January I drove down to Cooley Street to see Dennis and the rest of the commune. I arrived in my superstar girl friend's Jaguar wearing $50 bell bottoms, a $30 shirt, a $150 leather jacket, and $60 boots.

Dennis Sweeney took one look at me and walked out of the room.

On the last day in January, a string of National Liberation Front assaults on the Vietnamese battlefield did more in a week to undercut Lyndon Johnson's war policies than all the strategies of Allard Lowenstein, Dennis Sweeney, and David Harris combined.

For months, the Johnson administration had been reciting the litany that the National Liberation Front was on "its last legs" and "the end of the war" was "in sight." But a new enemy offensive beginning on the final day of Tet, Vietnam's most important holiday, gave the lie to that argument altogether. According to Defense Department statistics, the NLF and North Vietnamese Army put close to 100,000 troops in the field, attacking 36 out of 44 provincial capitals, 5 of Vietnam's 6 autonomous cities, and 23 American and South Vietnamese airfields and military bases, all at the same time. Most attacks were allegedly "repelled" within two or three days, but Army statistics later accorded the NLF "temporary control" of 10 provincial capitals. In Saigon, portions of the United States Embassy grounds had been held by Viet Cong sappers for 6 hours. In Hue, 4 North Vietnamese Army and 6 National Liberation Front battalions held off 3 battalions from the U.S. Army, 4 from the Marines, and 11 from the Army of the Republic of Vietnam until February 25. The United States command in Saigon later pointed to its statistics as proof that Tet was an "American and South Vietnamese victory," claiming that they had killed at least 50,000 Viet Cong and North Vietnamese Army soldiers and taken 6,991 prisoners while only absorbing 20,985 casualties themselves.

Now, however, it was obvious that the war would be a long and vicious haul.

The primary domestic reaction when Tet exploded in snippets of blood and gristle on the evening news was shock. Like a good portion of the country, Dennis Sweeney watched it happen on television. For all he knew, the Viet Cong casualties the announcer talked about included the people who had given him his ring the summer before.

Dennis and Rodney stationed themselves in front of Cooley Street's TV set while The Resistance presses ran in the garage. Another draft-card return date had been set for April 3, and the customary literature runs were being made. Dennis helped with those but not much else. More and more of his time was spent playing music with an informal band that had grown up among several commune members and outside friends. I was either off somewhere with Joan Baez or out of town giving speeches.

As "remaining pockets of VC" were being "cleaned up" in and around Saigon, CBS showed the chief of South Vietnam's national police grab a "VC suspect" by the hair, place his own snub-nosed revolver against the man's temple, and splatter the suspect's brains out the other side of his head.

"Those bastards," Rodney screamed, kicking at the wall.

Dennis Sweeney ground his teeth, jiggled his leg, and took his breath in sips. He didn't say a thing.

The Tet Offensive soon became something of a guiding light for Sweeney. The example of the NLF was also a hook for his need to strike out in a separate political direction, and that February he began doing so for the first time since we had organized The Resistance together the year before. His new strategy was carried out behind my back. David, Dennis told the others, was too tied up in this Joan Baez thing to provide the leadership he once had. The situation was ripe to break out into a whole new level of opposition, he claimed; only the spark to ignite it was missing, and rather than providing it, I was out riding around in fancy cars.

As Dennis perceived the situation that February, the government's credibility had been crushed once and for all, a dynamic that would make liberals ripe for defection leftward. To crystalize that sentiment required an act by "the movement" that somehow embodied a new anger and contempt for the war makers. In Dennis Sweeney's mind, that act was sabotage.

The idea took the first few people he mentioned it to by storm. One was Rodney from the commune. From him, it spread to a couple of other commune members and a few people from Berkeley as well. Dennis's proposed target was the naval ROTC clubhouse on the Stanford campus near the football stadium. Isolated in a eucalyptus grove, it would be, he claimed, easy and relatively safe to hit. The building was made of wood, so gasoline would be enough to set it off, late at night when it was empty. They would use the simplest possible ignition device, a burning cigarette wedged into an open book of matches. There were dry runs in Cooley Street's backyard. The would-be saboteurs calculated the fuse would give them a minimum of five minutes to get away from the scene before the burning started.

Gasoline was poured into empty plastic milk containers that could be left behind and incinerated in the ensuing combustion.

On February 18, while I was in Arizona giving a series of speeches for the two Resistance chapters there, Dennis and the others struck.

At approximately 1 A.M. they parked their car in one of the empty parking slots on the street flanking Encina Hall on the Stanford campus; carrying their gasoline, they crossed the lot where Humphrey had been chased and moved into the nearby eucalyptus grove, heading in the direction of the football stadium at a trot. No one was around the naval ROTC clubhouse. Sweeney and the others sloshed out gasoline, set their fuses, and took off for the car at a gallop. Sweeney hopped in behind the wheel and turned the engine over. And over and over. In his frantic attempts to get away, he had flooded it.

"Oh shit," Rodney yelled.

At that moment, the naval ROTC clubhouse went up in a "giant sheet of flame" that looked like an orange mountain on the other side of the trees. Dennis and the others immediately abandoned the vehicle and ran toward some bushes near the library to hide. Rodney told them to wait in the hiding place and went running for Roble Hall, a woman's dormitory, to borrow a car. A woman he knew was starting to pull her brand-new Ford pickup out of the parking lot when he dashed up. Her date of the evening was driving.

Rodney yanked the door open, told her it was an emergency and that he had to use her truck right now. She agreed and Rodney peeled out of the lot, leaving her to explain to her date just who that black man covered with sweat and smelling like gasoline had been.

Rodney picked the others up by the library and they all fled back to Cooley Street undetected.

Officially, the Stanford ROTC fire was one of the first such campus occurrences of the decade and remains an "unsolved arson" to this day. In September of 1968, more than six months after it happened, the FBI picked up information that Sweeney and Rodney had been involved, but the trail would be cold by then. Their suspicions would, however, keep agents hanging around Dennis's life for several years. By then, Sweeney would have long since decided that his effort at sabotage had been a "severe miscalculation." The arson threw suspicion on all Stanford's peace groups, and most made haste to denounce it in the strongest possible terms. On several occasions over the next few years, he would bring it up as an example of "a very serious mistake" he had once made, something that had put his whole political cause in jeopardy.

The guilt that "mistake" incited would also provide fertile ground for the incubation of Dennis's madness. The guilt grew as time passed, and when he eventually began to believe he was being "monitored" by what were at first only vaguely discernible nefarious forces, he was sure that his "mistake" was the reason why.

In New Hampshire, the manager of Lyndon Johnson's campaign had already made a serious blunder by telling the press that if McCarthy, who then was standing at 2 percent in the national polls, got even as much as 40 percent of the vote, it would be a "serious defeat" for the President. After Tet, "clean for Gene" students began to flood the state and the crowds showing up to see McCarthy became larger and more enthusiastic—enough so that McCarthy himself began to believe he might win and stepped up the pace of his activity.

About the same time, Allard Lowenstein visited Bobby Kennedy again at Hickory Hill and once again asked Bobby to run. Kennedy seemed torn but again said it couldn't be done. "Now," Bobby told him, "your friend McCarthy has ruined everything because he cannot win in New Hampshire—the result can only be that he will make Johnson even more powerful."

Lowenstein told Kennedy he was wrong about the power of Johnson and the weakness of the antiwar forces—but even if he weren't, the war had to be challenged for the sake of the country, whatever the politics involved. Kennedy was apparently moved, but not far enough to change his answer.

Lowenstein called Kennedy again several days later from New Hampshire on a McCarthy campaign phone. Still without a formal campaign position other than advisor, Allard was spending the weeks prior to the election running the local Portsmouth, New Hampshire, McCarthy for President office. The perch hardly befitted someone who thought of himself as the effort's original architect and quite possibly the next Senator from New York, but Allard apparently did not complain. "McCarthy's going to surprise some people," he predicted.

Kennedy said he doubted it strongly. It was February 29, and those doubts lasted another 13 days.

On March 12, McCarthy carried 42.2 percent of the New Hampshire Democratic vote, and when Republican write-ins were counted, his name was on a full half of the total ballots. "It was a miracle," the Kennedy biographer who had accompanied

Lowenstein to Hickory Hill in September exclaimed. "Ten thousand college students beat the President of the United States. . . . Gene McCarthy, who was a joke in January, became a myth in March. . . . Suddenly, Lyndon Johnson's renomination was in doubt."

It was a sweet moment for the junior Senator from Minnesota. Robert Kennedy telephoned with congratulations, and McCarthy told an aide that Kennedy had made "a tired crack about 'all those mornings at the factory gates.'" Even that didn't dampen McCarthy's spirits, and soon afterwards he left for his victory celebration downstairs in the ballroom.

The scene there was tumultuous. "The Children's Crusade," as McCarthy's troops had been dubbed, knew they had beaten Lyndon Johnson and they too thought it a miracle. Allard Lowenstein was among the group of dignitaries strung together on the back of the platform, rumpled from the drive from Portsmouth, but exuberant. He had planned to wear his one suit, but it had been stolen out of his car so he showed up in the same clothes in which he had spent the day walking precincts. There had been a movement among some of the Lowenstein partisans on the campaign staff to have Allard say a few words, but that had been quashed as "inappropriate."

When McCarthy came in, the crowd cut loose. He moved along the stage, shaking hands and exchanging greetings with most of the dignitaries, but his mood stiffened when he reached Lowenstein.

"Huh," he reportedly said with a tone of suspicion, "Lowenstein. Where were you in New Hampshire?"

10

No one grasped the new political reality engendered by Eugene McCarthy's 42 percent victory in New Hampshire more intensely than Robert Kennedy. At noon on March 13, Kennedy flew to Washington and, upon getting off the plane, was swarmed with reporters.

"I am actively reassessing the possibility of whether I will run against President Johnson," Kennedy told them.

To all intents and purposes he was now in the race. Bobby began by making a round of phone calls to his trusted advisors, summoning them to a meeting at his Hickory Hill home on the evening of March 15. One of those he called was Allard Lowenstein.

"Well, Al, baby," he said, "I've decided to take your advice and run."

Lowenstein would later claim that he was shocked at the declaration. In response, he mumbled something to the effect that people would think he was trying to steal the McCarthy kids' victory before they had even had a chance to celebrate it.

"Oh, come on, Al," Bobby chided. "Can't you find something more original than that to say? That's what all the papers are saying."

Despite the negative reaction, Kennedy wanted him at the Hickory Hill meeting, and Allard would never have considered missing it. Ten people were there for a previously scheduled dinner party, several Kennedy children were listening to the Jefferson Airplane on the stereo, and in the midst of it, Bobby and his advisors set about the business of trying to draft a speech announcing his candidacy. Lowenstein, according to one account, "warned that McCarthy would take the news badly and that the anti-Johnson forces might be so badly split that their efforts would cancel each other out." As one of McCarthy's best-known backers, Allard himself was in a delicate position. In order to preserve what he considered to be proper decorum in that potentially compromising circumstance, Lowenstein sat in a separate room during the actual drafting process. "I'm completely involved in the McCarthy campaign," he told one of the dinner guests, "but," he added, pointing through the door at Bobby, "that man ought to be President." As pieces of the speech were prepared, they were carried into the next room where Lowenstein reviewed them, trying to make the announcement as inoffensive as possible to McCarthy and his followers.

Despite Lowenstein's efforts, the McCarthyites were decidedly unmollified when the announcement speech was eventually delivered. Henceforth, the liberal presidential effort of 1968 would be split into two halves, with Allard Lowenstein inevitably caught in the middle.

His own spring offensive having been a failure, Dennis Sweeney soon formulated a new approach that reflected his increasing immersion in music. He and three other draft resisters, including Rodney from the commune, had formed a band called The Fool, after a character from the Tarot deck denoting infinity. Convinced that music was the perfect vehicle to draw uncommitted people into political circles, Sweeney envisioned rigging up a flatbed truck so that its back would serve as a stage and equipping it with generators. Using that truck, The Fool could haul into a location, play music, draw a crowd, and intersperse the sounds with short political messages, thereby mobilizing "the masses."

Unlike his plans for the naval ROTC building, Sweeney shared this strategy with me. He and I signed a fund-raising letter to The Resistance mailing list that spring, mentioning "a Resistance road show composed of a band, guerilla theater group, speakers, literature, and a library of films." We listed $1,000 "for the purchase of a truck or bus for a traveling education project" among immediate expenses. Soon a used 1941 Diamond Reo flatbed truck was purchased, and work to recondition and modify it was begun immediately.

On March 18, Dennis Sweeney watched Robert Kennedy's announcement on Cooley Street's television.

"He'll never be President," Dennis said. "They'll kill him first."

By then, Joan Baez and I had launched our nationwide campus speaking tour. Eventually I was able to reconstruct it from FBI files captioned "DAVID VICTOR HARRIS: SEDITION."

Since my induction refusal, I had increasingly become a focus of scrutiny. Federal agents now tracked my comings and goings, noting the cars I rode in, the houses I visited, the things I said.

The "Director, FBI" sent an "airtel" to the San Francisco office when the Joan Baez/David Harris tour was announced, ordering it to "immediately conduct necessary investigation to determine activities and itinerary of . . . subjects. . . . Coverage of these individuals should be detailed so that statements made by them be reported verbatim to insure that any statements they make may be taken into consideration in determining whether prosecutive action should be taken. . . ."

The FBI airtel about BAEZ and HARRIS went on at length but made no mention of the two subjects' love affair.

Frankly, I was not all that sure of where it stood myself. When we left San Francisco, she told me that things were through between us, but a day later the affair was on again. Four days after that it was back off and two more days later back on. Another week after all that and we were married.

Much of the magnetism both attracting and repelling us was a function of the tour. We traveled in an entourage which also included the co-director of her Institute for the Study of Nonviolence, her manager, and her secretary. In the towns where we stopped, she would usually give a concert and we would both speak at a campus lecture, hold a press conference, and appear on local TV and radio shows.

Where I alone might draw a crowd of 200 if I was lucky, having Joan on the stage with me multiplied those numbers by at least four to five times. Where I alone might get a short mention in the back pages, as her political partner I was part of a feature story with pictures. She was treated as a legend wherever she went, and I was swept up in some of that charisma. Having a woman everyone else seemed to want was, at the age of 22, an overwhelmingly seductive proposition. Two months away from a felony trial at which I knew I would be found guilty, I felt as if I had little to lose.

For her part, she reportedly thought I was the best speaker she had ever heard. I was something of a hero, too, and that charisma had its effects. Linked with me, she was now the beneficiary of the credibility generated by The Resistance's willingness to sacrifice for what we believed in. For someone as wrapped up in her political identity as she was, that must have been exceedingly attractive. Since I was facing a five-year felony charge, it was also a relationship that had a somewhat temporary cast to it from the beginning, however much we may have denied it to ourselves at the time.

Now that I am 36 years old and married for a second time, it is hard to look back to a divorce ten years in the past and see love on the other side, but I am sure it was there. In her words, we made "a great alliance." The legend of Mr. and Mrs. Peace in America was about to be born.

During the third week of March, the first of what would become a succession of newspaper stories appeared, claiming that Lowenstein was about to abandon McCarthy for Kennedy's campaign and citing "a source high in the McCarthy organization." Allard fired off a string of denials and renewed pledges of his loyalty to the Senator from Minnesota.

One of the people to whom Lowenstein had to deny the reports was Bobby Kennedy. On March 22, the two men were both on the bus returning prominent Democrats to New York City from a party dinner in upstate New York, and Allard sat next to Bobby for a while. Kennedy wanted to know if it was true Lowenstein was ready to switch. According to the biographer traveling with them, "Lowenstein wanted to. McCarthy had cut him out of his campaign and had told ugly stories about him. But he told Kennedy that publicly he had to stay with McCarthy awhile longer. For a few minutes, Kennedy brooded about this, about how he should have run earlier, and how Lowenstein understood loyalty. Then he scrawled a note to Lowenstein on a sheet of paper and passed it to him at the back of the bus." The note read:

> For Al,
> who knew the lesson of Emerson and taught it to the rest of us: "They did not yet see, and thousands of young men as hopeful, now crowding to the barriers of their careers, did not yet see if a single man plant himself on his convictions and then abide, the huge world will come round to him."
>
> From his friend,
> Bob Kennedy

Several days later, Lowenstein saw one of his old Yale protégés. He talked about how the stories continued to come out and how he had to continue to deny them. Allard claimed the "source high in the McCarthy campaign" was McCarthy himself, planting stories in an attempt to "force" him "out of the campaign." It was funny, Lowenstein said. To the public it looked like Bobby was the brutal one and McCarthy the nice guy, but in his own experience, it was almost exactly the opposite. McCarthy, he claimed, was behaving in "very bad ways" and being "incredibly rude." Kennedy, on the other hand, was being "very conciliatory." Then Allard's face softened into a hopelessly exuberant smile. "Look what he gave me," he said, producing the note. Germinating idol worship was obvious.

Allard Lowenstein would keep that note from "his friend, Bob Kennedy," on his person for months, pulling it out and showing it again and again when the mood struck him.

On March 26, Joan Baez and I were married in New York City. We flew a number of relatives and friends out from California for the ceremony and put them up at an expensive Midtown hotel. Among the friends were five members of the commune, including Dennis Sweeney. Until then, the commune did not have a clear idea of the luxury of my new circumstances, but the hotel made that obvious. They were the only people wearing Levis in the entire building.

"Jesus, David," Dennis blurted, looking at the $60-a-night room my soon-to-be-wife had rented for them and shaking his head.

The commune chose to treat the luxury as a momentary amusement and soon discovered that if you dialed a certain number on the house phone, whatever food you wanted would be delivered to the door. That night, the commune contingent ran up a $300 room service bill, ordering, among other things, a giant baked Alaska. I sat around with them for a while, but couldn't get with it. Nor did the commune seem at ease with me. By getting married, I was saying good-bye to that part of my life and they knew it as well as I. Joan was in no way willing to consider living in a commune with twelve scruffy men in their early twenties.

The next day, all the guests for the wedding were driven in limousines to a Manhattan "peace church" for the wedding. The commune was dressed in its finest. Dennis was wearing his velvet coat. Timmy had ratted his mane of hair so it stood out for a foot and a half on all sides of his head. People stopped and stared as he crossed the lobby. I wore a three-piece, dark blue Brooks Brothers suit, purchased two days earlier on my wife's credit card. The ceremony took 15 minutes, and after a brief reception, I returned to our suite and ordered lobster from room service. After I ate, I threw up.

There was no honeymoon.

On March 28, according to FBI field office file 25-68927, JOAN BAEZ AND DAVID HARRIS, now married, addressed an 8:30 P.M. meeting at Harvard University.

On March 21, Lyndon Baines Johnson announced that he would no longer seek his party's nomination.

With that, Allard K. Lowenstein's name went into the history books. He would be given almost exclusive credit for initiating the overthrow. During the next six months, a variety of national news publications would call him "the moving force behind Dump Johnson," "prime mover of the Democratic revolt," "the original Dump Johnson apostle," and even, in headlines, "The Man Who Ran Against Lyndon Johnson."

That fame automatically made him a principal player in the dogfight which then took over the Democratic party's presidential primaries. It pitted Eugene McCarthy, the man Lowenstein had asked to run and continued to endorse, against Hubert Humphrey, the man for whom Lowenstein had campaigned in 1964, and Robert Kennedy, the man Lowenstein was coming to worship.

On April 2, McCarthy carried the Wisconsin primary outright. According to *New York Post* columnist James Wechsler, a longtime friend of Allard's, "On primary night, Eugene McCarthy publicly thanked Lowenstein, whose organizing of students and other concerned citizens, he said, had been crucial to his lonely, successful combat."

It must have been a tribute to the magnanimous feeling that carrying Wisconsin had evoked in the Senator. By then, the two men, in fact, had little use for each other.

The overthrow of Lyndon Johnson was the first major political earthquake in the spring of 1968.

The second occurred just days after the first. On April 5, 1968, Martin Luther King, the country's foremost black leader, was assassinated in Memphis, Tennessee. Ghettos all over the country broke out in riots as the news spread, and in several cities, National Guard units had to be dispatched to maintain order. Lyndon Johnson went on national television in an attempt to calm things. Joan and I watched his speech from a motel room in Ithaca, New York.

We had participated in a New York City demonstration marking The Resistance's third national draft-card return two days earlier and then flown upstate to be part of a similar Resistance ceremony there. After our performances in Ithaca were over, we had planned to rent a car and drive back to New York City but were unable to secure a vehicle. According to an airtel to "DIRECTOR, FBI" from "SAC, ALBANY, (25-13114)," Ithaca's rental car offices and airline counters were under instructions to notify the FBI before selling any tickets or renting any vehicles to Joan Baez or David Harris. When I subsequently appeared at Ithaca's Hertz outlet, the clerk referred to a note taped near the cash register indicating "no cars available," with our names and another notation, "call FBI." The clerk told me all their cars were tied up, and so we went back to the hotel for the night and watched Lyndon Johnson on television.

The President looked straight at the camera. "My fellow Americans," he promised, drawing words out in grave Texas tones. "We shall overcome."

I picked up a glass full of water from the bedside table and flung it at the television set. As far as I was concerned, he had defiled the words just by putting them in his mouth.

By the first week of April, Allard Lowenstein had made up his mind to escape the Kennedy-McCarthy crossfire by running for elective office himself. Abandoning his Senate aspirations, he settled on the Fifth Congressional District, covering part of Nassau County on Long Island. Allard rented a comfortable brick house for his family in Long Beach, New York, and soon became the first resident of that town ever to run for Congress. The district's Democratic incumbent was retiring, but the primary would nonetheless be a hard uphill fight. Allard was by no means the candidate of the "Nassau Democratic machine," which intended to run its own man.

Lowenstein would later explain that he had only come into the race after being invited to do so by a group of Nassau County "McCarthy Democrats," but in this race, as in most of those to follow, he would throughout the campaign have to face charges of being a carpetbagger. He was not running for alderman, he responded. He was running for Congress, an office in which experience on a national level, such as his own, was of overwhelming importance. To further counter his interloper image, Allard personally designed a leaflet that he carried with him everywhere. "AT LAST!" it was headlined, "A CONGRESSMAN FROM LONG BEACH."

Allard's official announcement appeared in the *New York Times* on April 11. The next day it was the subject of a long column in the *New York Post*, written by Lowenstein's friend, James Wechsler. "No other individual did more than Lowenstein to set in motion the sequence of events climaxed by Mr. Johnson's formal withdrawal," it stated flatly.

For Lowenstein, his friend the columnist also noted, the decision to run for Congress "represents a very real personal turning point. . . . This unusual citizen . . . must now settle down for a long political siege on a limited landscape. No doubt there will be intermittent flying trips to McCarthy campaign fronts in other states, but his immediate major mission is clear. Now this fiery battler for others will be speaking for himself and he isn't running for exercise."

The New York Democratic primary was scheduled for June 17, 1968, 13 days after the California winner-take-all presidential balloting where Robert Kennedy and Eugene McCarthy were expected to wage their most crucial battle.

The three basic elements of Allard's Fifth Congressional District campaign were basically the same as in all his political exploits.

The first was Lowenstein himself. *New York* magazine described him as "short, balding and near-sighted, with the beginning of a paunch that oozes gently over his belt. He wears wash-and-wear slacks, nondescript sports coats, flapping woolen neckties, dusty brown Hush Puppies and a harassed look."

"I am," the candidate told his audiences in the district, "neither rightist, leftist nor liberal. I'm an independent, a mainstream McCarthy Democrat. . . . I don't want to be dramatic, but I think this country faces the very serious possibility of falling apart if it continues on its present course. That's what motivates many of us who are not normally politicians to get involved so deeply this year trying to affect events through elections. My faith is that the electoral process in the United States can work."

The second element was Lowenstein's widespread political connections. Despite the McCarthy trappings, the most important of his connections were with Bobby Kennedy. He was fond of telling reporters that Bobby had urged him to wait and become part of his presidential cabinet rather than try for Congress.

Kennedy himself never appeared on Lowenstein's behalf, but he dispatched several nationally known Kennedy surrogates to campaign for him and frequently asked his staff for updates on just how Lowenstein appeared to be doing. As spring progressed, Lowenstein's Kennedy identification had become so strong that the machine opposition switched tactics and derided Allard as "Kennedy's man," apparently in hopes of splitting away the district's McCarthy voters, who had allegedly issued Lowenstein his "invitation" to run in the first place.

The final element in Lowenstein's 1968 congressional campaign was, as usual, students. One journalist described him: "He is 39 years old, seems younger, and has surrounded himself with an enormous crowd of damp-skinned young people who are convinced that with Al Lowenstein to lead them, they can reshape the world." Fifteen-year-olds answered the Lowenstein-for-Congress phones, 18-year-olds leafleted shopping malls, 22-year-olds walked precincts, 21-year-olds called reporters to complain about campaign coverage, and 10-year-olds handed out fortune cookies with Lowenstein's name inside to returning commuters on the Long Island Railway depots. On any given night, a floating group of anywhere from five to 50 volunteers sprawled out on the floors and couches of the Lowenstein house in Long Beach, although Allard himself often left for Manhattan in the evenings to make the political rounds there and then spend the night at his West Eighty-second Street apartment. According to veterans of the campaign, it was a nonstop string of 18 and 20-hour days.

In that immense tangle, all lines led back to Lowenstein. The young people thought he was "selfless" and "understanding." He was like a father to them. "He's great," one teenager told a reporter. "All he wants to do is shape things." Years later, the same tone was used to describe him from memory, even by those of his workers who eventually fled the campaign, desperate to retrieve some sense of identity that was not dominated by Allard.

One remembered, "All that energy he had—enough, it seemed, to run the whole country—was overwhelming when confined to a congressional district. The way everything was arranged, it was hard for both you and Allard not to start thinking of your life as an extension of his own. It became a pattern you just sank deeper and deeper into. Allard always had someone for you to be. He never forced you, but if you hung around him, he was just impossible to resist. When things really got intense, that started burning people out."

Another veteran of that primary recalled what they called the "wonder kid" phenomenon:

> It was just this thing that Allard did over and over, it seemed like once a week almost. He would be out in one of the local offices, say in Massapequa, and would find some young guy stapling leaflets or something and Allard would discover him. I mean he would say things like "How could someone with your talent be stapling leaflets?" and immediately he pulled him off that job and put him to work driving him around. In that spot, Allard was pretty overwhelming for some 19- or 20-

year-old guy. They got to be privy to Al's meetings with big-time politicians, see all his influence up close. Inevitably at some point, when the wonder kid's worship of Allard was at its peak, he would be given some hopelessly difficult task to do like "Go see politician X and get me on the delegate list" or "Y and Z are telling incredible lies about me. Go find them and put a stop to it." The tasks were always beyond what the wonder kids could do, and so inevitably they failed and had to come back and report their inadequacy to Allard. They always felt terrible. That was followed by rejection. Allard was upset—not angry, just disappointed. Usually the wonder kid would be assigned to do something besides drive Allard for a while. Then, usually after a few days, he would forgive him and accept him back. I mean, from the wonder kid's point of view, the debt you owe that kind of "understanding" and "generosity" is immeasurable. "Hooked" is a mild word for the effect. It was a pattern of control that was beyond belief.

A few of these "wonder kids" later, in their most private conversations, mentioned encounters with Allard at the West Eighty-second Street apartment similar to Dennis Sweeney's in the motel and mine in Big Sur Hot Springs. Though often confused by the encounters, most only ended up working even harder in the galloping onslaught of Long Beach's first congressman.

Despite the killing pace of the campaign, Lowenstein seemed to thrive. By May, he had risen from underdog to even money, maybe better.

I was now living with my new wife in her house in Carmel Valley. My trial was scheduled for the 27th of May. Dennis Sweeney drove down to visit me in late April. Until then, most of the political difference and personal disapproval Dennis felt had gone unexpressed between us. When he left, he would to all intents and purposes have no relationship left.

Sweeney came inside the house gingerly, staring at the custom shape of the place and the hand-painted wall tiles. Joan stayed upstairs the entire time he was there. Sweeney motioned with his arms at the surrounding house.

"How can you do this, David?" he asked. "I mean look at all this."

I knew exactly what he meant. The incongruity of my politics and my new physical situation haunted me, and Joan and I had already fought over the question dozens of times. "What can I say?" I answered. "I'm going to have to work all this out with her. Now I'm just trying to deal with it as best I can."

Dennis snorted through his nose. "In the meantime, you're living like some kinda fucking king up on top of a hill in a palace."

"I guess so," I said.

Dennis snorted again and didn't push the subject any further. When we started up again, it was about the other subject that had been bothering him.

"What are you going to do about your trial?" he asked.

I would plead not guilty, I told him, on the grounds that simple refusal is not in and of itself enough to convict. The law clearly stated that I had to have done what I did with "intent and bad purpose." I would defend myself by explaining my reasons for doing what I did. That way, I pointed out, I could use the trial as a political forum.

"What do you think the jury will say?"

"Guilty," I said. I also speculated I would get 18 months, the standard draft sentence being handed out in San Francisco courts.

Dennis chewed his lip and looked at his feet for a moment. "Why go to jail?" he finally asked, leaning forward on his elbows with great intensity. "Organizers are needed on the streets, David. You're just throwing yourself and the movement away in jail." He suggested using a legal technicality to escape conviction.

"You're not supposed to let them take you, David. You're supposed to stay out, however you can," he said.

"I don't believe you're saying this, Dennis. If I felt that way I'd still have a deferment. I've given all kinds of speeches telling people they ought to join The Resistance, and there are people in jail for doing what I told them to. If I let them go to jail while I stay out, that makes it all just so much hypocritical bullshit."

"No," Dennis insisted, "that's not true. As long as you keep organizing. Otherwise you're just being a martyr, and we martyrs are no good to anybody."

"You sound like Stop the Draft Week," I snapped.

"You sound like Joan Baez," he snapped back.

We glared at each other for a minute, and the conversation never went much further.

In the next few days, Dennis told several people that I had "sold out" to my rich and famous wife and lost touch with "the people" and "the movement," not unlike the Joshua who had gone Barbados

Dennis used to sing about. I had a Jesus complex, he added, and wanted to be "nailed to a cross."

We were to have only two more discussions of any length before losing touch altogether. Both of those would be strained.

B y May, Sweeney's "mobile education project" was blossoming. The Diamond Reo's engine had been rebuilt and a new bed constructed that folded down into a stage. Using money raised for The Resistance by a Joan Baez benefit, The Fool had purchased amplifiers and instruments, including a Gibson electric guitar for Dennis. He was the band's rhythm guitarist and by far its least proficient musician. He had what other guitarists called "heavy hands." He could keep up with the others but had to practice very hard to do so.

At the same time, Dennis also arranged The Fool's logistics and was the principal articulator of its ultimate mission of roadside liberation. During the spring, word had spread through the movement grapevine that a coalition was being put together to demonstrate at the Democratic National Convention in Chicago in August, and Sweeney argued that The Resistance road show ought to be part of it, driving slowly East, stopping in towns along the way to play and picking up converts. In a paper titled "The Long March," which he circulated around the organization, Sweeney called the Chicago confrontation, "an act symbolic of the revolution America must have to restore its humanity and end its exploitation of people around the world" and "an opportunity to talk with thousands of people who share our determination to turn this society from its path of death and destruction, but to whom we are distant creatures of a strange culture." His shorthand name for the road show's participation was "The Caravan."

The name stuck, but the idea of going to Chicago was greeted with suspicion by a number of Resistance organizers, myself included. It was commonly believed that Chicago's mayor, Richard Daley, would not allow the gathering to take place—and traveling 2,000 miles to get beat up made no sense. To turn that sentiment around, Dennis Sweeney arranged a meeting of himself, me, and an organizer who would eventually be one of the Chicago Seven and had given the impassioned speech at the final banquet in Bratislava the summer before. I drove up from Carmel Valley and we met in an East Palo Alto steak house.

The organizer said that they had already begun negotiating with the city over assembly and parade permits. Up to a million people would come, he claimed. Faced with that huge wave of citizenry, Mayor Daley would have to accede the right to congregate.

The conversation lasted until the Chicago Seven man had to leave for a meeting in Berkeley. Afterward, Sweeney and I went back to Cooley Street. I told Dennis right away that I didn't go for it. The whole scheme was going to end up getting people stomped by the Chicago police department, just like in Oakland. Unsuspecting people would get creamed, and then it would all be praised as "the radicalization process."

Dennis disagreed, but I had the advantage. I was the western Resistance's principal spokesman and fund raiser. Whatever he felt, Sweeney had none of my leverage inside the organization, and it was a foregone conclusion that my arguments would win.

I could have stayed the night in one of Cooley Street's extra beds but instead used one of my wife's credit cards to rent a motel room. I felt uncomfortable at the commune, and the commune was no longer at ease with me.

On May 27, 1968, the trial of David Victor Harris for violation of Title 50 United States Code, Section 462, commenced in the federal court for the Northern District of California. From an attorney's point of view, I was a great handicap as a client. I expected to be convicted and pleaded not guilty solely to make the most direct political statement I could. As a consequence, shortly after the prosecution began its case, I stood up and absolved Local Board 71 of responsibility for any violation of its own operating regulations in their decision to order my induction. My lawyer had found at least four such violations already, any one of which would have been sufficient to force the government to drop charges and repeat the entire induction process. I stated for the record that I was aware of those legal technicalities, but I wanted to have my guilt or innocence decided on the basis of the real issue, the war for which I was being drafted. The state's case consumed the trial's first day.

The second day belonged to the defense. It would be, I told the reporters waiting in the hallway that morning, "its own kind of prosecution," putting the government's actions on trial, not mine. I appeared for court in a new brown suit with Joan on my arm. Cameras whirred and interviews were given. The spectator section was full of local peace movement and Resistance members, including Dennis Sweeney and Rodney from the commune.

As a means of pursuing my announced goal of putting the

government on trial, my "intent and bad purpose" strategy was, in fact, hardly adequate. The judge ruled that no testimony about Vietnam, the war there, the foreign policy of the United States, the American peace movement, or the organization called The Resistance was relevant, so the entire defense case, in effect, consisted of me on the witness stand trying to express myself with sufficient abstraction for my testimony to be admissible. Perhaps my most cogent statement during the hour and a half I was on the stand came in response to a question from my lawyer about something the prosecution's FBI agent had attested to the day before.

"The F.B.I. testified that you made a statement [in front of the induction center] about tearing the building down," my lawyer noted. "What did you mean?"

"That building is a symbol to me," I answered. "It is a symbol of death and oppression. . . . It has taught people to forget their lives and the lives of others. . . . We've all been taught fear. . . . We live in a politics of fear and . . . that fear makes it possible for us to ignore all the dead and dying. . . . I think each of us has to refuse that fear. If we don't, we will live with it for the rest of our lives. . . . Each of us is a seed for the liberation of mankind. . . ."

After the second day was over, Dennis and Rodney headed back to the commune with Rodney driving. Dennis steadily mocked what I was doing.

"Fucking David," he finally said, sticking his arms out and lolling his head to the side like a man crucified.

Rodney broke out laughing and so did Sweeney. He repeated the gesture over and over and laughed harder with each repetition.

When the jury went out the next day, three jurors—an accountant, a housewife with a son in Vietnam, and a 50-year-old domestic—voted not guilty and held their ground for eight hours. Finally the judge called the jury back in and instructed them that not submitting to an order for induction was proof in and of itself of both intent and bad purpose. After that, it was only another half an hour until a verdict was returned, "guilty as charged."

The judge then asked if I had anything to say before he pronounced sentence.

I made a short statement about how, though I accepted the judgment of the jury, history too would judge, and it would judge the law, not David Harris, guilty. My only crime had been not to commit an even greater crime. For me, the words were reflexive, a blur in the area of my lips. It was hard to concentrate on talking. I just wanted to find out what my future amounted to.

The judge spoke next. "You have made [this decision]," he began, "and let it be said that you made it, no one else. . . . You were going to be here or in some other court in this kind of situation, if I may use a term, come hell or high water."

"Here's hoping high water comes first," I joked nervously.

The judge ignored the interruption and cleared his throat. "A sentence in this kind of situation," he continued, "insofar as . . . having any rehabilitative purpose is of no value whatsoever as far as you are concerned, because you don't have to be rehabilitated and you don't want to be rehabilitated and you won't be rehabilitated, and I don't know there is any reason that you should be rehabilitated. . . . The sole purpose of the penalty here is punitive. . . . Punitive to say that you shall not do this without suffering a penalty, and secondly, to be a warning to others that they will be punished if they do the same. . . . It has to be stark and real and just as hard and tough as you are."

Then he got to the sentence itself.

"Three years in the custody of the attorney general of the United States," he said, "at whatever facility of the Bureau of Prisons he may dictate." The sentence was twice the length of any handed out in the Northern District of California for the crime of draft refusal in the last ten years.

I had to work at not wincing.

"You've talked a great deal about a new world," the judge added. "Well, I'd like to see it. One thing I'm sure of, it will have to have order, and you can't have order if you break any law you don't like."

The next day, my lawyer informed me that I could either start serving my sentence when the two weeks allowed for filing an appeal had lapsed or I could appeal and stay out on bond. If I appealed, it would be a year before the appellate court decided, and I could, of course, take it to the Supreme Court after that. I said I had no interest in the Supreme Court, but I would like the year it would take at the appellate level. I wanted the time, I said, to try and get "my family life together."

On May 31, 1968, the FBI office in San Francisco filed an initial parole report on David Victor Harris with the Federal Bureau of Prisons.

"There are," it stated flatly, "no known mitigating circumstances."

June 4, 1968, was primary election day in California. As a convicted felon, I had no right to vote in it and made no attempt to do so.

Kennedy, McCarthy, and Humphrey had come into California, but the only real contest was between the two peace candidates. Robert F. Kennedy was in his suite full of well-wishers in Los Angeles' Ambassador Hotel when initial reports of his narrow 4½ percent victory over McCarthy began coming in. Looking for a place to talk in private, Kennedy took his chief speech writer into a bathroom and closed the door.

"I've got to get free of McCarthy," he said. "While we're fighting each other, Humphrey's running around the country picking up delegates. Even if McCarthy won't get out, his people must know after tonight that I'm the only candidate against the war that can beat Humphrey."

In Kennedy's eyes, the list of "McCarthy's people" apparently began with Allard Lowenstein, and at 11 P.M., he had his speech writer place a call to Allard's house in Long Beach. Lowenstein was not there. Before heading downstairs to the ballroom where his celebrating supporters were waiting, Kennedy told the speech writer to place another call to Lowenstein and tell him that Bobby himself would call as soon as he came back from making his victory speech.

Then it was down to the Ambassador's kitchen, into the narrow corridor connecting the kitchen to the ballroom, and out into the glaring television lights and screams of adulation. Behind the podium, Kennedy flashed his famous smile and the crowd roared.

At that point, the committed delegate count stood at Humphrey 944, Kennedy 425, McCarthy 204, 872 uncommitted, with the big Northeastern primaries still to go. Robert F. Kennedy's last words to the crowd before heading back out through the kitchen corridor were, "On to Chicago."

The cheers shook the rafters.

By then, Allard Lowenstein was back at his Long Beach home, sitting near the phone with his wife, Jenny. They talked about Bobby while they awaited his call.

"I don't know why I love Robert Kennedy so much," Allard told her, "but I guess I love him as much as anybody in public life since Mrs. Roosevelt."

The telephone rang just as he finished the statement.

"He certainly chose a good line to come in on," Jenny joked.

Allard answered. It was a reporter from the *Wall Street Journal*. "Kennedy's been shot," the reporter said.

Allard Lowenstein rushed to the airport and caught the next plane to Los Angeles. The third and last of the spring's political earthquakes had happened.

O f all the hundreds of times Allard Lowenstein had flown back and forth across the United States, that flight early on the morning of June 5, 1968, was surely the loneliest.

The shooting of Robert Kennedy provoked the most overwhelming sense of loss in all of Allard's adult life. He would talk of that night whenever he was in a mood to think about what might have been.

Allard dashed from Los Angeles International to Kennedy's hospital in a cab, talked his way through the various lines of security personnel, and reached the floor Bobby was on, just as his now dead body was being wheeled into the corridor, surrounded by several friends and family, including Ted Kennedy, the incumbent Senator from Massachusetts and the last of the Kennedy brothers. Lowenstein joined them and would later talk at great length about the feeling in the elevator with Bobby's body. Emotions were stripped raw and Allard was sobbing along with the rest.

When Lowenstein finally spoke, it was to Ted Kennedy.

"Now you're all we've got left," Lowenstein told him, "and you're not good enough."

O nce Bobby Kennedy was buried in Arlington National Cemetery near his brother, Jack, he was also ensconced forever among Lowenstein's pantheon of idols. Of those four, only Norman Thomas and Frank Graham were still alive, and Thomas was fading fast. On the night before the New York primary, Allard visited the dying Socialist in the hospital.

"Win this one for me, Al," Thomas reportedly said.

The next day, 25,000 Democratic votes were cast in the Fifth Congressional District. Allard K. Lowenstein, "attorney," "McCarthy backer," and "co-chairman of the Conference of Concerned Democrats," defeated the "Nassau machine's candidate" by a 4,000-vote margin.

In most political campaigns, a period of calm would have followed in which the spent troops were allowed to regroup and catch their breath. Not, however, in Lowenstein's. Allard now threw his band of youngsters back into the national political fray in a last-ditch effort to "get things together" for the Democratic National Convention in August.

His principal strategy was called the Coalition for an Open Convention. To get the process rolling, a dozen students were installed in a series of Chicago pay phones, where they proceeded to call a long list of people around the country, announcing a meeting of some 1,200 "disaffected Democrats" in Chicago on the last two days of June. Most of the calls were billed to a telephone credit card number belonging to the Humphrey-for-President organization, which had been pirated by a former Ivy League student leader. When convened, the meeting was to pass a resolution opposing the nomination of Hubert Humphrey and make plans to try and block it in the weeks they had left. "We are not potential troublemakers who won't accept the verdict of the people," Allard explained. "We are the verdict of the people."

To remind the party of how widespread antiwar feelings were, Lowenstein also put in motion something called "the August Primary." It was a planned poll of voters throughout the state of Ohio in August by an army of student volunteers that, even though unofficial, Lowenstein predicted would discredit Humphrey completely.

Yet another Lowenstein strategy was aimed at the apparent assumption of the press that with Bobby gone, the peace forces would never regroup. To overcome that attitude, Lowenstein went so far as to have "McGovern" buttons made up and then distributed during lunch hour in the neighborhood of the *New York Times* building. It would, he said, convince the *Times* that a new wave was swelling in the Democratic ranks.

Lowenstein also had to fight to keep what had already been won from being stolen as well. On June 28, the New York State Democratic Committee met at the Commodore Hotel in Manhattan to distribute the delegate seats at the upcoming August convention, and it was apparent that the party regulars were out to turn the revolt to their own purposes. In Nassau County, six of the seven "McCarthy" seats were awarded by the party bosses to people who had actually opposed McCarthy in the primary. Allard Lowenstein, the most visible of McCarthy's Nassau public supporters, was not named to the delegation, but the "machine boss" whose candidate Allard had defeated was. The Commodore meeting was held in a stuffy, overcrowded room and quickly became a cascade of denunciations.

"You spit in the face of the notion that this convention is democratic," Lowenstein screamed.

Some of the regulars laughed, others booed, one shouted, "Sit the hell down!"

Eventually, the reformers walked out in protest, and Lowenstein caught a plane the next day for the founding Chicago meeting of Coalition for an Open Convention.

Lowenstein had to fight all the way up to the opening day of the convention to secure a seat on the New York convention delegation. What time he had left over from that and the rest of his national strategy he would spend back in the Fifth District, getting his general election effort under way.

In the middle of July, Dennis Sweeney and I had what amounted to our final conversation. Two-thirds of my time was now spent speech making across the western United States, building for another draft-card return on November 4. I was increasingly uncomfortable in my new life-style and wanted to move out of the house in Carmel Valley. I eventually won that argument, and by the end of the summer, Joan and I moved into a much less pretentious cabin in the mountains in back of Palo Alto.

When I saw Sweeney at Cooley Street in July, he was preparing to move into the same neighborhood. The Fool had now decided to take over the commune's mountain house, "to get their sound ready." Still planned to take place at the same time as the Chicago convention, though not aimed at it, the Caravan itinerary now included several warm-up jaunts around the Bay area and then a musical procession that would cross the mountains to the San Joaquin Valley, follow its entire length south, then hop the mountains again into L.A., Orange County, and finally San Diego. Sweeney was excited when I saw him. He said The Fool was really "cookin'."

He also said that the scene at Cooley Street was becoming a drag. It was obvious from his remarks that the commune had begun to split at the seams. The Buddhist and political wings were headed off in different directions. The Buddhists were a majority at Cooley Street now. Dennis called them "space cadets" and was looking forward to getting some distance from the trend.

The last thing he and I talked about was the Caravan. I declined a token offer to come along and told him they ought to skip the San

Joaquin Valley. That was my home turf, I said, and folks there would just think they were weird and run them out of town.

Sweeney did not take my advice. A month later, a caravan of eight or nine battered vehicles following a 1941 Diamond Reo flatbed with "The Resistance" painted on the doors advanced on California's farm country. Most of the two dozen or so people involved would look upon Dennis Sweeney, The Fool's rhythm guitarist, as the man in charge.

I now carried out my own work completely separate from Dennis or the commune I had helped found. My schedule was full and arranged under the premise that The Resistance had first call on my time. Mostly, I gave out two-week chunks of my presence to local chapters as they requested it. I flew in, was met by the chapter's principal organizer, and the rest was work. Often I gave as many as nine speeches in nine different locations before my day was over. When my wife was along, we usually stayed in hotels. When I was by myself, I ended up on someone's spare bed. I had long since shifted back full time to Levis and cowboy boots, and I felt more like myself again. By the summer of 1968, most of my friends were people who met me at the airport, wherever I might be.

I still have special feelings for those friends, though we have all scattered in different directions now. I remember a seemingly endless succession of frantic car rides with them, finishing one speech and rushing to another 20 miles away. I always rode shotgun and we all laughed a lot. Though the talk was politics, it was an intimate experience. We were carrying out big decisions in one another's company. Where our fathers had become men at war, charging a hill with a rifle in their hands, we were trying to do the same thing by dropping the rifle, stopping the war, and saving the hill. We had no models to go by, and it took courage to fly in the face of everything John Wayne stood for.

Aside from those regular swings, I also spoke at special events. One of those, in August 1968, was the NSA Congress in Manhattan, Kansas. I accepted the invitation with a sense of nostalgia. I had given my first speech calling for draft resistance at the congress held two years before, and much had changed since then. A lot of rhetoric about fighting with the police in the streets was now going around campuses, and as a consequence, the formerly radical people such as I who broke the law by practicing civil disobedience rather than violence were considered "moderate." From "radical" to "moderate" was a long distance to come without ever once having changed your stance, but it was typical of the times.

At the 1968 NSA Congress's program on draft resistance I repeated myself one more time.

As was his annual habit, Allard Lowenstein also attended that congress, arriving shortly after I left. He traveled there with the national journalist he had run into in Saigon the year before and who was now assigned to cover Lowenstein himself. They arrived at 1 A.M. and, according to the journalist, were met by five young "Lowensteinites, college graduates, all part of his great apparatus, all enthusiastic. . . . It is like being with the star football player when he returns to campus after a year's absence."

Late the next afternoon, Allard crossed paths with the Chicago Seven radical whom Dennis and I had met with in May. Allard and the journalist sat in the audience during the radical's speech to a congress workshop; noticing their presence, he made a pointed remark about the "professional CIA-oriented politicians who occupy one part of McCarthy's campaign." That evening, the roles were reversed and the future Chicago Seven defendant sat and listened while Allard spoke.

For Lowenstein, the occasion fell almost exactly a year after he had first come to NSA and formally launched Dump Johnson, and his speech was an assessment of the intervening gains and losses. We had, Allard said, punctured

> the inevitability of Lyndon Johnson's election and we might have done more except for June fourth. We did it without a major name, money, or the mass media. We showed that the system is not so resistant to change but that it is badly corroded. . . .
>
> The McCarthy people turned around public feeling on the war, made the opposition to it respectable, and only a small minority in the country now believes it can be won. . . . We did change some things, we learned some things, and the fact that Bob Kennedy was murdered and Gene McCarthy was disorganized doesn't show me that the system won't work. . . . The exalting fact is that ordinary people in a complex society felt they could affect the honor and the future of their country and they did.

His annual contribution to the National Student Association made,

Lowenstein returned to New York and then traveled west again to Chicago with his wife, Jenny.

In Chicago, Allard Lowenstein was in his element. "Everything is disorganized," the journalist with Allard would later explain. "A convention is not sane at all. It is a matter of who functions best at 2:00 A.M., who bears best the lack of sleep. . . . Lowenstein naturally thrives on this. The rest of the world has come round to his way of living."

From the time he arrived on Friday, August 23, it was obvious to Allard that the Kennedy-McCarthy split still existed, and McCarthy was too "proud," "stiff," and "distant" to bridge it. Lowenstein immediately began attempting to fill the vacuum, attending meetings with everyone about everything. To help keep his act together, Allard relied on a "coterie" of young men who rendezvoused with him at regular intervals and were dispatched on errands.

The strategy was to stop a Humphrey victory on the first ballot. To do that, obviously more than McCarthy would be needed, and soon "Draft Teddy" buttons began appearing on the convention floor. Teddy Kennedy's entrance would break Humphrey's back, Allard maintained. "The greatest miracle of our time is about to happen," he told one pessimistic friend.

While on their way to a quick dinner break on Sunday evening, August 25, Lowenstein and the journalist dogging his footsteps were stopped by a delegate from Wyoming who wanted to introduce Allard to his wife.

"This is the man I told you about, Margaret," he explained. "The one who came out last year and made that speech about Johnson. Said it could be done and, by god, he was right. Well, young fella, you're all right."

Allard deflected the compliment by saying it was really people like the Wyoming delegate who had done it.

"Everyone will now act according to character," Lowenstein predicted to the rapt couple. "Johnson will try to screw Humphrey, because he's Johnson. That coalition will shatter. McCarthy will hold his strength but not pick up. Then they will turn to Teddy."

The next day, the Caravan reached Delano, California, and set up in a local park. The Diamond Reo was parked in an assembly area, its stage folded down, and several Caravaners went into

Delano distributing handbills inviting the residents to come out in the evening to hear some music and talk about the war and social change.

When the program finally began, about a hundred Delano natives stood around in front of the flatbed stage. The men were all short-haired or duck-tailed. A lot of the women wore pedal pushers. Rodney and the lead guitarist did the singing and Dennis stood behind them, intently jumping from chord to chord, sometimes looking at his fingers on the Gibson's neck to make sure they were in the right place. No one applauded, not even politely. Next came a slide show about Vietnam that emphasized the suffering of the Vietnamese people and displayed scenes of bombing rubble, decimated villages, and crippled peasants. Muttering began to break out in the crowd and increased when Dennis Sweeney got up behind the microphone and started a short rap continuing the themes from the slide show. Shouts of "Commie" and "traitor" were heard from the back. Dennis decided to cut it short, The Fool came back for a final number, and the program ended.

Afterward, Dennis said it was probably best that they leave Delano immediately. The Caravan agreed, and when all the trucks and automobiles were loaded, they headed south on the state highway. At the edge of town, several cherry bombs were tossed down on them from an overpass, and the procession immediately pulled over to inspect for damage. Dennis and Rodney were standing next to each other on the roadside when suddenly a chopped and lowered Chevy, full of local low riders, swerved onto the shoulder, forcing everyone to scatter. One of the Chevy's occupants pulled his pants down and stuck his bare ass out the back window as they roared past.

"Hippie freaks," the driver shouted, slinging a beer can in Sweeney's direction.

Dennis turned to Rodney. "This is just like goddamn Mississippi," he said.

The next afternoon, The Resistance road show was in Bakersfield and decided to skinny-dip in the reservoir outside of town. The local sheriff was waiting when they got out of the water. The "hippies" were given the choice of being locked up on charges of lewd conduct or immediately packing up this "Caravan" of theirs and getting out of Bakersfield altogether. The Caravan chose the latter and fled over the Tehachapis and into the L.A. basin.

Back in Chicago, it was apparent that Lowenstein's Sunday night optimism had been misplaced. Teddy would not risk asking for the nomination, and everything else was being handled

Chicago style. The demonstrators outside numbered closer to 10,000 than the 1,000,000 the organizers had predicted, but the police were hunting them everywhere and initiated bloody skirmishes all over the city. Inside the convention, the security forces manhandled delegates and press alike, provoking Walter Cronkite to describe them as "thugs" on national television. Lowenstein himself was arrested while entering the convention floor and detained for 30 minutes on charges of carrying an issue of the *New York Times*, an alleged fire code violation.

Wednesday morning, Hubert Humphrey's name was placed in nomination and, as the balloting approached, the nomination appeared to be his. Simultaneously, demonstrators converged outside the convention hall and were being truncheoned by the police. Their ranks by then included a number of young, angry McCarthyites calling the whole process a sham and a railroad. Before the votes could be tallied, Lowenstein attempted to make a motion adjourning the convention until someone put a leash on the Chicago police. First, he went to the microphone in the New York delegation, but the state chairman refused to let him use it.

Lowenstein then headed for the podium. The journalist hustling along behind him reported, "But the Illinois delegation blocks it, and the Illinois delegation is blocked by great circles of plainclothesmen. As Lowenstein moves forward, he is hemmed in by the plainclothesmen. . . . 'I'm a delegate from New York trying to make a motion,' he says. 'No, you're not,' one says. 'You're not going to make a motion.' He pushes forward again. 'Listen sonny. Be a good boy. Push off,' one of them says. 'There are federal agents here and they know what you're doing and you're going to be in trouble.'"

Hopelessly cut off, Allard finally retreated and was soon grabbed by an angry and somewhat hysterical Reform Democrat.

"Why isn't Teddy being put in nomination?" she screamed.

"Because the big shots don't want it," Lowenstein answered.

"The big shots didn't want Lyndon Johnson beaten and that didn't stop you," she screamed even louder. "Why don't you do something?"

"I don't know who appointed me Jesus Christ," Allard snapped. "Isn't there anyone else here?"

Off the floor, he told one TV interviewer that "this convention elected Richard Nixon President of the United States tonight."

He then proceeded to a last meeting of McCarthy delegates, where they agreed to make a candlelight march on the convention hall, now sealed off from the public by Chicago police and National Guard troops. Lowenstein had already arranged for a Chicago synagogue to donate the candles.

Allard and Jenny finally returned to their hotel room around 5 A.M.

Thursday morning. She was exhausted, but Lowenstein had also promised the room to a bunch of McCarthy students, and at 6:30, the McCarthy students showed up, pounding on the door. Allard let them in and said he and his wife were about to leave, but Jenny got furious.

"I don't care if they're wounded," she objected. "I don't care if they're dying."

Allard gave them the room anyway.

"He kept introducing them to me," Jenny later told the journalist, "and I kept refusing to be introduced."

A number of the students had only met Allard once or twice before.

"What do you think he's running for?" one of them asked Jenny.

"Some minor deity," she cracked.

"Are you sure it's minor?" the student asked.

Early Thursday afternoon, August 29, Eugene McCarthy made a farewell statement and left Chicago.

The wave had crested and was now breaking up into disconnected fingers of surf racing up the beach for the high-water mark. Perhaps its deepest penetration before it was altogether spent would be the election of Allard Lowenstein in New York's Fifth Congressional District, an achievement on which he would spend the rest of the autumn.

The obvious conclusion that things had finally played themselves out was reinforced in Lowenstein's physical condition after McCarthy's final concession. In the previous 18 months, according to the calculation of the journalist who had spent the convention shadowing him, Allard had given 2,367 speeches, traveling 288,021 miles in the process.

By 6 P.M. that Thursday, Allard Lowenstein had laryngitis and had to communicate by written note for the remainder of the convention.

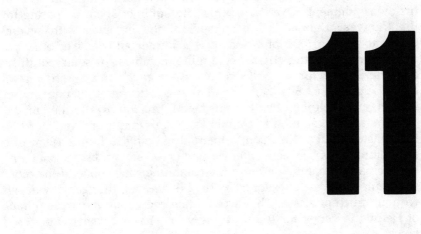

When the Caravan straggled back in early September, Dennis Sweeney's career as a political organizer, now almost six years old, was essentially over, and he threw himself totally into his music. The Fool was now the group identity in Sweeney's life, and he hoped to take the rock 'n roll band out on the club circuit that fall. One of the drawbacks to that plan, at least as the other band members saw things, was that Dennis's third-rate skills acted like an anchor on The Fool's music. At first, however, no one made a move to break up the band, and they returned to practicing for long hours at the commune's mountain house.

Later in September, Sweeney was visited by two agents from the FBI. They wanted to talk about the previous February's Stanford ROTC arson.

Sweeney's name had come to their attention through an error in his own judgment. Over the spring and summer spent preparing for the Caravan, Dennis had been sporadically involved with several different women, one of whom was a former girlfriend of Stuart, a friend and one of the original commune members. At some point, he had told Stuart's former girlfriend about the attack on Stanford's naval ROTC clubhouse. She had eventually mentioned it to one of her friends, and the friend had turned the information over to the FBI.

The agents came on to Dennis as though they were convinced he had masterminded the arson, apparently hoping to frighten him into self-incrimination. Sweeney denied any involvement, using as an alibi that he had been sitting around the commune; since none of the other commune members questioned by the FBI cracked, the agents were left without much of a case. They would, however, continue to keep track of Dennis Sweeney for the next few years, hoping something would break.

S hortly afterward, Dennis Sweeney saw Armin Rosencranz, the 1962 Stanford student body president who had known both him and Allard in what were already being called "the old days."

The two men talked at random about what they had each been up to since they'd last seen each other four years before. Dennis mentioned his band and then took an unexpected tack. He said he had taken "many, many doses" of LSD during the preceding year and that it was "hard for that much acid not to change one's head."

When they were later informed of Dennis's comment, it would strike many former commune members as odd, since the period of time Sweeney referred to had been one in which most commune members, myself included, had stopped using LSD. Although Dennis had continued to dabble, his use was in no way remembered in the "many, many doses" range.

That day in September, Rosencranz didn't linger on the issue. After more conversation, the subject of Allard Lowenstein came up. There was some mention of how Lowenstein was doing in his congressional race, and then Dennis interjected the issue of Allard and sex, one of no more than a half dozen times in his life the normally reticent Sweeney ever initiated that subject.

"So what do you think of our former assistant dean's sexual interest in young men?" Sweeney asked.

The question came out of the blue. Rosencranz said he had known lots of men in Allard's "sort of entourage" and had heard stories of various kinds of "hugging incidents," but had never heard of anyone who had actually had sex with him.

"Well, I think I know one who has," Dennis offered.

"Who?" Rosencranz asked.

"David Harris," Sweeney answered.

I didn't learn of the remark until twelve years after it was made. Since my experience with Allard had been the same as his own and Dennis knew it, I view the comment as a sign of how badly he felt about me. I am not surprised.

M y famous wife and I were living less than three miles further into the mountains than Dennis, but he and I were no longer in touch. I spent most of the fall on the road, boosting the last of The Resistance's national draft-card returns. One of the questions always asked me was about going to jail.

I said it was the price I had to pay to be my own person and that I was prepared to pay it. The Resistance, I claimed, would carry on its struggle in jail and out. Our bodies might be locked up, but we would continue to organize. I claimed that when I was taken off to serve my sentence, others would pick up my work where I left off.

That last statement was typical of the well-intentioned but hollow rhetoric that seemed to overtake much of the Sixties that fall. On November 4, 1968, The Resistance managed to turn in about the same number of draft cards as the previous December. Afterwards, it would collapse as an organization.

On November 5, Richard Nixon narrowly defeated Hubert Humphrey to become the thirty-seventh President of the United States, and in New York's Fifth, Allard K. Lowenstein was elected the first congressman ever from Long Beach, New York. As positions went, this would be Allard's peak, but none of that topping out was apparent in November of 1968. In his district office, opened immediately after the election by changing the sign on his campaign headquarters door, someone had already put a plastic collection bucket out on the table with "Congressman Lowenstein for President" lettered on its side.

"Jenny and the children will live in Long Island," the *New York Post* noted, "while Lowenstein commutes [to Washington]." "We just can't afford to maintain two homes," Allard explained. "I'm going to contribute one-third of my [$30,000] salary to pay my staff better wages. You can't expect good people to sacrifice for you unless you can sacrifice something too."

He would be the only member of the Ninety-first Congress to serve his entire term while residing on the spare beds or living room couches of his friends around town.

Meanwhile, the fortunes of Lowenstein's former protégé, Dennis Sweeney, began their long drop off the edge. The final event precipitating the downturn was the dissolution of The Fool. Belonging to a "community" had been a dominant theme in Dennis's life since he had signed on as one of Allard Lowenstein's Original Sixteen at Stern Hall in 1962. The end of The Fool was the theme's final frustration. As had become Sweeney's pattern, he had invested all of himself in a mutual identity, and it, in turn, went belly up.

The dissolution had been insisted upon by Rodney and hurt Dennis a lot. Rodney told him that it was nothing personal, but Dennis felt betrayed and he said so. To the extent that the breakup had a climactic scene, it occurred between the two of them late in the fall, when Dennis showed up at Rodney's and demanded that Rodney give him the amplifier he had used with The Fool. The amplifier was the Caravan's community property, Dennis insisted, and since he was the one who had put the Caravan together, it rightfully belonged in his custody. Rodney said he didn't give a shit what it was, he had his amp, and he was going to keep it. Sweeney eventually stormed out looking like he had lockjaw.

Dennis would have liked to pick up with another band, but there were few if any such options for a player of his experience, age, and expertise. That vacuum in his music scene was apparently one of the motives behind Sweeney's decision in December to leave California, go East, and out of nowhere resume the career in filmmaking he had envisioned for himself in Natchez three years earlier. Ed Pincus, the filmmaker, was in Cambridge, Massachusetts, where he had recently finished editing some of the footage from the summer of 1965 into the documentary *Black Natchez*. Dennis knew that there was another collection of film, shot in Panola County that summer, that Pincus had not used in *Black Natchez*, and he had visions of cutting it into another movie himself when he reached Cambridge. He traveled there with a woman from Boston he had been "doing a thing" with since the Caravan.

Another factor impelling him East at the end of 1968 was that FBI agents had been by to see him several more times, and it was, he figured, a good time to disappear for a while.

If 1968 was the year when everything seemed to come together, 1969 would be a year in which a lot of it seemed to come apart.

During the second weekend of January, I attended my last organizational meeting of The Resistance. It was supposed to be a conference of chapter representatives from all over California. I arrived with Joan when the conference was well into its second day. By then, the conference had split into two mutually antagonistic camps.

The first faction, the proto-Leninists, wanted to give up draft-resistance organizing and turn to something more "militant" and "working class." They were now into theories of "oppression" and "imperialism." The second faction, the space cadets, wanted to give up draft-resistance organizing in favor of "alternative life-styles." They talked about founding communes in New Mexico and co-ops in Mendocino County and commencing the new world immediately. The space cadets had complicated everything even further by ignoring the conference rules. Each Resistance group was supposed to send only two representatives, and all of them had complied except this new-age lobby, virtually all of whom were from Los Angeles. They brought up two dilapidated school buses full of people who spent much of the conference either consuming immense amounts of brown rice, chanting "oooooommmmmmmmmmm" in unison, or piling on top of each other in 30- and 40-person heaps. All of these activities were put forward as a means of emitting "peace vibrations" into the atmosphere.

I knew right then that 1969 would be a crazy year. After six hours of conference, Joan and I split.

"At least I don't have to worry about the organization falling apart after I go to jail," I joked during the drive home.

Three days later, Allard K. Lowenstein was sworn into the Ninety-first Congress. He and Eugene McCarthy, still a senator from Minnesota, were featured speakers at a Brooklyn conference of the still active remnants of the 1968 Kennedy and McCarthy efforts.

Lowenstein took the rostrum first and made a big point of lauding the Senate's selection of Ted Kennedy as majority whip. The choice, he claimed at length, would prove pivotal in levering open the new Nixon administration's hold on the war policy it had inherited from Lyndon Johnson.

When McCarthy's turn came, he began his remarks with a slash at Lowenstein. "It's nice to know," he observed, "that after three days in Congress, Al Lowenstein is an authority on the Senate. If I had known how important the whip was, I wouldn't have gone into New Hampshire."

If the antagonism between McCarthy and Lowenstein was still private prior to that remark, it remained so no longer.

"I was deeply grateful and touched when he made the fight last year," Allard told a reporter from the *New York Times Magazine*, "but . . . wherever I go, I find I have to defend McCarthy against rather bitter comments. New Hampshire was a turning point, but we haven't finished the turn. There are new people to be persuaded every day. . . . I don't like to take potshots at Eugene McCarthy, but I'm afraid he's brought it on himself. I remember him historically, but I've forgotten him as a contemporary."

With 1969 less than a month old, the two men whose convergence had touched off much of what would later be remembered of 1968 were no longer on speaking terms.

A llard Lowenstein would call his term in the House of Representatives "the proudest achievement" of his life.

In one way, Congress certainly seemed to present no adjustment difficulties for him. He probably started his career there more skilled at the arts of trade-off, negotiation, coalition building, and maneuvering than many of the men who had been there twenty years. His wide intellect dealt easily with the spectrum of congressional issues, and his burgeoning national reputation gave him a visibility far beyond any other freshman's. Congress also filled the one glaring hole in Allard's public persona to date. "Most of the doubts about Al," one old friend explained, "came not so much because of his causes, but because with his causes he had no normal job. . . . People looked at Al and there he was . . . just running around with causes. . . . And they had their doubts. People will be more sympathetic [now] because he'll have a title and a position and they'll be reassured."

Congressman Lowenstein would not make any kind of reputation as a legislative architect. He was a persuader first and foremost; as such, perhaps his greatest effect was on a circle of young congressmen, most of whom were Republicans. They would remember his example of "dedication to principle" as an "inspiration" and regret that he had not served longer. "He was ideal for the job," one explained, "and it was ideal for him."

A congressman's identity also presented Allard with heretofore unknown dilemmas. When free-lancing, Allard had always been able to juggle his myriad of causes and connections by moving between them on his own initiative, arriving suddenly, setting his own context, and moving on. The technique allowed his army of friends, sympathizers, protégés, fans, and allies to be at his disposal much more than he was at theirs. As a congressman, he was suddenly in one place, burdened with votes and committee meetings, a sitting target for the by now thousands of people around the United States who each thought his own relationship with Allard was "special." In the first few months of his term, it seemed that at least 90 percent of them wrote at least one letter, all assuming that their personal relationship with Allard would assure immediate attention.

The crush was often more than Lowenstein's familiar style could cope with, but, according to his early staffers, Allard could never bring himself to admit as much. He still expected to deal personally with every item, large or small, and as a consequence soon had a hopelessly growing stack of letters to answer and phone calls to return, all of which Allard refused to let his staff answer on the grounds that they pertained to "friends." In the meantime, "friends" all over the country were feeling put out because they had not even received a form letter response. Several of the staff tried unsuccessfully to call him on his behavior, arguing that people would understand how busy Allard was and wouldn't be insulted by a staff response, at least as a stopgap measure until Allard himself got time. Lowenstein reportedly dealt with such confrontations by sloughing them off, promising to change, and then not changing. When confronted from the other end, he told clumsy lies and put it off on "bad staff work." Eventually, several of his staff would leave for other jobs over the issue.

That small dilemma was reflective of the times themselves. As the Sixties rushed toward a new decade, the base that had brought Allard Lowenstein this far would begin to shift under him in ways that, pinned down in Congress, he could no longer move fast enough to keep up with.

From my own early 1969 perspective, a decade's worth of escalation had built up a momentum that now seemed on the verge of going out of control on all fronts. 536,100 American soldiers were in Vietnam, the Nixon Administration had made it clear from its first days in office that it would deal harshly with dissent, and what had once been "the movement" was now awash in rhetoric about "going underground" to wage "armed struggle." The sound of hatches battening down was everywhere.

I responded by tying up my own role and getting ready to be imprisoned. In February and March, Joan Baez and I made our last campus speaking tour. When it was over, she was pregnant and I entered a holding pattern, hanging around the house, being recognized when Joan and I went down the hill to eat, writing a book, and waiting for the appellate court to order my arrest. I did my best in the meantime to prepare for disappearing from the world as I knew it.

Ed Pincus had not heard from Sweeney since Natchez and was surprised to see him when he showed up at his office in the MIT film department in early 1969. The two of them had not been particularly close, but Pincus still thought of Dennis as a friend. He agreed with Dennis's idea of cutting the leftover footage and arranged for him to get access to an editing machine.

While in Cambridge, Dennis and the Boston woman he had come East with lived in a big house that David Newman, Pincus's former partner, had rented. As Newman remembers it, Dennis and the Boston woman argued regularly. Sweeney was also "totally into his music." Newman played the guitar and the two of them jammed a lot. "Still waters run deep," Newman said later, "and Dennis was some very still waters." An old friend who saw Dennis then described him as "quieter and more withdrawn." When asked what he had been up to over the last few years, Sweeney just answered, "Working in the movement," and left it at that. He was broke most of the time, and Newman, flush from a recent job as cameraman, didn't charge him and the Boston woman any rent.

By March, Dennis had a rough cut of his 45-minute documentary ready and showed it to Pincus. Pincus was very critical.

Anxious, Dennis showed the rough cut to several other people in hopes of a different judgment. Two of these were a couple who had once been active in SDS. The woman had been a friend of Dennis's former wife, Mary, and had last seen him while they had still been living together on Channing Street in Palo Alto. The man had known of Sweeney but had never really talked with him before. After watching, they offered their assessment, some of which was good, some bad. Sweeney's reaction to the critique struck them both as "strange."

According to the woman, he became "very weird." The man described the response as "anguished" and tried to reassure Dennis that the film "had some good stuff in it" and that he had "enjoyed seeing it," but the reassurance did not quench Sweeney's obvious anxiety. For the former SDS man, that was the one troubling aspect of what had otherwise been a "positive contact." "The film was okay for what it was," he would later explain. "I just thought Dennis should let go of it a little and loosen up."

After tinkering with the film some more, Dennis brought it back to Pincus and said it was done. Pincus viewed it and told Dennis the cut was not even worth making a print of, much less showing in public.

Rather than go back to the cutting room for another try, Sweeney somewhat abruptly decided to return to California. He and Newman had been discussing collaborating on a screenplay about the civil rights movement. In April, Newman got a camera job on a feature that was about to be shot in Mendocino County, California; Newman thought he could get Dennis a job on location operating a boom, and they could work on the screenplay in their spare time. Sweeney got enough cash together to purchase a used Matchless 650 motorcycle, and he and the Boston woman headed back to California on it.

When he finally arrived at the feature's location, Newman was unable to get him hired, and, out of money, Dennis and the Boston woman headed south for San Francisco to find work.

Congressman Allard Lowenstein (D-NY) traveled to San Francisco around the same time to address an ADA meeting. He was now widely recognized as the nation's "bridge to youth," who "understood" what young people "were going through" and could "channel their dissatisfaction" into "good causes." He tried to rush in and play that role in Berkeley, and the ensuing encounter in some ways exemplified the extent to which times were changing and pulling the rug out from under him.

Berkeley was in the midst of its most explosive disturbance since the Free Speech Movement six years earlier. The issue this time was something called "Peoples Park," a controversy over a formerly vacant lot owned by the university where students and Berkeley street people had begun to cultivate small vegetable and flower patches. The university's decision to fence the space off from the public in preparation for turning it into a parking lot led to a series of campus rallies. One of those rallies spontaneously headed down the street to demolish the fence, setting off a month-long succession of clashes with Alameda County sheriff's deputies in the course of which one Berkeley resident was killed by police shotgun fire and several more wounded. California's governor, Ronald Reagan, quickly issued a statement to the effect that if the people on the streets of Berkeley wanted war, they would get it. The National Guard was then mobilized and Army helicopters hovered over Berkeley, spraying a brand of tear gas supposedly banned for use anywhere outside of Vietnam. Mass arrests had become common, and rarely a day or two passed without fresh battles of one sort or another.

In the middle of all that, Allard Lowenstein showed up, hoping to mediate between the students and the university, just as he had been attempting to do when I first met him in the spring of 1965. This time, he called a woman then at Berkeley who had served as his press secretary in the Fifth District primary and asked her to arrange a meeting with a "broad cross section" of campus sentiment. He didn't, he said, want his being in Congress to keep him from being "useful" in "whatever was going on." The group she put together to meet with him included a nationally known environmentalist then teaching at the university's school of design, one of the Stop the Draft Week's principal organizers, and the university student body president. Congressman Lowenstein was more than two hours late for the meeting.

At first, he gave the impression of knowing little about the park struggle, treating it as some kind of "hippie gardening" issue, until it was pointed out to him that a broad and active coalition had been put together around the question. He then expressed his desire to help mediate. According to one participant, "Everyone in effect told him he was irrelevant." There was no reason for his involvement, they said. What could he do for them?

Lowenstein said he had connections to the university administration, but the students pointed out that the issue was no longer even in administration hands. Ronald Reagan was calling the shots, and Reagan had made it clear that the only choice he offered was the chance to back down or get gassed. Allard said that he also had good connections in Washington, D.C. Someone answered that Bobby Kennedy's former chief political operative was already lobbying for them there and Lowenstein's connections weren't any better than his. Finally, Allard added that he also had "forces" he could muster out here in Berkeley, but since every political group from the Young Democrats left was already involved in the Peoples Park coalition, the gathering remained unimpressed.

According to one participant who had stood slightly in awe of Lowenstein when the conversation began, "Allard's indispensability disappeared." He now seemed "just another liberal congressman, no more [and] no less."

This response was bound to be somewhat disquieting to someone who had been a "spiritual transfusion" less than two years before. Allard returned to Washington that night.

D ennis Sweeney and the Boston woman found a place to live in San Francisco at a house in the Mission District that Stuart from the commune and several other refugees from the Stanford antiwar scene were sharing. Dennis also found work driving a cab and talked a lot about "the scum" he had to encounter every day on the job. According to one of his housemates, Dennis "brooded most of the time." He also adopted a scruffy little brown dog that barked fiercely at the sight of any black person. Rodney, the defunct Fool's former bass player, drove up from Palo Alto to visit Dennis on several occasions, and each time, Sweeney's pet attacked him and had to be tied up. By all accounts, Dennis no longer had any "active politics" to speak of.

On Memorial Day, 1969, Sweeney and Rodney attended a march in Berkeley, "just to watch what was coming down." At one point, they ended up on a curb as buses full of helmeted deputy sheriffs roared by. Rodney flipped them the bird.

The gesture pissed Sweeney off. "Don't do that," he snapped. "I learned that in Mississippi. Shit like that just makes them crazier."

He and Rodney continued watching until Dennis had to get back to San Francisco to pull his shift with Yellow Cab.

Back in Washington, pieces of the personal network Allard had constructed around himself during Dump Johnson continued to drop away. His old friend, Curtis Gans, had split with Allard the year before over Lowenstein's keeping a foot in both McCarthy and Kennedy's camps, and Lowenstein now began having differences with the two former seminarians who had spearheaded the Campus Coordinating Committee.

Earlier that year, the two had put together another letter from "student leaders" pledged to refuse induction if called, and Lowenstein had offered his Capitol Hill office for the group's press conference. In the course of that fresh liaison, the two former seminarians tried out on Allard an idea they had pretty much decided to spend the summer organizing around. They called it a "Moratorium Against the War." It amounted to setting aside a day when students all over the country would call a halt to all normal activity and spend the day protesting the war. A month later, they would repeat it for two days; two months later, for three days. They were thinking of setting the first one for sometime in October.

Allard said they should do it on the Fourth of July. The former seminarians objected that July was much too soon and, with schools in summer session, the base would be insufficient.

Allard said it should feature a centerpiece demonstration in Washington, D.C., at which everyone would carry American flags; and the rules should be constructed in such a way as to exclude the "more left" and "irresponsible" elements of the peace movement. The two younger men said the exclusion smacked of "red-baiting" and disagreed. As long as a group was against the war, they said, it should be welcome and allowed to carry whatever signs, flags, or banners it chose.

Allard suggested the two ought to come onto his congressional staff and use his office as an organizing base. They said frankly that anything coming out of a congressman's office would be suspect on campuses and lack credibility.

The rejection chafed at Lowenstein, but the two former seminarians stood firm. They wanted to do their own idea, not Allard's. That June, they began putting their Moratorium together. It ended up spawning 350 demonstrations around the country on October 15, 1969, by far the widest national participation yet in the course of the war.

Not content to leave the field to his former lieutenants, Allard attempted to organize his own demonstration to compete with theirs.

In the second week of June 1969, the court of appeals confirmed my conviction by a 2 to 1 vote. I greeted the news with a certain amount of relief. I was tired of waiting. By law, I had a three-week grace period in which to file further appeals, but I filed none. I had spent the last three years knowing prison was coming and I wanted to get on with it.

Everything seemed to be catching up with me. Celebrityhood had left me at great distance from where I had started, and I was tired of having to live in the midst of my famous wife's reputation. In my more honest moments, I admitted that it had injected a degree of pretentiousness into me that was as disagreeable as it was insecure. I figured that once I was a convict I would be busy just being David Harris again, and I looked forward to that as well. I was credible and respected because I had taken an honorable stand and was prepared to accept the consequences. Now the consequences part had come due. Dealing with it would confirm that the rest was real, and I wanted that confirmation more than I wanted anything else.

In the first week of July, I received a telephone call from the federal marshal's office ordering me to come down to the Federal Building in San Francisco and turn myself in. I told them the least they could do was pick me up.

They did.

At 10 A.M. on July 15, 1969, two federal marshals showed up at our cabin in the Santa Cruz mountains with a warrant for my arrest. I had been up since early that morning, watching the rocket blast-off carrying the first men to the moon. The marshals padlocked a chain around my waist, attached a pair of handcuffs to the chain, and then put the handcuffs around my wrists. For having fought my own kind of war instead of theirs, I was now embarking on my own kind of journey into space.

While I was sharing 3-Tank, A Block, San Francisco County Jail, with a bank robber, a pimp, and three junkies, Dennis Sweeney found a new job sorting mail at the post office. He also involved himself in a venture with Stuart and several others. When the world's first moon flight landed, the Mission District house manufactured souvenirs of the occasion for sale to novelty shops. Their "moon plaque" consisted of a piece of plywood with a picture of the moon on it and a paper with the quotation left behind by the moon landers. No one made a dime from it, but Sweeney's role in the enterprise became tangential anyway as his relations with Stuart floundered.

Dennis was still involved with the Boston woman, and Stuart was living with his former girlfriend again, the same one with whom Dennis had had a brief fling earlier in 1968. Now the situation repeated itself, and a tense triangle reportedly developed among Dennis, Stuart, and the girlfriend. Sweeney and the woman from Boston broke up and got back together several times as well.

Around the same time, the FBI showed up at the post office where Dennis was working. The agents told him they didn't intend to make any trouble for him at his new job, and if he kept "his nose clean" everything would be all right. They just wanted to get back "in touch" and remind him that they knew where he was.

As it turned out, the reminder was something Sweeney would never be able to forget.

L ate in my second week on A Block, I was in my first prison strike. The precipitating incident occurred when the pimp in 3 Tank developed some kind of pleurisy condition. By 8:30 P.M. he was having trouble breathing, so we yelled for the cop on duty. When he finally came, he said he would be right back with medical attention and left. There was still no sign of a doctor when the lights were turned out at 10, so A Block began banging its tin coffee cups on the bars. Suddenly, the lights went on and eight cops in riot gear rushed down the hallway to our tank. After the pimp had been moved to a holding cell in another part of the jail, the duty officer announced that all of A Block would lose its visiting privileges for a month because of the disturbance we had created.

The next day, A Block refused to eat any more of the jail's food until our visits were returned. The strike lasted eight days. According to jail officials, I was the "instigator." The day it ended, federal marshals signed me out of San Francisco County Jail, drove me across the bay to Oakland, and deposited me in the jail there for another two days. Then they came back to haul me to the Swift Trail Federal Prison Camp outside of Safford, Arizona, 1,000 miles away.

For the journey, a chain was again locked around my waist and my wrists shackled to it. The Oakland jail was on the top floor of the courthouse, and to leave it, the marshals and I rode the public elevator to the front lobby. My clothes were rank and I had a week's growth of stubble on my face. One marshal waited with me by the entrance while the other brought the automobile around.

One passerby approached. She looked at the way I was chained up, then at my face, and back to the chains. "What'd you do?" she asked.

"I didn't kill anybody," I explained.

Back in the nation's capital, Allard Lowenstein's conflict with the two former seminarians—who had once been among his most trusted lieutenants—was heating up.

One of the key aspects to their moratorium plan was the broadening of their student coalition by securing a number of antiwar congressmen and Senators as sponsors. While the seminarians circulated around the Hill trying to line up sponsors, Lowenstein was telling the same set of people that he knew the Moratorium organizers quite well and that they were "good kids," but they wouldn't be able to keep things in control. "Other elements" were sure to make their way into the event and distort, even discredit it. The two former seminarians, however, had their own relationships with the congressmen and Senators in question and managed to convince a number of them despite Allard's opposition.

Lowenstein also set in motion his own plan for the fall, notwithstanding the fact that large sections of the student network he hoped to use had already signed up with the Moratorium and were unavailable to him. To build a new network, he hit upon using the student interns in Washington for the summer as a nucleus. Allard could recruit them without having to fly around the country, and they would all be back on their respective campuses in the fall. By August, he had put together a series of recruiting meetings in sympathetic congressmen's offices.

At a typical one in the office of Republican Congressman Paul "Pete" McClosky of California, Allard began by praising the former seminarians extravagantly. They were, he said, two of the finest young men he knew. His own objection was not to them, but to their plan. It could, he warned, easily fall into the hands of "the wrong people" and get "out of control." What was needed was a demonstration that was "antiviolence" before even being "antiwar." It could, he said, be a rallying point for the clean-cut, nonviolent students whose faith in democracy was still intact. On top of everything else, Allard added with an air of total assurance, the former seminarians would "never" pull their plan off. It was beyond their skills, however much Allard himself might like them.

Some of the intern group seemed persuaded, but others were not. One student pointed out that the Moratorium was already being organized on his campus and indeed, judging from its present strength, would definitely be pulled off. Another added that if all they talked about at a national demonstration was the peace movement's dilemma about nonviolence instead of expressing their anger over Vietnam, they were letting the government off the hook and acting like the peace movement was the problem instead of the war. A former student body president at Berkeley argued that the wider the participation, the less likely it was that trouble would occur; exclusion for the purposes of nonviolence was self-defeating. The discussion seesawed back and forth but remained polite.

Within a month, Allard's plan fizzled completely and disappeared as though it had never existed. Within another month, news accounts listed Representative Allard K. Lowenstein among the national legislators endorsing the upcoming Moratorium Against the War.

By then, I had settled into the Swift Trail Federal Prison Camp outside of Safford, Arizona. It was a minimum security institution with no walls to speak of, desert on three sides, and Arizona's Graham Mountains on the fourth. Three hundred prisoners were housed in six cinder-block barracks and built roads into the nearby national forest five days a week. Except for monthly visits from my increasingly pregnant wife, that spot in Arizona was my whole world. I followed other events through four-day-old San Francisco newspapers and several subscriptions to national magazines.

Such was the nature of both the outside world and Allard Lowenstein at the time that I could not track one regularly without encountering the other. Shortly after I arrived in Safford, I ran across a reference to my former mentor in two six-inch Associated Press columns headlined, "Congressman Hit by Gas 4 Times." It was datelined Prague, Czechoslovakia. According to the story, Congressman Allard K. Lowenstein had been tear-gassed on four different occasions while "observing" antigovernment demonstrations. His "assistant," a young man from Columbia Law School, was "arrested, clubbed, and held for 14 hours." Apparently the two of them were in Prague as part of what AP described as Lowenstein's "private trip around the world."

About a month later, a string of stories concerning the approaching Moratorium came out, and among them was the news of Congressman Allard K. Lowenstein's endorsement. Also among them were accounts of how Richard Nixon was trying to undercut his antiwar opposition by announcing the withdrawal of 20,000 American soldiers from Vietnam, and Allard's name popped up as part of the antiwar movement's response, a reaction the *San Francisco Examiner* labeled, "Nixon Peace Acts Stir Up War Foes." The gist of the article was that instead of "placating antiwar elements," the withdrawal had "spurred them to call angrily for more." Among the "indications of deep dissatisfaction" cited were the sudden rise of interest in the Moratorium, a report that an unnamed Senator would soon introduce a bill cutting off all funds for the war by the end of 1970, and plans by two Republican congressmen to introduce a bill repealing the 1964 Gulf of Tonkin Resolution. At the top of that list was the news that "Rep. Allard Lowenstein (D-NY) plans to announce tomorrow a 'change in attitude' toward the President's policies and perhaps a move as dramatic as his eventually successful 1968 crusade to drive former President Lyndon Johnson from office."

I scoured the next newspapers that reached me to find out what Allard's new twist amounted to, but found nothing until a reference appeared more than two months later under the headline "Antiwar Vote Plans." In it, Lowenstein announced plans for a "nationwide referendum on Vietnam." According to the congressman, he was, at that moment, simultaneously negotiating with various antiwar groups and the Nixon White House about the idea. The referendum was "planned for April," when "most college students will be home on Easter vacations," and he called it "an invitation" to the President "to measure how much support he has" by a "valid, constitutional procedure."

Like the demonstration he had set out to organize the summer before, nothing would come of this idea either.

D ennis Sweeney worked for the post office all fall. Sometime in October he was visited by Ed Pincus, the filmmaker from Cambridge, and David Newman, Pincus's former partner. Newman was still in Mendocino County, and Pincus had come West to see him. Newman suggested they go down to San Francisco and drop in on Sweeney. When they arrived, Dennis noticed that Pincus's former partner had the symptoms of a bad cold and commiserated, saying everyone had been sick. The "disease," he claimed, was a result of "some gas" that had been sprayed on Berkeley by the CIA. Now the winds were spreading it all over California. Then Dennis produced a small, round, red pill. These, he said, were the only things that could combat the effects. Thousands of them were coming through the post office every day and Sweeney had ripped off a handful. He said he didn't know what they were, but everyone he had given them to had been cured.

Newman declined the offer.

After staying awhile longer at Sweeney's, the three men drove across the Bay Bridge to Strawberry Canyon behind Berkeley for several hours and then headed back to San Francisco to try and catch a Buster Keaton movie. Newman drove, and Dennis and Pincus sat in the backseat and talked.

As they crossed the bridge, Sweeney began to confess in general terms to what he had done to the naval ROTC clubhouse, and Pincus was surprised to be told. He was not a good friend of Sweeney's and there was no reason he ought to know what Dennis was telling him. Dennis was nervous and furtive as he talked. He did not say exactly where or what he had done, only referring to it once as a "terrorist" act, another time as a "bombing." What he said had contradictory implications: that he was into a whole "underground" scene but also that the "bombing" had been an isolated, one-time act. It was a "terrible" thing and had, he claimed, single-handedly caused liberals to turn against radicals and had hurt "the movement" badly.

Before going on to another subject, Sweeney added that FBI agents had recently interviewed both a woman he'd had an affair with and the woman's father, looking for evidence. The feds didn't have anything on him directly, Sweeney added, but they were on his trail.

A side from paranoia, isolation would be Dennis Sweeney's most prominent feature when he finally stumbled out of the woodwork ten years later to assassinate Allard Lowenstein. That pattern had already begun in 1969.

He shared a house with Stuart, and Rodney still came up occasionally to visit, but they were the only two members of the old Peace and Liberation Commune he still saw. The relationship with Stuart was clouded by the triangle they had both been a part of; by late fall, Sweeney's rivalry kept him from saying much more than hello to Stuart. His relationship with Rodney was also on the rocks before the year was up. Not long after Pincus's visit, the Boston woman was raped by a black man while hitchhiking in the Palo Alto area and became pregnant. She and Sweeney reportedly had furious arguments about the incident. He didn't believe her rape story and was convinced that she had been sleeping with Rodney. This conclusion soon made Dennis turn on Rodney directly, and the two men virtually broke off communication.

Eventually, Dennis and the Boston woman decided to terminate the pregnancy, and on December 2, 1969, Sweeney accompanied her down to the Stanford Medical Center where she reportedly checked in for an abortion.

That same December 2, my wife was at the Stanford Medical Center entering labor. She passed Dennis Sweeney and the Boston woman in the hallway leading to the delivery room. There was a moment of recognition, but nobody stopped, nobody said anything.

That was the last I heard of Dennis Sweeney for almost four years.

A llard I could not help but follow as long as my newspapers kept coming.

"Rep. Lowenstein's office has become a 'Mecca' for antiwar activists"; "Rep. Lowenstein backs the 19-year-old vote amendment"; "N.Y. Congressman Allard K. Lowenstein was selected as '70 Senior Class Fellow at the University of Notre Dame."

As the worst of winter closed in on eastern Arizona, I followed the stories from my bunk. The barracks I lived in held 50 men, distributed among four long rows of single beds. The air inside was full of cigarette smoke, armpits, and stray steam from the communal shower.

For all of Lowenstein's seeming eminence, it was apparent from close reading that as 1970 got under way, he was also in political trouble in the Fifth Congressional District. New York's congressional districts had been reapportioned under the leadership of Republican Governor Nelson Rockefeller, and the Fifth had been stripped of several of its heavily Democratic Jewish enclaves, transforming it into what looked like solidly Republican turf. Allard's congressional seat had, in effect, been snatched out from under him after he had spent little more than a year in office. Local Nassau County Republican party leaders immediately began publicly harping on the fact that Lowenstein, the quintessential liberal, no longer truly represented his supposed constituency. Typically, Allard tried to use the development to advance his own agenda.

On February 16, 1970, the Associated Press transmitted a story eventually run as "Rep. Would Quit For Vote On War" with a Washington, D.C., dateline. "Rep. Allard K. Lowenstein (D-NY)," it read, "offered today to resign from Congress on condition that Gov. Nelson Rockefeller agree to call a special election in 60 days. He said it could provide a test of sentiment on the war in Vietnam and other issues. Lowenstein, a liberal Democrat who organized the movement to dump President Johnson in 1968, said he would run for reelection. . . . 'If we can get a special election, win or lose,' Lowenstein said, 'I believe I will have done more to make democracy more viable.'"

Had the gambit come off, Lowenstein's reelection would have become the national antiwar vote he had mentioned to the press in November. Nelson Rockefeller never took him up on the offer, calling it a "political game."

W ithin two weeks after that, I switched prisons and lost access to newspapers for a while. Again, I was identified as an "organizer" of a strike and, along with three other convicts, immediately shipped out of Safford to the La Tuna Federal Correctional Institution, La Tuna, Texas, 10 miles outside of El Paso and a mile from the New Mexico line.

The correctional institution was housed in two stories of concrete and included eight dormitory wings, four cell blocks, assorted outbuildings, and an exercise yard, all surrounded with 12 feet of chain-link fence topped with triple rows of concertina wire and watched over by gun towers. Built to hold 360 prisoners, it held 780. I and the others from Safford were immediately installed in the "disciplinary" cell block, where we were kept locked up for the next month and a half. While there, I filed for transfer to a prison in California, but the La Tuna authorities and the Bureau of Prisons headquarters in Washington, D.C., both rejected the request. To outflank them, I tried writing all the people I knew who might have enough influence to get the decision reversed. One of them was Allard Lowenstein. He never answered my letter.

Nor did I ever get a transfer. Along with a collection of other convicts identified as potential "troublemakers," I was assigned to C Block, the maximum-security unit, 24 cells, holding one man apiece. Five days a week, 7:30 A.M. to 3:30 P.M., I worked with a crew that stacked bales of hay on the prison farm just outside the institution's walls. Once I was established in that routine, my flow of newspapers recommenced and I learned that Allard had been busy.

In response to an outbreak of police attacks on campus demonstrations around the country that spring, he raced between schools, conducting his own one-congressman "unofficial hearings." In Alabama, 2,000 students crammed into a meeting hall to tell story after story of assaults by uniformed officers on "peaceful" marchers. In Tennessee, he arrived in the wake of a huge Billy Graham rally at the university's football stadium at which Richard Nixon had appeared. A relatively tiny number of demonstrators had held up signs saying, "Thou shalt not kill," and, according to the student witnesses, "The police singled out individuals active in civil rights and peace movements, arresting some the next day who weren't even in the stadium."

Lowenstein held hearings, and the Republicans in New York's newly gerrymandered Fifth District seethed.

In May, an issue of *Look* magazine was sent to me, which reportedly caused great consternation to the guards charged with censoring the incoming mails. The picture on the cover was of myself, my wife, and our newborn son, taken several months earlier in the visiting yard at Safford. "Joan Baez and David Harris," the tagline went. "A family kept apart by conscience." The question of whether I ought to be allowed to read about myself was debated by the guards all the way to the warden's office before being resolved. I received that issue of *Look* more than two weeks late.

It is probably necessary to have been in prison to understand just how curious an experience reading about myself was that May. My world was now so much smaller in scope than that of the David Harris in that article that he seemed like someone else. The real me saw Joan once a month in the visiting yard, and the distance between us increased each time. I was a convict with something of a reputation for the strikes and my time in isolation. I had my friends I hung out with, I played basketball and occasionally smoked a little smuggled reefer out on the exercise yard. And that was it. That there was another me circulating out on the streets at the same time was dislocating and made me somewhat uncomfortable. People survive prison by not pretending they are anyplace else; for a moment, *Look* made that a little more difficult. I probably wouldn't have minded, except in principle, if the warden had decided to keep the magazine for himself.

Reading the story made me think about Joan for a while and then about the old Peace and Liberation Commune before I had met her. I remembered how we all had once sat around at Cooley Street and talked about doing time together. That I was the only one of us who had actually been locked up lent an ambivalence to my memories. Especially about Dennis Sweeney. In his case, I felt more than a little let down.

Whatever Dennis had been up to during those first few months of 1970, by May it was apparent that it had not worked out. Early in the month he showed up by himself at Rodney's house in Palo Alto, saying that he and the Boston woman were "going East," but he didn't specify why or where or what they planned to do there. Dennis explained that he had just stopped in to say good-bye.

The two men talked briefly and then walked together down to a nearby grocery to buy some cigarettes. Inside, they continued talking by the store's newsstand. At some point in the conversation, Dennis noticed the *Look* magazines arranged on it. The cover featured me and my wife.

"David," Sweeney interjected with a motion at the magazine. Then he went on to speculate that having gone to prison would prove an asset to me. He talked with an air of indifference and abstraction about the public symbol I'd become. "You watch," he predicted. "David will get out, run for Congress once and lose, then run again and win." Both disgust and grudging respect were carried in Dennis's voice. To Rodney, he seemed despairing. Everyone else from the old commune had found a new tangent to pursue, but Dennis seemed to have remained stuck "with his cock in his hand and no place to go."

The conversation died, Sweeney paid for his cigarettes, and the two men walked out to the store's parking lot. There, Dennis said good-bye, and they didn't lay eyes on each other again.

Shortly thereafter, Sweeney also took leave of Stuart's former girlfriend. They met in one of San Francisco's small neighborhood parks and sat on the grass, talking. Then Dennis suddenly made a comment that would stand out ten years later as his first direct articulation of the shadow that would soon obscure everything else in his life.

Dennis, his manner offhand, told her that he sometimes thought "someone" had "planted an electrode" in his head, in order to "monitor" and "control" him.

The woman thought the remark was a bad joke. She giggled nervously and shrugged it off.

Dennis did not follow up on it.

In the years to come, this "electrode" acquired transmission capabilities, filling his head with voices that drowned out everything else. At first, the voices were numerous, but as the years wore on they were dominated by that of his former mentor, Allard Lowenstein.

The onetime girlfriend to Dennis and Stuart did not see him again until March 15, 1980, when she opened a newspaper and saw Sweeney sandwiched between two New York police detectives, identified as a 37-year-old homicide suspect.

A llard Lowenstein was now 41 years old and three-quarters of the way through his one and only term in Congress. Along the way, his feelings about "the proudest achievement" of his life had become a little mixed. "You get used to seeing things happen in the House that you don't believe," he told one reporter late that spring. "On anything significant, they rarely give you a reported vote. The procedures lack any fundamental democratic quality. The average age of the committee chairmen is three years beyond the compulsory retirement age of most companies."

That same impatience and ambivalence marked Allard's behavior at a barbecue for the Nassau County Democratic Central Committee at his house in Long Beach early that summer. About an hour before the occasion was scheduled to begin, an old journalist friend stopped by and Allard eventually suggested they go out to Baskin-Robbins for an ice cream cone. The journalist wondered if Allard had time before the barbecue started, but Allard assured him that there was "no problem." After a while at Baskin-Robbins, the journalist again asked Lowenstein whether they ought to return to his home, since his guests must all be there waiting. Allard sloughed it off and said they ought to stop by Nathan's Hotdog stand. There, Lowenstein bought a Coney Dog and got involved in a long series of discussions with the kid behind the counter and several others of the largely teenage patrons.

When the journalist again suggested they leave and return to the house, Allard resisted until the journalist finally stated flatly that he had to get back to Manhattan, whatever Allard's plans were. The two of them subsequently returned to the Long Beach house. The barbecue was over, hosted entirely by Jenny, and the Democratic committeemen were all either already gone or just leaving. A number must have been at least slightly insulted by the way they had been treated, but Allard didn't seem troubled in the least. The attitude struck the journalist as strangely dysfunctional. Lowenstein needed all the friends he could make.

The Nassau County Republicans were preparing an election

campaign in which Allard Lowenstein would be villified as Congress's "chief apologist for the Black Panthers" and linked to everyone from SDS to Ho Chi Minh. Nevertheless, Lowenstein continued to fly around the country, supporting those things he deemed important and ignoring everything else.

On one of those trips, he stopped in El Paso, rented a car, and came out to La Tuna to visit me. In response to that gesture, the Republicans would later tar him as someone who abetted "draft dodgers."

I, the "draft dodger" in question, had no warning he was coming. I was down on the prison farm stacking hay when he arrived. A guard in a pickup truck was dispatched to bring me back. "I've got a call out for Harris, four six nine seven–one five nine," he told my work boss. "Some big shot from Washington's here to see him."

I was ordered to the administration offices in the front hallway, where Allard was waiting. It was the first time we had been face to face since he had reclaimed his box of *Brutal Mandate* copies at Cooley Street in May 1967.

"How are you?" he asked with an embarrassed-seeming shuffle.

"All right," I responded.

The interchange was still limping when one of the prison case workers interrupted. It was approaching four o'clock, he said, one of the times during the day when all prisoners had to be locked into their cells to be counted. Allard said that was all right, he would go to my cell with me; since he was a congressman, it was allowed. He and I were locked into my cell together for the next hour and a half until the cell block was released for dinner.

He sat on the bunk, I on the toilet seat. We had little to say to each other.

"How are you getting along?" Allard repeated nervously. "Your letter sounded terrible."

It didn't matter, I said. I had served 14 months of my sentence and was due to appear in front of the parole board in another 45 days. I asked him how he liked Congress.

He said it was okay.

Silence kept interrupting until uneasiness prompted one or the other of us to try and fill it. As was always the case between us, dislike was not at issue, though I'm not sure what was. Perhaps it was just an inevitable outcome of abandoned protégéhood. He had become a stereotype in my eyes, and I'm sure I had in his as well. When I asked

him why he had stopped by, Allard blushed and explained that he
hadn't wanted to "abandon" me. I felt like reminding him that I was
not his to "abandon," but I didn't want to seem ungrateful. I just
thanked him for coming and lit a cigarette. He passed most of the time
by telling me about the lives of a whole list of people he said we both
knew but half of whom I couldn't remember. When the cell door finally
opened, we were both relieved. I walked him down to the now locked
gate leading to the administration wing. The guard in the control room
buzzed it open.

"Good-bye," he said.

"So long," I answered.

With that, he headed off for the front door and the lot under the
gun tower where his rent-a-car was parked. I turned and walked for the
exercise yard. On the steps of the chow hall, one of the Albuquerque
junkies I had become friends with approached me.

"Who was that dude?" he asked.

"Just some congressman I used to know," I said, not breaking
stride.

Everyone involved in the decade would have their own date for
when the Sixties ended, and that cell time with Allard Lowenstein
would be mine. It had been ten years with little in the way of simple
summations to explain it once it was over. The best and worst in us had
fought it out with the best and worst of ourselves. No one had won and
no one had lost. Nothing had changed, but everything was different.

12

The rest amounted to aftermath:

Stanford University, where Dennis and Allard first met in 1961, went on to become, in the estimation of one national news magazine, "the equal" of Harvard in every aspect except "endowment" and "social life."

Stern Hall, the men's dormitory where Lowenstein was director, is now coed.

Armin Rosencranz, the Stanford student body president 1962–63, is now a writer and foundation executive in Marin County, California.

SNCC disappeared as an organization before the Sixties were over.

Bob Moses, SNCC's foremost Mississippi hero, lived in Africa for several years, taught school, and is now back at Harvard doing more graduate work.

James Forman, the most visceral of Lowenstein's SNCC critics, teaches at Cornell University.

One of the young Yale Freedom Vote volunteers who had been arrested with Lowenstein late one night in Jackson in 1963 later graduated from Boalt Hall, the University of California law school. After becoming an attorney, he was suspected of smuggling a pistol to one of his black militant clients in San Quentin Prison, disappeared from sight, and now lives underground.

The National Lawyers Guild, whose participation Allard vehemently objected to during preparations for the Mississippi Summer Project, continues to provide legal aid to political organizing efforts.

Frank Graham, one of Lowenstein's idols and the man whose intervention he sought in order to "save" the Summer Project, later died of natural causes.

The Yale protégé who drove Lowenstein and Graham back from New Haven together is now a professor at Duke University.

The young black SNCC staffer who ran the McComb, Mississippi freedom school in which Dennis Sweeney taught was found almost ten years later, already stiff from rigor mortis, in an abandoned automobile parked on a Newark, New Jersey, city street.

J.D., Dennis's best friend on the McComb Project, is now a ranch hand in Idaho.

The Harvard protégé who drove Allard from NSA to the Atlantic City Democratic National Convention is now an attorney in Washington, D.C.

Rose, the woman I was in love with when I volunteered for the second Freedom Vote, eventually committed suicide.

The Stanford undergraduate who first insisted that I meet Allard Lowenstein when he came through campus in the spring of 1965 is now on the staff of a congressional committee in Washington, D.C.

The *Daily* editor whom Allard assisted in writing the "true story" of what had gone on in Mississippi is now a professor at a state college in New Jersey.

The 173rd Airborne Division, first dispatched to Vietnam in 1965, later engaged in the largest concerted mutiny of the war when ordered to retake a spot on the map called Hamburger Hill.

David Newman, Ed Pincus's partner in the shooting of *Black Natchez*, now works in the film industry in Hollywood.

Mary King, Dennis Sweeney's wife for a little less than a year, went on to pioneer in the development of community-based health-care delivery systems, remarried, and was later one of the highest-ranking female presidential appointees in the Carter administration.

The Encampment for Citizenship, directed by Allard Lowenstein in 1965, continues to hold summer programs for students around the country.

The American aerial bombardment of Southeast Asia, already an issue when the 1965 Encampment was being held, continued for another ten years. It would leave more than four and a half million Indochinese civilians killed, wounded, or homeless. In proportion to the populations of North Vietnam, South Vietnam, Laos, and Cambodia, an average of more than 250 pounds of high explosive per person were dropped before the onslaught came to an official halt in 1973.

Stokeley Carmichael, the SNCC chairman who stayed with Dennis and Mary during his visit to Stanford in early 1966, now lives in West Africa.

The Stanford undergraduate who talked me into running for student body president now teaches at the University of Wisconsin in Madison.

The Dominican Republic, where Allard implemented Norman Thomas's Committee for Free Elections strategy in 1966, has continued to hold regular elections, although intimidation remains a strong fact of political life there. The PRD, Juan Bosch's former party, is now the party in power, although they have moved considerably to the right since the days of Bosch's leadership. Bosch himself has denounced the PRD, now calls himself a "Marxist-Leninist," and runs a popular radio show broadcast from Santo Domingo.

The IILR secretary-treasurer whom Lowenstein had told his former protégé to contact upon arrival in Santo Domingo to open the Committee for Free Elections headquarters later admitted that he had once done work for the CIA.

The house on Cooley Street became a hippie crash pad before finally falling vacant. During its vacancy, the house was ransacked by neighborhood teenagers, and several fires set, which turned it into a charred shell. The lot where it once stood is now occupied by five stucco two-bedroom units. The fallen tree in the backyard has long since become firewood.

The Guava bomb, technological successor to the Pineapple bomb we learned about in 1966, was itself eventually superceded by a "fragmentation device" manufactured from plastic. The plastic's advantage was that the fragments it subsequently imbedded in Vietnamese could not be located with an X-ray machine, thereby "tying up" even more "enemy personnel."

The Selective Service Act of 1948, having been enforced for 18 years when I first violated its provisions, lasted another seven before being suspended, not long after the Paris Peace Agreements were signed between the United States and North Vietnam. Of the estimated 26,800,000 young men subject to the draft throughout the duration of the war in Southeast Asia, 8,720,000 chose to enlist and another 2,215,000 were drafted. 1,600,000 served in combatant and 550,000 in noncombatant roles in Vietnam. Fifty-one thousand were killed, 270,000 were wounded. Of the 15,980,000 men registered with the Selective Service who saw no military service, 15,410,000 were deferred, exempted, or disqualified, and 570,000 violated the Selective Service Act. Of those, 209,517 were prosecuted, 8,750 were convicted, approximately 3,000 became fugitives, and 197,750 had their cases dropped. Of those convicted, 3,250 were imprisoned and 5,500 were given probation or suspended sentences. Of those in prison, 1,500 served less than six months, 1,500 served between 7 and 24 months, and 250 served 25 months or more. In 1979, compulsory registration for conscription was resumed.

The National Student Association steadily sank in stature, budget, and prestige, until it eventually merged with a newer rival student organization and moved its headquarters back to Madison, Wisconsin, where it had been located when Allard Lowenstein was president from 1950 to 1951.

William Dentzer, the friend of Allard's who had originally made the connection with the CIA that would end up discrediting NSA, was, at last report, still employed by the Department of State.

The minister who helped officiate at Lowenstein's wedding to Jennifer Lyman in 1966 was later unsuccessfully prosecuted by the federal government for conspiracy to violate the Selective Service Act.

One of the editors of the *Stanford Daily* during my term as student body president was shot down as a Navy pilot over North Vietnam and spent seven and a half years as a POW.

The student body vice president who assumed the presidency when I resigned in February 1967 was at last report an insurance executive in the Dallas–Fort Worth area.

Lenny, one of the Berkeley founders of The Resistance, now sells real estate in Alameda County, California.

Curtis Gans, who helped conceive and carry out Dump Johnson, was, by 1969, somewhat resentful of how Lowenstein seemed to have taken exclusive credit, but he attempted a rapprochement. Antiwar Democratic party circles were then grappling with possible wordings for a proposed congressional resolution demanding withdrawal from Vietnam, and Gans had worked up some language he was showing around to Democratic office holders. In the course of that, he approached Allard. Lowenstein said that he had been working with Senator Frank Church on questions of wording and suggested Gans take his language to Church's office. At Church's office, an aide asked Gans whether he was the one who had brought over "the Lowenstein draft." Gans immediately left, called Allard, and demanded every copy of the wording back. The two old friends didn't speak to each other for another five years. Gans is now a columnist and political consultant based in Washington, D.C.

Of the two former seminarians who organized the Campus Coordinating Committee in 1967, one got back on good terms with Allard shortly after their conflict over the Moratorium, but for the other it took longer. One became American director of Amnesty International, the other became state treasurer in Colorado and, later, director of the federal agency overseeing Vista and the Peace Corps.

Former President Lyndon Baines Johnson died of a bad heart, former Vice President Hubert Horatio Humphrey of cancer.

The Chicago Seven defendant who gave the impassioned address at the Bratislava banquet became an unsuccessful candidate for United States senator from California nine years later.

The Ivy League protégé who drove Allard to the airport after his brilliant announcement of Dump Johnson at the 1967 NSA Congress became a State Department official in the Carter administration.

Gerald Hill, the CDC chairmen who, along with Lowenstein, was one of the co-chairmen of the Conference of Concerned Democrats, later ran unsuccessfully for Congress on several occasions.

Julian Burroughs, the deserter who spent the last day of Stop the Draft Week in jail with Dennis Sweeney and then fled East, was discovered by Andy Warhol in a New York City phone booth and appeared in Warhol's film *Naked Cowboy* before fleeing to France.

"DAVID VICTOR HARRIS/SEDITION" was dropped as an active FBI investigation in 1971, four years after its inception.

The United States Embassy in Saigon, parts of which were held by the Viet Cong during the 1968 Tet Offensive, was eventually abandoned for good when Saigon became Ho Chi Minh City in 1975.

The naval ROTC clubhouse attacked by Dennis Sweeney and several others in February 1968 was later partially rebuilt, was heavily damaged by another unsolved arson, and was then razed.

The custom-built house Joan Baez and I lived in for the first six months of our married life was sold.

The white ex-convict found guilty of Martin Luther King's murder is still serving a life sentence in a Tennessee penitentiary.

James Wechsler, whose April 1968 *New York Post* column trumpeted Allard Lowenstein's decision to run in Nassau County's Fifth Congressional District, later became editor of the *Post*'s editorial page. After Lowenstein's death, Wechsler would be one of his principal "defenders."

The East Palo Alto steak house where Dennis and I met with the future Chicago Seven defendant was later remodeled and now houses St. Samuel's Church of God in Christ.

The judge who sentenced me to three years in prison later oversaw the trial of Patricia Hearst and died shortly thereafter.

The Palestinian immigrant convicted of Robert F. Kennedy's murder is serving a life sentence in a California penitentiary and will be eligible for parole in 1984.

Ted Kennedy tried for the Democratic presidential nomination in 1980 and was defeated by the incumbent Jimmy Carter.

The Diamond Reo flatbed truck used on the Caravan was eventually sold for scrap to an Easton, California, junkyard.

One of the student canvassers recruited by Allard for the 1968 "August Primary" in Ohio later became mayor of Cleveland.

The journalist who followed Lowenstein around the Chicago convention later won a Pulitzer Prize for a book about Vietnam.

The woman from Boston who went East with Dennis is one of the country's leading young documentary filmmakers.

Stuart's former girlfriend inherited a sizable amount of money and became a society figure in the western city in which she finally settled.

The former press secretary who set up Allard's meeting about the Peoples Park works for the *Los Angeles Times*.

Ronald Reagan, the governor of California who dispatched the National Guard on Peoples Park, is President of the United States.

Peoples Park itself is a hangout for Berkeley's floating population of derelicts, street people, and transients. Three rapes were committed there during 1981.

The attorney general into whose custody I was committed in July of 1969 eventually served six months in prison himself for "obstruction of justice."

Look magazine, which featured Joan Baez and David Harris on its May 5, 1970, cover, ceased publication less than a year afterwards.

The journalist who ended up hanging around with Allard at a Long Island hotdog stand while the Nassau County Democratic Committee waited for Lowenstein to arrive at his own barbecue later served as a foreign correspondent for the *New York Times*.

I was paroled on March 15, 1971, almost nine years to the day before Allard Lowenstein's death, despite having one of La Tuna's worst disciplinary records. Joan Baez and I separated and began divorce proceedings three months later. After the Paris Peace Agreements were finally signed in 1973, I began a career in journalism which, with the exception of standing as the Democratic party's unsuccessful nomination for Congress in California's Twelfth Congressional District in 1976, I have pursued ever since. In 1977, I married Lacey Fosburgh, a novelist and *New York Times* reporter, with whom I continue to live happily today.

My son, Gabe, born five months after I went to prison, is now twelve, likes computers, and makes plastic models of the airplanes that used to bomb Vietnam.

13

Between the years 1970 and 1980, the *New York Times* information bank registered 381 entries and cross-references under Lowenstein, Allard K. Caught freeze frame, new decade or not, he was still a blur. When it finally came time to remember him, he was also still beyond easy categorization.

Intensity is never a simple proposition, and in Lowenstein's case, trying to untangle its roots only leads further into contradiction. He was generous and caring to a fault, yet found it difficult to sustain an interest in conversations he did not dominate. He had absolute faith in the superiority of his own judgment, but made everyone else's case better than he made his own. He cared nothing for titles, yet spent a great portion of his remaining life pursuing them. He was a genuinely selfless server of causes, but he arranged his life so 95 percent of the situations he encountered centered on his own presence. He could work up a plausible strategy for winning the presidency in ten minutes, but when it came to organizing a trip to the movies, things inevitably ended up with nine people waiting on nine different street corners while Allard himself was two hours late and in a phone booth, calling Nairobi collect.

During the Seventies, Lowenstein served as a member of the Democratic Party National Committee, president of ADA, and ambassador for special political affairs to the United Nations, but none of his successes came close to matching either his aspirations or his history. He never lost faith in his own capacity to concoct political miracles like the one in 1968, but no more miracles were attributed to him.

In 1972, he talked to friends about running for President of the United States himself. Instead, he eventually launched the Dump Nixon movement, which culminated in California Congressman Paul "Pete" McCloskey's winning a total of one delegate in the New Hampshire Republican primary. In 1976, Lowenstein was instrumental in the Democratic presidential bid of California Governor Jerry Brown; Brown won five of the six primaries he entered but was unable to block Jimmy Carter's nomination. In 1980, Lowenstein was a spokesman for the unsuccessful presidential challenge of Senator Ted Kennedy.

The string of losses in his own electoral career began in November 1970 when the Republicans' gerrymandering counterattack caught up with him: after a pitched political battle, he was defeated for reelection. In 1972, a group of voters "invited" him into the Brooklyn congressional district of a well-entrenched Democratic machine incumbent, and he lost that primary by 1,000 votes. The results were thrown out by a New York Court two months later, and when the primary was repeated, Lowenstein lost again. Undaunted, he became the Brooklyn district's Liberal party candidate in the 1972 general election and lost for the third time in six months. In 1974, he journeyed back to Long Island and ran unsuccessfully in the district that included some of the Democratic enclaves the Republicans had stripped from his old Fifth Congressional District. That lack of success was repeated in the same place in 1976. In 1977, when Manhattan Democratic Congressman Ed Koch was elected mayor of New York City and his seat vacated, Allard competed in the Democratic party's procedure to choose a candidate for the ensuing special election and lost. In 1978, he ran in the regular primary and lost again. In March 1980, he was preparing for another race in the same district.

The list of disappointments eventually took their toll on Lowenstein's reputation; by 1980, he was being treated in the media as someone who had once been a giant killer but had since fallen on harder political times. Ironically, only what Dennis Sweeney did seemed to stem the deterioration. A dead Lowenstein's contribution, in the eyes of everyone who talked about him publicly, transcended his own personal losing streak. The conclusion was appropriate.

Like all creatures nine parts presence and only one part position, Allard's impact must finally be appraised as much by the reflection of those he moved as by his own achievements. About 50 former students he introduced to politics are serving in state legislatures. Twenty times that many are at work in the executive branch, state administrations, interest lobbies, newspapers, federal agencies, social organizations, and Democratic party central committees. The army of young men whose enthusiasm marked Allard's trail through the Sixties is no longer young, but it is still on the march.

It was to be the final irony of Allard Lowenstein's life that it ended at the hands of one of those same young men.

The Dennis Sweeney of the 1970s was far more easily labeled than his former mentor. The conclusion of all psychiatric evaluation would be that Sweeney was a "paranoid schizophrenic of the chronic type."

Originally called *dementia praecox*, or precocious dementia, this disorder's statistical track shows fewer cultural variables than any other disorder treated by psychiatry. On a computer, paranoid schizophrenia of the chronic type looks something like a universal condition. Its symptoms appear among 1 percent of any studied population, be it in Java or the Bronx. They also appear only in a certain age range, from the late teens through roughly the third decade of life. Agreement on chronic paranoid schizophrenia's strict age limitations is such that the most recent American Psychiatric Association diagnostic manual is able to assert flatly that if the first development of any such symptoms occurs in anyone over 35, it must, by definition, be some other disorder. There is also general professional agreement about the symptoms and the pattern of their onset. All chronic paranoid schizophrenics sooner or later hear voices. They all develop elaborate paranoid fantasies, usually involving a conspiracy of which the chronic paranoid schizophrenic is the central object; in addition, among males, confusion about sexual identity and intense fear of homosexuality are also common attributes. The symptoms emerge over a long period and don't become all-encompassing until relatively late in their development. Even then, they continue to exist side by side with much of the afflicted's nonderanged mind. Chronic paranoid schizophrenics don't blither and are perfectly capable of rational conversation that becomes noticeably strange only when it cuts across the chronic paranoid schizophrenic's conspiratorial logic. Once in the paranoid schizophrenic pattern, few ever emerge again.

Professional consensus begins to disappear when the causes behind the disorder's symptoms are discussed. They spring seemingly from no common experiential base, and the most recent research has increasingly focused on the chronic paranoid schizophrenic's body chemistry. Symptoms seem to coincide with either an over- or underabundance of certain amphetaminelike chemicals in the brain. Symptoms can be duplicated by withdrawal from extreme and continuous methedrine addiction and from being under the influence of the drug PCP, widely known as angel dust. The symptoms occasionally diminish temporarily in response to the crude blood-filtration process involved in kidney dialysis. The most radical working thesis is that the disorder may be a viruslike infection of the central nervous system present at birth, but with an extraordinarily long incubation period. Other more accepted theses combine notions of biochemical predisposition with the variables of induction by emotional trauma or prolonged stress.

Using the current state of scientific understanding as a guideline, the most that can, in fact, yet be said by way of an explanation of

Dennis Sweeney is that his procession of bad luck, political shortfall, emotional battering, and poor decisions was next combined with a random statistical calamity, not unlike being hit by a falling building while waiting for the street light to change.

Instead of going East as he had said he would in the spring of 1970, Dennis Sweeney and the Boston woman apparently went to L.A. and then back North again. That fall, they visited the former SDS couple who had previewed Dennis's film in Cambridge and were now living in the mountains in back of San Jose. As the man remembered the visit, Dennis didn't seem to have any direction and seemed to need "a place to be nowhere in." Sweeney also seemed "untogether" in comparison to the woman he was with. "He was in her dust, that much was obvious. She was going somewhere and he wasn't."

Sometime during the next year, Sweeney and the Boston woman finally broke up for good. In late 1971 or early 1972, one of his old Stanford classmates saw him at a Berkeley coffee shop, and Dennis said he was sharing a room with a Filipino merchant seaman in San Francisco. The former SDS couple saw Dennis again around the same time, and he told them he was going to move to Oregon. Also around the same time, two Federal Bureau of Investigation agents approached one of Sweeney's former radical friends living in the East Bay, saying they had some questions to ask Dennis but couldn't find him. Later in 1972, one of Sweeney's former Stanford professors talked with him in Portland. Dennis said he was resuming his education at Portland State and washing dishes to support himself. He reportedly seemed "like he had been through a hard time."

Although he didn't mention them, the voices had already begun to haunt Dennis, accompanying him wherever he went. Just what the voices said was never recorded. Apparently, he first conceived of them as "radio signals from outer space." They made school impossible, so he went to Cambridge but shortly moved back to Portland again. By then he had reportedly had the last sexual encounter of his life. He later told his lawyer he'd had no woman since 1972, because, he said, the voices had "sapped" him of his "power." Henceforth, the principal object in his life would be to escape them.

In early 1973, Sweeney apparently concluded that the voices were emanating from a "sensor" lodged in his teeth. Sometimes he thought it had been there since birth and, at other times, that it had been implanted in an operation his parents had arranged when he was five years old. He had as yet developed no explanation for why it had been done.

Sometime early in 1973, Dennis Sweeney attempted to rid himself of the "transmissions" by using a pair of pliers to tear the denture bridge out of his mouth where it had been "permanently" wired by the civil rights movement dentist in 1965. When he finished, all that was left in the middle of his upper jaw were the filed down stubs of his own front teeth. Dennis Sweeney's mouth would look like a relic from trench warfare forever after.

That act of self-inflicted ugliness so shocked Dennis's mother and stepfather that they took steps to have him treated at the Oregon State Mental Hospital. He was held for a ten-day observation period, but there was insufficient evidence of disorder to commit him on anything but a voluntary basis. Sweeney later bragged that the time he spent in the mental hospital had taught him how to escape being committed against his will. "Just don't talk about your transmitter," he explained.

The "transmissions," however, did not stop. Out of the hospital but still in Portland, he reached the decision that if the source wasn't in his teeth, it must be somewhere else in his body and began looking for a doctor to locate and remove it. He now suspected that the FBI or the CIA might be involved in the network that was trying to control and monitor him.

While Dennis was trying to find his transmitter, I was living by myself in a house in East Palo Alto, just a block and a half from the lot where the Cooley Street house had once stood. It was the fifth residence I had had in the two years since my release from La Tuna, and I felt like I had done hard time in all of them. Starting a new decade had been as difficult for me as it had for everyone else, and rubble from the Sixties was still piled up all around my head. My marriage had collapsed into acrimony and child custody disputes after I had been back on the streets for three months. I had thrown myself into several different antiwar organizing efforts and made considerable money on the college lecture circuit, but I felt as though I was just going through the motions. I considered myself obliged to continue as long as the war ground on, but I did so in something of a daze, drifting about, waiting for a sign that it was all over.

I greeted the Paris peace accords signed by the United States, North Vietnam, South Vietnam, and the National Liberation Front on January 27, 1973, as something of a personal liberation. I suddenly had options again; upon examining myself in the cold light of what was being called "peace," I thought it was obviously time to move on. I was an ex-convict, ex-husband, ex-civil rights worker, ex-student body president, and ex-organizer against an ex-war. I was proud of what I had done, but I somewhat desperately wanted a future to go with my past. Within two weeks, I arranged to write a story for *Rolling Stone* magazine. Within three months, I had won a contributing editor's contract and with it, a job description in the present tense.

At about the same time, I learned of Dennis Sweeney's sojourn at the Oregon State Mental Hospital from an old Stanford friend of us both. The man called looking for contributions to help send Dennis to a highly regarded private psychiatric institution in Connecticut. He said Sweeney was "seriously disturbed." I gave what I could. Sweeney visited the facility but returned to the West Coast as soon as it was apparent that the doctors were unwilling to extract his electrode.

Later that spring, he wrote me a letter from Portland. It was short and would be the last thing I heard of him for the next seven years. He said that he now knew that no American doctor would be willing to buck the forces at work and give him the "proper treatment," so he was preparing to leave for France. I wrote back and told him to stop by and see his old friends first.

I never got an answer.

Sweeney wrote letters to several other people from his past that same spring. The most comprehensive example to survive was the one addressed to the former SDS couple:

> We were never really close friends, I realize, but I need some trustworthy advice so that I can begin to plan my life again instead of being perpetually on the run. . . . I don't know any more poetic way of saying it, but I am at the lowest ebb of my life now because of the psychological warfare that is being made on me, since about two years ago. I don't believe I am alone in that respect, but since I am alone and have been prior to leaving California in '72 my perspective has become entirely subjective. The specific way in which this psych war has been effected has been a revelation. I am simultaneously attuned to and programmed electronically, apparently,

causing obliteration of an already weak ego, social objectification and ostracization, and a freeze on my ability to reintegrate myself intellectually for not being able to sort out my own thoughts from the impulses running through my skull. I am fairly certain that I have software that I wasn't born with. I have done everything I can think to do to locate it and remove it. My efforts have all been failures and usually self-destructive.

No doubt in the Sixties I was a party to some behavior that was politically irresponsible. If that incurred a social debt then I am willing to pay it in reasonable terms with some sense of limits such as definition of what constitutes rehabilitative service and duration of same, as opposed to bureaucratic sadism and infinite guilt which is what I see confronting me.

More likely, I think, is that my whole life since early childhood is tangled into a kind of self-aborted preparation for social democratic leadership, where the lines of responsibility for thought and action are very muddy. Unwilling to live my life on the terms that have been revealed recently, that is as a component in a vast communication system, I think I am simply being pressured to leave the country. . . .

I take it that I cannot undo myself from this system within the system. If that is not an absolute rule then I am open to suggestions as to how to go about it, for I really don't feel up to starting over at age thirty in another culture. If that is the reality of the situation, though, I would like to know where you think I might travel to find the medical help I want. . . .

I know we're all up against it now, and I wish I were not so divided from humanity that I can't pitch in. I hope you are both in considerably better shape than me, and if I can work this out we will see each other again. Excuse me for being overly familiar with this letter, but there are some situations in which everyone seems almost equi-distant and a reach might be excusable. I hope I hear from you, and that your lives go well through the next three years.

Sincerely,
Dennis Sweeney

Whether Sweeney ever made it to France is not clear. If he did, he was only there a matter of weeks. Later in 1973, he turned up in Cambridge and phoned two old Stanford friends, saying, very "mysteriously," that he had something he wanted to talk about. They had dinner and the two old friends were shocked by his mouth. Eventually, Dennis got onto the subject of his sensor. He was convinced one had been implanted in him somewhere and was still talking about the operation he might get in France. He wasn't sure who was responsible but speculated that it likely included both the FBI and the CIA. All of this was said in a "terribly matter-of-fact" voice.

"Apart from that delusion," one of the friends remembered, "he seemed only mildly depressed and withdrawn. He still had extremely good manners, always very polite. It was terribly, terribly sad was all. He just couldn't apply himself to finding something that mattered to him. He had no idea what he was going to do but on the other hand, didn't seem very troubled by that."

Dennis rented a tiny apartment in Cambridge and got a job turning burgers at a fast-food joint on Harvard Square where he stood at a grill in the front window; for a while, one of his Stanford friends got together with him fairly regularly. "He thought people were watching him but admitted that that might be because of his teeth," the friend explained. "He was cool about his delusion too. I just got so that whenever he brought it up, I just told him I didn't want to talk about it and he accepted that. He talked about it the same way as everything else. On the one hand, he seemed lonely. On the other hand, you had to go out of your way to draw him in because he was so withdrawn."

Quietly, Dennis Sweeney was arranging his life around his need to escape the voices inflicting themselves upon him with increasing frequency, and people who couldn't help out with that were discarded. The old Stanford friend and Dennis played basketball together once a week or so, but then Dennis stopped showing up and left his job in the burger shop as well. The Stanford friend tried to locate Sweeney on several occasions as the Seventies progressed but never saw him again.

Ed Pincus, the Cambridge filmmaker, saw Dennis Sweeney around this same time, in 1973. He showed up at Pincus's home, told Ed and his wife, Jane, the story of his "transmitter," and explained that he had come to see them because he was sure Pincus would know of a doctor who could cut it out. Dennis compared himself to a woman searching for an abortion and being unable to find anyone to perform it.

Ed and Jane Pincus were moved by the spectacle and followed their initial impulse to help out. Ed saw Sweeney as "flotsam of a failed revolution. . . .It had gone wrong," he later explained, "and Dennis was left holding the bag. He hadn't hedged his bets at all, and when the movement was no longer there, he had nothing." Ed spent hours trying in a rational way to convince Sweeney that no technology such as the one he had described even existed. Jane tried to convince him that he had just internalized a series of metaphors. Both expressed sympathy and took his dilemma with great seriousness.

Pincus referred Dennis to an MIT psychiatrist but later realized that the requests for "help" kept coming his way because Sweeney was becoming convinced that Pincus himself was somehow involved in his transmission network and would know how to free him of it. He was apparently already hearing the filmmaker's voice among the cacaphony inside his head. When the psychiatrist Ed had recommended refused to operate, Sweeney simply returned to Pincus looking for more hints. His conclusion that Pincus was involved grew rapidly and ensured that while Dennis Sweeney's other ties to people from the "old days" would evaporate by the end of 1973, he would stay in touch with Pincus, someone who had been at best a tangential friend during the Sixties themselves.

The connection would evolve into a nightmare for Ed Pincus. Over the next seven years, Dennis would check in with him about every six or nine months, and with each encounter, Dennis's delusions seemed to escalate.

During 1974, Sweeney visited Pincus even more often. Once, Dennis explained that when he was in movie theaters he became transparent and radioactive. When Sweeney's mind wandered from the picture, people around him would all cough quite angrily to let him know they knew he wasn't watching. Women on buses whispered his thoughts to one another as part of their own conversations.

Another time, Dennis appeared shortly after it had been publicly revealed that the CIA had, over the previous two decades, experimented on unwitting people with LSD.

"You see?" Dennis said. He treated the new information as "confirmation that his own LSD use had somehow been conspiratorially induced."

Dennis habitually ended each visit by promising, "I won't come back to see you again until I can talk about something else," and each time he returned and talked about the same thing.

These repeated exposures to Dennis's condition had left Pincus somewhat alarmed at how absolutely bent Sweeney's mind had become, so he called a nationally known psychologist with whom he was friends. Specifically, the filmmaker wanted to know whether Sweeney was dangerous.

The psychologist told him not to worry. There were millions of guys like Dennis floating around, he said, and 99 percent of them, though weird, were harmless.

Perhaps the only other person out of his past whom Dennis visited in 1974 besides Ed Pincus was his former mentor, Allard Lowenstein. Sweeney was working in a mattress factory in Lynn, Massachusetts, at the time, and Allard was back on Long Island, running for Congress.

As usual, the Lowensteins' house was choked with young campaign workers. Just being 31 years old made Dennis stick out, and that difference was only intensified when the youngsters in the house got a look at his mouth. When his story about how a transmitter had been wired into his head got around as well, jokes were made about him out of his hearing. It was just a final absurd craziness in Allard's biannual pell-mell election madness to them. Some guy showed up saying the CIA had wired his teeth, so he had torn them out, the kind of story that easily brought on hysterical laughter at the end of a long day in the precincts. Dennis also told someone that all the evil in the world was flowing out of the electrode in his skull.

The depths to which Dennis had fallen pained Allard intensely. When Sweeney explained about the transmissions, Lowenstein said he should see a doctor and offered to do whatever he could to help him find the right one.

Dennis turned the offer down and headed back for Lynn on the bus.

In 1975, Ed Pincus first heard from Sweeney by letter. Dennis was now in Philadelphia, living in the home of a United Church of Christ minister and working as a free-lance carpenter, picking up odd jobs wherever he could.

Allard Lowenstein also heard from Dennis while he was in Philadelphia. Lowenstein's communication was a phone call, apparently made from a pay phone in the Philadelphia train station. Over the last five years of his life, Allard would tell and retell the story of that call to everyone he saw who had known Dennis Sweeney. By now, Lowenstein's former protégé was convinced that the CIA was deeply involved in his tribulations. There were people watching him, and he feared that they meant to kill him. Dennis's tone on the phone was much more hateful and angry now, very different from the confusion he had exhibited at Long Island the year before.

"Call your dogs off," he warned Allard.

Allard said that what Dennis was saying made no sense.

Dennis said he was tired of being hounded and wouldn't put up with it much longer.

"Dennis," Allard agonized, "let me help you. I know people who can help you. I would be happy to get you that help. I'd like to do it."

Sweeney apparently did not appreciate being told he was deluded. "So you too," he growled. "So you too."

Later in 1975, Ed Pincus received a phone call in which Dennis said that he was leaving Philadelphia and moving back to Massachusetts. There was something he had "to talk about."

When the two men got together, Sweeney went straight to the heart of his concern. He asked Pincus point-blank whether he was behind all this.

Pincus had to laugh. "You can't be serious," he said. "Of course not."

Dennis then wanted to know whether Pincus's former partner, David Newman, was.

Pincus told him he was sure Newman wasn't. When Pincus asked why he suspected them, Sweeney explained that they were both involved in the "media" and hence familiar with "transmissions." He added that Pincus's own voice was now transmitted to him "twenty-four hours a day."

When asked how Dennis could be sure it was Pincus doing the transmitting, Dennis answered that it wasn't just his voice, it was also his "hidden personality."

All of this was said to Ed Pincus in Sweeney's traditional Bob Moses style: quiet, calm, undramatic, and polite. To Pincus, it seemed everything from "silly" to "uninteresting," but not "dangerous."

That last conclusion would change shortly.

By the time of his next visit, a note of terror had entered Dennis Sweeney's aura. It was, no doubt, the first time he had ever terrorized anyone face to face in his life.

The next meeting came sometime in early 1976 at Ed Pincus's MIT office. Pincus was frightened from the moment Dennis walked in and sat down. Just looking at him made the short hairs on the back of Pincus's neck stand on edge. Sweeney's demeanor was that of a snarling dog. The stoic front was still there and the quiet voice, but it seethed with anger. His back teeth clamped together when he talked. He said he was tired of Pincus's denials. He said he was now sure Pincus was behind all of it, and if he wasn't, he wanted Pincus to tell him who was. The voices of the filmmaker, the filmmaker's wife, Jane, and even the Pincuses' five-year-old son had all been broadcasting to him 24 hours a day. It had to stop.

Pincus immediately feared for his life and wondered whether Dennis had a gun. Eventually, he had to go to the bathroom and his kidneys began to ache, but he was too frightened to stand up and turn his back, much less leave for the bathroom down the hall, so he sat glued to his chair, waiting for Dennis to explode into outright violence. It lasted the next four hours. Pincus tried to keep Dennis talking throughout.

"Surely if these people who are after you are so powerful," he objected, "they could mimic my voice."

"It's not just your voice," Sweeney repeated, "it's your whole hidden personality." The proof was all in James Joyce's novel, *Finnegans Wake*.

Pincus offered that he had never been able to finish the book.

"What do you want?" Dennis snarled. "A skeleton key?"

Ed Pincus did not push the subject.

Sweeney continued on his own. Pincus, he pointed out, was part of the "killer elite, on the run since Watergate." It was an "international Jewish conspiracy," all part of Jews' "paternalism toward the white race."

"Dennis," Pincus exclaimed, "I can't believe you're saying all this. I don't believe my own ears."

"It's what you've done to me," Sweeney answered.

Pincus tried to change the subject and asked Dennis whether he had visited his aunt and uncle, who live somewhere in the Boston area.

Sweeney said he had tried, but when he approached their house, the messages had become so strong that he'd had to turn back. Pincus and his wife, Jane, were there, naked, doing "obscene dances," and telling him to do "awful things."

Ed Pincus was afraid to ask what the awful things were.

All of this, Dennis continued, was part of a continuing plot to marry him off to a "Jewess." He had not, he claimed to Pincus, "had a woman" in years. That too was part of the same plot.

Pincus asked why he would want to marry Dennis to a Jewess.

Coupled together, Sweeney pointed out, their electrodes would be a much more powerful base from which to transmit.

Pincus tried once again to convince Sweeney that no such technology existed, but Sweeney responded by calling Pincus a liar.

"But I'm nobody. How could a small-time schmutz like me be involved? Could I really do all these things you think I'm doing by myself?"

"You aren't alone," Dennis answered. "You're in it with Allard Lowenstein and Angela Davis." The three of them had conspired together to destroy "the movement" and make "an example" out of him. Because of that conspiracy, Dennis charged, he had become "isolated" from all of his friends. They were making him an "object lesson" in the "futility of left struggle." The movement was dead, he lectured. Why not leave him alone now? Why bother to continue making an example of him?

This was the first time in the 11 years since they had met that Ed Pincus had ever heard Sweeney mention Allard Lowenstein's name. Pincus did not realize what a major figure Lowenstein had been in Sweeney's life until after Lowenstein had been shot to death.

Finally, after repeating his warning about Ed's having to stop, Dennis ended his siege and left.

Immediately afterward, Ed Pincus moved his family to a new location, which he kept a strict secret, changed his home phone number to an unlisted one, and bought a gun for protection.

Nnone of Pincus's maneuvers kept Dennis Sweeney from pursuing his trail. Sweeney soon called the MIT office again, insisting to the secretary that he had to talk to Ed Pincus and that it was "terribly important," but Pincus hid behind excuses delivered through office personnel. Dennis continued his stalking throughout 1976. Once, he sat outside Pincus's old house for three days in the hopes that Pincus would show up. His calls to the MIT office also became increasingly insistent.

"I can't stand this anymore," Dennis told his secretary. "It has got to stop."

Ed Pincus consulted the police, but they informed him they were powerless to do anything until Sweeney himself acted. It was not against the law to want to talk to someone.

By January 1977, Pincus had decided that the only way to get Sweeney off his back was to agree to see him face to face.

They met for the last time on a street corner in Cambridge near a subway stop. Pincus had insisted the meeting be outside in public view and for his own safety had two friends stationed there to keep an eye on things. Pincus got to the corner first. Then Sweeney arrived.

Dennis walked directly up to him and demanded that the film-maker take his glasses off.

The demand was music to Pincus's ears. To him, it meant that Sweeney had no weapon and only planned to attack him with fists.

Pincus did as he was told, and Sweeney immediately began pummeling him. The blows were surprisingly weak, and Ed Pincus did not attempt to fight back. Instead, he fell to the ground and assumed the protective fetal position once taught to all of Mississippi's civil rights workers. While thrashing him with his arms, Dennis claimed Pincus was still broadcasting "24 hours a day," then corrected himself, saying that Pincus didn't in fact broadcast while Sweeney was asleep.

Then Pincus's friends intervened and pulled Dennis off. Sweeney made no move to resume. His parting shot was a reference to transmissions.

"The next time you've got something to say to me," Dennis warned, "say it to my face."

With that, he turned on his heel and disappeared into the subway.

In retrospect, it appears that the attack on Ed Pincus at least partially dislodged Dennis's obsession from the filmmaker he had first known in Natchez in 1965 and sent it drifting even further back in his personal history, until it came to rest on Allard Lowenstein. As much would seem apparent in the decision Sweeney now made to move once again. This time Dennis chose Mystic, Connecticut, halfway between Pincus in Cambridge and Lowenstein in New York.

Still shaken by Sweeney's obsessional assault, Pincus remembered his reference to Lowenstein and tried to send a warning to Allard. Jane's mother apparently knew one of Lowenstein's relatives, and through her Pincus passed on a message that Dennis Sweeney should be considered dangerous and should not be met with alone.

There is no record of whether the message ever reached Allard himself.

In January 1977, I saw Allard in California. It was our last encounter.

Fittingly, it came on the tail end of an exercise that in retrospect looks remarkably like a throwback to my days as his protégé. In 1975 I had decided to take time off from journalism and run for Congress in the 1976 elections, a decision made on an impulse. I had always badmouthed electoral politics while the war was going on, but recently California had passed a law returning the right to vote and hold public office to convicted felons, and it seemed somehow appropriate that on the 200th anniversary of the American revolution, my generation should begin assuming the reins of power. "We need a congressman who went to jail before he went to Washington instead of after," I said. In the year and a half that followed, my initial impulse was gradually worn to a nub. I shook hands, begged contributions, wore suits, and tried to remember everyone's name. I found it a dispiriting exercise and thought the process itself seemed to evoke mediocrity in everything it touched.

I had had one brief phone conversation with Allard shortly after I decided to run. He was then in California working for Governor Jerry Brown as a "consultant." I told him what I planned to do and he was frank, saying he preferred my opponent, Pete McCloskey, to me. Since he had once supported McCloskey for President, I found that perfectly understandable. I didn't ask for an endorsement, and he, obviously, did not offer one.

When I finally lost the general election in November of 1976 with about 34 percent of the vote, I had gained 35 pounds, developed bags under my eyes, and was grateful that victory had eluded me. I looked forward to returning to my typewriter. My last duty as a Democratic party congressional nominee was to act as a delegate at the California State Central Committee Convention in Sacramento that Janaury. It was there that I crossed paths with Allard.

My wife, Lacey Fosburgh, and I joined several friends for breakfast one morning in the coffee shop of the hotel where the convention was headquartered. The place was full and noisy. We had been sitting at our table for several minutes before Lacey noticed Allard halfway across the room.

"Isn't that Allard Lowenstein?" she asked. She had known him a little in New York and had last seen him at a peace rally there in 1969, where she had been quite impressed.

I looked in the direction she indicated and spotted him seated at a table with four or five young men. He looked tired, cluttered, and wore an ill-fitting sports jacket. The young men were all blond, collegiate, and, as Lacey remembers them, "looked like they belonged on a beach." They were paying a great deal of attention to Allard, but he seemed distracted, blindly turning the pages of his newspaper. Occasionally he looked up and scanned the coffee shop, but with a restless, disjointed air. The young men eventually left, and, as they did, Lowenstein noticed us across the room. He stuffed his paper into his hopelessly crammed traveling bag, left a tip, and, walking toward the lobby, stopped at our table along the way.

He and I exchanged warm greetings, and each of said it had been a long time. Allard declined the offer of a chair, saying he was on his way to meet someone in the lobby, but he stood by the table and made political small talk. There was none of the discomfort that surrounded our last face-to-face conversation in my jail cell almost seven years earlier, but neither was there the former sense of connection between us. Our talk was perfectly pleasant. Then Allard said good-bye and walked on out the lobby door.

After several minutes, he returned to the coffee shop. Apparently, whomever he was supposed to meet was late, and Lowenstein took a seat at the counter by himself. Again, Lacey noticed him. I only looked briefly and returned to the conversation at our table, but she kept watching. He seemed to be in some private place inside his head, she said, paying little attention to the political polyester eddying around the counter. Lacey would later remember him vividly as looking "lost," not "on" in the theatrical sense, like a piece of "flotsam." He stayed perched there in his mental bubble for several minutes and then left to try the lobby again.

After he was gone, Lacey brought his name up and, with a strong feeling of human affection, commented on the "intense sadness of this man."

"I have a feeling he's failed at something," she said.

"Times change," I shrugged. Off the top of my head, I could think of nothing better to say.

I have since learned that at the time I last saw him, his marriage was in its final stages of collapse. According to several people he talked to about his divorce from Jenny, it was an extremely painful, confused, and demoralizing experience for him.

Not long after our coffee-shop encounter, Allard assumed the last full-scale "position" of his life. Newly elected Jimmy Carter asked him to serve as the United Nations delegation's so-called "fifth ambassador" for special political affairs, overseeing "human rights" and "decolonization." Lowenstein reportedly had doubts about Carter and whether he himself could function in a hierarchy like the State Department. Even so, he accepted the offer.

He would keep the job for less than a year. Lowenstein was not a good administrator and did not fit easily in the State Department pattern. He was used to doing things quickly and having his own way, neither of which were features of a fifth ambassador's rank. One of his first tasks was to represent the United States at the United Nations Human Rights Commission meeting at Geneva, and he returned feeling that he had made "great strides" on the issue of Soviet dissidents, but those "strides" soon came to nothing. The problem, he told his friends, was that he had received "no administration backing." Similar complaints would dot his term in office.

Perhaps Lowenstein's greatest frustration was over South Africa. While still at the UN, he traveled there at what was apparently the South African government's informal invitation. He was given radio time by his hosts, which he used to give an address calling for the release of South Africa's black nationalists from political prisons. One American who was in South Africa at the time called the performance brilliant. Allard also reported to his superiors that while there, he had met with a group of Afrikaner officials, whom he was invited to address. Lowenstein claimed he had been introduced to the group of white South Africans as "one of our greatest enemies," and they all had copies of his 1962 book, *Brutal Mandate*. The question they put to him was what South Africa had to do in order to gain acceptance from the West. Allard claimed he answered by suggesting a round-table conference at which the Afrikaner government would deal directly with the black nationalist leadership they now kept imprisoned. To his surprise, the Afrikaners, Allard alleged, then said that they would be willing to negotiate secretly with the United States on the possibilities of such a move and wanted his personal assistance in initiating the process. Lowenstein returned to New York from Johannesburg feeling that South Africa was at a "turning point." He was enormously excited.

His superiors, however, were not. No official action was ever taken on Allard's reported breakthrough, and no authorization to pursue it would ever be given. It was reportedly the State Department's position that South Africa was just using Lowenstein's own optimism to generate the illusion of serious intentions when they, in fact, had none.

owenstein's frustrations at the United Nations soon led to visions of moving on to another arena. About six months after he had become fifth ambassador, a journalist witnessed one such sign when the two had lunch at Sardi's Restaurant in New York City. While they were eating, a woman Allard had never met before approached their table.

"Aren't you Allard Lowenstein?" she asked.

Allard said he certainly was.

"Well, I hope you'll pardon my interruption," she continued, "but I just wanted to say I admire you a lot and I hope you run for Ed Koch's seat."

Koch had just finished first in the primary for mayor, and his Manhattan congressional seat would soon be open.

Allard said he would love to talk to her about that later and cleared his afternoon schedule at the UN to do so.

The journalist was surprised at all this, and, several days later, when the two men had lunch again, Allard said he was "strongly considering" resigning from the UN to run for Koch's seat.

The journalist offered that Lowenstein might be better off staying put. Wasn't Allard worried about becoming "the Harold Stassen of New York congressional politics"?

Allard said he wasn't. This was a seat he could "win" and "step right into."

Not long afterwards, Allard revealed his plans and predicted victory to an old friend from his Stanford days. Then he told the Stanford man the story of what had become of "poor" Dennis Sweeney.

Allard said it was "one of the great tragedies of the decade."

There were other indications that year that Dennis's fate haunted Allard in a very personal way.

One of Lowenstein's duties as fifth ambassador was to travel around the country making speeches under the auspices of the United Nations Association. On May 16, 1977, he came to Stanford and, while there, granted a short interview to a history professor who was collecting oral accounts of the civil rights movement. In the middle of several questions about his own relationship to SNCC, Lowenstein started talking about Dennis Sweeney. Allard said:

I remember one of the most bitter experiences I had in
Mississippi in personal terms came about because one of the
people who went down to Mississippi as a result of my efforts
at Stanford was a guy called Dennis Sweeney. . . . It's a
very,very illustrative story in terms of an autobiography. It's
too long to tell you now, but the basic point of it was that he,
after he got there, became very radicalized. He was sent to
McComb. He was in very great danger physically. He was
arrested when they blew up the Freedom House, and in the
course of that decided that Norman Thomas and I and other
figures were . . . the enemy, much more than the white
power structure. And since Dennis and I had been quite close
friends, it became a very, very personal thing. . . . Dennis
and I had been good friends at Stanford when I was here,
among the people that I worked with trying to end a lot of the
social injustices here. He had been in the forefront of that. A
very talented person. He went to Mississippi during the
period when SNCC was getting into "black power" and,
during the period when I was becoming the sort of villain in
their eyes, became very much the spearhead of their
campaign against me in a lot of ways. We met under very
ugly kinds of circumstances in places where he would attack
me from a very personal feeling. . . . He, after becoming very
much involved with SNCC, ended up being thrown out of
SNCC himself because he was white and, as the thing
radicalized further, it became more black. They ended up
accusing him of all the things that he had accused me of
except it was done after he had put all of his emotion into
SNCC, and it very, very badly damaged him. . . .

He called me from Philadelphia maybe two years ago out
of the blue and told me that people were trying to kill him. It
was a very sad sort of end for a very talented person that
hacked out the fillings of his teeth because he said the CIA
were using those fillings to damage his brain. And he just
simply had gone to the point where I don't know if there's
ever any way he could be reclaimed from this tragedy. . . .
That whole situation . . . produced genuine paranoia and very
often very deeply bitter and permanently damaged people. It
was not limited to ideology. There was a very interesting
overlap between ideology and psychology in that whole
thing. . . . That people didn't snap under [the pressure] is
incredible because the stresses were just constant. . . . If you
understand all of that, there isn't any way that you can ever
underestimate the reasonableness of going crazy.

By the middle of the summer of 1977, Dennis Sweeney was earning a living in Mystic as a carpenter and staying in a rooming house on Jackson Street down near the water, where he would stay for the next two years. The house he lived in was five bedrooms with a shared kitchen and shared bath. Sweeney was remembered by his fellow roomers as "strange" and "definitely a loner." The strangest thing about him was his ritual of locking himself either in his room or the communal bathroom and screaming back at the voices in his head. One of the Jackson Street residents remembered a lot of "stuff about his father" among the rantings, all of which were "angry," "full of obscenities," and "antagonistic." One of the words he screamed a lot was "kikes."

When one of these shouting fits had passed, Dennis made a point of apologizing very politely to everyone in the house for the noise. He explained that it was something he had to do in order to chase away the people in his head and get them to stop bothering him. His tone of voice implied that it was nothing more unusual than a disagreeable daily chore. Several other roomers tried to communicate more with him about his troubles but met with very little success. One who had several such conversations remembered them as "totally off the wall, shit about martians with ray guns and like that. Very weird." Once Dennis told his fellow roomers that the people watching him had "turds for brains" and "look through a telescope." He said the remark as though they could hear it and he was saying it anyway.

Sweeney filled up most of his spare time in Mystic with an interest in woodworking. The Jackson Street house had a garage, where he sometimes worked at making furniture until 2 or 3 A.M. His other recreation seemed to be drinking an occasional beer and listening to 1950s rock'n'roll on the radio. He read books, magazines, and newspapers, and impressed the other roomers as being "well educated." Other than that, they knew surprisingly little about him. He was originally from Oregon and had been living in Massachusetts. Various conversations led them to believe that he had once been "a political activist" or something, and in the only political discussions he had there, he "went on about how angry he was that there were poor people and poverty," saying that the government "protected the rich and the corporations." He seemed deeply offended by those political problems but was otherwise calm. He drove an old Chevy pickup, rolled his own cigarettes, was a reliable carpenter, and was never late to work.

During the two years Sweeney lived on Jackson Street, he had almost no contact with everyone he had once known. A rumor that he had committed suicide in 1974 even began making the rounds in the old "movement" circles in which he had once circulated. Dennis did call Ed Pincus's office on several occasions but never got further than the secretary.

He also wrote a letter to Allard Lowenstein. According to the Lowenstein assistant who read the letter, it contained nothing unusual, just a lot of talk about what Sweeney was doing now and questions about Allard's own political plans. There seemed to be nothing obsessive about it. Back in Mystic, however, there was at least one piece of evidence that Dennis had begun to focus his paranoia on his former mentor.

Sometime late in 1978, Sweeney was in an accident at work. The jack holding up a scaffolding had toppled onto his head and opened a gash it took several stitches to close. Within days of the event, Sweeney had apparently concluded that Allard Lowenstein had arranged for the accident to happen.

B y then, Allard had resigned from his UN post and made two unsuccessful attempts to become the Democratic nominee for Ed Koch's congressional seat. He was on the verge of turning 50, and much of the luster had disappeared from his legend.

"I hated to see him get old," one longtime friend later confided. "He wasn't going to settle down and be a lawyer in New York. His family was broken up. He wasn't going to be successful at politics. I was afraid he was just going to become someone ridiculous, a guy who was always running for office. By the last year of his life, he was no longer taken seriously in a lot of circles, was looked upon as someone who once was, as a creature of the past tense, not the present."

Lowenstein would probably have been somewhat hurt to hear those thoughts about himself. He had lost no faith in his own destiny. To friends, he talked at length about Churchill and Wellington, both of whom had undergone long political exiles before finally coming to power. So it would be with him, he suggested, and his pace never slackened.

The one apparent concession he made to nostalgia as his fiftieth year approached was an occasional gathering of friends from "the old days" together at his brother's restaurant in Manhattan. One group he got together with in 1978 and 1979 was composed of students from his assistant dean days at Stanford from 1961 to 1962. He repeated to them the story of Dennis Sweeney and the sad fate that had befallen him. To one person, Allard agonized out loud about the "mystery" of why Dennis had come to "hate" him so much.

In early 1979, Allard Lowenstein threw himself into the last major project he would carry through in his lifetime: setting out on his own both to negotiate a solution to the Zimbabwe/Rhodesia civil war and to pursue the opening from the white South Afrikaners he felt he had chanced upon while still at the UN. When, after his death, the *New York Times* foreign desk queried its correspondent in Salisbury about those efforts, the correspondent summarized the trip in a memo sent by cable on March 15, 1980.

> Al Lowenstein visited South Africa and Rhodesia at least twice in the past year offering himself in an honest broker role. He came with knowledge of Secretary of State Vance and other senior State Department officials but no commission other than encouragement to do whatever he could and to report back if he found openings into which diplomats could move. He was in Rhodesia for "internal" elections in April 1979, and again about three months later. On each occasion, he preceded his visit with stops in black capitals . . . involved in Rhodesia problem and met there—and in Salisbury—with the very top people—Ian Smith, Kenneth Kuanda of Zambia, Julius Nyerere of Tanzania, Bishop Abel Muzorewa, etc. His idea was to develop a peace formula for settling war between Patriotic Front and Salisbury government and step back to allow Britain and the United States . . . to move in and bring things to fruition.
>
> In South Africa, where he spent several weeks trying to bring together parties to the racial dispute—ruling white Afrikaners, white liberals, tribal black leaders, and black nationalists. . . . the effort was hopeless from the beginning (as, to speak bluntly, it was in Rhodesia too, coming as it did from a private American citizen with a strong ground in politics . . . but little influence).
>
> Privately, many who dealt with Lowenstein on his trips felt that he was motivated by a desire to promote a new political career for himself at home (New York Senate bid?). Al did not deny this. Can't give you any refusal on-the-record quotes because most of those I got fell into this category, but perhaps you can make do with . . . a Rhodesian foreign office

official, a white, who was the liaison here when Al came through on his swings: "I think Al saw himself as sort of a king maker for the future Zimbabwe—a sort of catalyst around which the future Zimbabwe . . . would form, but unfortunately for Al, he was overtaken by events. . . . Al was out on his own, looking for a breakthrough and hoping that if all went well he'd get the kudos. The State Department knew about it and encouraged him, but only on the understanding that if anything went wrong they could wash their hands of it. He had a sincere concern for the future of the area and was trying to be constructive, but the problems were greater than could have been resolved by anyone."

In July 1979, when Lowenstein was still in Africa, Dennis Sweeney left Jackson Street in Mystic and moved across the bay to New London, Connecticut, where he rented a room at 33 Granite Street, one of two rooms for single men on the second floor of a converted barn. New London's American Legion Post No. 9 was a half block away.

Dennis's room was approximately 15 feet square, painted green and furnished with a dresser, a table, a small icebox, and a single bed. Its principal decoration was a rug with pink flowers laced over a turquoise background. The air in the shared bathroom carried the antiseptic stench only years of continuous Lysol applications can generate. The rent was $150 a month. Dennis always paid by check. His landlady was in her late sixties and lived in the larger house nearby. When she first met him, she guessed his age at 27, ten years younger than he actually was.

The landlady told him right away that she was strict—absolutely no female visitors—but Dennis said that would be no problem. He told her he was from Oregon. When she asked why he had left home, Sweeney told her that there had been some "trouble" between his friends and his family and he had come East to "get away" from it. The landlady was impressed with Dennis's manners and would remember him as a "very polite young man."

"He always paid his rent on time," she told one of the reporters who suddenly swarmed out to Granite Street in March of the next year. "He was very fair in his dealings. If he owed you a dime, he paid it. He built furniture downstairs in the barn, sometimes until real early in the morning. Said he couldn't stand to be idle. He was quiet, never made a bit of noise. No bad language. I don't think he had any social life. I never saw him with another person. He kept his room very neat and had his own phone. I have nothing ill to say about the poor boy. I wish every roomer I had was so nice."

She had only one conversation with him that was unduly "strange."

While paying the rent one month, he told her all the different places he had lived.

"Why don't you stay put?" she asked.

"I can't," he said. "They're following me. You can't see them, but they're there."

B y the fall of 1979, the "they" in Sweeney's head had largely been transformed into Allard Lowenstein. Dennis wrote another letter to Allard during this period, but it, like the previous one, was inconsequential in the eyes of the person sorting Lowenstein's mail.

Dennis's obsession with Lowenstein had begun to coalesce around a feeling that he needed to intersect with Allard face to face.

In late October, Lowenstein was scheduled to appear at a conference sponsored by Milsaps and Tougaloo colleges in Mississippi, on the history of the civil rights movement and the 1964 Mississippi Summer Project. Somehow, Sweeney found out about it. The week before the conference began, one of its organizers received a phone call from a youngish-sounding man who identified himself as Dennis Sweeney. Sweeney said he had been with SNCC from 1963 to 1965 and was interested in coming to the conference. He was trying to arrange enough time off from work so he could take the bus down to Jackson. He was particularly interested in the appearance of Allard Lowenstein and wanted to know just which days "Mr. Lowenstein" was going to be in attendance. Despite the phone call, Sweeney made no appearance at the Milsaps and Tougaloo conference.

Lowenstein's role there was volatile. The audience at the panel on which Allard was scheduled to appear was full of SNCC veterans, most of whom were seething that he, of all people, was going to stand up there and pass historical judgments about "their" movement. Lowenstein sensed the antagonism and, at first, tried to duck it. The original speakers order had placed Allard first, but he had the emcee move him back to second, then third, then fourth, and finally last place as the panel proceeded. His hope was apparently that SNCC's antagonism would play itself out before he took the podium. Instead, it intensified. Shortly after he finally stood up to speak, people in the audience began shouting that Lowenstein had no right to be on that panel saying whatever he was going to say. There were accusations hurled at his "destabilization efforts" in the 1964 Summer Project and epithets about his "red-baiting" and "sabotage" as well.

Having been effectively shouted down, Lowenstein was not, however, without recourse. He had strong contacts among Milsaps College undergraduates as a consequence of having spoken there several times in the previous two years, and by the next evening, his Milsaps lieutenants set up a rump meeting in a campus hall where Allard could make his own case. Several hundred people attended. Lowenstein's remarks were largely autobiographical and concerned his own role in the civil rights movement. He still claimed to have been the inventor of the Summer Project. Few former SNCC members showed up to dispute the claim, but those who did were vehement in their objections to his version of history.

Of all the antagonisms in Allard's life, the one with SNCC continued to be the most bitter. After 16 years, the venom between them was still fresh. When it came time to mourn Allard Lowenstein's passing, only a few former SNCC members would show up, and even those few confessed to having decidedly mixed feelings.

Despite that encounter in Mississippi, there was more reconciliation than recrimination in Allard's life that fall. He enjoyed recapturing the old days and sent several long messages to people he had broken with or lost touch of, trying to get relationships back together.

One involved a former protégé now living on the East Coast. During the Sixties he and Lowenstein had been very close, but that intimacy had diminished in the decade that followed. The former protégé had, since his undergraduate days, struggled with ambivalence about his own sexual identity, and Allard, among others, had counseled him about it. After a divorce, the former protégé had finally turned openly "gay" and felt much better for it. His own sense of distance from Allard now had sprung from stories he had heard about his former mentor in homosexual circles. Allard had always insisted to his former protégé that he, Allard, was not "gay," but now the protégé kept hearing of reports from gay men who claimed to have had sex with Lowenstein. It bothered him very much that Allard seemed to have misled him.

That fall, Lowenstein gave several speeches in the former protégé's hometown and arranged to see his old friend. They finally got a chance to talk alone at 2:30 A.M. Both were feeling good about being back in touch. The gay protégé then told Allard about the stories he had heard and how angry that had made him feel.

Allard confessed frustration about those stories himself. He had always, he said, tried to be truthful with his friends and such rumors destroyed that trust. The stories were inventions, he said. They made him feel "funny" about the people who told them. He was "different," he claimed, not "gay."

Lowenstein went on to talk about the loneliness of not being with Jenny anymore. He said the divorce had left him feeling like a failure. In his relationships with women since then, he said, the women had been "terribly needy."

The former protégé commented on the difficulties he had had with women after his divorce and discussed his own subsequent decision to be with men exclusively. Then he asked Allard directly why he himself had not made the same decision.

Lowenstein's response led the protégé to believe that he had indeed had experimental sexual encounters with men, but that none of them had been either "successful" or "satisfying."

Then the subject switched to Eleanor Roosevelt, the monarch of Allard's pantheon. Recently, news accounts had appeared about "the intimate nature of a friendship" that had gone on for thirty years between Mrs. Roosevelt and her "close friend," Lorena Hickock, a reporter and author. Ms. Hickock and Mrs. Roosevelt's correspondence had just been made available to historians by the Franklin D. Roosevelt Library in Hyde Park, New York, and included statements like, "I remember the feeling of that soft spot just northeast of the corner of your mouth against my lips. . . ."

Talking about those letters, Allard told his gay protégé that the people from the Roosevelt Library had been in touch with him for advice and that he had responded that it was a fit subject for public discussion and couldn't be stopped anyway. That night, he added that in some way, it was probably "salutory."

Allard's comment led the discussion back to sexuality. Allard described himself as "odd" but then retracted the word. It wasn't odd to want to be physically close with someone else, he said. Didn't everybody want that? At the same time, he was confused because "so few" men seemed to respond comfortably to that attitude.

The protégé then asked Allard about his habit of spending most of his time with men. Wasn't part of that attraction physical?

"Of course," Allard answered, very much so. He liked touching men and he loved sleeping in the same bed with someone. He liked hugging and being held. Then he repeated that he was "odd." Maybe, he speculated, he was out of another time. Maybe he would be different if he had been born later. He wanted physical contact with men, but he didn't want "anything more" than that. Gays, he said, found that unsatisfactory, and straights were alarmed. Sex, he said, was the obstacle to his closeness with men. They wanted either "too much" or "too little."

At some point, the issue of Allard's manipulated encounters with young men came up, and it seemed clear to the former protégé that Allard felt guilty about them but didn't have much "understanding" about it. He knew he had been manipulative at "some level" but obviously didn't want to talk about it. There was, according to the gay former protégé, "a lot of not seeing what he was doing" on that particular subject.

The conversation then reverted back to Eleanor Roosevelt. Allard speculated that she must have wanted her letters to be discovered or she would never have let them survive. The revelation about her sexuality was, in effect, "her own doing." As such, he said, it made Allard happy.

By now, it was after 6 A.M., and Lowenstein had to catch a plane at 9. For the last two hours of his stay, he and his former protégé went to bed together and fell asleep in each other's arms. As the protégé would later remember, "There was nothing sexual about it," just a brief comforting before leaving on the run.

Allard Lowenstein ran as hard in 1979 as he had 10 and 20 years earlier. He occasionally indulged in fantasies about moving to Florida and working on a book about Africa, but no one who heard him talk about the "retirement" believed it would happen soon. Another presidential election year was beginning soon.

By December of 1979 Lowenstein was already flashing around the country boosting Ted Kennedy's campaign. Allard's role, as remembered by the assistant who ran Lowenstein's corner of the Manhattan law office he made his personal headquarters, was that of troubleshooter and speaker.

On Christmas Day, 1979, the *San Francisco Chronicle* ran a long interview with him.

> Lowenstein vociferously challenged the current "inquisitorial mood" in examining the private lives of political figures. . . .
> A similar obsession with the private lives of the nation's founders "would've deprived us of the services of Thomas

Jefferson, Alexander Hamilton, and probably George
Washington," Lowenstein said. "So far as I know, Richard
Nixon had a superb private life and I have no reason to think
Tricia or any of the other heroines of the Nixon family have
ever engaged in any conduct that would be considered
inappropriate, but that had nothing to do with the quality of
Nixon's administration."

Early in January 1980, Allard came to California to work the
Democratic Central Committee convention personally, and from there
he proceeded on to Florida. His appearances on the Eastern seaboard
were occasionally carried on local New York City television stations'
late-night campaign wrap-ups. Dennis Sweeney reportedly watched
him several times while down at New London's Dolphin Café trying to
enjoy a beer and escape the voices.

The event that seems to have finally impelled Sweeney
through the final steps leading up to homicide occurred on
February 24, 1980. That day, Gerald Sweeney, Dennis Sweeney's
stepfather, dropped dead in Portland from a heart attack, and Dennis
Sweeney flew home for the funeral. He knew before he left Connecticut
that the voices were responsible for what had happened. They had told
him so themselves, and Allard Lowenstein's was chief among the
chorus. Dennis would later tell police investigators that Lowenstein
had harassed his father to death by suing him in court and trying to
take all his money. No such lawsuit ever existed.

His obsession was only deepened by the events in Portland after
he arrived. One of these and the decision it precipitated would later be
touched upon by Sweeney in a letter from his cell in Riker's Island
Prison to Jeffrey, one of the Peace and Liberation Commune's former
members.

> Dear Jeffrey,
>   I got your card yesterday and have no trouble answering
> immediately with all the time I have. . . . As you may know, I
> have been troubled for the past ten years by "voices" which
> interfere with any unarticulated stream of consciousness. The
> group whom the "voices" represent have made a prescenium
> [sic] of my life for the presentation of their own lifestyle to the
> American public. Among those voices, most of whom I can
> identify, has been yours. Among the last impressions I had

*before I made the decision to drive down to N.Y. with a gun
in my possession to see Al was a memory of being home in
Oregon for my stepdad's funeral just two weeks previous.
After a visit to the funeral parlor to view the open casket, I
was running an errand for my mother and as I strolled
through a supermarket, yours and David's voices were
presented to me as darting around the aisles hinting at
complicity with my stepdad's death. I was very depressed
about the addition of your consent to the "voices" who were
already claiming responsibility for his heart attack. I came to
the conclusion that I couldn't drag that scene around the
continent anymore as it appeared to be involving an
increasing number of deaths and injury every day. I don't
know with what amount of consent your voice has been used
over the past years, but I was pleasantly surprised to receive a
note from you. I was glad to hear that despite everything else
you are still the same person you were fifteen years ago. . . .
Write again if you like, or until then,*

> Yours truly,
> Dennis

Dennis Sweeney left Portland the day after his stepfather's
funeral and returned to Connecticut. On March 3, he
entered Raub's Sporting Goods on Captain's Walk in New London's
refurbished old-town section near the train station, one of the small
city's six gun dealers. There, in official terms, the commission of his
felony began.

Sweeney went to the case displaying pistols and selected a Llama
.380, a seven-shot, .380-caliber automatic of Spanish manufacture,
costing $130. In order to take possession of a handgun in Connecticut,
it was first necessary for Sweeney to fill out an "Application to
Purchase, Pistol or Revolver," in accordance with section 29-33 of the
Connecticut General Statutes, Revision 1965. Sweeney also filled out
the "Firearms Transaction Record/Intrastate Over-the-Counter" required by the Federal Bureau of Alcohol, Tobacco, and Firearms. To
question "E" on the federal form, "Have you ever been adjudicated
mentally defective or have you ever been committed to a mental
institution?", Dennis answered, "No." The state form had to be sent to
the New London police for a check on his felony arrest record. When
that was returned with an okay, the clerk told Sweeney he could

purchase the Llama and take it home. The process could take anywhere from six days to two weeks.

Back at Granite Street, Dennis Sweeney told his landlady that he was going to be moving back to Oregon soon, but he wasn't yet sure when. He asked if he could arrange to pay his rent by the week until he left, instead of by the month as had been his practice, and she agreed. He also called the law offices of former Congressman Allard K. Lowenstein and made an appointment for 4 P.M., Friday, March 14.

Despite making that appointment, there is evidence that Sweeney was still confused about which voice should be his target. In the first two weeks of March, he made several frantic phone calls to Ed Pincus's office. He reportedly told the secretary who answered that he knew Pincus lived in Vermont and just wanted the address. The secretary put him off.

On Tuesday, March 11, 1980, Dennis Sweeney returned to Raub's Sporting Goods, paid $130 cash, and picked up his Llama. He also purchased a 50-round box of standard .38-caliber ammunition.

That same Tuesday was primary election day in Florida and Allard Lowenstein had been there for a week, stumping in the Miami area as part of Kennedy's final push. His trip was paid for by the Dade County Coalition for Human Rights, the group first formed to campaign for a local gay rights ordinance; it later got national exposure when it opposed the ultimately successful fundamentalist Christian drive to repeal the ordinance, headed by former singer and orange-juice-industry spokesperson, Anita Bryant. According to several Coalition members later interviewed by the *New York Native*, a gay biweekly tabloid, Allard's Florida effort gave hints that he wanted to increase his involvement in gay politics.

The *Native* claimed that "Lowenstein was viewed by Kennedy staff as a trusted emissary to the gay community," and that "gays viewed him as their emissary back to the Kennedy campaign." In Florida, he pursued his usual crowded schedule and was the featured speaker at a major gay rights rally in the Club Miami bathhouse on the night before the election. Lowenstein also had a number of conversations with gay leaders in which he reportedly discussed his "hopes of participating further." "He talked about the importance of the gay community doing educational work beyond the political," the national coordinator of the Gay Vote 1980 project was to recall. "He said he would like to do a retreat with gay leaders about where the gay movement should be going, about how to educate for the coming generation." Allard's sensitivity was trusted, and it was clear to all those he dealt with that he had an affinity for the issues involved.

According to the *Native*, Lowenstein was described by "some of his close gay friends and coworkers" as also "having an intensity that brought forward a special intimacy 'that went beyond camaraderie.'" The tabloid would offer as an example the conversation Allard reportedly had with a former Mr. Gay America contestant who was among those assigned to assist him. "We sat down in the office and he was making phone calls," the gay man recalled. "He started talking about my music, it was like giving me a psychology trip, that I should believe in myself." The former Mr. Gay America contestant later indicated that after several hours of such talk, he felt as close to Lowenstein as he did to his own lover. "He mentioned, 'I'm not gay, but you know, a funny thing happened to me.' He said there was one person he used to lay down and hold, right after he got out of the service. As the hours went by, he said how close we felt, how we had opened up our lives, and how he would like to just lie down and hold me, if that could ever be, and then he gave me his phone number in New York City."

On the evening of March 11, Lowenstein was ensconced in the Kennedy headquarters taking calls as precincts began to report. The returns indicated a victory of sorts. Although his candidate did not carry the state, the gays among whom Allard had campaigned turned out heavily for Kennedy. Further, the head of the Dade County Coalition was elected to the county's Democratic Party Executive Committee, and six other gays were selected as either delegates or alternates to the national convention. "It was," the *New York Native* reported, "the first political victory for gays in the 1980 campaign and coming in Florida made it especially sweet."

Lowenstein's critical role in it was apparently greatly appreciated. After his death, the six gay delegates to the convention dubbed themselves the "Lowenstein memorial delegation," and the Dade County Coalition for Human Rights renamed its political arm the Allard K. Lowenstein Political Action Committee.

On Wednesday, March 12, Allard Lowenstein's flight from Miami was met at La Guardia Airport by his assistant. The circles under Allard's eyes were deep and black. It was twelve years to the day since Eugene McCarthy had first punctured Lyndon Johnson's presidency. During the drive into Manhattan, Lowenstein looked through the mail that had come to the office in his absence. One of the letters was from a New Hampshire woman at whose home he had spoken on behalf of the Kennedy campaign. She had included a snapshot taken of Allard on that occasion. Lowenstein examined himself in the photograph and joked about how exhausted he looked.

"I look like Frank Graham did a month before he died," Allard said. "Do you think I've only got a month left too?"

The assistant filed the remark away with a number of similar speculations Lowenstein had made about his own death in the last few years. It was a trait shared by many men fresh to their fifties.

On the morning of Friday, March 14, 1980, Dennis Sweeney approached his landlady and told her that the day had come when he was finally going to leave for Oregon. It seemed sudden, but his rent was paid up for the week so she raised no objections. He told her he was packing his things; when they were ready, with her permission he would like to pull his truck up on the lawn by the barn to make loading easier. The landlady said that would be fine.

Dennis then went back to his room and packed up all his worldly possessions in a suitcase and several boxes. According to a later New London police inventory, they included a sales slip from Raub's Sporting Goods, several bundles of letters, a Massachusetts driver's license, a Connecticut driver's license, a hot plate, a few clothes, a potted fern, an address book with Allard Lowenstein's number in it, several boxes of other books, a collapsible woodworking bench of Sweeney's own design and construction, and a 50-round carton of ammunition with seven cartridges missing.

At noon, the landlady looked out of her back window and saw Sweeney drive his pickup onto the lawn next to the barn and bolt up the stairs to his room. He was wearing Levis, work boots, a plaid shirt, and a blue nylon windbreaker. He still looked no older than 27.

She expected to see him return to the truck with boxes, but instead he returned with nothing in his arms, jumped into the cab, and drove off down Bristol Street. She had no idea he was headed for New York City. When the local police arrived that evening, they found Sweeney's shaving kit set out, as if he intended to freshen up with it on his return. A clean change of clothes was arranged neatly on the bed.

Dennis Sweeney arrived at Lowenstein's office on time, but Allard was running a little late, so Sweeney took a seat in the outer office. Dennis would be remembered by one of the office workers as "expressionless" and "calm." He smoked a Winston.

Unbeknownst to anyone besides himself, his brand new Llama .380 was hidden in his windbreaker pocket.

Allard eventually came out, greeted Dennis with a smile and a handshake, led him into his private office, and closed the door behind them. There is no surviving record of just what the onetime mentor and protégé said to each other. If it held to past form, Sweeney asked Lowenstein to tell the voices to cease and desist, stop this merry-go-round, and let him off. Allard agonized and pleaded with Dennis to let him help him get the treatment he needed. It is known that they were seated on opposite sides of the desk while they talked. It is also known that after 10 to 20 minutes, Sweeney stood up and shook the hand of the former Stanford assistant dean of men. No doubt Allard thought he was about to leave. Instead, according to police sources, Sweeney pulled his $130 automatic, fully loaded, a round in the chamber, and the safety off.

"We've got to put an end to this, Al," he reportedly said.

Allard shouted, "No," and threw his left arm up to try and protect himself.

There was no mercy left in Dennis Sweeney. He fired all seven rounds. Five hit Allard, three apparently while he was lying on the floor.

When he was done, Sweeney walked back into the stunned outer office, laid his empty pistol in the receptionist's work tray, took a seat, lit another Winston, and waited for the police to arrive. In the office, former Congressman Allard K. Lowenstein bled profusely and called out weakly for help. Dennis Sweeney didn't say a word, just sat there with his lips pressed together as tight as a suitcase lid.

Allard Lowenstein was rushed, unconscious but alive, to St. Clare's Hospital on West Fifty-first Street. His left arm was broken and one lung was irreparably mangled. He was shot in the gut and his heart had two holes in it. One was two inches in diameter, the other half that size. Upon arrival, his eyes responded to light. A breathing tube was inserted into his windpipe, and tubes for a blood transfusion were stuck in his one good arm and both legs. His heart stopped once, but it was revived with an electric shock. He was wheeled into surgery at 5 P M

The police took Sweeney to a Manhattan stationhouse, where he was interrogated for 57 minutes.

"He's been controlling my mind for years," Sweeney said. "Now I've put an end to it."

He also told police he had grievances against six other people but declined to give their names. He told the police Lowenstein had hounded his stepfather into a heart attack and caused the accident at Dennis's job site. Lowenstein was also responsible, he said, for the deaths of Robert Kennedy and Thurmon Munson, the Yankee catcher killed in a 1979 plane crash.

Afterward, they took Sweeney to Bellevue Hospital for the night, then shipped him off to the mental wing of Riker's Island Reformatory for Men.

Lowenstein was on the operating table at St. Clare's for five and a half hours. Surgeons patched his heart, removed one lung, sewed up his hemorrhaging stomach wound, and set his arm. Allard consumed 29 pints of blood and was still alive when he was taken on to the intensive-care unit.

By then, old friends from all over New York had converged on the hospital. Some were in the sixth-floor waiting room with his ex-wife, Jenny, and their three kids. Others were on the sidewalk outside the building. As time dragged on, it was hard not to believe Allard might pull off yet another miracle. People remembered his wrestler's body and his seemingly indomitable will, and it seemed possible. Allard had never been an easy opponent; it was thought that even death itself would find him no different a match. Certainly he did not give in. He held on for a while after the grueling tour in the operating room, but in the end, 29 pints was more blood turnover than his body could tolerate, and "complications" developed.

At 11 P.M., Jenny and the doctors emerged from a room and she told her children their father was dead. People began to cry and evacuate the waiting room to give the family privacy. When the news reached the sidewalk outside, they cried too.

No one hung around St. Clare's for long. They scattered across the slick street in groups of one, two, or three. All of them were convinced they had lost someone special and irreplaceable. Allard Lowenstein had died a hero's death, they would say, just like Bobby, Martin, and even Jack himself.

"With his endless energy," Senator Ted Kennedy said of Allard in a speech in New York, "with his papers, his clothes, his books and seemingly his whole life jammed into briefcases, envelopes and satchels—all of it carried with him everywhere—he was a portable and powerful lobby for progressive principles. All by himself, he was more effective than an organization of thousands. He was a one-man demonstration for civil rights; even when he walked alone, he was a multitude marching for peace. He had a gentle passion for the truth."

The tributes were many. The *New York Times* gave former Representative Allard K. Lowenstein and his assassination treatment not unlike that prescribed for the death of a sitting Senator. President Jimmy Carter issued a statement from the White House. "This senseless and violent death," it read, "has cut short a life devoted to reason and justice. From the sit-ins to the campuses to the halls of Congress, Al Lowenstein was a passionate fighter for a more humane, more democratic world. In the civil rights and antiwar movements, his eloquent dedication to nonviolent change inspired many thousands of Americans. As my administration's representative to the United Nations Commission on Human Rights and United Nations Trusteeship Council, he was an effective spokesman for democracy around the world and for justice and reconciliation in southern Africa. I deplore the act of violence which took Mr. Lowenstein's life, and Rosalynn and I extend our deepest sympathy to his children and to the countless friends he made in a life of service to his fellow human beings."

On March 16, 1980, the Lowenstein family held a private funeral ceremony.

On March 17, a public memorial service was held at Central Synagogue on Fifty-fifth Street, near Lexington Avenue, attended by 2,500 people. It was a remarkable group, including United States Senators; Jewish housewives from Long Island; Stanford alumni; reporters; folk singers; artists; Yale, Harvard, Chapel Hill, and City College of New York alumni; veterans of Johannesburg in 1959, the UN in 1960, Palo Alto in 1961, North Carolina in 1962, and Jackson in 1963; ambassadors; congressmen; veterans of Atlantic City in 1964, Berkeley in 1965, the Dominican Republic in 1966, NSA in 1967, New Hampshire, Long Beach, and Chicago in 1968; newspaper editors, publishers, and reporters; ADA, NAACP, SCLC, IILR, CCD, CCC, and ACT members; guys from the University of North Carolina wrestling team; Notre Dame, UCLA, University of California, UT alumni, UF alumni, UW alumni; USC, WSU, MSU, RPI, TSU, USU, VMI, and AIA and T alumni; old friends; people who had not seen each other in years; waitresses; secretaries; former protégés, organizers, and precinct workers; former allies and former antagonists; Republicans, liberals, Democrats, independents, Socialists, and libertarians; the dogmatic, the uncommitted, and everything in between.

On March 18, Allard Lowenstein's body was buried at Arlington National Cemetery with full military honors. His grave site is as close to John F. Kennedy's in one direction as Jack's own brother Bobby's is in the other.

14

The same day Allard was laid to rest, I engaged in a series of phone conversations with my editors at the *New York Times Magazine.* I said that working out what happened to Allard and Dennis would make a great story, but before I took the assignment, I wanted to warn them that I would have to deal with the incident between Dennis and Allard in the motel in 1964. Given that it was a pivotal encounter between two parties to an eventual homicide, I didn't see that there was much choice. They agreed and said only to make sure anything I wrote was within the boundaries of good taste and "*Times* standards."

A few days later I left my home in California and started following the story East. I wanted to attend a court appearance by Sweeney in early April.

As it turned out, I was setting out on a reporting journey that would end in a magazine article and later this book. It brought me face to face with both the absolute isolation Dennis had fallen into and the hold Allard still had over those who had known him. His remarkable network of friends and connections, as I would learn, continued even after his death.

When the day came for Dennis's appearance in court, I sat in the front row of the dingy courtroom. It was only a brief legal motion, his lawyer told me, and Dennis would be present for ten minutes at most, but he promised to try and get me a brief courtroom visit when the appearance was over. Dennis eventually came in from the holding cells dressed in his street clothes, his upper lip pulled down to cover the wreckage in his mouth. He listened with interest until the proceedings were over, and then the judge granted a one-minute courtroom visit.

I wasn't sure whether Dennis would even remember me. As yet, I had no idea he had been visited by my voice in a Portland supermarket only two months before. When we were face to face, Sweeney made no introductory remarks, even though we had last seen each other in 1968. He just looked straight at me.

"Ten years without change," he said. "Such a long time without change and now all this on top of it."

I dealt with the "sexual question" in two places in the copy I eventually filed with the *Times Magazine*. One paragraph included what apparently happened in the motel room, how Dennis characterized it, its effects as reflected in his discussion of it with other people, and an allusion to the fact that several of those other people had themselves had the same experience with Lowenstein. No generalizations were drawn or big words used. This paragraph summarized what information I had then, prior to undertaking the extensive reporting effort for the book. The second paragraph, elsewhere in the piece, was an explanation of chronic paranoid schizophrenia, in which I mentioned that paranoia regarding a homosexual approach was a symptom.

Within several days after the piece was filed, the magazine's editorial offices received phone calls from a national columnist based in New York, a New York City councilman, and a former member of the U.S. delegation to the UN. All of them said they wanted to make it "clear" that any allegations that Allard Lowenstein was a "homosexual" were absolutely "unfounded" and amounted to character assassination. Not long thereafter, I got my first phone call from the magazine asking for an explanation, which I provided.

Dennis Sweeney told the story of that encounter to at least five people, including me, and I had talked to the rest. All of their conversations with Dennis occurred prior to any overt symptoms of his chronic paranoid schizophrenia. Interviews I conducted with a half dozen other protégés who had had similar experiences with Lowenstein substantiated that his approach to Dennis was consistent behavior, rather than an isolated occurrence. I myself had had such an experience, and numerous other sources said they had heard stories of similar incidents. I pointed out that the word "homosexual" was not even used in what I had written. In total, 150 words were involved.

In another vein, I also argued it was not character assassination to indicate that people, Lowenstein included, are complex. Besides, this was a homicide committed by a man suffering from a mental aberration, one of whose symptoms in men is sexual confusion and extreme paranoia about homosexual approach. The victim in this case was someone the perpetrator believed had once made such an advance. If it had happened between two Puerto Ricans with knives on the subway, I noted, there would be no question but that the subject would be recognized and dealt with.

The editor at the magazine agreed with everything I said and hung up. Several days after that, the editorial offices of the *Times Magazine* received a message from a onetime columnist and former press secretary for Bobby Kennedy who had also been a friend of Allard's. He just wanted to let the *Times* know that this guy they had working on the Lowenstein story was also collecting money for the Dennis Sweeney Defense Fund.

I called the former press secretary back myself. I pointed out that there was no such thing as the Dennis Sweeney Defense Fund. No money for legal defense was being collected by anybody, much less me. I was surprised he hadn't bothered to check that out himself, I said. I also pointed out that my profession was journalism; I was good enough at it to have a contract with the *New York Times Magazine*, knew the rules of reporting, and had followed them in every story I had ever written. I did not collect money for anybody I was writing about. On top of that, since he and I had met several times, he knew how to get my phone number, and I said I thought he owed me a call before slandering me to my employer.

He wanted to know whether I was going to write anything about Lowenstein with "sexual connotations."

I said I would write whatever I thought was relevant to the homicide I was being paid to explain.

He said allegations of that sort would be a "cheap shot," taken when Allard could no longer defend himself from "vindictive" attempts to "ruin his good name."

I said that complex sexuality did not discredit a person. People who assume it does are manifesting a level of intolerance that Allard himself certainly never shared.

But there was a family with young children involved, he said.

I said I was sorry about that.

He said that nothing on the subject was worth mentioning. If I went ahead and used it, he and I must be "different kinds of journalists."

I agreed that we probably were.

By the end of May, my story was finished, had gone through the editorial process, and was ready to be published, but it was still not yet scheduled for any particular issue. Around that time I had a long phone conversation with one of Allard's former protégés now living in California. I mentioned to him the people who were swarming around my story like jackals on fresh meat.

"Amazing," he said. "That's exactly the kind of shit I used to do for Allard twelve years ago. It's the protégés first duty. Allard always had to be defended from 'spurious attack' by people with 'questionable motives.' Now that's you."

I said nothing.

"Lowenstein speaks from the grave," he added, attempting a joke.

I did not laugh.

My story eventually ran in the August 17, 1980, issue of the *New York Times Magazine* under the title "Bloody End of '60's Dream." As printed, it contained no reference to any encounter in any motel room between Allard and his assassin in 1964.

The only account of that "sexual question" to reach print during the first year after Allard's death was in a long story written by Teresa Carpenter, published in the *Village Voice* on May 12, 1980, and reprinted in a shorter version by the *Washington Post* on May 18. Carpenter wrote:

> There was a suspicion, even back in Stanford, that
> Lowenstein never dealt quite honestly in personal matters.
> There was an undeniable tension between Lowenstein and
> the young men in his following. "I know that many of us,
> most of us, had passes made at us from Al," says a friend of
> both Sweeney and Lowenstein from the Stanford period.
> Often they weren't overt proposals, "but clearly testing . . . to
> be offered an overnight room and to discover that there was
> one bed." After the shooting, in fact, there were rumors that
> Lowenstein and Sweeney had fallen out as the result of a
> lover's quarrel. . . . (Now, from his cell in Riker's Island,
> Sweeney denies they ever had a relationship. Once while he
> and Lowenstein were traveling through Mississippi together,
> they checked into a motel. According to Sweeney, Lowenstein
> made a pass and Sweeney rebuffed it. Sweeney is not angry
> with Lowenstein, he claims. Nor does he feel any shame. It's
> just that Lowenstein wasn't always aboveboard.)

Several weeks later, a response to Carpenter's allegations appeared in a letter to the *Washington Post* signed by 15 members of Congress. "Measured against even the loosest journalistic standards," they wrote, the *Voice* story was "grossly deficient," "rife with unsubstantiated assertions and gratuitous innuendo," "deeply offensive," and "completely at odds with reality." "Dennis Sweeney's life is certainly worth examining," the letter continued. "But the examination should . . . not include farfetched and ridiculous gossip. . . . Many of her assertions are not only unsubstantiated but patently false." With the letter's publication, the "controversy" over Allard's sexuality disappeared for the rest of 1980.

It surfaced again in 1981 as an offshoot of that year's Pulitzer Prize scandal. The Pulitzer committee's first choice for the feature award, a story about an eight-year-old heroin addict by a woman writer from the *Washington Post*, turned out to have been fabricated, and the committee's replacement was an entry from the *Village Voice* of three stories written by Teresa Carpenter. One of them was "From Heroism to Madness," her story about Dennis Sweeney and Allard Lowenstein. Although at least one member of the selection panel later claimed that the award had been for "the best of the entries," an account of a murder committed by a released mental patient, and not for the article about Lowenstein and Sweeney, Carpenter's selection reactivated Lowenstein's "defenders."

This time the "defense" was led by James Wechsler, a *New York Post* associate editor and a friend of Lowenstein's for over 20 years. On April 12, 1981, he went after Carpenter in a *Post* column. "Miss Carpenter," he charged, "was guilty of irresponsible defamation of a dead man . . . a melange of unattributed gossip-mongering and political malice that could shadow the lives of Lowenstein's family—and especially his three children, now 13, 11 and 10." It was reportedly Wechsler's hope to generate enough pressure to force the Pulitzer committee to withdraw her award. In the interest of discrediting Carpenter's story, both Wechsler and Larry Lowenstein, Allard's brother, also filed complaints with the National News Council, an "independent" body funded by several foundations, whose self-designated purpose is investigating citizens' complaints about their treatment by the news media. The Council normally operated under a rule that no complaints can be filed more than 90 days after publication, but, according to its later report, awarding the Pulitzer to Carpenter "clearly" made such restrictions "moot." In their complaints, both Larry Lowenstein and Wechsler said that "the *Voice* article was a distorted portrayal" of Allard.

In investigating the complaints, the News Council staff identified four issues of contention. The second of the four was "whether there was validity in incorporating homosexuality as a potential motive in the slaying." When their final report was issued, the News Council cited six different sources by name who all said that the question of "homosexuality" was "inaccurate," "the sort of thing you would hear from people who were hostile to him," and a "kind of gossip or keyhole rumor." I too was contacted by the staff—but no part of my information was woven into the final conclusion. I told the Council officials that Sweeney had told me about an "approach," that I had interviewed several other people to whom he had told the story, that I myself had experienced a similar "approach," and that I had interviewed more than a half dozen young men who had had the same experience. I said I thought Carpenter's piece had problems, not the least of which was that it created the impression that she had interviewed Sweeney when in fact she had not; nevertheless, if the News Council came out saying the question of sexuality had no bearing, they would be inaccurate and embarrassed. None of my statements was mentioned in their report, and the Council concluded, with one dissenting vote out of 15, that "the complaints" were "warranted."

The embarrassment began not long after the Council issued its report. Instead of suppressing the sexual question or causing the Pulitzer committee to rethink its award, the activity of Lowenstein's "defenders" provoked a second round of media curiosity. This time, the issue of sexuality was interwoven with reports of possible behind-the-scenes manipulation of the press and efforts at censorship. Several articles on censorship appeared; others were researched but not published or aired by at least one national magazine, one newspaper, and one national television program.

The apex of this second media wave came in July 1981 with the appearance of a long article in the *New York Native,* a small but respected gay newspaper.

Starting with the assumption that homosexuality was not discrediting to anyone, the *Native* was apparently able to locate a number of gays who were prepared to discuss their contact with Allard on the record. "Holding a man was what he told me he liked to do," said one man identified by name. "It was something he liked to do with men he cared about. It was something he felt comfortable doing with men who felt comfortable doing it with him, as part of the intimacy. He did have a type that he was intimate with: Wasp, jock, and it helped if you were a student body president."

Perhaps the most moving comment in the *Native* article came from a former director of the National Gay Task Force. "He [Lowenstein] asked if he could talk to me privately," the man recalled. "He looked to see that he was out of earshot, and said, 'You have been through a lot with your family, and your wife, and I wonder if I could talk to you about that.' He said it might be better to meet someplace less obvious." The two men then had a series of three private meetings in the mid-1970s. The gay organizer recounted:

Each time it was to talk about the fact that he was bisexual,

that he loved his wife very much and loved his family. He
wanted to know about my experience with my kids. I think
his biggest concern was how my kids had reacted when I told
them. . . . He did indeed have gay relationships; he made it
very clear that he did. He made it very clear that that was
how he perceived himself. The only thing we talked about in
his personal involvement was whether one could sustain a
bisexual relationship. He wanted to know if it was possible to
have [his wife] know and approve and make space for a male
somewhere on the scene. I told him I thought it was
theoretically possible, but my observation was that it really
didn't work. That was upsetting to him. . . . As far as I could
tell, he hadn't told much of anyone. Our conversations were
predicated on nobody knowing. . . . He was seriously and
deeply concerned about what the costs of a public disclosure
would be to him and his family and only a little bit about the
cost to his political career. . . . He . . . said he wished others
didn't have to go through the hell he was going through.

The controversy has ebbed since the *Native*'s story appeared, but it
will no doubt linger for a long time around the edge of conversations
where the late Allard Lowenstein's name comes up. Nowhere in the
course of the controversy has Dennis Sweeney made a public comment
on Lowenstein or the murder, and the chances of his doing so seem
increasingly slim.

The closest thing to such a comment is kept in a manila file in
the Manhattan district attorney's office. The file contains the
reports of three psychiatrists who examined Sweeney and a 31-page
letter written in 1980 by Sweeney and addressed to his attorney. During
1981, the D.A.'s office allowed a National News Council member and
Teresa Carpenter to examine the documents. The Dennis Sweeney the
paperwork describes was clearly deranged by even the most stringent
of legal and psychiatric standards.

"Born in 1943," one psychiatrist noted, "he stated that his birth
took place in a military camp since his father was in the service. The
defendant stressed the importance of this information because at the
time the military was carrying out secret experiments and that he was
used as a subject. He believes that devices were implanted in him at
that time."

The "devices" eventually generated "voices," and much of the file is devoted to trying to track and analyze Dennis's private chorus. According to another examining psychiatrist, Sweeney's "auditory hallucinations are derogatory, threatening, and insulting to his masculinity with an implication of homosexuality." According to Sweeney, the voices can be divided into two general categories: The first were those of "family and friends," and the second was "a small group of Jews from New York directing me to whom I should marry. Since I was being treated like a guinea pig with a bombardment of sound waves, they extrapolated that I should be married like a guinea pig and, judging from the treatment I was getting, provide a family of experimental rats whose origin could not be thought of as having anything to do with myself and who would be the result only of . . . self-preservation such as inmates experienced in the Third Reich. . . . Had I more understanding of the racial antagonism felt toward gentiles by Jews," Sweeney noted, "and the vanity some Jews feel . . . my depression would have been lessened."

Needless to say, the voices only intensified as time passed. "Voices in the shower," Sweeney wrote, "would remind me of a coworker's mistake and suggest 'wouldn't you like to give him the bump?'. . . . a female [sic] voice would say, 'you're wasting yourself. You should be working for us.' And another implied that I was effeminate and making homosexual overtones to the neighbor by having cleaned the shower in the bathroom which we shared . . . One of them kept referring to me as Sben Whoona which I took to be a Jewish nickname for recalcitrant, blue-eyed, Aryan types." One of the psychiatrists reported that "in 1973, Mr. Lowenstein's voice became distinct among all the voices. He [Sweeney] saw him [Lowenstein] . . . and told him how the persecution interfered with his life and relationships with women, how when he was near a woman the effect was to cause him to say 'wrong words which come to my lips: obscene remarks about their bodies; do you want to screw?; should I buy a prophylactic?'" At his stepfather's funeral, the voices, another of the reports maintained, "also designated images or gestures as if defecating on the coffin."

Apparently, the voices Lowenstein was leading made a qualitative leap into new dimensions in 1978 or 1979. As Sweeney explained, "Mr. Lowenstein's voice over the previous six years had been telling me with whom I should be spending my time and whom I should marry. Of late, it had grown weary of peering down at me so I decided to interpret his claim . . . as an expression of frustration of trying to make me a feudal liege, so I wrote him a letter. I said I had no respect for any of the movements or ideologies he had lived to spawn in the 1970s and that I would not even be a member of his following. I told him I wanted to be forgotten as soon as possible." Henceforth, as one psychiatrist observed, "the Lowenstein forces would demonstrate their own power and punish him for being recalcitrant by attacking others." In Sweeney's words, "the man [was] killing others to make me feel like a coward."

Dennis held Allard responsible for the Chicago plane crash on Memorial Day of 1979 in which almost 200 people were killed, a collision between a Coast Guard cutter and an oil tanker off Florida in February of 1980, and several other disasters. After the death of Thurman Munson, he heard Allard say, "I have killed the most popular Yankee but no one in New York City will stand up to me or stop me." Over and over again, he heard Lowenstein repeat, "Why didn't you stand up to me? I am inflicting violence and harm on people and no one will stop me." Finally, Dennis noted, "the pattern of these New York Jews insulting and fighting with my family when it was me they had been acquainted with overcame my restraint against wasting time." Sweeney, one report stated, "now felt that not only his own life was in danger but that of many people in the world. He had to confront the perpetrators."

Dennis Sweeney's account of the final denouement in Lowenstein's office was matter of fact in tone. "I explained to him that I wanted to return to my home in Oregon," Sweeney wrote, "but that before I could so with any ability to function, I needed his word that insofar as he was aware of any anger or vendetta against me by himself and a few others, that he restrict it to myself and not cause any harm to anyone near or dear to me. He said that he couldn't give me that kind of pledge and that he thought I should see a psychiatrist. If I needed any help in doing so, he would be glad to assist. He said I had to begin by helping myself. . . . I then took the gun out of my pocket and said that in the light of what I had seen, his statement was not good enough for me, and I began to fire."

I made my last attempt to visit Dennis in May of 1980. I had prepared to visit him three times before, but each time, I called ahead to Riker's Island at the last minute only to find that 844-80-833, Dennis Sweeney, had been switched to another unit or his visiting days changed. My fourth attempt was made from Washington, D.C. This time my phone call confirmed that he would be available for visiting the next day, and I took the first shuttle flight up to La Guardia in the morning.

Riker's Island can be seen as one lands at the airport, but none of the La Guardia cabbies knew how to get me there. Finally, one got directions and, after a five-minute ride, dropped me at the guard post commanding the foot of the causeway connecting the prison island to the mainland. A drizzle was falling, interspersed with sharp gusts of wind. I waited for the public bus to take me to the institution. At the visitors' entrance I took a number and waited my turn to sign in at the reception windows. When my number was finally called, I registered to visit Dennis Sweeney, was cleared through the metal detector, and moved into a second room where I waited for a prison bus to take me and the other visitors out to the unit getting visits that day. By then, I had been at Riker's for an hour and a half.

The prison bus finally stopped at a big, gray building; visitors passed first through a chain-link fence that was locked behind us, then through a solid steel doorway and into a concrete waiting area lined with benches. I didn't know what I was going to say to Dennis. By my calculations, he was guaranteed to spend at least the next 30 years locked up somewhere. Finally, one of the custodial officers came out of a door in the far end of the room and asked who was here to see Sweeney.

I said me.

He said Sweeney had been moved that morning to the prison hospital wing and couldn't have a visit until the next Wednesay.

It took me another hour to extricate myself from Rikers Island and get back on the public bus across the causeway. At the bus stop, I stepped out into the rain and paused for a moment to look back at the tangle of wire and gun towers behind me.

I suppose it was somehow fitting that Dennis Sweeney was unreachable to me. His is one of the saddest stories I know. According to one of the district attorney's psychiatric reports, Sweeney still "believes Mr. Lowenstein is not dead, that 'the bullets were tampered with or he [Lowenstein] was wearing a bulletproof vest.' He believes this because [Sweeney says] 'I hear his voice in the atmosphere . . . pushing women at me, threatening my life by using other inmates against me.' [Sweeney] believes no new tragedies have occurred because he 'stood up to them like a man.' "

On February 23, 1981, Dennis Sweeney was finally found "not responsible by reason of disease or defect" and committed to the New York State mental health system, where he remains hospitalized today.

I made my only visit to Allard's Arlington grave in June of 1980. It was a muggy day, not unlike the one on which Allard had arrived in Jackson, Mississippi, 17 years before. His final resting place was easy to locate just by flowing with the flood of tourists headed for John F. Kennedy's memorial.

Kennedy's grave sits on the top of a gentle knoll and is marked by an eternal flame. As you face it, the left-hand slope drops off most sharply, pitching down to a shaded glen where the only headstone is that of the President's brother, Bobby. To the right of John's marker, the knoll slopes away more gradually to a concrete walk and then an open buffer of grass before a hillside of simple white headstones begins. The place for JFK is set apart and protected by a chain strung from stanchions. Right outside the chain, closer to it than any other, is Allard Lowenstein's grave. That section of graves had apparently been closed for years, but a spot for Allard was arranged by a call from the White House.

When I was there, no permanent marker had yet been planted, and the location was marked by a green metal name holder stuck in the sod. "Lowenstein," was handwritten on a card attached to the frame. I noted that Allard's closest neighbors were Augustus Joseph Wellings, Rear Admiral, USN, 1897–1956, and Robert Staling Mathers, Commander, USN, 1913–1957. Before I could see much more, the guards came up and said I was not allowed to walk on the grass. I pocketed my notebook and headed back for the parking lot.

I am sure a more formal headstone has been erected for Allard by now, but I prefer to remember the temporary one he had that June. It looked as if he still might up marker and catch the first flight out, having merely rested briefly before his next call.

I will miss Dennis and I will miss Allard. They were both extraordinary people who lived through an extraordinary time, and the extraordinary thing that happened between the two of them finally convinced me that the extraordinary time had come to an end. I will miss it, too.

I am indebted to a number of sources in addition to my own recollections for the information in this book.

First and foremost among them are the memories of some 50 other veterans of the Sixties with whom I conducted more than 150 hours of interviews. They trusted me with their knowledge and for that I am deeply grateful. I owe special thanks to Clayborne Carson, William Evers, Teresa Carpenter, and The Data Center in Oakland, California, all of whom made pieces of their own original research available to me.

I also made extensive use of daily news coverage by the *New York Times* and the *Stanford Daily*. Coverage by the *Portland Oregonian*, *Wall Street Journal*, *New York Post*, *San Francisco Chronicle*, *Newsday*, *San Francisco Examiner*, *New London Day*, *New York Daily News*, *Washington Post*, *Los Angeles Times*, Associated Press, and the Collegiate Press Service was also of great help.

I was also aided by accounts of the time previously published in a number of fine books. They are:

Bonds, Ray, ed. *The Vietnam War*. New York: Crown, 1979.

Carson, Clayborne. *In Struggle: SNCC and the Black Awakening of the 1960's*. Cambridge: Harvard, 1981.

Carter, Hodding. *So the Heffners Left McComb*. New York: Doubleday, 1965.

Chester, Lewis; Hodgson, Godfrey; and Page, Bruce. *An American Melodrama: The Presidential Campaign of 1968*. New York: Viking, 1969.

English, David. *Divided They Stand: The American Election 1968*. Englewood Cliffs, N. J.: Prentice-Hall, 1969.

Ferber, Michael and Lynd, Staughton. *The Resistance*. Boston: Beacon Press, 1971.

Forman, James. *The Making of Black Revolutionaries*. New York: Macmillan, 1972.

Goff, Fred and Locker, Michael. "The Violence of Domination: U.S. Power and the Dominican Republic." In *Latin American Radicalism*, edited by Irving L. Horowitz, et al. New York: Random House, 1969.

Good, Paul. *The Trouble I've Seen*. Washington, D.C.: Howard University Press, 1975.

Harris, David. *I Shoulda Been Home Yesterday*. New York: Delacorte/Seymour Lawrence, 1976.

Herzog, Arthur. *McCarthy for President*. New York: Viking, 1969.

Knappman, Edward, ed. *Presidential Election 1968*. New York: Facts on File, 1970.

Lowenstein, Allard. *Brutal Mandate: A Journey to Southwest Africa*. New York: Macmillan, 1962.

McCord, William. *Mississippi: The Long Hot Summer*. New York: Norton, 1965.

Newfield, Jack. *Robert Kennedy: A Memoir*. New York: Dutton, 1969.

Plimpton, George, ed. *American Journey: The Times of Robert Kennedy*. New York: Harcourt Brace, 1970.

Schlesinger, Arthur. *Robert Kennedy and His Times*. Boston: Houghton Mifflin, 1978.

Von Hoffman, Nicholas. *Mississippi Notebook*. Port Washington, N.Y.: David White, 1964.

Witcover, Jules. *85 Days: The Last Campaign of Robert F. Kennedy*. New York: Putnam, 1969.

At various points in this book, I placed great reliance on a number of magazine accounts and occasionally quoted from some of them at length. They include:

Bennett, Roy. "The Issue: Vietnam; The Target: Johnson." *ADA World Magazine*, 21, July 1967.

Berriault, Gina. "The New Student President." *Esquire*, 68:93, September 1967.

Brownmiller, Susan. "Gene McCarthy Is Waiting for a Sign." *New York Times Magazine*, 10–11, July 20, 1969.

Bush, Larry. "The New Legacy of Allard Lowenstein." *New York Native*, July 13–26, 1981.

Carpenter, Teresa. "From Heroism to Madness: The Odyssey of the Man Who Shot Al Lowenstein." *Village Voice*, 25: 1+, May 12, 1980.

Cowan, Paul. "What Makes Al Lowenstein Run?" *Ramparts*, 7:45–51, September 7, 1968.

Halberstam, David. "The Man Who Ran Against Lyndon Johnson." *Harper's Magazine*, 237: 47–62, December 1968.

Harris, David. "The Bloody End to a 60's Dream," *New York Times Magazine,* 34–37 +, August 17, 1980.

Hedgepeth, William. "We're Just Non-Violent Soldiers." *Look,* May 5, 1970.

Powers, Thomas. "A Chance Encounter." *Commonweal,* 107: 261–2, April 11, 1980.

Ramparts. How I got in, and why I came out of the cold"; "How the CIA turns foreign students into traitors." Editorials, March 1967.

Schechter, Leonard. "The Teenie Power of Al Lowenstein." *New York Magazine,* August 12, 1968.

Shereff, Ruth. "Crisis Over the Dominican Republic: Liberals in Wonderland." *Commonweal,* 86:198–9, May 5, 1967.

Shereff, Ruth. "The Committee for Free Elections in the Dominican Republic." *Liberation,* November 1966.

Stern, Sol. "NSA: A Short Account of International Student Politics and the Cold War with Particular Reference to the NSA, CIA, Etc." *Ramparts,* 5:29–38, March 1967.

White, Neal. "The New NSA." *New Republic,* 157:11 August 2, 1967.

In compiling these resources I made use of the Stanford University libraries. Preparation of the manuscript would have been impossible without the assistance of Beth Haisler of Menlo Park, California.

David Harris